# False Prophets

# The Past in the Present

Richard Bonney

# False Prophets

## The 'Clash of Civilizations' and the Global War on Terror

Peter Lang Oxford

*Cover design:* Dan Mogford

First published in 2008 by Peter Lang Ltd
International Academic Publishers, Evenlode Court, Main Road,
Long Hanborough, Witney, Oxfordshire OX29 8SZ, England

www.thepastinthepresent.com, www.peterlang.com



British Library and Library of Congress Cataloguing-in Publication Data:
A catalogue record for this book is available from the British Library, UK, and the Library of Congress, USA.

ISBN 978-1-906165-02-4 (Paperback)
ISBN 978-1-906165-07-9 (Hardback)

Printed in Hong Kong

*This book is dedicated to my wife, Margaret, in our twenty-first year of marriage: may there be many more. Particular thanks are due to Alexis Kirschbaum for her enthusiastic support and to Bernard Dod for his useful comments and attention to detail. The errors remain mine.*

# Contents

# Preface

> *Interviewer*: What is your opinion about what is being said concerning ... the 'Clash of Civilizations'? Your constant use and repetition of the word 'Crusade' and 'Crusader' show that you uphold this saying, the 'Clash of Civilizations'.
>
> *Osama bin Laden*: I say there is no doubt about this. This is a very clear matter ...
>
> Al-Jazeera interview with Osama bin Laden (October 2001)[1]

> One of the things that attracted a lot of attention in *The Clash of Civilizations* was my use of the phrase 'the bloody borders of Islam'. But if you look around the Muslim world you see that in the 1990s Muslims were fighting non-Muslims in Bosnia, Kosovo, Macedonia, Chechnya, Azerbaijan, Tajikistan, Kashmir, Indonesia, the Philippines, the Middle East, Sudan, Nigeria, and other places. Muslims have been fighting one another also ...
>
> Samuel P. Huntington (17 June 2002)[2]

In another era, the main arguments of this book might have seemed delusional. Yet in the first decade of the twenty-first century, truth really is stranger than fiction. When Samuel P. Huntington's article entitled 'The clash of civilizations?' was published in 1993, the intellectual community 'dismissed it as somewhat strange if not downright wrong'. Then came the terrorist attacks of 11 September 2001 known in the US as the events of '9/11'. After these atrocities, which were regarded as a national disaster comparable to Pearl Harbor in 1941, everything changed: 'the mainstream media in the USA automatically, implicitly and unanimously' adopted Huntington's paradigm to explain the terrorist attacks. The media remembered Huntington's use of the phrase 'the bloody borders of Islam'. That was enough. A paradigm does not have to be true to become conventional wisdom.[3]

The late Pope John Paul II once observed: 'a clash ensues only when Islam or Christianity is misconstrued or manipulated for political or ideological ends.' In the interview given to al-Jazeera in October 2001, the month after he had authorized the most notorious terrorist atrocity of all time, Osama bin Laden took it as axiomatic that Huntington's idea was correct: 'there is no doubt about this.' 'The people of Islam' had awoken, he asserted, realized that they were the main target of the 'Zionists and Crusaders', and decided to fight back. When, on 16 September 2001, on the South Lawn of the White House, George W. Bush declared the 'war on terror' a 'Crusade' he took the words out of Osama's mouth – according to bin Laden himself.[4] In an address in Atlanta, Georgia, on 8 November 2001, President Bush defined his 'war to save civilization itself' as a campaign against terrorists operating in more than sixty different countries. 'Is the Islamic world not around 60 states? ... Did they not say that they want to change the region's ideology, which vents hatred against the Americans? What they mean by this is Islam and its [defenders] ...'[5] Bin Laden has consistently attempted to project the conflict not as 'between the al-Qaeda organization and the global Crusaders' but as between 'the people of Islam' and the global Crusaders.[6] It was his duty to provoke the clash of civilizations analysed by Samuel P. Huntington and others.[7] 'If we don't want this to be a war of civilizations,' commented the head of the State Department's intelligence bureau under President Clinton, 'we have really got to get rid of [the] person who is intent on making it that way.'[8]

*False Prophets* is about the influence of ideology on foreign policy, and in particular examines how a group of advisers committed to a fixed ideological viewpoint – the neo-conservatives and their allies among the Christian Right and the American pro-Israel lobby – could take control of decisions in foreign policy of the world's only remaining superpower at a moment of crisis in 2001. It is also about how they, and their supporters in a supine press and extraordinarily superficial electronic media, could so trumpet the alleged virtues of their policy that any opposing voice was not only shouted down but accused of national disloyalty. The ramifications are far-reaching for those families who have lost loved ones in a conflict that was manageable but in the event was mismanaged; for those who live in the increasingly illiberal democracies in the West which have suffered a loss of civic freedom as a result of the so-called 'war on terror'; and for those who have suffered the dreadful consequences of the implementation of deluded and misguided policies abroad, especially the ordinary people of Afghanistan and Iraq.

# Introduction
## Are We Fighting World War IV Against Islamo-Fascism?

> The Cold War was World War III, which reminds us that not all global conflicts entail the movement of multi million-man armies, or conventional front lines on a map. The analogy with the Cold War does, however, suggest some key features of that conflict: that it is, in fact, global; that it will involve a mixture of violent and non-violent efforts; that it will require mobilization of skill, expertise and resources, if not of vast numbers of soldiers; that it may go on for a long time; and that it has ideological roots.
>
> Eliot A. Cohen (20 November 2001)[1]

> The war we fight today is more than a military conflict; it is the decisive ideological struggle of the twenty-first century. On one side are those who believe in the values of freedom and moderation – the right of all people to speak, and worship, and live in liberty. And on the other side are those driven by the values of tyranny and extremism – the right of a self-appointed few to impose their fanatical views on all the rest. As veterans, you have seen this kind of enemy before. They're successors to Fascists, to Nazis, to Communists, and other totalitarians of the twentieth century. And history shows what the outcome will be: this war will be difficult; this war will be long; and this war will end in the defeat of the terrorists and totalitarians, and a victory for the cause of freedom and liberty.
>
> President George W. Bush, Address to the American Legion National Convention, Salt Lake City, Utah (31 August 2006)[2]

*False Prophets* seeks to analyse the interaction of political ideology on the formation of policy, principally in the US and to a lesser extent the UK, in the aftermath of the terrible events of 11 September 2001. Those events, we now know, were master-minded by two men, Osama bin Laden and Ayman al-Zawahiri, using Khalid Sheik Mohammed as their agent[3] – men inspired by Abdullah Azzam's idea of a global *jihad* for the defence of the

Muslim lands,[4] and who were committed to provoking a conflict between the Sunni Muslim world and the United States. Afghanistan for Azzam was essentially a training ground for the revolutionary vanguard, which would lead the Muslim *ummah* in a war of resistance against the West. Azzam's slogan was simple but ferocious: 'there will be no solution to the Palestinian problem except through *jihad*.'[5] In *Join the Caravan,* he proclaimed: '*jihad* and the rifle alone: no negotiations, no conferences and no dialogue.' For Azzam, every ideology requires 'a vanguard (or foundation = al-Qaeda) that gives everything it possesses in order to achieve victory'. He returned repeatedly to this theme, which was taken up by bin Laden. In his statement of 7 October 2001, bin Laden specifically referred to the 11 September attackers as a 'vanguard of Islam ... rendered successful by Islam'.[6]

Marc Sageman is among those who have emphasized the extent to which Ayman al-Zawahiri has taken over the intellectual leadership of the global jihadist movement since the death of his rival Azzam.[7] The new *jihad,* al-Zawahiri declares in *Knights under the Prophet's Banner* (2001), is a struggle between Islam and the hostile global forces of the West (including Russia), using a 'number of tools' including the United Nations; friendly rulers of Muslim-majority states; multi-national corporations; the international communications and data exchange systems; the international news agencies and satellite media channels; and the international relief agencies, which are used as a cover for proselytizing, coup planning, and the transfer of weapons. The one slogan that had been well understood by the whole Islamic nation (*ummah*) over the past fifty years was the call for *jihad* against Israel, to which had been added in the last decade the call for *jihad* against the US presence in the Islamic lands. 'The fact that must be acknowledged is that the issue of Palestine is the cause that has been firing up the feelings of the Muslim nation from Morocco to Indonesia for the past fifty years.' It also served as a rallying point also for 'all Arabs, be they believers or non-believers, good or evil'. The 'new reality', al-Zawahiri argues, is that the 'Jewish–Crusader alliance, led by the United States' will 'open a battlefield ... that includes the entire world' against 'any Muslim force' seeking 'to reach power' in any of the Muslim-majority countries. To adjust to this 'new reality', the jihadist movement must concentrate on inflicting 'the maximum casualties against the opponent, for this is the language understood by the West'. The battle must be moved 'to the enemy's grounds to burn the hands of those who ignite fire in our countries'.

'Taken as a whole', Michael Scheuer observes of bin Laden's statement issued on 23 April 2006, it 'seeks to draw the sharpest possible case for the existence of a "clash of civilizations ... [that] has been carried out by their civilization [the West] against our [that is, the Sunni Muslim] civilization", and seems to augur near-term attacks against the United States, its allies and their publics.'[8] Or, as Huntington himself observed in 2002: 'undeniably, the terrorist actions of Osama bin Laden have reinvigorated civilizational identity. Just as he sought to rally Muslims by declaring war on the West, he gave back to the West its sense of common identity in defending itself.'[9]

By what term do we describe our 'enemy' after 11 September 2001, if we agree that bin Laden's authorized attack put his group and those of his ilk beyond the pale? There is no consensus on terminology. Speaking at the National Endowment for Democracy on 6 October 2005, President George W. Bush stated:[10]

> Islamic terrorist attacks serve a clear and focused ideology, a set of beliefs and goals that are evil, but not insane. Some call this evil Islamic radicalism; others, militant Jihadism; still others, Islamo-fascism. Whatever it's called, this ideology is very different from the religion of Islam. This form of radicalism exploits Islam to serve a violent, political vision: the establishment, by terrorism and subversion and insurgency, of a totalitarian empire that denies all political and religious freedom ...

Although the columnist Joseph Sobran calls Islamo-fascism 'an empty propaganda term',[11] it is the one most commonly used in the United States. Its origins are contested. Manfred Halpern used the expression 'neo-Islamic totalitarian movements' in 1963. The term 'Islamo-fascism', Roger Scruton claims, 'was introduced by the French writer Maxime Rodinson (1915–2004) to describe the Iranian Revolution of 1978'. It was not, though, a precise analytical term (he talked of a *type de fascisme archaïque*). Rodinson was a Marxist, who described as 'fascist' any movement of which he disapproved.[12] Nor was the term used much even in the 1990s. Malise Ruthven wrote on 8 September 1990 in the *Independent* that 'authoritarian government, not to say Islamo-fascism, is the rule rather than the exception from Morocco to Pakistan.' Ruthven, however, uses the term 'fundamentalism' for his own study of extremism.[13] In an interview within a month of 9/11, Daniel Pipes declared that 'Islamism is Fascism': 'Islamism is a totalitarian ideology. An Islamist is a danger in the same way a Fascist is a danger.'[14]

From this time on, the term has been used frequently by neo-conservatives, though their opponents use alternative descriptions – most recently and intriguingly (though the term is unlikely to catch on because it alludes to a different historical era) John Gray's 'Islamo-Jacobinism.'[15] Timothy Garton-Ash is correct in arguing that 'in identifying those trying to kill us, we should choose our words carefully'.[16] Neither 'Islamo-fascist' nor 'Islamist' is the right label. 'Most Islamic terrorists are, in some sense, Islamists, but most Islamists are not terrorists,' Garton-Ash argues. Since *jihad* can be used in the sense of a 'crusade for education',[17] the only correct term is 'violent jihadist', with perhaps 'jihadist' as an acceptable abbreviation – the term *jihadi* is frequently used by the many innocent Muslims whom they attempt to murder and terrorize in Muslim-majority countries.[18] Brian Michael Jenkins concurs that '"jihadists" may be the most appropriate term for the adherents of th[is] ideology. These are individuals for whom *jihad* has become the sole reason for existence.'[19]

Whatever the precise terminology, the more the language has turned towards Islamic or Islamist terrorism, the more the religion of Islam itself appears to be implicated in the definition of the enemy. The positive role of this world religion is forgotten, ignored, or denigrated. In some measure, therefore, it may appear that something akin to a 'clash of civilizations' was precipitated by 9/11. Ostensibly, the Huntington thesis seems to have been, if not proven, remarkably prescient. Closer examination, however, will reveal that this is much less clear-cut than is commonly supposed. In answer to President George W. Bush's claim that '11 September changed our world', 'rather it was America's reaction to 11 September that changed the world'. The US 'suffered a terrorist attack unprecedented in its scale and destructiveness and in so doing lost its sense of security'. It also 'lost its sense of perspective'.[20] It became a society ill at ease with itself and fearful of the outside. Though more Americans were killed in 2001 than in 1941, 9/11 was not a second Pearl Harbor.[21] That other 'day of infamy' (7 December 1941) was a pre-emptive attack launched by a state (fascist Japan), which may have been provoked by the United States but had not given warning of its intentions.[22] No Middle Eastern or other Muslim-majority state attacked the US in 2001. The al-Qaeda network – an extremist terror group motivated by a political ideology – not the Taliban-controlled state of Afghanistan, let alone the Afghan people, launched the attacks of 9/11; and it had given notice of its intentions to attack the United States as far back as 1996 and 1998.[23] ('There is no evidence of the involvement of the people of Afghanistan in what happened in America,' bin Laden affirmed on 7 November 2001.)[24]

The Taliban regime in Afghanistan was attacked as a 'rogue-state' sponsor of terrorism by the US and its allies in retaliation for the events of 9/11,[25] but the majority of the hijackers on 11 September were Saudi nationals, not Afghans, and Mullah Omar, the ruler of Taliban-controlled Afghanistan, was betrayed by bin Laden, who authorized the attacks in contravention of explicit assurances that he would not do so.[26] The attacks of 9/11 were preventable had the al-Qaeda warnings been heeded and appropriate security arrangements, particularly regarding Saudi nationals, been put into place.[27] They were not, largely through a lack of imagination within the intelligence community, a fatal lack of co-ordination between the CIA and the FBI and the absence of proper debate within the US government and Congress: no national intelligence estimate on the terrorist threat was produced between 1997 and 2001, while powerful neo-conservatives in government such as Paul Wolfowitz had belittled the al-Qaeda threat.[28]

Once the attack had occurred, over-reaction was the order of the day. Echoing the terminology of Alexandre de Marenches, the former head of the French secret service during the presidencies of Georges Pompidou and Valéry Giscard d'Estaing,[29] the prominent neo-conservative Eliot A. Cohen wrote an opinion page for the *Wall Street Journal* on 20 November 2001 entitled, 'World War IV: Let's Call this Conflict What it is'.[30] Following Cohen's arguments but not necessarily his tactics, Norman Podhoretz wrote an article for *Commentary* magazine entitled 'How to Win World War IV' in February 2002. 'Whether or not Iraq becomes the second front in the war against terrorism, one thing is certain', he contended: 'there can be no victory in this war if it ends with Saddam Hussein still in power.' 'The real enemy in this war', Cohen argues – as Daniel Pipes has also so persistently and authoritatively done at greater length – 'is not the generalized abstraction "terrorism", but rather "militant Islam"'. Podhoretz failed to notice the contradiction between his two statements – and that Saddam Hussein was a curious target, since he was no militant Islamist; bin Laden called 'socialists' such as Saddam 'infidels, wherever they may be ... in Baghdad or Aden'; he also called him a 'thief' and an 'apostate'.[31] Podhoretz sought instead to reinforce his arguments with a quotation from Bernard Lewis, 'the greatest contemporary scholar of the Islamic world'.[32] Podhoretz's diatribes against 'Islamo-fascism' and depiction of the struggle after 9/11 as World War IV, have continued since.

In September 2004, Podhoretz wrote a retrospective narrative ('World War IV: How it Started, What it Means, and Why We Have to Win') for *Commentary*, to which we will have cause to refer in the discussion of neo-conservative politics and ideology in Chapter 7.[33] 'The military face of the strategy is pre-emption and the political face is democratization,' he contends. 'The stakes are nothing less than the survival of Western civilization, to the extent that Western civilization still exists, because half of it seems to be committing suicide.'[34] In September 2007, Podhoretz published his summation on the theme, *World War IV. The Long Struggle against Islamofascism*. Here the same arguments return with greater elaboration. He dismisses the Bush administration's self-description of the struggle: the 'Global War on Terror'. '... GWOT – as it mockingly, and deservedly so, became known – made no more sense than calling the enemy in World War II "the blitzkrieg" rather than "Germany", or "the dive bomber" rather than "Japan".'[35]

His conclusion or 'epilogue' as he calls it – there can be no 'conclusion' until World War IV is 'won' - is central for our discussion. World War IV, according to Podhoretz, 'will almost certainly go on for three or four decades', and thus Americans are called upon to be far more patient than they were in World War II, when the US was only involved in the conflict for four years. The Islamo-fascists are 'even more elusive than the Communists', so a comparable degree of patience will have to be exercised as in World War III (the 'Cold War'). Podhoretz recalls that in his first State of the Union Address, President George W. Bush affirmed that history had called America to action and that it was both 'our responsibility and our privilege to fight freedom's fight', a fight he also characterized as 'a unique opportunity for us to seize'. Subsequently he reminded his audience that 'we did not seek this war on terror' but that the United States was now trying to meet the 'great demands' that 'history has placed on our country'.

Podhoretz contends that in his use of language and repeated references to history, George W. Bush echoes the concluding paragraphs of George F. Kennan's article, written in 1947 at the start of the Cold War, entitled 'The sources of Soviet conduct'. (Since he was then director of the State Department's policy planning staff, Kennan wrote under the pseudonym 'X'. The essay has thus come to be known as the 'X article'.) Kennan (1904–2005) argued that the Cold War presented the United States with a historic opportunity to assume leadership of what would eventually be described as the 'free world':[36]

> The issue of Soviet-American relations is in essence a test of the overall worth of the United States as a nation among nations. To avoid destruction the United States need only measure up to its own best traditions and prove itself worthy of preservation as a great nation ... the thoughtful observer of Russian–American relations will find no cause for complaint in the Kremlin's challenge to American society. He will rather experience a certain gratitude to a Providence which, by providing the American people with this implacable challenge, has made their entire security as a nation dependent on their pulling themselves together and accepting the responsibilities of moral and political leadership that history plainly intended them to bear.

For Norman Podhoretz, 'substitute "Islamo-fascism" for "Russian–American relations" and every other word of this magnificent statement applies to us as a nation today.' He continues:[37]

> Now, 'our entire security as a nation' – including, to a greater extent than in 1947, our physical security – once more depends on whether we are willing to accept and ready to act upon the responsibilities of moral and political leadership that history has yet again so squarely placed upon our shoulders. Furthermore, and to a greater extent than in 1947, it is almost entirely on *our* shoulders that the burden rests ... Do we, the American people of this generation, have it in us to beat back the 'implacable challenge' of Islamo-fascism as the 'greatest generation' of World War II did in taking on the Nazis and their fascist allies ... ?

Another convert to the idea of the struggle post-9/11 as 'World War IV' is James Woolsey, formerly the Director of the CIA under President Bill Clinton. In a speech delivered on 16 November 2002,[38] Woolsey warned Muslim extremists that

> they have to realize that now for the fourth time in 100 years, we've been awakened and this country is on the march. We didn't choose this fight, but we're in it. And being on the march, there's only one way we're going to be able to win it. It's the way we won World War I fighting for Wilson's 14 points. The way we won World War II fighting for Churchill's and Roosevelt's Atlantic Charter and the way we won World War III fighting for the noble ideas I think best expressed by President Reagan, but also very importantly at the beginning by President Truman, that this was not a war of us against them. It was not a war of countries. It was a war of freedom against tyranny. We have to convince the people of the Middle East that we are on their side, as we convinced Lech Walesa and Vaclav Havel and Andrei Sakharov that we were on their side.

Interviewed on 10 October 2005, Woolsey added that Eliot A. Cohen had been correct in describing the struggle as a long war, 'decades not years ... I have come now to start calling it "the long war of the 21st century"'. The Committee on the Present Danger (CPD) was relaunched on 20 July 2004, for the third time since the end of World War II – the previous occasions were in 1950 and 1976 – under the chairmanship of Woolsey to combat what he called 'a totalitarian movement masquerading as a religion'. At a press conference in January 2006, when an Iran Policy Paper was presented, Woolsey added: 'the militant Islamists cannot be appeased; they will wage war until they are stopped.'[39]

Working backwards from the conclusions of this book, we maintain at the outset that the hypothesis of a permanent clash akin to World War III (for David Selbourne, Tim LaHaye, and George W. Bush – particularly in the circumstances of Iran's acquisition of nuclear weapons)[40] or World War IV (for Eliot A. Cohen, Norman Podhoretz, James Woolsey, and the neo-conservatives who embrace the concept of an endless, ongoing war as a deliberate act of choice)[41] is a false one. Was the Cold War ('42 long years' of 'war' according to Norman Podhoretz) a genuine world war (World War III)? George F. Kennan lectured at the National War College in 1946–7 on the theme 'Measures Short of War'.[42] In an interview for CNN in May–June 1996, Kennan clarified that the containment of the Soviet Union was not the same thing as war: 'I'm sorry that in the telegram I did not emphasize more that this did not mean that we would have to have a war with Russia,' he said; 'but we would have to find a way of dealing with them which was quite different from that which had been going on.' Asked whether he was 'satisfied [with] the success of the policy of containment', Kennan answered in the affirmative: 'if the alternative was to have a great military conflagration, I could see no good coming out of this ... You must remember my view of warfare: that everybody is a defeated power with modern warfare, with [nuclear] weapons.' Significantly, he added that his 'thoughts about containment were of course distorted by the people who [mis]understood [the idea] and pursued it exclusively as a military concept; and I think that that, as much as any other cause, led to [the] 40 years of unnecessary, fearfully expensive and disoriented process of the Cold War.'[43] Robert G. Kaufman, a proponent of the Bush doctrine, contends that Truman had a 'more enlarged, enlightened and realistic concept of our true national interest' than had Kennan. Although Kaufman, too, uses the term 'World War III', he admits that Ronald Reagan 'resolutely pursued a policy of vigilant containment and ideological warfare' – but neither rearmament nor 'ideological warfare' is open war.[44]

Kennan, the architect of 'containment' rather than 'World War III' is, by his own admission, a strange authority for Podhoretz to cite in the context of an alleged new 'World War IV'. It is bin Laden who, on 28 December 2004, proclaimed that 'World War III' was raging in Iraq.[45] There is no case for the neo-conservatives to echo his language, any more than there is for the President of the United States to refer to bin Laden, let alone quote his words, as he did at Fort Bragg on 28 June 2005.[46] At this South Carolina Air Force base on 24 July 2007, the President referred to bin Laden and al-Qaeda 118 times in 29 minutes! Dan Froomkin argued in the *Washington Post* that the President had become al-Qaeda's 'best publicist': 'like any terrorist organization, al-Qaeda wants attention. It wants to be perceived as powerful. And it particularly wants Americans to live in fear.'[47]

Instead of arguing at the outset that the proponents of the 'clash of civilizations' are 'false prophets', we will attempt to outline the arguments presented by a number of the theoreticians of the movement which has been called 'neo-conservative' and suggest reasons why many of their views are based on faulty logic or a misreading of either history or current events. We will not pursue the ambiguities of the terms 'terrorism' and 'war on terror(ism)' since this has been done elsewhere ('explain[ing] what "they do to us" [is used] to justify what we "do to them"').[48] Only in the last chapters – Chapters 8, 9, and 10 – and the conclusion will the whole thesis of the 'clash' be challenged in its various ramifications and a counter-model suggested. But first we must place the debate in context, by suggesting something of the tradition of hostility between the West and Islam and the reasons why in 2001 the United States, while woefully unprepared for the attacks on New York and Washington DC, was prepared to respond so vigorously to what it perceived as an unprovoked declaration of war against it by the forces of Islamic extremism.

# Chapter One
# The Context of the Clash

> When it comes to the common rights and needs of men and women, there is no clash of civilizations. The requirements of freedom apply fully to Africa and Latin America and the entire Islamic world. The peoples of the Islamic nations want and deserve the same freedoms and opportunities as people in every nation. And their governments should listen to their hopes.
>
> Remarks by President George W. Bush at the 2002 Graduation Exercise of the United States Military Academy, West Point, New York (1 June 2002)[1]

> The great struggles of the twentieth century between liberty and totalitarianism ended with a decisive victory for the forces of freedom – and a single sustainable model for national success: freedom, democracy, and free enterprise.
>
> US National Security Strategy, 2002 *(NSS-2002)*[2]

> The American people have chosen, consented to, and affirmed their support for the Israeli oppression of the Palestinians, the occupation and usurpation of their land, and its continuous killing, torture, punishment and expulsion of the Palestinians ... The freedom and democracy that you call [for] is for yourselves and for the white race only; as for the rest of the world, you impose upon them your monstrous, destructive policies and governments, which you call the 'American friends'. Yet you prevent them from establishing democracies ...
>
> Osama bin Laden, Letter to the American People (6 October 2002).[3]

> This struggle has been called a clash of civilizations. In truth, it is a struggle for civilization.
>
> President George W. Bush, Address to the Nation (11 September 2006)[4]

The relationship between values such as democracy and human rights, faith and culture is a complex one; the primacy of a 'Western' understanding of either democracy or human rights cannot be imposed on other parts of the world without the risk of oppression. The global 'leadership' of human rights and religious freedom discourse has been appropriated by successive American administrations. The championing of both values can, in certain circumstances, lead to the multiplication of wrongs in the world rather than increasing the human good – the case of the intervention in Iraq in 2003 appears to demonstrate this. Anthony Woodiwiss argues that under the present 'rules', the rights of only some members of the human race are protected, while those of others are ignored – one can suggest that the rights of the innocent victims of war in Afghanistan and Iraq fall into this category. For true justice to emerge in the world, a far wider range of humanity must be protected. It is desirable to support true freedom of expression; economic, social, and cultural rights as having equal status to political and civil rights and the right to freedom of religion; and to recognize that indigenous peoples are entitled to a degree of protection while also allowing them the capacity to develop. Rights and freedoms are thus much more complex and universal than allowed for within the current American paradigm.[5]

There are many legitimate paths towards national and cultural self-determination rather than a single path which all are obliged to follow. In his early writings, Francis Fukuyama – at that stage an unrepentant neo-conservative – may not have meant to endorse the thesis that there is 'a single sustainable model for national success', but many of his readers took him to imply just this, when he talked of 'the end point of mankind's ideological evolution' and 'the universalization of Western liberal democracy as the final form of human government' (see Chapter 2). By 2006 it became clear that Fukuyama had dissociated himself from ideas which, in Stephen Holmes's words, had been 'hijacked and deployed by the Bush administration to support policies that Fukuyama now heartily condemns'.[6]

### *The Legacy of the Past: Orientalism and the Western Lust for Empire*

For the period of the Middle Ages until the seventeenth century at least, the 'Christian' powers of Europe were as warlike and expansionist as their Muslim counterparts – and throughout those centuries of warfare, there were plenty of occasions when Christian and Muslim powers reached alliances of convenience against a common enemy. Virtually every Muslim jurist writing on *jihad* of the sword in the Middle Ages conceived of two worlds in conflict, one the House or Abode of Islam (*Dar al-Islam*), the other the House or Abode of War (*Dar al-harb*), with at best an indeterminate area of negotiation known as the Abode of Truce (*Dar al-sulh*). Similarly, Christian jurists could not conceive of a state of peace with the 'infidel'. In his treatise *On the Law of War* (1532), Francisco de Vitoria pronounced that all captured infidel combatants should be killed and their women and children enslaved.[7] Professor Norman Daniel demonstrated nearly fifty years ago that the negative stereotype of Islam was created by Christian scholars in the period of the twelfth, thirteenth, and fourteenth centuries as war propaganda in support of the Crusades. He further argued that there has been a very long survival of the 'medieval concepts' into modern times.[8] The late Christian priest and scholar of Islam, Professor William Montgomery Watt, who died on 24 October 2006 at the formidable age of 97, contended that this distorted image identified by Norman Daniel was 'a negative aspect of European identity', by which he meant that it was 'an image of what Europe [was] not'. This negative stereotype was contrasted to the positive identity of being a Christian. Professor Watt attributed 'the tenacity of the prejudice' to the fact that this distorted image of Islam 'was an essential aspect of the emergence of European identity'.[9]

Watt's view is confirmed by the research of Tomaz Mastnak, who argues that there would be no 'European history in the strict sense of the word' without its hostility towards the Muslim world. 'Western, Latin, Christians' hostility toward the Muslims – anti-Muslim sentiments, ideas, calls for action and action – played a key role in its formation.'[10] Nasir Khan reminds us that there was more than one 'Christian' response to the Islamic advance and that the polemic emanating from (Orthodox) Byzantium – a literature from which Pope Benedict XVI quoted directly in his notorious lecture at Regensburg on 12 September 2006 – was if anything worse than that of the Latin West: 'the implication is that Satan himself was the moving force behind Islam. The Qur'an in a like manner was regarded as a false scripture that Muhammad composed with the help of a [renegade Christian, possibly Arian] monk ...'[11] Thus when Benedict XVI quoted the words of the Byzantine emperor Manuel II Paleologus c.1391 – 'show me just what Mohammed brought that was new, and there you will find things only evil and inhuman, such as his command to spread by the sword the faith he preached'[12] – he was quoting the customary polemic of a bygone age. What is open to question was the wisdom of the Roman pontiff, in the context of a lecture on faith and reason, in drawing the world's attention to the hate literature of the past at a troubled time in the relations between the West and the Islamic World.

Norman Daniel commented that 'the condemnation by Edward Said in his *Orientalism* [1978] of the assumed superiority and cultural intolerance of the Orientalist tradition in the West was not only laudable but overdue.' He considered nevertheless that the 'great Orientalists meant to achieve impartial judgements', and just to attempt impartiality 'was itself a major achievement', even if their views 'by no means broke entirely with those of the Middle Ages'. The chief lesson might be that 'scientific' methodology may be unable to escape from 'its bundle of inherited prejudices of all kinds'.[13] In fact critics, both at the time and since, have been stern towards Said and his unverified assertions. He fails to demonstrate, for example, that 'Orientalism is fundamentally a political doctrine' and that 'for every Orientalist, quite literally, there is a support system of staggering power', considering the ephemeral nature of the myths that Orientalism propagates; nor does he demonstrate that 'this system now culminates in the very institutions of the state.'[14]

Keith Windschuttle criticizes Said's approach in three areas. First, he questions his assertion that Orientalism, although purporting to be an objective, disinterested, and rather esoteric field, in fact functioned to serve political ends. Orientalist scholarship provided the means through which Europeans could take over Oriental lands: 'colonial rule was justified in advance by Orientalism, rather than after the fact.' Windschuttle concedes that Orientalism provided the West with a command of Oriental languages and culture, plus a mindset that convinced it of its cultural and technological advance over Islam, but 'these are far from sufficient causes of imperial conquest since they explain neither motives, opportunities, nor objectives.' 'Said provides no support at all for his contention that "colonial rule was justified in advance by Orientalism"', Windschuttle contends, 'because he fails to cite evidence about the actual causal sequence that led to the annexation of any of the territories occupied by England or France in the nineteenth century. Where real historians have attempted this, they have come to quite different conclusions, with trade, investment, and military causes predominating.'[15] Extraordinarily, Said fails to discuss the German school of Orientalism – yet the Germans were among the most prominent Orientalists. Did he omit them consciously, because Germany never went on to become an imperial power in any of the Oriental countries of North Africa or the Middle East?

Secondly, Windschuttle attempts to refute Said's claim that Orientalism led the West to see Islamic culture as static in both time and place, as 'eternal, uniform, and incapable of defining itself', which gave Europe a sense of its own cultural and intellectual superiority. In attempting this refutation, however, Windschuttle pays insufficient attention to the long tradition of anti-Islamism, and its role in creating a European identity.

And thirdly, Said contended that Orientalism produced a false description of Arabs and Islamic culture as isolated from the mainstream of human progress in the sciences, arts, and commerce. In contrast, Windschuttle contends, with Bernard Lewis, that 'rather than being necessarily ethnocentric and racist, Oriental Studies was one of the first fields within European scholarship to overcome such prejudices and to open the Western mind to the whole of humanity'.

Christopher de Bellaigue is willing to allow that there is a closer relationship between Orientalism and Empire than some of Said's critics, such as Windschuttle and more recently Robert Irwin, are prepared to admit.[16] Silvestre de Sacy, who became professor at the Paris École Spéciale des Langues Orientales Vivantes in 1795, is regarded as the 'father' of Orientalism. De Sacy laid the foundations for a syllabus for students of Arabic, helped start the Société Asiatique and wrote copiously (and far from favourably) about heterodox Muslims such as the Druze. He was an adviser to the Foreign Minister, translated into Arabic the bulletins of the Grande Armée in Egypt and also the Imperial proclamation that was issued after France's occupation of Algiers in 1830. Clearly, the work of Sir William Jones, who made the genealogical link between Sanskrit, Latin, and Greek, in 1786, and who presided over the Asiatick Society of Bengal, influenced the development of British imperialism: the founder of the Society was none other than Warren Hastings, the Governor of Bengal. Christopher de Bellaigue adds that in the nineteenth century, 'two diplomats who were prominent in promoting Britain's influence over Iran, Sir John Malcolm and Sir Gore Ouseley, the latter a founder of the Royal Asiatic Society, made serious scholarly contributions to the study, respectively, of Iranian history and poetry.'

In the same tradition, after World War II, Orientalists continued to offer advice to governments seeking 'regime change'. De Bellaigue notes that

> Ann [K.S.] Lambton won renown as a Persian grammarian and a student of Iranian land tenure. In 1951, while she was a lecturer at [the School of Oriental and African Studies], she advised the British Government on ways to oust the Iranian Prime Minister, Mohammad Mossadeq, who had nationalized the Anglo-Persian Oil Company. On Lambton's recommendation, an Oxford Persianist, R.C. Zaehner, was dispatched to Tehran to make preparations. (In the event, it took the CIA to topple Mossadeq, in 1953.)

Robin Zaehner, Fakhreddin Azimi informs us, 'readily mixed scrupulous scholarly pursuits with inevitably unscrupulous meddling in the shady underworld of covert operations'.[17]

According to Bernard Lewis, one of 'the roots of Muslim rage' is the 'feeling of humiliation – a growing awareness, among the heirs of an old, proud and long dominant civilization, of having been overtaken, overborne, and overwhelmed by those whom they regarded as their inferiors'.[18] Here was the genesis of Lewis's seminal polemic, written before the events of 9/11, but published afterwards, entitled *What Went Wrong?*[19] Bernard Lewis fails to emphasize the fact that growing industrial power in the nineteenth century allowed Europeans to colonize far faster and on a far larger scale than was previously possible. As John Darwin argues, 'it gave them the means to penetrate new markets and crush old competition. It enlarged their ability to collect information and exploit it efficiently. Above all, it enhanced their capacity to project their physical power over far greater distances and at much lower cost.' Not only did the arrival of the steamship and the railway remove much of the reality of strategic remoteness. There was also the new possibility of indirect control: 'invisible sway: the systematic accumulation of predominant influence over regions and states whose rulers were left with a purely technical sovereignty.'[20] Some might argue that this kind of 'informal empire' remains very much alive in the present era.

The European colonizing experience imposed an unequal relationship on other parts of the world: the raw materials of the colonies were cheap, while the industrial goods produced in Europe were expensive; the one fuelled the other, and was intended to do so. Whether directly or indirectly ruled in the imperial system, the colonies or semi-colonies became increasingly impoverished. Thus when Bernard Lewis and others talk in terms of 'modernization', it must be recognized that modernization in the European – and later American – mould came at a huge price. As John Darwin comments: 'it seems possible (some would say obvious) that Europe's expansion amounted in part to a deliberate assault on the modernizing venture of other peoples and states. Perhaps it was not Europe's modernity that triumphed, but its superior capacity for organized violence.'[21]

Bernard Lewis virtually ignores European colonization of the modern Middle East and large parts of what is now the Islamic world. He alleges that it was 'comparatively brief and ended half a century ago.'[22] The French ruled Algeria from 1830 to 1962. The British were present in what is now Bangladesh from 1757 to 1947. The British controlled much of the Indian sub-continent directly from the nineteenth century until a mismanaged partition and ignominious end to colonial rule there in 1947 which continues to carry a heavy cost in relations between India, Pakistan, and Bangladesh some sixty years later. As Juan R. Cole writes, 'while Britain only formally ruled Egypt from 1882 to 1922, it was already making and breaking its rulers in the 1870s, and continued to play a heavy-handed role in Egyptian politics and in the Suez Canal until 1956. Radical Islamism was first provoked to terrorism in Egypt precisely by the arrogance of British power there, beginning a genealogy of violence that leads through Ayman al-Zawahiri directly to 11 September 2001.'[23] And why did Britain occupy Egypt? It was a key zone astride a maritime highway, the Suez Canal, which provided the cheapest and fastest connection between Britain/Europe and India. As late as 1956, President Eisenhower condemned the arrogant colonial interventionism of Britain and France in the Suez crisis: 'if those fellows start something, we may have to hit 'em – and, if necessary, with everything in the bucket.'[24] This was an American rejection of Eden's proposed regime change for Egypt. Eden had written to Eisenhower that 'the removal of Nasser and the installation in Egypt of a regime less hostile to the West, must ... rank high among our objectives.'[25] For his part, while he shared 'in general the British and French opinions of Nasser', Eisenhower considered that they had chosen 'a bad time and incident on which to launch corrective measures'.[26]

European colonialism was seen by Eisenhower as a relic of the past, but this did not mean that the United States did not have its own Orientalist agenda for the Middle East. It was displayed in the paradox of Franklin Roosevelt's policy in 1945, his last year in office. He was committed to the establishment of 'a free and democratic Jewish Commonwealth'; but he was warned that his 'continued support of Zionism may ... lead to actual bloodshed in the Near East and even endanger the security of our immensely valuable oil concession from Saudi Arabia'. FDR met King Abdul Aziz Ibn Saud on board the USS *Quincy* in Egypt's Great Bitter Lake on 14 February 1945, in what was the official beginning of US–Saudi diplomatic relations. 'Ibn Saud made the point that he had no trouble with native Palestine Jews,' Roosevelt told an aide, 'but the immigration from Europe was more than he could cope with and if things went wrong the millions of surrounding Arabs might easily proclaim a *jihad* [Roosevelt used the incorrect translation 'holy war'] and then there would be no end of trouble.'[27]

On 16 February 1943, President Roosevelt had declared that 'the defence of Saudi Arabia is vital to the defence of the United States', thereby making possible the extension of the Lend-Lease Act to the kingdom.[28] The US petroleum giant ARAMCO was already well placed in Saudi Arabia by 1945, using racist employment practices and taking a firm line against dissent – the first strike of Saudi workers occurred in that year. Saudi Arabia was to remain 'America's kingdom' for as long as possible; and once the Saudis grew restless and wanted to nationalize their oil industry, Saudi petrodollars would be recycled in the form of American arms sales.[29] From the beginning of the relationship until the present, the

United States has had to balance the concerns of its two main client states in the Middle East. If US military technology supplied to Saudi Arabia fell into the 'wrong hands' it could harm US forces in the Middle East and threaten Israel.[30]

Chalmers Johnson noted in January 2004 that 'the Pentagon currently owns or rents 702 overseas bases in about 130 countries,' and estimates the likely total on 'an honest count' as probably in excess of 1000. 'Once upon a time, you could trace the spread of imperialism by counting up colonies,' Johnson concludes; 'America's version of the colony is the military base. By following the changing politics of global basing, one can learn much about our ever larger imperial stance and the militarism that grows with it.' Even so, for some military planners in the Bush administration such as Andy Hoehn, the US 'military footprint' is still not big enough: 'we don't look particularly well-positioned to deal with the problems we're now going to confront.'[31]

This leads us to consideration of the term 'American empire'. Eisenhower clearly tried in 1956 to distance the United States from the old colonial regimes of France and the United Kingdom and for the most part in their history Americans have convinced themselves that they – unlike the wicked Europeans – have not really had an empire worthy of the name. The experiment of US colonial state-building was short-lived and had ended before World War II: it was confined to Haiti (1915–33), the Dominican Republic (1916–24), Cuba (1899–1902, 1906–9), and the Philippines (1899–1935). Some commentators, such as Michael Walzer, consider imperial rule an exercise of futility in the contemporary world. Americans have no stomach for the economic or military costs of empire. The American public commitment to democracy 'makes imperial rule very hard to justify and equally hard to manage'. Other governments are capable of opposing the policies of the hegemonic power and therefore the endeavour to create a new empire is certain to fail.[32] Martin Walker is less certain. Has not perhaps the United States embarked on a new project, a 'virtual empire', the like of which the world has not seen before? If the war on terrorism shifts the virtual empire into the reality of rule, 'the new beast is likely to find its rule as vulnerable as the empires that have disappeared'.[33]

For others, who are consistent critics of US policies abroad, such as Noam Chomsky, there is no question as to the US search for hegemony; the American Empire project seeks to document, and criticize, the endeavour.[34] In his response to the tragedy of 9/11, entitled 'Blowback', Chalmers Johnson employed a CIA term first used in March 1954 in a declassified report on the 1953 operation to overthrow the government of Mohammad

Mossadeq in Iran. 'It is a metaphor for the unintended consequences of the US government's international activities that have been kept secret from the American people.' Of George W. Bush's rhetoric on 11 and 20 September 2001, Johnson comments: 'This attempt to define difficult-to-grasp events as only a conflict over abstract values – as a "clash of civilizations", in current post-Cold War American jargon – is not only disingenuous but also a way of evading responsibility for the "blowback" that America's imperial projects have generated.'[35] Subsequently, Chalmers Johnson has developed his theme in a *Blowback* trilogy on the costs and consequences of the American Empire in the broadest sense.[36] (The 'blowback' argument was reinforced in the speech delivered by the Dubai chief of police to the Crans Montana global security forum in November 2007, when he argued that the Americans had 'created the Satan' in the first place: Western experts had taught the al-Qaeda forerunners in the Afghan resistance to Soviet occupation 'how to make and explode bombs'. This version of events is vigorously contested by the former CIA operative Marc Sageman, who served in Islamabad in the years 1987–9, and argues that explosives were introduced 'much later, around 1992'. The assassination of Abdullah Azzam by a huge car bomb on 24 November 1989 emerges as a key event because of the absence of such attacks before then.)[37]

Finally, there are a (limited) number of voluble neo-conservative defenders of the new American empire. Max Boot is one of the best-known of these. Writing four days after the 9/11 attacks, Boot argued that 'the most realistic response to terrorism is for America to embrace its imperial role.' The attacks were the 'result of insufficient American involvement and ambition; the solution is to be more expansive in our goals and more assertive in their implementation.'[38] Boot argues, in answer to the question, does the US need an empire?: 'North Korea, Iran, Syria, Libya, and other states pose a major threat to world peace and to American lives. So do terrorist networks like al-Qaeda. If we don't stop the bad guys, who will? If we don't police the world, who will? The job of policing these distant lands – places full of failed states, criminal states, or simply a state of nature – ultimately falls to us, which means that whether we like it or not, liberal imperialism appears to be in our future.'[39] Even in the twenty-first century there was a case to be made for imperial occupation by benevolent American neo-imperialists:[40]

> Most successful examples of state building begin by imposing the rule of law – as the United States did in the Philippines, and Britain in India – which is a prerequisite for economic development and the eventual emergence of democracy. Merely holding an election and leaving will likely achieve little, as the United States learned in Haiti in 1994. For occupation to have a

> meaningful impact, it should be fairly lengthy; if Americans are intent on a quick 'exit strategy', they might as well stay home …
>
> We can only wonder what might have happened if, after the Soviet Union was driven out in the early 1990s, the United States had helped build Afghanistan into a viable state. It might not have become the home of the Taliban and al-Qaeda, and the World Trade Center might still be standing.

## *'Reverse Orientalism' or 'Occidentalism':*[41] *the Rise of the Conflict of Civilizations Thesis in Muslim-Majority Countries*

There were many European colonialists who denigrated the achievements of other civilizations, including that of Islam. But there were also others – a significant number at first, gradually fewer and fewer in the later period of colonization and as the process of colonization itself came under greater scrutiny from the governing elites in Europe – who were willing to recognize the achievements of non-Christian societies. As the trend increased towards a sense of racial superiority among the European governing class in colonial societies, so the reaction set in and affected profoundly even those Muslims, such as Allama Muhammad Iqbal (1877–1938), who admired much of Europe's cultural achievement and drew upon its intellectual traditions. In his poems, entitled *Persian Psalms* (*Zabur-i 'Ajam*) written in 1927, Iqbal bemoaned the cultural predominance of the West:[42]

> Against Europe I protest,
> And the attraction of the West:
> Woe for Europe and her charm,
> Swift to capture and disarm!
> Europe's hordes with flame and fire
> Desolate the world entire … (Part 2, no. 19)
>
> Fool! Is there then such hope in thee
> Of winning Europe's sympathy?
> The falcon grieves not overmuch
> About the bird that's in his clutch … (Part 2, no. 61)
>
> Eschew the West, and do not be
> Bewitched by Europe's wizardry;
> Not worth a barley, in my view,
> Is all her ancient and her new … (Part 2, no. 62)

Yet Iqbal was inconsistent in his critique. Writing in *The Reconstruction of Religious Thought in Islam* (1928), he was much more positive. 'The most remarkable phenomenon of modern history is … the enormous rapidity with which the world of Islam is spiritually moving towards the West,' he wrote. 'There is nothing wrong in this movement,' he continued, 'for European culture... is only a further development of some of the most important phases of the culture of Islam.'[43] Not everyone would have agreed with this assessment, or with Iqbal's championing of Atatürk's authoritarian reforms in Turkey.

The Turkish Revolutionary struggle under Kemal Atatürk failed to achieve the unanimity of support it had sought. Early on there was criticism that his policy was blindly Western-oriented and imitationist, detached from its own roots, seeking to attain the title 'civilized' at all costs, prepared to glorify the achievements of the Greco-Roman heritage while neglecting the historical achievements of non-European peoples across the Mediterranean basin and the fertile crescent. Atatürk's critics equated Westernization with giving up one's status as a member of a worthy and powerful nation with a proud history. Turkish people, it was alleged, were forced to live 'like the French while being ashamed of even mentioning their Turkishness'. Mehmet Dogan's manifesto *The Treachery of Westernization* (1975), which has gone through several subsequent Turkish editions, pointed out the dangers both of alliances with Europe and admiration of European ways, norms, and values. Nergis Canefe and Taninodotl Bora stress 'the intertwined traditions of Turkism, Islamism, cultural puri[ty], defensive nationalism and reverse Orientalism' as a long-standing phenomenon in Turkish political culture. They conclude that it can be categorized as the 'Oriental' re-enactment of the Huntington thesis on the 'clash of civilizations'.[44]

A similar form of 'reverse Orientalism' or 'Occidentalism' is to be found in Jalal al-i Ahmad's *Occidentosis* (*Gharbzadegi*), a work which brought him to the attention of those most active in the Iranian Revolution of 1978–9.[45] This biting criticism of the Westernization of Iran and other Eastern societies was first published in a limited edition in 1962 and then posthumously in its complete form after the revolution led by Ayatollah Khomeini. Jalal al-i Ahmad's interpretation is at times penetrating, and at other times naïve. Writing in a period well before the end of the Cold War, he perceived that the age in which he wrote was no longer one of 'clashing "isms" and ideologies',[46] but one subordinated to what he termed 'the realm of mechanization' (or 'mechanosis'), which in our time would be called variously the globalized economy or the capitalist system. Machines required oil, so Iran had something sought by the West: Jalal al-i Ahmad correctly pointed to the first oil concession in 1901 made to William Knox D'Arcy as the beginning of its modern downfall.[47]

'This is what we call *following* in politics and economics,' Ahmad proclaimed. 'To follow the West – the Western states and the oil companies – is the supreme manifestation of occidentosis in our time. This is how Western industry plunders us, how it rules, how it holds our destiny ... They take away the oil and give you whatever you want in return – from soup to nuts, even grain.'[48] A dependent economy and thought process was the inevitable outcome: 'now that we are an oil-producing country and the European brings us everything from soap to nuts on a silver platter, why should we go to the trouble of building factories, heavy industry, with all the attendant problems ...?'[49] Jalal al-i Ahmad's 'occidentotic man' was one who was devoid of belief or convictions, a faithful partaker of the West's consumer goods, potentially a servant and broker for the oil interest, and, like the Orientalist, 'a parasite growing on the root of imperialism'. 'He has no faith, no direction, no aim, no belief, neither in God nor in humanity. He cares neither whether society is transformed ... nor whether religion or irreligion prevails.'[50]

Sayyid Qutb's entire life work was dedicated to countering the irreligion characteristic of Jalal al-i Ahmad's 'occidentotic man'. Since the events of 11 September 2001, readers of the *New York Times* and even scholars such as John C. Zimmerman have been obsessed with Qutb (1906–66) as being in some way the intellectual progenitor of Osama bin Laden and mastermind of the 9/11 atrocities.[51] They are misguided in their search for such an affiliation.[52] Instead, we should view Qutb's anti-Westernism against the background of Islamic reformist discourse from Jamal al-Din al-Afghani (1838–97), through Muhammad Abduh (1849–1905) to Muhammad Rashid Rida (1865–1935).[53] Qutb divides the concept of 'civilization' (*hadara*) into two elements: culture (*thaqafa*), which includes religion, art, and ethical norms; and materialism (*madariiya*), which comprises sciences and their applied results. He acknowledges the difficulty of distinguishing the two terms but cites the example of Japan as a country which was able to preserve its *thaqafa* while adopting the latest in European *madariiya*.[54]

In its quest to establish a universal order, Islam confronts another 'system' with equally universalist ambitions: what Qutb calls 'modern material civilization'. The separation between the worldly and the divine, stipulated as the bedrock of the 'modern material civilization', is particular to the history of Christianity in Europe; it is not inevitable that all civilizations must go through it on the road to progress. Qutb also addresses the 'moral failure' of the West. The notion of 'perpetual progress' is the product of the historical circumstances of the Christian-European context. Material profit becomes the sole criterion, not only of the acceptance or the rejection of things, but also of existence or non-existence. This implies a state of affairs in which man loses all nobility, where he is no more than an instrument. Western thought, Qutb argues, not only stands on a 'materialistic basis that is contrary to the Islamic theory of life', but is essentially inimical and in opposition to Islam. Qutb argues that the US wants an 'Americanized Islam', but a castrated one: 'the Americans and their allies in the Middle East reject an Islam that resists imperialism and oppression, and opt for an Islam that resists only Communism.'[55] Iqbal 'never dehumanized the West', but for Ian Buruma and Avishai Margalit the idea of the West as less than human is what makes Qutb a 'high priest of Occidentalism'.[56] 'The sociologist Gershon Shafir believes the world today is divided between the followers of Leo Strauss and the followers of Sayyid Qutb. No doubt this will be news to many.'[57] Anne Norton explores the insights and ironies of this observation. The followers of Qutb

> stand in the advance guard of those who fought in Afghanistan. Most of those who have set themselves in opposition to the West, and many of those engaged in violent attacks on Western targets, see themselves as followers of Sayyid Qutb. They are, they believe, engaged in a struggle of more than worldly significance. The followers of Strauss [see Chapter 7] see themselves symmetrically: standing of the defence of the West, for the revival of ancient teachings and a lost morality.[58]

It is in this tradition of ferocious anti-Westernism, rather than in theology or attitudes to violence, that a link between Sayyid Qutb's analysis and that of Osama bin Laden may be perceived. Whatever the resonance of bin Laden's rhetoric, a group such as Hizbu'llah (the Party of God) in Lebanon is more representative of Islamist opinion in the Arab world. Hizbu'llah's 'statement of purpose' issued by its press office on 20 March 1998, while seeking to rid itself 'of the pressuring threats practised by the foreign Zionist Entity [= Israel], which has been thrust upon the Islamic, and the contemporary Arab nation', nevertheless seeks a form of Islam that 'recommends communication among civilizations and rejects divisive collision between those civilizations'.[59] Hizbu'llah does not deny the legitimacy of Western states as it does that of Israel, but it conceives of the West as a counter-civilization confronting Islamic civilization. The party's struggle with the West is justified as a defence of 'our religion, existence and dignity'. 'Ali Fayyad, one of the party's theoreticians, nevertheless considers that it is possible to move from an irreconcilable 'conflict' (*khilaf*) to a civilizational 'disagreement' (*ikhtilaf*), which implies coexistence and harmony. Yussef Meri' goes further, and suggests that it is possible for the party to become reconciled with any Western state that changes its regional policy.[60]

These comments suggest that the remarks of Richard Armitage, the US Deputy Secretary of State, in September 2002, that Hizbu'llah had become 'even more dangerous' than al-Qaeda and had 'made the A team of terrorists', while al-Qaeda had been relegated to the B team, were seriously misplaced.[61] Armitage underestimated the ongoing challenge of al-Qaeda and at the same time obfuscated the reality, which was that Hizbu'llah, Ayatullah Fadlallah, its spiritual leader, and Iran had all condemned the 9/11 attacks. Fadlallah added that neither offensive nor defensive *jihad* could justify such acts, which were not sanctioned by any religion, civilization, or human logic.[62] There is some evidence that bin Laden once met Imad Mugniyeh, Hizbu'llah's chief arms smuggler; but co-operation between the Sunni al-Qaeda group and the Shi'ite Hizbu'llah seems to be unproven.[63]

In spite of the possibility of change within a body such as Hizbu'llah, the liberal Syrian author Nidhal Na'isa depicts the Middle East as 'an intellectual disaster area after the surging fundamentalist tsunami swept through it'. 'A great part of the fiery, devout, [Islamic] revivalist discourse ...', he declares, is based on the claim that the 'infidel' West is 'our mortal arch-enemy, that it hates us with the greatest hatred, and that it does not let any opportunity pass for hatching conspiracies and striking at us'. Furthermore, the claim that 'all of the backwardness, misery, deterioration, decline, defeats, and baseness currently present in the Arab and Muslim worlds' is due to 'an uninterrupted flood of machinations on the part of those evil infidels' is made. Westerners target Islam 'because they have no religion, and because we are better than them in Allah's view'. According to the Islamists, Islam is, for this reason, the only civilization 'capable of destroying Western civilization, defeating it on its home ground, and wiping it out of existence'. Nidhal Na'isa rejects this reverse 'conflict of civilizations' thesis, noting that the West

> has contributed greatly – through material aid, technical expertise, and advisory assistance – to many of the amenities of life we enjoy. Tens of millions of humans have benefited from the West's achievements in the sciences, and Western universities have opened [their doors] to the multitudes of students arriving from all countries of the world. They have granted citizenship and inducements – material and other – to all of the outstanding, the gifted, and the creative to live in those countries – and even to those who were chased out of their own countries. For instance ... London has become a safe haven for fundamentalists fleeing the hell of Middle Eastern despotism. They release, from London, their fiery communiqués for the destruction of the infidel West ...

Nidhal Na'isa remains nevertheless something of a lonely voice in his rejection of the Occidentalist 'clash of civilizations' thesis, notwithstanding his fierce rejection of George W. Bush's counter-productive foreign policy.[64]

### *Without Moral Equivalence: Bin Laden's Critique Viewed on its Own Terms*

Tony Blair remarked of 9/11 in a speech on 5 March 2004: 'they killed 3,000. But if they could have killed 30,000 or 300,000, they would have rejoiced in it. The purpose was to cause such hatred between Muslims and the West that a religious *jihad* became reality; and the world [would be] engulfed by it.'[65] The impact of the attacks was so great not because of the actual numbers killed but the psychological impact. Brian Michael Jenkins notes that 'psychologists have learned that we rank such events by almost squaring the death toll per event ... The terrorist attack on 9/11, with nearly 3,000 dead, had the psychological impact of millions dying.'[66] Many American commentators are reluctant to analyse the writings of Osama bin Laden and Ayman al-Zawahiri because of 'moral equivalence'; they fear that, if their words are considered, a degree of 'justification' will be found for the unwarranted murder of 3,208 civilians in the three most significant al-Qaeda operations in the West prior to June 2004 (New York plus Washington DC on 9/11: 2,996 victims; Madrid, March 2004: 190 victims; Saudi Arabia, May 2004: 22 victims). This is nonsense. There can be no justification for gratuitous murder.

However, in order to know an enemy, his arguments should be studied.[67] Between 11 September 2001 and April 2006, in spite of being the world's most hunted man, bin Laden broadcast 24 statements.[68] Even George W. Bush has listened to the words of bin Laden (though it might have been preferable not to have told the world that he had done so, since terrorism needs no additional publicity). Hence the importance of Michael Scheuer's study *Through Our Enemies' Eyes*, the first systematic consideration of bin Laden's arguments from an intelligence specialist rather than a self-appointed pundit. In his second book, *Imperial Hubris*, Michael Scheuer discerns six main themes in Osama bin Laden's propaganda: (1) US support for Israel that keeps Palestinians in the Israelis' thrall; (2) the presence of US and other Western troops on the Arabian Peninsula; (3) the US occupation of Iraq and Afghanistan; (4) US support for Russia, India, and China against their Muslim militants; (5) US pressure on Arab energy producers to keep oil prices low, which is regarded as tantamount to oil theft; and (6) US support for apostate, corrupt, and tyrannical Muslim governments.[69]

To this list could be added (7) the notorious US 'double standard' (*al-izdiwajiyya*)[70] in its dealings with the Islamic world, particularly on the question of democracy, with Algeria in 1992 cited as the prime example; (8) the proliferation of weapons of mass destruction (WMD) and the largely unacknowledged existence of the Israeli nuclear arsenal; (9) arms deals between the West and Saudi Arabia and the Gulf states, further prolonging Western control over the Middle East long after colonialism has come to an end; (10) and finally, the suspicion that the United States and Britain seek to redraw the political map of the Middle East. The Bush–Blair 'axis' (his response to George W. Bush's 'axis of evil' speech) is compared by bin Laden to the Sykes–Picot pact of 1916. He reminds his audience that President Nixon had considered sending airborne troops to seize oilfields in Saudi Arabia, Kuwait, and Abu Dhabi in 1973–4 had the OPEC oil embargo not been lifted.[71] As Scheuer comments, bin Laden has been 'precise in telling America the reasons he is waging war on us. None of the reasons have anything to do with our freedom, liberty and democracy, but [they do] have everything to do with US policies and actions in the Muslim world.'[72]

Bin Laden's stated purpose is 'to liberate the land of Islam from the infidels and establish the law of Allah'. In his 'Declaration of War Against the Americans', he recognized the need to protect the oil wealth of the Middle East: 'I would like here to alert my brothers, the *Mujahidin* ... to protect this [oil] wealth and not to include it in the battle, as it is a great Islamic wealth and a large economic power essential for the soon to be established Islamic state ...' The huge Saudi oil resources represented 'a serious danger to the very existence of the Zionist state in Palestine' and were not to be attacked. That at least, was the truth according to Osama in 1998;[73] the situation had changed considerably by 2007, although the jihadist attack on the Saudi oilfields was foiled. On 16 December 2004, bin Laden returned to this theme:[74]

> Remember ... that the biggest reason for our enemies' control over our lands is to steal our oil, so give everything you can to stop the greatest oil theft in history from the current and future generations in collusion with the agents and foreigners ... oil, which is the basis of all industry, has gone down in price many times. After it was going for $40 a barrel two decades ago, in the last decade it went for as little as $9, while its price today should be $100 at the very least. So keep on struggling, do not make it easy for them, and focus your operations on it, especially in Iraq and the Gulf, for that will be the death of them.

America emerged from World War II as a net importer of oil because of greatly increased demand. US oil production did not peak until 1970,[75] and the US was still considered in 2005 to be the world's third largest producer, but it still relies on supplementing its own supplies with Middle East oil. It is only since 2007 that the Bush administration has recognized that oil dependency must be reduced, since the US requires a far higher percentage of the world's oil production to sustain its economy than any other country.[76] Michael T. Klare had argued the case the previous year for 'taking oil out of the equation': 'Osama bin Laden and his lieutenants understand full well that America's presence in their backyard is driven by our addiction to Middle Eastern oil, and that so long as we do nothing to curb this addiction we will continue to embrace policies that will generate ever more recruits for al-Qaida. Only through self-discipline and the elimination of our oil dependency can we break this cycle and so win the war against terror.'[77] By November 2007, the weakness of the US dollar, worries about the security of fuel supplies, continuing demand from China, and a relative dearth of supply (two million extra barrels of oil a day were required in 2008 and another two million in 2009) sent US oil prices above $98 a barrel, so that oil could be said to be 'on the cusp of $100 a barrel'[78] - bin Laden's dream price of 2004 had come to pass within three years.

The suffering of the Lebanese and Palestinian peoples is seen by bin Laden as a result of the creation of Israel with Western support. The notion of revenge is central to bin Laden's thinking:[79]

> The events that made a direct impression on me were during and after 1982, when America allowed the Israelis to invade Lebanon ... I still remember those distressing scenes: blood, torn limbs, women and children massacred ... The whole world heard and saw what happened, but did nothing. In those critical moments, many ideas raged inside me, ideas difficult to describe, but they unleashed a powerful urge to reject injustice and a strong determination to punish the aggressors.

Bin Laden regards the Zionist enterprise as an anachronistic extension of European colonization into the modern age. Since bin Laden's words were censored in the United States in the aftermath of 9/11, there was little or no reporting at the time of his claim that the attacks were a culmination of an eighty-year struggle;[80] that the action was to avenge 'our people killed in Palestine';[81] that it was Palestine 'which has sunk under military occupation for more than 80 years' (some commentators have assumed that bin Laden was referring to the abolition of the Caliphate in 1924); that 'the creation and continuation of Israel is one of the greatest crimes, and you – the United States – are the leaders of its criminals'; and finally that there was 'no need to explain and prove the degree of American support for Israel.'[82]

'You prevent [us] from establishing democracies', bin Laden told the American people in October 2002. The comment seems odd, considering that the Afghanistan and Iraq wars were supposed to be, at least in part, about removing tyrannies and establishing new democracies. His meaning becomes clear, when it becomes evident that he is referring to events in Algeria a decade earlier: 'when the Islamic party in Algeria wanted to practise democracy, and they won the election, you unleashed your collaborators in the Algerian army on them, and attacked them with tanks and guns, imprisoned them and tortured them – a new lesson from the "American book of democracy"'.[83] The elections in Algeria were overturned by the military, on the grounds that victory for the Islamic Salvation Front (FIS), as the former French Prime Minister, Alain Juppé, expressed it, was 'neither in the interest of Algeria nor in the interest of France'[84] and the other Western states. Such wilful double standards – that the majority of electors of majority-Muslim states cannot see the fruits of their election victory if the result is not to the liking of the United States or other Western powers – are particularly resented in the Islamic world. Indeed, the overturning of the Algerian elections in 1992 and the coup against Mossadeq in Iran in 1953 have become tests of Western sincerity in seeking the good of the Islamic world for disinterested reasons:[85] they are tests which the Western powers have decisively failed. Memories are long in the Middle East.

Bernard Lewis tries to turn the argument on its head by alleging that by definition the Islamist FIS was undemocratic and that the Algerian military's *coup d'état* of 1992 was indeed a case of double standards – but of the Muslim world against the West:[86] '... democrats are of course at a disadvantage. Their ideology requires them, even when in power, to give freedom and rights to the Islamist opposition. The Islamists, when in power, are under no such obligation ... Their electoral policy has been classically summarized as 'one man (men only), one vote, once'. In contrast, Samuel P. Huntington distanced himself from the interpretation advanced by other neo-conservatives such as Bernard Lewis and Daniel Pipes by asking:

> ... when the Algerian military cancelled the election that the Islamist party was clearly going to win, did they hear any complaint from us? Or the French? Or other Europeans? Not at all. We all sort of quietly said, 'Well done, well done'. That produced a disaster in Algeria, a civil war in which 100,000 people have been killed ... By cancelling the election, the Algerian military greatly strengthened the power of the extremists and the radicals in the Islamist movement. If we believe in democracy, then we ought to believe in a democracy that will allow Islamist parties to come to power.

Subsequent research suggests that the army in Algeria needs to 'reconsider its position as the depositary of popular sovereignty, which it can no longer sustain', while France needs to cease its covert obstruction of international initiatives seeking to facilitate a valid, internally achieved, solution.[87] Daniel Byman notes that the US information strategy should 'centre on the very real brutalities of the jihadists'[88] and many consider that the Algerian civil war a good example of such extreme violence – though the violence of the Algerian military has been as great as that of the militant jihadists they were seeking to quell.

Bin Laden's case concerning weapons sales and the acquisition of weapons of mass destruction (WMD) requires further elucidation. The terrorist leader is entirely correct to argue that the United States pursues a policy of double standards with regard to WMD:[89]

> As for the countries to which you give consent, such as Israel, they are allowed to keep and use such weapons to defend their security. Anyone else who you suspect might be manufacturing or keeping these kinds of weapons, you call criminals and you take military action against them.

The nature of the regime was indeed the essence of the US argument against Saddam Hussein's alleged possession of WMD, and also Iran's alleged pursuit of WMD. For George Weigel, one of the Bush Administration's chief Catholic supporters, 'some states, because of the regime's aggressive intent and the lack of effective internal political controls on giving lethal effect to that intent, cannot be permitted to acquire weapons of mass destruction' (see Chapter 8).

'When will the USA and the UK tell the truth about Israeli [nuclear] weapons?', George Monbiot asked in November 2007. 'Iran isn't starting an atomic arms race, it's joining one.'[90] 'The Israelis, who are one of the few peoples whose survival is genuinely threatened, are probably more likely than almost any other country to actually use their nuclear weapons,' Henry A. Kissinger, the US national security adviser, warned President Richard M. Nixon in a memorandum dated 19 July 1969. 'This is one program on which the Israelis have persistently deceived us', Kissinger continued, 'and may even have stolen from us.' The danger of pressuring the Israelis, however, was that the reason would have to be given. Doing so would mean that 'we will be the ones to make Israel's possession of nuclear weapons public with all the international consequences this entails' – that is, it might 'spark a Soviet nuclear guarantee for the Arabs, tighten the Soviet hold on the Arabs and increase the danger of our involvement' in a Middle East conflict.[91]

Bin Laden referred to arms sales in his message entitled 'Depose the Tyrants', directed to the Muslims of Saudi Arabia and elsewhere on 16 December 2004. This contained a denunciation of 'those who have entered into the alliance of global unbelief against the Muslims, as well as the plundering of the *ummah*'s public funds'.[92] The particular target was the UK–Saudi al-Yamamah ('the Dove') air defence contract which was signed on 9 February 1986, renewed subsequently and which bin Laden estimated was worth more than $30 billion. (Mike Turner, the Chief Executive of BAE Systems, stated in August 2006 that BAE and its predecessor had earned £43 billion over the previous twenty years from the contract and that it stood to earn £40 billion more.)[93]

The 'war on terror' has proved to be enormously beneficial for the arms sales of the US and the UK in the Middle East. The two allies have sought thereby to recoup their costs from military intervention abroad and the higher price of oil imports. Saudi Arabia, for example, has sought to pay for the al-Yamamah contract by the delivery of up to 600,000 barrels of oil a day to the UK government. A total of $21 billion in arms sales agreements were signed by the US from September 2005 to September 2006, compared with $10.6 billion in the previous year, according to data compiled by the Pentagon. Foreign military sales agreements had typically ranged from $10 billion to $13 billion a year since 2001. Then, in 2007, the US announced that it was to provide Saudi Arabia and five Gulf states – Bahrain, Kuwait, Oman, Qatar, and the UAE – with up to $20 billion in military equipment over ten years, with a further $30bn in new US aid to Israel and $13bn to Egypt, again both over ten years. All of this was said to be part of a regional strategy to bolster the position of US allies against what was seen as a more aggressive Iran, which was in the process of acquiring WMD.[94]

Bin Laden's comment on the al-Yamamah contract demonstrates his awareness of the poor showing of Muslim-majority states in the UN's human development index:

> If we estimate the number of unemployed at 100,000 [in Saudi Arabia], then we can divide the value of the deal, $30 billion, into 100,000, which comes to 1,125,000 riyals per head. If these funds were put into publicly owned companies in a legitimate way and into generating work for the unemployed, and if they were spent on their own people, like the poor, the miserable and those in debt, then the people's condition would improve.

Perhaps this is Osama bin Laden posturing for popular support. The US succeeds in generating its own arms race in the Middle East by ensuring that Israel continues to have a 'qualitative military edge' (QME) over its rival, Arab, states. Above all, arms transfers are a means of recycling Arab petrodollars while improving the US balance of payments. Saudi Arabia spent just over $9 billion on defence in 1975; by 1982, the figure had risen to $22 billion. In less than twenty years, military expenditure in the Middle East escalated from $4.7 billion in 1962 to $46.7 billion in 1980, nearly nine times the world average. Other capital projects, usually with foreign contractors providing the expertise, proliferated. Growth was confused with development, and the import of advanced technology with the acquisition of technological capacity. The wealthy and powerful were the principal beneficiaries of development expenditure. There was little investment in agriculture and next to no evidence, at least until recent times, that oil earnings were used productively in fostering inter-Arab trade. In spite of the demands for the creation of financial and monetary institutions appropriate for Third World development, and which would provide more favourable terms than those of the Western-controlled lending institutions, there was little support from the Arab states which had been enriched by oil earnings.[95]

In 2004, there were only five Muslim-majority states which had a human development index in the category 'high', and their combined population was a mere 6.5 million. Thirty states fell into the category of 'medium' human development, and they had a combined population of 893.5 million. There were a further 19 states in the category of 'low' human development, and these had a combined population of 468.9 million people. The development problems of Muslim-majority states with relatively low human development indexes are essentially similar to those of other developing states. Contrary to the thesis of Bernard Lewis and others, the problems are in the areas of indigenous economic development, in education, and in health care, rather than in any alleged cultural tendencies which produce underdevelopment. Altaf Gauhar argues that 'few Arab governments have any popular mandate; they are essentially dynastic and authoritarian. Security and self-perpetuation are their dominant concerns. National security efforts are directed as much, if not more, against internal revolt as against any external threat … The natural instinct of all authoritarian governments is to keep a substantial part of their wealth in safe havens.'[96] It must, however, be stressed, that many of these authoritarian governments are allies of the United States and essentially are propped up by its support. This is, in essence, bin Laden's argument:[97]

> … Karzai [President of Afghanistan after the overthrow of the Taliban] is a quisling brought in by America … here we should ask ourselves: what is the difference between a Persian Karzai and an Arab Karzai? Who was it that installed the rulers of the Gulf States? It was the Crusaders, the same

people who installed the Karzai of Pakistan [= Musharraf],[98] who installed the Karzai of Kuwait, the Karzai of Bahrain, Qatar, and others. Who was it that installed the Karzai of Riyadh and brought him in, even though he had been a refugee from Kuwait a century earlier, to fight on their side against the Ottoman state and its governor, ibn Rashid?[99] It was the Crusaders, and they are still holding us prisoner today. There is no difference between the Karzai of Riyadh and the Karzai of Kabul …

# Chapter Two
## Revisiting Huntington's 'Clash of Civilizations' Thesis Post-9/11

> Culture ... is the most strategically important element in the relation between nations. More than political and economic problems, those related to cultural communication are likely to generate conflicts in the future.
>
> Mahdi Elmandjra (1992)[1]

> [What is the explanation for the alleged propensity of Muslims for violence?] I don't think it has much to do with the [Qur']an or any other traditional religious teaching. I think it is largely a response to unsuccessful modernization in most Muslim societies, a product of the absence of pluralism and liberty and open politics in those societies. It is also a product of historic resentment, particularly among Arabs, over what they feel have been great injustices imposed on them by the West. And it is also, I think, a result of the division within Islam. Every other major civilization has a core state. What is a core state for Muslims? Who provides leadership to Islam?
>
> Samuel P. Huntington (17 June 2002)[2]

> History is once again witnessing a great clash. This is not a clash of civilizations. The civilization of Islam, with its humane traditions of learning and tolerance, has no place for this violent sect of killers and aspiring tyrants. This is not a clash of religions. The faith of Islam teaches moral responsibility that ennobles men and women, and forbids the shedding of innocent blood. Instead, this is a clash of political visions.
>
> Remarks by President George W. Bush at the United States Air Force Academy Graduation Ceremony, Falcon Stadium (2 June 2004)[3]

During the Carter administration, when Samuel P. Huntington was co-ordinator for security planning (1977–8), he wrote 'Presidential Directive 18', a comprehensive overview of US–Soviet relations which argued that the advances made by the Soviets in the 1970s were 'temporary, and that the West would eventually move out ahead'. His recommendation was a military build-up, which helped prevent the National Security Council (NSC) from taking an accommodationist stance toward Moscow. Subsequently, the NSC initiated the massive build-up of the last two years of the Carter administration and the entire Reagan presidency. In this respect, his policy recommendations and those of the Republican adviser Richard Pipes (see Chapter 4) were very much on a par.

And so it has remained, in broad outline, ever since. In 2006 the expenditure of the United States on its military establishment and armaments amounted to 46 per cent of total world defence expenditure in market exchange rate (MER) terms.[4] When the expenditure of other states is converted into purchasing power parity (PPP) figures, the other members of the group of highest spenders are a considerable way behind the US (528.7 billion); China (188.2 billion), India (114.3 billion), Russia (82.8 billion), and the UK (51.4 billion) are the next four, but their combined expenditure is less than that of the US. In fact, one has to combine the expenditure of the next seven states (that is, China, India, Russia, the UK, France, Saudi Arabia, and Japan) before the expenditure of the US is exceeded. No Muslim-majority state is in the same league: Saudi Arabia (36.4 billion), Iran (28.6 billion), Turkey (20.2 billion), and Pakistan (15.6 billion) are in the top fifteen in terms of PPP expenditure, but are dwarfed by the American expenditure, which vastly exceeds that of the whole Islamic world.

The scale of the American predominance is staggering. Yet the US seems able to sustain its current level of military predominance indefinitely and (within its own terms) inexpensively. Robert G. Kaufman observes that 'the United States now spends less than 4 per cent of its gross domestic product (GDP) on defence, compared with 13.5 per cent in fiscal year (FY) 1953 under President Truman, 8.7 per cent in FY 1969 under President Johnson, and 6 per cent in FY 1986 under President Reagan. The Bush administration's defence spending as a percentage of GDP is just slightly higher than that of the Roosevelt administration on the eve of Pearl Harbour [in 1941], when the United States remained unprepared and isolationist.'[5]

Charles Krauthammer, named as America's most influential commentator by the *Financial Times* in 2006, had caught the eye of the policy community with an article in 1990, which called for full exploitation by the United States of its ascendancy in its 'uni-polar moment'.[6] What did this mean in practical terms? What was the United States to do in the early 1990s without an ideological enemy of stature and a genuine threat to its power? When giving testimony to Congress in March 1993, James

Woolsey, the Director of the CIA, caught the mood of euphoria in the United States following the collapse of the Soviet Union but also the sense of bewilderment at the apparent absence of any powerful competitor to American power: 'we have slain a great dragon, but we now live in a jungle filled with a bewildering variety of poisonous snakes.'[7]

## *'Paradigm Lost':[8] the Search for a Common Enemy in US Foreign Policy after the Collapse of the Soviet Union*

This new threat of a 'bewildering variety of poisonous snakes' clearly required further clarification and this was provided by Huntington in 1993 in his so-called 'clash of civilizations' theory. Whatever the strengths or weaknesses of Huntington's analysis, it has been claimed that no thesis has had a comparable influence on Western, especially American, strategic thinking since the end of the Cold War. Mohammad Nafissi, for example, argues that though China and the so-called 'Sinic civilization' may pose the greatest challenge to Western hegemony in the longer term, the clash thesis 'would not have achieved its tremendous resonance without the spectre of a perceived Islamic threat'.[9]

One reason for this extraordinary influence is the unique character of American public institutions and the way in which well-placed academics can influence policy-makers and policy-making. No other political system has such effective political lobbies: we will have cause to examine one of these in more detail in Chapter 5. None has the range of well-financed 'think tanks', mostly of a distinctly conservative ethos, which produce commissioned and non-commissioned research either for direct advocacy and lobbying or indirectly to influence policy. The central position attained by the American Enterprise Institute under President George W. Bush has been attested by the president himself and will be considered in Chapter 7.

Huntington is said to have received $4.7 million over 15 years from the John M. Olin Foundation, 'a right-wing think tank that grew out of a chemicals and munitions business'. The industrialist John M. Olin (1892–1982) stipulated that rather than exist in perpetuity, his foundation should spend all of its assets within a generation of his death. According to data from Mediatransparency regarding funding up to the end of the year 2003, the John M. Olin Foundation had become the fourth largest conservative funder (having given a total of $305.4 million since 1985 to a range of 15 universities – most prominently Harvard, Huntington's own institution, which received $21.4 million – and another fifteen think tanks and advocacy groups, as well as other policy institutes). The $7 million donated by the Olin Foundation to the American Enterprise Institute and the $4 million donated to the Federalist Society assume considerable significance in retrospect, given their unwarranted influence on the George W. Bush administration.[10]

The reliance of successive presidents on individuals who belong to think tanks has varied considerably: nearly 200 members of America's leading conservative think tanks participated in Ronald Reagan's administration between 1981 and 1988 (55 from the Hoover Institution; 36 from the Heritage Foundation; 34 from the American Enterprise Institute; 32 from the Committee on the Present Danger; and 18 from the non-partisan Center for Strategic and International Studies).[11] In contrast, George H. W. Bush tried to 'insulate himself from think tanks that had established and maintained close ties to his predecessor'. Both Presidents Carter and G. H. W. Bush discounted the intellectual contribution of the neo-conservatives: 'in doing so, they excluded a lot of intellectual firepower, people like Jeane Kirkpatrick (1926–2006), Norman Podhoretz and Irving Kristol, who had inspired and invigorated the Reagan administration.'[12] President Bill Clinton relied on more centrist groups such as the Democratic Leadership Council (DLC) and Progressive Policy Institute (PPI).[13] For conservative voices such as Fukuyama and Huntington, these were lean times in terms of any immediate influence on government. However, what they lacked in influence they gained in research resources: John M. Olin Foundation funds assisted Fukuyama's production of 'the end of history' thesis and then Huntington's 'clash of civilizations' counter-thesis, 'the most important foreign policy debate in the aftermath of the Cold War' in the words of the commentator John J. Miller.[14]

The collapse of the Soviet system was construed – misconstrued, it might be argued – as a significant victory for American power and resolve. Thereafter, commentators tried to replace communism with an alternative threat to the American way of life. For Francis Fukuyama, 'the triumph of the West, of the Western idea', was evident first of all in the total exhaustion of viable systematic alternatives to Western liberalism. The twentieth century, that had begun 'full of self-confidence in the ultimate triumph of Western liberal democracy', seemed at its close to be returning full circle to where it started: not to an 'end of ideology' or a convergence between capitalism and socialism, as earlier predicted, but to 'an unabashed victory of economic and political liberalism'. 'What we may be witnessing', Fukuyama mused, was not just the end of the Cold War, or the passing of a particular period of post-war history, but 'the end of history as such: that is, the end point of mankind's ideological evolution and the universalization of Western liberal democracy as the final form of human government'.[15]

Yet if Fukuyama's theories were correct, what justification was there for the vast stockpile of weapons, weapons moreover of increasing expense and technical sophistication, that the United States was determined to maintain? How could strategic planners continue to redraw the world's maps into competing blocs if Western liberal democracy was indeed to become universalized? Where was the 'bewildering variety of poisonous snakes' in the jungle now to be found?

There was little substantive basis to Fukuyama's theories, the musings of a political economist rather than a historian, but they provided Samuel Huntington with the spur he needed. Instead of an 'end of history', which he argued was in reality no more than the end of a long-standing ideological conflict, he projected an alternative theory, that the next conflict, after the end of the Cold War, would not be an ideological one as such but a 'clash of civilizations'. 'It is my hypothesis', he wrote in a seminal article in 1993 that sought to replace George Kennan's 'X article' as the standard text for discussion by strategic planners, 'that the fundamental source of conflict in this new world will not be primarily ideological or primarily economic. The great divisions among humankind and the dominating source of conflict will be cultural. Nation-states will remain the most powerful actors in world affairs, but the principal conflicts of global politics will occur between nations and groups of different civilizations. The clash of civilizations will dominate global politics. The fault lines between civilizations will be the battle lines of the future.'[16]

### *Huntington's Lack of Originality and the Convenient Absence of the Israel-Palestine Conflict from his Theory*

'... a bunch of suicide pilots turned theory into practice on 11 September 2001 and sealed his reputation as the world's foremost scholar of the modern age' (Sarah Baxter). Such is the hyperbole that can be written about Samuel P. Huntington even in a newspaper with the reputation of London's *Sunday Times*.[17] It will be shown in Chapter 3 that Bernard Lewis formulated the term 'clash of civilizations' as early as 1957 and then returned to the theme in 1990. Nor was Lewis unique. Mahdi Elmandjra, a former Assistant Director-General of UNESCO, argued in 1991–2 that the Gulf War 'set the stage for the first civilizational war'. The Gulf War, he wrote, 'is but the first episode of a North–South conflict where the fundamental issue is basically of a cultural nature.' The main ingredients of Elmandjra's theory of a 'war of civilizations' were later included as basic assumptions in Huntington's thesis.[18] It is instructive to recognize that the 'clash of civilizations' argument was also formulated from a non-Western and non-Eurocentric viewpoint, since Elmandjra advocated increased recognition of the world's cultural diversity.[19] Regrettably, Huntington effectively turned Elmandjra's work on its head.

Ervand Abrahamian contends that when Huntington's article on 'The clash of civilizations?' was published in 1993, the intellectual community 'dismissed it as somewhat strange if not downright wrong'. The Islamic specialist, Roy P. Mottahedeh, in a compelling critique of Huntington's article written three years later, noted that 'civilizationalism, if not nationalism, has become the last refuge of scoundrels.'[20] Yet, after 9/11, everything changed in the US – although not in Europe: 'the mainstream media in the USA automatically, implicitly and unanimously adopted Huntington's paradigm to explain' the terrorist attacks.[21] Why did this happen? Abrahamian's conclusion is simple: laying stress on the 'clash of civilizations' and 'Islamic terrorism' conveniently removed any American responsibility for the grievances of Muslim radicals which, while not justifying the simultaneous attacks on the World Trade Center and the Pentagon, nevertheless explain the context in which they came about. Professor Fred Halliday, writing in the *Guardian* at the end of September 2001, noted that the crisis could be explained by political tensions within the Islamic world, especially over the Palestine issue, rather than by 'nonsense talk of clash of civilizations'. He recognized, however, that 'in the field of cultural speculation, the great winner has been the theory, first espoused by Samuel Huntington in 1993, that says we are entering an epoch that will be dominated by "the Clash of Civilizations".'[22] Halliday has always maintained that most, if not all, international disputes do not involve such a clash but are situated within the framework of one civilization[23] – an observation that has been borne out in the detailed research of Errol A. Henderson and Richard Tucker.[24]

It was precisely because he states the opposite that Huntington was so useful to the Bush regime and its supporters in the 'war on terror'. The rival clash of nationalities – Israeli and Palestinian – could be lost in the ambiguity of civilizational identity and the alleged fault lines between them. Even more conveniently, Huntington excludes Judaism from his list of civilizations. By sleight of hand, Israel is simply removed from the scheme of things. In his introduction to the Hebrew translation of Huntington's work, which became a bestseller in Israel for 20 weeks in 2004, Israeli journalist Dan Margalit suggests that *The Clash of Civilizations* raised and then skirted two questions of special interest from an Israeli perspective: whether Judaism constitutes a civilization, and in what ways the conflict between the Israelis and Palestinians relates to the larger war of civilizations. Peter Berkowitz comments:[25]

While Huntington says little about Judaism, his answers are implicit in his analysis: Judaism does constitute a civilization, though a minor one because of Israel's small size and the dispersion of the Jewish people. Indeed, because it is rooted in biblical faith and respects the dignity of the individual, Judaism should be seen as a part of Western civilization. The conflict between Israel and the Palestinians may exacerbate international tensions, but it is not the source of the fundamental clash between the West and the rest. On Huntington's account, the West would be facing a showdown with Islam even if Israel did not exist.

## *Huntington's 'Robust Nationalism'*

Huntington's political views can be defined not by looking first at the clash thesis and his opinions on foreign policy, but rather by his views on domestic issues – especially in an article he published in 1999 entitled 'Robust Nationalism'. 'Robust nationalism', he contended, 'is an alternative to divisive multiculturalism, xenophobic isolationism and wimpy universalism. It is a foundation on which conservatives could unite to promote American national interests abroad and national unity at home.'[26] Huntington mused that it might be possible for neo-conservatives and classic conservatives to 'agree on some assumptions and concepts, the totality of which distinguishes them from liberals and other non-conservatives. A set of conservative first principles would not necessarily provide definitive positions on specific policy issues, but could provide a framework within which conservatives could debate and to which they could relate their differences over policy issues ...'

What are these first principles? Huntington contends that 'three characteristics of conservative thought deserve emphasis: belief in God, [their] conception of human nature, and [their] commitment to the nation'. While conservatives may or may not actively practise religion or be members of a church, Huntington maintains that 'it is difficult to be conservative without being religious. By and large conservatives believe in God, and since Americans are overwhelmingly a Christian people with a small but important Jewish minority, the God of American conservatism is the God of the Old and New Testaments. In contemporary America, religious commitment and conservatism march arm in arm in battle against secularism, relativism and liberalism. In conservatism, man is not the measure of all things.'

Conservatives live in a Hobbesian, not a Lockean, world. Conservatives thus view conflict, and even violent conflict, as 'an inherent aspect of the human condition'. Whereas liberals tend to believe that the end of whatever is the current major conflict means the end of all conflict (hence the indulgence in euphoria in 1918, 1945 and 1989), conservatives 'know that the end of one conflict creates the basis for another one'. Belief in country is as important as belief in God:

> Given the nature of the world, conservatives rank devotion to country along with devotion to God. Patriotism is a – perhaps the – prime conservative virtue. Conservatives give their highest loyalty to their country, its values, culture and institutions. Unlike most liberals, they see international institutions not as good in themselves but good only insofar as they contribute to furthering the well-being of the American nation. Non-conservatives tend to degrade national identity either in favour of ethnic, racial, gender or other sub-national identities, or in favour of identity with supranational institutions and ideals. Conservatives believe that foreign policy should promote the national interest, although they may differ as to exactly how that interest should be defined. They also resist intrusions on national sovereignty by international organizations, courts or regimes ...

Huntington predicts that 'in the future serious external threats to America could arise from China, Russia, Islam or some combination of hostile states'. At the present, however, 'the principal threats to American unity, culture and power are closer to home. The appropriate response of both classic conservatives and neo-conservatives is to come together in support of a robust nationalism that reaffirms some basic truths. America is a religious country. Patriotism is a virtue, Universalism is not Americanism. Nationalism is not isolationism.'[27]

El-Din Aysha and others have noted that though once a severe critic of the theory of American decline, Huntington has 'shifted radically to the declinist camp with the end of the Cold War'. Cultural decay has to be tied to the global balance of power. Threats may become 'mirrors', exposing what is wrong on the home front and what needs to be changed, when the power of the adversary stems from the absence of these debilitating factors on its own territory. This, El-Din Aysha pronounces, is Huntington's 'unique and distinctive contribution to the conservative declinist school: his hope to reformulate America on Hamiltonian lines via a combination of concerns over moral decline and the growing power of other civilizations'.[28]

For short periods in his earlier career, Huntington was policy adviser to Presidents Lyndon B. Johnson and Jimmy Carter. His views are close to those of former National Security Adviser Zbigniew Brzezinski and former Secretary of State Henry Kissinger, friends of his from Harvard, and the so-called 'realist' or 'American primacy' school of international relations.[29] This policy, which held a united Europe in suspicion and preferred a special relationship with a client United Kingdom, was well formulated by Kissinger in a lecture delivered at Chatham House in May 1982:[30]

> I do not claim that the United States is always correct in its perceptions. But Europeans ought to take care not to generate such frustrations in America that either an embittered nationalism, or unilateralism, or a retreat from world affairs could result …
>
> In recent times the United States may have appeared unintentionally callous towards the danger of nuclear wars or insufficiently alert towards the opportunities for peace. But the United States has nevertheless been more nearly correct than its critics in warning that those who seek peace not backed by strength will sooner or later find the terms of peace dictated to them; that peace to be meaningful must be just; that nations live in history, not utopia, and thus must approach their goals in stages. To ask for perfection as a precondition for action is self-indulgence, and in the end an abdication.

'Realism' or the pursuit of American primacy could take, in Henry Kissinger's case, the form of failing to allow a democratic election result in Chile to stand if it did not serve American interests (Kissinger famously demeaned Chilean sovereignty with his comments that 'the issues are much too important for the Chilean voters to be left to decide for themselves' and 'I don't see why we need to stand by and watch a country go communist due to the irresponsibility of its people'); in Zbigniew Brzezinski's case, it could take the form of unleashing the genie of a violent *jihad* ('some stirred-up Muslims' he called them) to overturn the Soviet occupation of Afghanistan.[31]

The late Edward Said denounced Huntington as an Orientalist and a reductionist, 'an ideologist … who wants to make "civilizations" and "identities" into what they are not: shut-down, sealed-off entities that have been purged of the myriad currents and counter-currents that animate human history, and that over centuries have made it possible for that history not only to contain wars of religion and imperial conquest but also to be one of exchange, cross-fertilization and sharing. This far less visible history is ignored in the rush to highlight the ludicrously compressed and constricted warfare that "the clash of civilizations" argues is the reality.'[32] Huntington, he stated, 'argues from the standpoint of Pentagon planners and defence industry executives' who might have stood to lose their jobs with the ending of the Cold War but who are now firmly back in place because Huntington has 'discovered a new vocation for them'. Huntington, he claims, 'writes as a crisis manager, not as a student of civilization or as a reconciler between them'. No consensus existed – or exists – as to his postulated eight civilizations (Western; Confucian/Sinic; Japanese; Islamic; Hindu; Slavic-Orthodox; Latin American; African), which cannot stand up to analytical scrutiny. Above all, Said denounced the idea of an 'exclusionary civilization': 'the more insistent we are on the separation of cultures and civilizations, the more inaccurate we are about ourselves and about others. The notion of an exclusionary civilization is … an impossible one.'[33]

### *Huntington Mark I and Mark II: the Confusion over the Role of Religion and of Islam in Particular*

From Churchill's 'Iron Curtain' speech at Fulton, Missouri, on 5 March 1946, until the fall of the Berlin Wall on 9 November 1989, American strategists could point at a map and define a clear enemy, whether or not there was officially a policy of *détente*. Huntington published a map of the Cold War World in the 1960s in his 1996 book *Clash of Civilizations* (including, incredibly to any Black African, South Africa under apartheid as part of the 'free world' – that is, the anti-Soviet camp).[34] An understanding of the world based on competing ideological blocs as in Cold War years could not easily be replicated in the 1990s when the challenges proved to be quite different. Nor could they be mapped coherently. (Indeed, it may be argued that Huntington's geopolitical vision is weakened by his failure to incorporate a more effective sense of geographical realities, a weakness that had also been present in Kennan's analysis.)[35] As Huntington commented in a debate at the Ethics and Public Policy Center conference in Florida in January 2002:[36]

> During the Cold War we had a clear bipolar situation: two superpowers, two rivals. What do we have now? Political scientists debate whether we have a uni-polar or a multi-polar situation. I think we can best describe the existing structure of global power as uni-multi-polar: one superpower, then six or eight major regional powers, then secondary regional powers, and then the rest. The structure of global power is pyramid-shaped, with the single superpower at the top. The superpower has veto action on almost any big, global issue.

After the fall of the Berlin Wall and the dissolution of the Soviet Union and the system of control it had exercised, no easy geographical depiction was available for planning purposes, although this did not stop political theorists from attempting the impossible. In 1993, Huntington had suggested a map of the 'fault line' between Western and Eastern Orthodox Christianity c.1500 as an example; in 1996, he went further and suggested that this map represented the eastern boundary of Western civilization (with Greece playing no role in 'Western' civilization, since it was Orthodox and therefore placed in the east).[37] He further proposed a map of the world civilizations post-1990.[38]

Huntington's post-1990 map clearly has problems, for example in its depiction of India as a 'Hindu culture': though only 12 per cent of the population, more Muslims live in India than in any country of the world apart from Indonesia. Proponents of a 'secular' India would contend that India's culture is inherently pluralist and multicultural, with an interaction between its various religions and cultures. Amartya Sen notes that it is 'impossible to think of the civilization of contemporary India without taking note of the major roles of Muslims in the history of the country'. India's 145 million Muslims amount to more than the population of Britain and France combined, and India has many more Muslims than nearly every country within Huntington's definition of 'the Muslim world'. Moreover, the 'simplistic characterization of India along an artificially singular religious line remains politically explosive, in addition to being descriptively flawed'.[39]

One set of borders requires far more examination than any other. These are the so-called 'bloody borders' of Huntington's postulated Islamic civilization ('Islam's borders *are* bloody, and so are its innards', he wrote in 1993).[40] 'No single statement in my *Foreign Affairs* article attracted more critical comment than "Islam has bloody borders"', Huntington later recognized. He claimed that he 'made that judgement on the basis of a casual survey of inter-civilizational conflicts'. Quantitative evidence 'from every disinterested source', he contended, 'conclusively demonstrates its validity'.

Though remarks such as 'the underlying problem for the West is not Islamic fundamentalism. It is Islam' seem clear enough,[41] Huntington claims that his views have been misunderstood. On criticisms of his use of terminology, he commented:

> I'm aware that there's an inherent ambiguity in the term 'clash of civilizations'. Are we talking about simply differing views, different types of cultures and customs, different religions? Or are we talking about violent conflict? What we want to aim for is to prevent these differences in culture and civilization from leading to violent conflict.

We may have to talk in terms of a Huntington Mark I (pre-11 September 2001) and a Huntington Mark II (post-11 September 2001) interpretation. The true importance of 9/11 for Huntington is that it[42]

> dramatically symbolized the end of the twentieth century of ideology and ideological conflict, and the beginning of a new era in which people define themselves primarily in terms of culture and religion. The real and potential enemies of the United States now are religiously driven militant Islam and

> entirely non-ideological Chinese nationalism. For Americans the religious component of their identity takes on new relevance in this environment.

Huntington's post 9/11 statements about Islam suggested an earlier confusion, or a subsequent realization of just how profoundly dangerous his comments had been. 'I don't think Islam is any more violent than any other religion ...', he commented in 2001, in what might seem a *volte-face* from the position he had adopted in 1993–6. People such as bin Laden could seize on statements in the Qur'an 'as commands to go out and kill infidels. But the Pope did exactly the same thing when he launched the crusades.' Wars involving Muslims did not arise from the 'inherent nature of Islamic doctrine and belief', because as with Christianity, 'adherents can use' doctrines 'to justify peace or war as they wish'. Rather, 'the causes of contemporary Muslim wars lie in politics, not seventh-century religious doctrine.' A major civilizational war between Islam and the West 'is clearly the goal of Osama bin Laden', Huntington declared after 9/11; but he refrained from arguing that this event was the confirmation of his thesis. He clearly did not wish to bring about a conflict of civilizations. Indeed, he feared that a prolonged military response to 9/11 'could produce Muslim unity' against the West, which was what Osama bin Laden wanted.

Rather than pursue a strategy of conflict, the West should display realism and recognize the 'long history of Muslim and Arab states [losing out] at the hands of the West' and the 'manifest failure of secular or moderately religious states across the Muslim world' to develop and catch up with Western economic and technological development. There was a 'reaction of Muslim peoples to their own corrupt, ineffective and repressive regimes', while the US gave its opponents a grievance because of its persistent favouritism towards Israel. American troops should not be left in Saudi Arabia, since this provided an additional grievance and had turned Osama bin Laden into an anti-American terrorist. In addition, 'unless truly vital national interests are at stake', states 'belonging to one civilization should not become involved in military conflicts between states of another one'. The logic of Huntington's position might seem to be that American forces should not be present in the Persian Gulf, except that he affirms that vital national interests were indeed at stake in the conflict of 1991.[43]

Responding to critics of his thesis, Huntington poses two questions: if not a clash of civilizations, then what is the alternative overarching hypothesis? (Curiously, he rejects the evidence for ideology among violent jihadists such as Osama bin Laden.)[44] Secondly, he asks how it might be that his thesis of a clash of civilizations could become a self-fulfilling prophecy? Everything 'depends on how people react'.[45] Regarding his own analysis, Huntington professed himself 'very pleased that what I said about the "clash of civilizations" stimulated a lot of talk, maybe some action, about dialogue between civilizations. I've been invited to conference after conference involving people from different civilizations to try to promote a dialogue between them. The government of Iran sponsored a resolution in the UN General Assembly declaring 2001 "the year for dialogue between civilizations". I think that's great! That's the sort of thinking I would like to encourage.'

In a debate at the Ethics and Public Policy Center in Florida in January 2002, Huntington refined his arguments considerably by suggesting four main changes that had occurred 'in global politics over the course of the past decade'. The first was the decline of ideology and its replacement by 'culture': 'this is the main theme of my book *The Clash of Civilizations*, and I think it is a tremendously significant development …' The second is the resurgence of religion: 'nowhere has religion become more important in shaping identity than in the world of Islam, and the Islamic resurgence is a major development in our world.' The third change cited by Huntington was the collapse of the Soviet Union and its implications for the balance of power, while the fourth was the changing nature of warfare – the relative scarcity of inter-state wars and the growth of 'communal wars', that is, 'wars among ethnic and other national groups', in a large number of which 'religion is a very important dimension'.

Since religion, according to Huntington Mark II, is 'the principal defining characteristic of civilizations, fault line wars are almost always between people of different religions'.[46] Eric Hanson remarks that 'there is no question that the break-up of the ex-Yugoslavia is the great example of Huntington's splitting of a country along the fault line of three civilizations: Western [Croatia], Orthodox [Serbia] and Islamic [Bosnia]. However, most conflicts do not fit this dynamic ...'[47] Even Hanson's apparently clear demonstration of Huntington's thesis – the break-up of Yugoslavia in the 1990s – is categorically rejected in Vjekoslav Perica's detailed study of religion and nationalism in the three main constitutent states. Perica emphatically rejects the notion that a 'clash of civilizations' – or religions as such – played a central role in fomenting the aggression which led to the break-up of Yugoslavia. Rather, it was the religious *institutions* which destabilized the country in the pursuit of socially destructive forms of nationalism – the Islamic community leaders (though these were relatively moderate), the Croatian Catholic Church, and the Serbian Orthodox Church (both of which were effectively fundamentalist). They denied legitimacy to the post-Tito Yugoslav state and stirred up ethnic nationalism and hatred among their members, the result being ethno-religious and ethno-national conflict. 'The three largest religious organizations', Perica writes, '... were among the principal engineers of the crisis and conflict.'[48] Norman Cigar similarly shows that the Serb nationalist intellectuals sought to depict their 'Muslim problem' as part of a broader, unified Muslim threat applied to the entire (and unsuspecting) West. Serbia was only trying to deal with the same problem as Britain, Italy, and France, which were being 'flooded' and 'suffocated' by Muslim immigrants.[49]

Huntington's *The Clash of Civilizations and the Remaking of World Order* (1996) might have become known as the seminal text which placed religion at the heart of a modern understanding of the international relations system, but for two factors. One was that Huntington Mark I went to considerable lengths to avoid using the term 'religion' in it,[50] and has only done so since. The other is that he failed to analyse the nature of the causal relationship between religion and politics in the various world cultures, and 'how religion and politics affect each other in contemporary international affairs'.[51] Huntington's first corrective came in a piece he penned for a collective volume entitled *The Influence of Faith,* which appeared just a few weeks before 9/11, and was devoted to the subject of world-wide religious persecution.[52] In this essay, Huntington noted the ways in which, for more and more governments in the world, religion is the chief source of, or threat to, their legitimacy. States seek to control religion, if necessary through repression and persecution, precisely because religion is becoming more important.

Christianity in particular is, around the world and in almost all its forms, the carrier of democracy and political liberalization. Huntington cites a Chinese government publication of 1992 which, after taking note of the (Catholic) Church's role in the collapse of Soviet Communism, pointedly concludes: 'if China does not want such a scene to be repeated in its land, it must strangle the baby while it is still in the manger.'[53] And strangling religion is precisely what the Chinese regime is determined to do. Huntington is left with the need to encourage tendencies in non-Christian religions that are supportive of religious freedom, in the hope that the 'ecumenical personality' of such religions will prevail over their 'darker personality'. 'Moving in this direction would at best be a long, slow process, but it may be the only practical one.' 'Religious liberty', he concludes, 'is an issue where it is difficult to be optimistic without being utopian.' Indeed it is: in June 2007 it was reported that MI6 had informed the Pope and other religious leaders that potentially 200 million Christians were at risk world-wide from increasing religious persecution.[54] The figure of 200 million Christians at risk was the estimate of Paul Marshall ten years earlier.[55]

## *The Huntington Thesis Subjected to Empirical Test*

Various empirical tests can be applied to Huntington's theory to assess whether it can be substantiated for the period up to 2001. No test, of course, will be able to demonstrate its longer-term applicability, and though Huntington himself has applied certain caveats to the argument, it is arguable that the events of 11 September 2001 and their aftermath have strengthened his case. Huntington observed in 2002 that the terrorist actions of Osama bin Laden had reinvigorated civilizational identity.[56] In another sense, the Iraq war of 2003 might be construed as fitting his model, if it is argued that 'nation states will remain the principal actors in world affairs but ... their alliances will be civilizational and the civilizational nature of these alliances will dominate world politics'.[57]

However, Huntington differs from other proponents of the clash thesis, such as Bernard Lewis, on the question of intervention abroad. In 1996, he declared that '... Western intervention in the affairs of other civilizations is probably the single most dangerous source of instability and potential global conflict in a multi-civilizational world.'[58] Huntington (a life-long Democrat) refused to join ranks with the Republican administration in support of a preventive war in Iraq in 2003. On the fifth anniversary of 9/11 he was asked if he remained critical of the application of the Bush doctrine to foreign policy and whether he saw any way for the US to extricate itself from the quagmire:[59]

> Yes. I didn't see the need to go in. Sure, Iraq is an important oil producer. Obviously, we want to have stability in the Persian Gulf area. We want to counter the expansion of the influence of radical Iran. But I didn't see the need for us to go into Iraq ... There are many ways to get out. The question is how to get out in a fairly responsible fashion that won't produce even worse consequences than our being there. And that won't be easy. But I think setting a timetable, which we wouldn't necessarily have to announce in advance, of gradual withdrawal, and trying to shift some of the responsibilities for dealing with Iraq to other countries, other Gulf states, or the European Union would be a start.

How, he was asked, can we defuse tension with the Muslim world?

> I think we have to take a calmer attitude and try to understand what their concerns are. I think we have to recognize that there are tremendous divisions within the Muslim world, between different varieties of Islam and different states. It is a very pluralistic world. We should recognize it as such, and deal with the individual segments of that world, and try to accommodate, to the extent that we can, their particular interests.

The future cannot be predicted; but the conflicts of the past can be analysed to judge whether or not they fit the model Huntington has outlined. Errol A. Henderson and Richard Tucker provide a detailed list (which Huntington does not) of states which have existed at some point between 1816 and 1992 and the civilization to which each might be presumed to belong. (The exercise demonstrates the practical difficulties posed by the categories, leaving aside the larger intellectual objections to the paradigm.) Henderson and Tucker argue that three propositions emerge from Huntington's analysis which can be subjected to empirical test. The first is that in the era before the Cold War, inter-civilizational difference was associated positively with an increased likelihood of inter-state war. The second is that during the Cold War, inter-civilizational difference was associated negatively or insignificantly with the likelihood of inter-state war. And the third is that in the era since the end of the Cold War, inter-civilizational difference is associated once again with an increased likelihood of inter-state war.

Henderson and Tucker's work suggests that while the period of the Cold War bears out some of Huntington's arguments, namely that the superpower stand-off kept a lid on inter-civilizational clashes, the pre- and post-Cold War periods do not. They conclude that 'viewing the world through civilizational lenses is more likely to blind decision-makers to both the divisions within civilizations (including their own) and the cross-cutting cleavages among them which might provide opportunities for co-operation.' Furthermore, 'a policy of cultural containment is likely to foment inter-state conflict by encouraging more aggressive policies towards states of different civilizations while creating a false sense of security that members of the same civilization will have convergent interests.'[60]

Henderson and Tucker concur with Stephen M. Walt, who challenges Huntington's view that the first Gulf War was a harbinger of the fault-line wars that are supposed to happen in the post-Cold War era. Huntington's interpretation here is untenable on his own terms. The war began as an intra-civilizational dispute between Iraq and Kuwait. And it continued as an intra-civilizational dispute, with Kuwait, tacitly supported by Israel, the United States, and a coalition which included Egypt and Saudi Arabia among Muslim-majority states, evicting Iraq from its lands, though at considerable cost to its oil infrastructure.[61] In suggesting that the Gulf War was a harbinger for subsequent conflict Huntington agrees unwittingly with bin Laden's view.[62] (Huntington's error arose from the fact that here he was trying to incorporate the interpretation of Mahdi Elmandjra into his analysis.)

Further detailed analysis of Huntington's work, by means of other empirical tests, has been undertaken by Jonathan Fox.[63] Fox argues that looking at ethnic conflict strictly from the perspective of the West, the number and proportion of ethnic conflicts with Islamic groups have increased since the end of the Cold War. However, from a more global perspective, civilizational conflicts, at least since 1945, have been and remain a minority of ethnic conflicts. Moreover, from the perspective of the alleged 'Islamic civilization', there has been little change since the end of the Cold War. 'Thus, while the small increase in ethnic conflict between the Western and Islamic civilizations can seem very important to Western eyes, such as those of Huntington, from the global and Islamic perspectives it is merely a small increase that has occurred in the context of a general rise in ethnic conflict ... the overall picture shows that these conflicts are a minority of the ethnic conflicts in which Islamic ethnic groups are involved.' However, Fox has been studying 'only "fault line" conflicts within states'; he has not addressed '"fault line" conflicts between states or "core state conflicts"'.[64]

Fox argues that Huntington's concept of civilizations is insufficient to explain domestic conflict in the post-Cold War era. 'Civilization' may have had a small influence on domestic conflicts, but this 'clearly does not reach the level of the paradigmatic claims made by Huntington'.[65] Religion is a more significant variable, but even so, 'religious conflict is, overall, less common than non-religious conflict'.[66] From detailed analysis of the evidence in specific datasets of conflicts, Fox concludes that 'while some individual aspects' of the analysis are not inconsistent with Huntington's theory, 'the balance of evidence' is strongly against the prediction that civilizational conflicts will become the defining type of conflict in the post-Cold War era. Islamic groups have tended to fight non-civilizational conflicts more often than civilizational ones (i.e., as in Iraq, fratricidal conflict between Sunni and Shi'ite groups is more common than a unified front against non-Muslim enemies). There has been no evidence at all to justify Huntington's prediction of an Islamic-Sino-Confucian alliance against the West. There is only one exception to the rule that so-called civilizations did not engage in higher levels of violence in the post-Cold War era, and that is the case of so-called 'Hindu civilization', which has experienced the phenomenon of extreme right-wing *hindutva* violence on a significant scale. To prove the predictive value of a paradigm, dramatic and uniform changes in conflict patterns consistent with the theory have to be perceived. They clearly are not, Fox argues. Instead, the more modest (and non-paradigmatic) claim that the influence of religion, as one factor among many in conflicts, has increased since the 1980s can be demonstrated from the evidence.[67]

More recently, Fox has summarized other quantitative studies of the clash of civilizations theory as well as showing that 'religious conflicts – including religious wars like those in Afghanistan and Algeria, which are not civilizational but clearly between factions within the same religion – are consistently more common than civilizational conflict and became a majority of all conflicts starting in 2002. This rise in religious conflict as a proportion of all domestic conflict is not a post-9/11 phenomenon, but is, rather, the result of processes that date back at least to the late 1970s.'[68] The increasing role of religion in state failure is also emphasizd by Fox: prior to 2002, religious conflicts were a minority of all domestic conflicts, but since then (at least until the end of 2004) they have become a majority of them. Fox notes that there are 1.75 times as many Christians in the world as there are Muslims, and about twice as many Christian-majority as Muslim-majority states in the world. Making allowances for these facts, Muslims participated proportionately more than Christians in intra-state violence, with most of this being between Muslim and Muslim (e.g. Sunni Muslim versus Shi'a Muslim). It is therefore likely that an increase in religious violence will be particularly marked between Muslim groups in the future (a view that coincides with that of other scholars such as Vali Nasr, whose analysis is discussed in the Conclusion).[69]

The weakness of Huntington's specifically cultural (as distinct from religious) analysis is fully revealed by Dieter Senghaas.[70] Huntington, Senghaas contends, 'assumes civilizations to be some kind of "beings" at the macro-level ... he regards civilizations as not adaptable and changeable over centuries. Deep down, they remain constant, and they tend to process external influences so as to guarantee continuity.' Senghaas points out that Huntington's thesis, 'which regards the clash of civilizations as the crux of international policy, does not explain why specific civilizations, or the states representing them, have to clash at all as a consequence of cultural characteristics.'[71] Senghaas concludes that 'there will be no clash of civilizations or cultural regions – and how, indeed, could there be? There will be cultural struggles in many places. But it would be wrong to inflate the realities of such cultural struggles into a geocultural fiction, or to confuse the theory of the clash of civilizations with reality.'[72]

'Fault lines do occur at the micro-level', Senghaas concedes, 'but they are not automatically based on cultural differences ...' Rather, they are 'created by socio-economic problems involving systematic discrimination'. Senghaas calls these 'distribution conflicts'.[73] Religion 'gains momentum and becomes a rallying point, a resource in desperation, only when promising life perspectives do not emerge otherwise'. Successful societies, Senghaas contends, are the reverse of the monocultural model which Huntington postulates in his subsequent study *Who are We?*, with its forebodings about a crisis of national identity in the US. Instead, for Senghaas,[74]

> successful societies inevitably become pluralistic societies, although in an unplanned way. This also changes, naturally, their 'cultural soul' (if it is ever identifiable) into a pluralistic one. The question of identity, however, does not go away. On the contrary, it becomes a permanent point of discussion – without a chance to solve it. This leads to a perfectly acceptable situation, to an endless self-reflection about identity – a condition well documented today in Western societies.

# Chapter Three
# 'Bring Them Freedom or They Destroy Us': Bernard Lewis and the Evolution of the 'Lewis Doctrine'

> [After 9/11] the public arena was left to the one prominent Middle East specialist who very much reinforced Huntington's paradigm – namely Bernard Lewis. If Lewis failed to cite Huntington by name it was because of intellectual property rights, not because of intellectual differences …
>
> Ervand Abrahamian (2003)[1]

> I think that the cause of developing free institutions – along their lines, not ours – is possible. One can see signs of its beginning in some countries. At the same time, the forces working against it are very powerful and well entrenched… I think that the effort is difficult and the outcome uncertain, but I think the effort must be made. Either we bring them freedom, or they destroy us.
>
> Lecture delivered by Bernard Lewis on board the *Crystal Serenity* (16 July 2006)[2]

'Scholarship or Sophistry?' The question has been asked of Bernard Lewis's *œuvre* by a Muslim scholar, who accuses him of leadership of the neo-Zionist Orientalist movement, which seeks to 'paint Islam and Islamic … societies as innately hostile to the West, modernism, democracy, tolerance, scientific advance and women's rights'.[3] In his more senior years,[4] Lewis chose to relaunch his theory of conflict between an alleged 'Western' and alleged 'Islamic' civilization, as if these existed in watertight compartments, in September 1990.[5]

The year he chose to do so in itself seems significant. With the destruction of the Berlin Wall the previous year, symbolizing the collapse of Communism, where was the new ideological enemy, against which the military-industrial complex of the West could justify its ceaseless pursuit of ever more destructive and more expensive weapons? As Charles Glass comments, 'the Christendom-Islam split found an audience among American cold[-war] warriors only when they lost their Soviet nemesis'. 'What better opiate than an enemy in the form of another civilization that had always resisted the West?'[6]

*Bernard Lewis, the Originator of the 'Clash of Civilizations' Thesis*

Lewis did not coin the phrase 'clash of civilizations' in 1990 but thirty-three years earlier, in 1957, at a Middle East conference at Johns Hopkins University. Then he had pronounced: 'we shall be better able to understand this situation if we view the present discontents of the Middle East not as a conflict between states or nations, but as a clash between civilizations.'[7] The concept was therefore not new in 1990 but was a central part of his *œuvre*, particularly in the years when his writing had become, in Edward Said's phrase, 'aggressively ideological'. Lewis wrote in 1990: 'this is no less than a clash of civilizations – the perhaps irrational but surely historic reaction of an ancient rival against our Judeo-Christian heritage, our secular present, and the worldwide expansion of both.'[8]

In the 1990 essay, Bernard Lewis added two important cautionary points – which he later chose to ignore and which other proponents of the clash thesis have also failed to note. He wrote:

> ... It is crucially important that we on our side should not be provoked into an equally historic but also equally irrational reaction against that rival ... The movement nowadays called fundamentalism is not the only Islamic tradition. There are others, more tolerant, more open, that helped to inspire the great achievements of Islamic civilization in the past, and we may hope that these other traditions will in time prevail.

Before the issue would be decided, Lewis pronounced, there would be 'a hard struggle, in which we of the West can do little or nothing'. Even the attempt to intervene might do harm, he observed, 'for these are issues that Muslims must decide among themselves'.

If only Bernard Lewis had been prepared to leave the matter there! For in these cautionary remarks several warnings were issued which later went unheeded. First, it is important that if one side in a conflict is perceived in an entrenched and irrational way, the other side does not follow suit: that serves merely to exacerbate the problem. Secondly, Western intervention in the affairs of the Muslim world is almost always likely to be counter-productive unless there is a prior wish for co-operation. Thirdly, the most important thing above all is to 'avoid the danger of a new era of religious wars, arising from the exacerbation of differences and the revival of ancient prejudices'. And fourthly, we must strive on each side to learn about each other's history and culture so as to gain a better understanding of what we talk about: the risk otherwise is a clash based on preconceptions, prejudices, and ignorance.

'Make no mistake, those who are unwilling to confront the past will be unable to understand the present and unfit to face the future.'[9] Bernard Lewis's comment is a wise one, though everything depends on the clarity of judgement with which one confronts the past. In his encomium on the eve of the master's ninetieth birthday, Fouad Ajami accepted that Lewis had played an active political role but was disinclined to attribute a precise influence, so as to protect his hero from any obloquy which the political actors with whom he was associated (Vice-President Cheney among others) might suffer:[10]

> Some of his detractors, with an excessive belief in his talismans, have attributed to the historian all sorts of large historical deeds. For some, he is the godfather of the accommodation of years past between Turkey and Israel. For others, he inspired the Iraq war, transmitting to Vice-President Dick Cheney his faith in the Iraq campaign as the spearhead of an effort to reform the Arab world … In more recent writings on the historian, George W. Bush's 'diplomacy of freedom' in Arab-Muslim lands is laid at Mr Lewis's doorstep ...

For Halper and Clarke, Lewis has been 'an influential, tactical and partisan player in the contemporary policy debate', who, for example, was among those consulted as to whether Islam should be the state religion of the reconstituted Iraqi state.[11] The presence of Vice-President Dick Cheney at the reception for Lewis on his ninetieth birthday, and the words he spoke in his honour, leave little doubt as to his influence on the administration of President George W. Bush.[12]

## *The Lewis Doctrine Helps Define the Shift in US Foreign Policy under George W. Bush*

Lewis's critics are much less reticent than his admirers about his influence. For Scott Thompson and Jeffrey Steinberg, writing in 2001, he was nothing less than 'the British Svengali[13] behind the clash of civilizations' thesis,[14] while for Peter Waldman, writing in the *Wall Street Journal* on 3 February 2004, it was the 'Lewis Doctrine', the idea that democracy could be 'sown' by the West in the Middle East, that was facing a severe test in Iraq. It was taken for granted that the Lewis Doctrine – that is, that most Islamic countries had failed miserably at modernizing their societies, beckoning the Americans to intervene – was now US policy. Indeed, Waldman contended that Lewis's diagnosis of the malaise in the Islamic world and his advocacy of war in Iraq 'have helped define the boldest shift in US foreign policy in fifty years'.[15] For in his diatribe on the clash between Islam and modernity, *What Went Wrong?*, Lewis's willingness to risk the 'hazards of regime change' is made patently clear.[16] This willingness to take big risks was not new. Much earlier, in 1979, Lewis had presented the secret Bilderberg group with a plan for redrawing the borders of the larger Middle East into a mosaic of competing mini-states, thereby weakening the power of the existing republics and kingdoms. The urge to redraw the maps of the larger Middle East has become a dangerous obsession among policy strategists in the United States, as will be discussed further in the Conclusion.

According to Michael Hirsh, 'America's misreading of the Arab world – and our current misadventure in Iraq – may have really begun in 1950. That was the year a young University of London historian named Bernard Lewis visited Turkey for the first time.'[17] For Hirsh,

> today, that epiphany – Lewis's Kemalist[18] vision of a secularized, Westernized Arab democracy that casts off the medieval shackles of Islam and enters modernity at last – remains the core of George W. Bush's faltering vision in Iraq. As his other rationales for war fall away, Bush has only democratic transformation to point to as a *casus belli* in order to justify one of the costliest foreign adventures in American history. And even now Bush, having handed over *faux* sovereignty to the Iraqis and while beating a pell-mell retreat under fire, does not want to settle for some watered-down or Islamicized version of democracy. His administration's official goal is still dictated by the 'Lewis Doctrine', as the *Wall Street Journal* called it: a Westernized polity, reconstituted and imposed from above like Kemal's Turkey, that is to become a bulwark of security for America and a model for the region …

Bulwark of security for America or bulwark of security for Israel? The question has to be asked because of Bernard Lewis's well-publicized 'Lebanonization' thesis, whereby most of the states of the Middle East with the exception of Israel were conceived as potentially on the verge of collapse:[19]

> Most of the states of the Middle East … are of recent and artificial construction and are vulnerable to such a process. If the central power is sufficiently weakened, there is no real civil society to hold the polity together, no real sense of common national identity or overriding allegiance to the nation-state. The state then disintegrates – as happened in Lebanon – into a chaos of squabbling, feuding, fighting sects, tribes, regions and parties.

Lewis's analysis of 1992 reads with hindsight as an uncanny prophecy of what might follow the US-led intervention in Iraq in 2003, an intervention which he himself advocated, the risks of which he seems to have forgotten.

Such views have led to his lionization in Israel and by the Israel lobby in the US. On 19 February 1996, Lewis was feted in Jerusalem, where he delivered the ninth annual B'nai B'rith World Centre 'Jerusalem Address' on the theme of 'The Middle East Towards the Year 2000'.[20] Noting that the 'rejectionists remain a powerful force and have the capacity to delay' an Israel–Palestinian peace, Lewis emphasized the rival perceptions of the conflict:

> Another problem is the ignorance of the other side's point of view. While very few in Israel are aware of the sense of outrage that most Arabs feel over the very existence of Israel in the region, Arabs have very little knowledge about Jewish history or modern Zionism. Bookstores in the Arab world carry, almost exclusively, leftovers from the Third Reich, including the *Protocols of the Elders of Zion*. These kinds of books are all the Arabic reader has to choose from in order to learn about the connection between Jews and the Land of Israel although a number of books about Israel have been translated of late.
>
> The level of mutual fear and distrust is immense and therefore difficult to overcome. The translation of these mutual fears creates very different perspectives: Israel perceives itself as a small country surrounded by countries with overwhelmingly large populations armed to the teeth waiting for an opportunity to destroy it while Arabs perceive it as a powerful, technologically advanced, economically dominant country awaiting an opportunity to extend its imperial rule over the whole Arab world. There is a real fear that the old military menace which Israel posed is gone only to be replaced by an economic menace. Over-enthusiasm by Israelis has encouraged, rather than allayed these fears …

Yet 'over-enthusiasm by Israelis' is never really considered by Lewis as a possible reason why, in Edward Said's phrase, 'Muslims (or Arabs) still will not settle down and accept Israeli hegemony over the Near East'.[21] For Bernard Lewis, hostility against Israel stands in for complaints about economic privation and political repression in other parts of the Muslim Middle East 'and as a way of deflecting the resulting anger'.[22]

Any misdeed against Palestinians – even Ariel Sharon's 'indirect responsibility' for the Sabra and Shatila massacres in 1982, in the words of the Kahan commission established in Israel – has, in Lewis's account, to be 'balanced' by atrocities committed by Muslims against Jews or others.[23] If Palestinians were evicted from their homeland in 1948, then so were Jews from some of the Muslim lands. If there is to be justice for Palestinians, then this will result in the end of the state of Israel. It is not Israeli intransigence and military aggression which has led to the devouring of more and more Palestinian land; no, the Palestinian problem has defied solution because of the encouragement given by the United Nations to the Palestinian refugees. The Palestinians have not accepted their fate, which is somehow to be integrated into other (Muslim) states which do not wish to receive them permanently. Because it has not gained unquestioned international support in its search to establish a religiously unified state within self-defined defensible borders, Israel unaccountably receives the blame![24]

In a perceptive analysis published in 2005, entitled 'War is too important to be left to ideological amateurs', Robert Gilpin is scathing of Lewis's influence on American foreign policy and his tendency to absolve both the US and Israel for any responsibility for their actions. Gilpin distinguishes between hatred of the US for 'what it is' and hatred of the US for 'what it does'. Lewis's 'clash of civilizations' model presupposes that the US is hated, and was attacked on 11 September 2001, for what it *is* rather than what it *has done*. 'The implication of this interpretation of Islamicist terrorism is that anti-American terrorism arises from a failed civilization, is inevitable, and cannot be prevented through any attempt to resolve political disputes' between the Islamic world and the United States. 'An especially pernicious aspect of the "clash of civilizations" thesis', Gilpin continues, 'is that it absolves Israeli and US policies of any responsibility for contributing to anti-US terrorism.' Diplomatic initiatives are thus dangerous, and could even embolden the terrorists. The only solution to the problem of Islamicist terrorism is the transformation and democratization of Middle Eastern societies. 'If so', Gilpin concludes, 'we are indeed entering an era of civilizational conflict that will be very long and extremely dangerous.'[25]

Bernard Lewis had no more anticipated the events of 9/11 than had any other commentator, but he was swift to comment on them. He did so in person to Secretary of State for Defense Donald Rumsfeld, in an urgent meeting convened at the Pentagon while it was still smouldering from the attack. 'It was like a war zone', one participant recalled. 'You could still smell the smoke.' An account of the meeting runs that[26]

> they met in Rumsfeld's conference room. After a CIA briefing on the 9/11 attacks, [Richard] Perle introduced two guest speakers. The first was Bernard Lewis, professor emeritus at Princeton, a long-time associate of Cheney's and Wolfowitz's. Lewis told the meeting that America must respond to 9/11 with a show of strength: to do otherwise would be taken in the Islamic world as a sign of weakness – one it would be bound to exploit. At the same time, he said, America should support democratic reformers

> in the Middle East: 'such as', he said, turning to the second of Perle's guest speakers, 'my friend here, Dr Chalabi' ... At the meeting Chalabi said that, although there was as yet no evidence linking Iraq to 9/11, failed states such as Saddam's were a breeding ground for terrorists, and Iraq, he told those at the meeting, possessed WMD.

Lewis was not just an advocate of force in meetings such as this, but also in print. Two pieces were rushed to press in the remaining months of 2001, one purporting to explain to the bemused American public 'the revolt of Islam', when it began and how it might end;[27] the other on 'learning the lingo', explaining the concepts of crusade and *jihad*.[28] In the latter article, Lewis argued that President George W. Bush's 'use of the term "crusade" in calling for a powerful joint effort against terrorism was unfortunate, but excusable'. In fact it was disastrous. It demonstrated ignorance of sensitivities in the Middle East and elsewhere as well as ignorance of the very history which Lewis himself sought to impart. Bush's reference to a 'crusade' against terrorism, which passed almost unnoticed by Americans, rang alarm bells in Europe. As Peter Ford of the *Christian Science Monitor* noted, it raised fears that the terrorist attacks could spark a 'clash of civilizations' between Christians and Muslims. 'We have to avoid a clash of civilizations at all costs', commented French foreign minister Hubert Vedrine. '[We have] to avoid falling into this huge trap, this monstrous trap,' which he said had been 'conceived by the instigators of the assault'.[29]

European fears were also raised by the term 'war' used freely by the White House for an unconventional enemy without a clearly defined territorial base. Bush's terminology of 'war on terrorism' was a potentially fatal confusion of concepts at the outset, which Bernard Lewis did nothing to clarify.[30] It elevated Osama bin Laden and his terrorist group to the status of an inter-state protagonist to be defeated by the full might of the world's sole remaining superpower, instead of downgrading them to what they were and are, a band of criminal terrorists who could have been brought to justice by effectively co-ordinated international military action of a 'police' nature. Lewis talked of crusades and *jihads* as 'holy war' not 'sanctified violence', implying that in the past they had been solely about religion and not also about the possession of territory. Yet Lewis quoted Osama bin Laden's statement from 1998 on this very point: 'for more than seven years [that is, since the end of the first Gulf War in 1991] the United States is occupying the lands of Islam in the holiest of its territories, Arabia, plundering its riches, overwhelming its rulers, humiliating its people, threatening its neighbours, and using its bases in the peninsula as a spearhead to fight against the neighbouring Islamic peoples.' It was 'in view of this' (Lewis's words) that Osama bin Laden issued the command that 'to kill Americans and their allies, both civil and military, is an individual duty of every Muslim who can [do so], in any country where this is possible, until the Aqsa mosque and the Haram mosque are freed from their grip, and until their armies, shattered and broken-winged, depart from all the lands of Islam, incapable of threatening any Muslim.'

Lewis was correct in pointing out that 'the laws of *jihad* categorically preclude wanton and indiscriminate slaughter'. He continued:

> what the classical jurists of Islam never remotely considered is the kind of unprovoked, unannounced mass slaughter of uninvolved civil populations that we saw in New York two weeks ago. For this there is no precedent and no authority in Islam. Indeed it is difficult to find precedents even in the rich annals of human wickedness.

Lewis's honesty in this respect has brought criticism from others in his lobby, who had wanted him to vilify Islam.

In his article on the 'revolt of Islam', Lewis sought to back-peddle somewhat on that 'conflict of civilizations' he had warned was inevitable:

> President Bush and other Western politicians have taken great pains to make it clear that the war in which we are engaged is a war against terrorism – not a war against Arabs, or, more generally, against Muslims, who are urged to join us in this struggle against our common enemy. Osama bin Laden's message is the opposite. For bin Laden and those who follow him, this is a religious war, a war for Islam and against infidels, and therefore, inevitably, against the United States, the greatest power in the world of the infidels.

After a long digression on Islamic history, including many of the elements of what would appear in print as *What Went Wrong?*, Lewis deftly wove an apparent web of connections which might serve to deceive the unwary reader:

> Osama bin Laden and his al-Qaeda followers may not represent Islam, and their statements and their actions directly contradict basic Islamic principles and teachings, but they do arise from within Muslim civilization ... Bin Laden and his followers clearly have no ... concern [about US retaliation], and their hatred is neither constrained by fear nor diluted by respect. As precedents, they repeatedly cite the American retreats from Vietnam, from Lebanon, and – the most important of all, in their eyes – from Somalia ...
>
> If bin Laden can persuade the world of Islam to accept his views and his leadership, then a long and bitter struggle lies ahead, and not only for America ... If bin Laden is correct in his calculations and succeeds in his war, then a dark future awaits the world, especially the part of it that embraces Islam.

As Christopher de Bellaigue observes, 'the predictions and generalizations in this passage are so vast as to make it almost worthless; there is much that is mischievous and misleading in Lewis's positing the inevitability of conflict.'[31] The deftness of Lewis in drawing together disparate themes without commonalities is well demonstrated in the remainder of the article on the 'revolt of Islam': he draws parallels with Hitler and Nazism, giving the impression that any failure to stand up to bin Laden in the way Lewis advocates would be akin to the appeasement of totalitarianism; Baghdad, the seat of the Caliphate until 1258, was brought into the discussion of Arabia without any obvious connection except as a holy place in the world of Islam (and serving as a pointer to the fact that Saddam Hussein, the secular 'tyrant', was in current occupation of that capital city); previous American defeats, in Vietnam, Lebanon, and Somalia, were recalled because at all costs these precedents must be avoided; and, as the *coup de théâtre,* Saddam Hussein was introduced as the 'real' enemy, a formidable one, who for that reason has not yet been confronted as he should. Finally, most irresponsibly of all, Bernard Lewis suggested that there were viable 'democratic oppositions capable of taking over and forming governments', such his friend Ahmed Chalabi in Iraq and his band of self-serving, well-heeled supporters – the notorious 'Gucci Guerillas' from London – who carefully supplied the American administration with snippets of dubious intelligence which it wished to hear (and later claimed that all they had done was for the greater good: to get rid of Saddam).[32] Lewis produced no evidence of any link between Iraq and al-Qaeda, between the source of the terror attack on the United States and Saddam Hussein, because there was none; whether or not Saddam Hussein offered a 'bounty' to suicide bombers in Israel,[33] the reality was that there was no common ground between the secular ideology of Saddam Hussein and the religious-inspired language (though not necessarily religious-inspired ideology) of Osama bin Laden. There was no link between intervention in Iraq and the 'war on terror'. On the contrary, it was a diversion of military resources away from Afghanistan. No matter: 'freedom' must be supported.

### *Bernard Lewis, the Imposition of Democracy, and the Iraq War*

In September 2002, in an article entitled 'Time for Toppling' published by the *Wall Street Journal,* Bernard Lewis returned to his task of advocating the overthrow of Saddam Hussein:

> Democratic governments are elected by the people and are answerable to the people, and with exceedingly rare exceptions, the people prefer peace ...

> It is equally true, but less recognized, that dictatorships do not make peace. The world war started by the Axis ended with its defeat. The Cold War started by the Soviet Union ended with its collapse.
>
> In the same way, the dictatorships that rule much of the Middle East today will not, indeed cannot, make peace, because they need conflict to justify their tyrannical oppression of their own people, and to deflect their peoples' anger against an external enemy. As with the Axis and the Soviet Union, real peace will come only with their defeat or, preferably, collapse, and their replacement by governments that have been chosen and can be dismissed by their people and will therefore seek to resolve, not provoke, conflicts.

As polemic or propaganda, the piece read well. But where was the new and decisive argument for the overthrow of Saddam Hussein? Lewis purported to show respect for the argument of those who feared that 'even a successful attempt at regime change in Iraq would have a dangerously destabilizing effect on the rest of the region, and could lead to general conflict and chaos'. Why should we feel threatened by such a change?, he argued:

> the overwhelming evidence is that the majority of our terrorist enemies come from purportedly friendly countries, and their main grievance against us is that, in their eyes, we are responsible for maintaining the tyrannical regimes that rule over them – an accusation that has, to say the very least, some plausibility. Apart from Turkey and Israel, the two countries in the region where the governments are elected and can be dismissed by the people, most of the countries of the Middle East can be divided into two groups: those with what we are pleased to call friendly governments, and therefore increasingly hostile people who hold us responsible for the oppression and depredations of those governments, and, on the other hand, those with bitterly hostile governments, whose people consequently look to us for help and liberation.

Among the so-called 'friends' of the West were some fellow-travellers whose company no respectable Westerner would wish to keep, the Wahhabis of Saudi Arabia. Lewis was scathing on 'petrodollar Puritanism', as it has been called:

> Imagine that the Ku Klux Klan gets total control of the state of Texas. And the Ku Klux Klan has at its disposal all the oil rigs in Texas. And they use this money to set up a well-endowed network of colleges and schools throughout Christendom, peddling their peculiar brand of Christianity. You would then have an approximate equivalent of what has happened in the modern Muslim world.

(In fact, the Saudis have become increasingly concerned about 'deviant ideology', as they call it; in November 2007, Saudis who had been approached by 'deviant ideologists' [*sic*: = militant jihadists] were asked to contact the nearest security agency if they were in the Kingdom or the nearest Saudi mission abroad to clarify their own standpoint.)[34] Lewis's attack on the Saudis was no more than an interim statement. His real concern was to back the campaign to impose democracy on Iraq, and above all to put the Iraqis back in charge:[35]

> Fortunately, the nucleus of such a government is already available, in the Iraqi National Congress, headed by Ahmed Chalabi. In the northern free zone during the [19]90s they played a constructive role, and might at that time even have achieved the liberation of Iraq had we not failed at crucial moments to support them… It took years, not months, to create democracies in the former Axis countries, and this was achieved in the final analysis not by Americans but by people in those countries, with American encouragement, help and support. Ahmed Chalabi and the Iraqi National Congress deserve no less.

In what way is the cause of democracy advanced by imposing your own candidate from abroad? Lewis had already expressed his confidence in his 'good friend' Ahmed Chalabi in the aftermath of 9/11. Yet Chalabi and the Iraqi National Congress had little or no indigenous support in Iraq. In the end, he even fell foul of his American protectors and blamed them for the delay in ceding power to Iraqis. While a secularist, he was certainly no Iraqi Kemal Atatürk, no strong man who could take decisive action against foreign overlordship. If anyone was likely to play that role, apart from the Sunni insurgents, it was the sinister Shi'ite cleric opposed by the Americans, Moqtada al-Sadr.[36] The real democratic following, against all the expectations of Bernard Lewis, was commanded by the supreme Shi'ite cleric, Grand Ayatollah Ali al-Sistani, who had little difficulty in outwitting the experienced but ineffective American proconsul, L. Paul Bremer III.[37]

Reflecting on the Iraq war a year on, in a lecture delivered in Rome on 9 March 2004, Bernard Lewis reaffirmed his view that the Iraq war was primarily concerned with preventing terror and bringing 'freedom' to the Arab world ('I prefer to use the word "freedom" rather than the word "democracy" because the word "democracy" has been much misused in our time').[38] Lewis admitted that some of the expected benefits arising from the invasion by Coalition forces had not yet come to fruition, largely because of unexpected delays in capturing Saddam Hussein, which had encouraged the Sunni insurgents and created uncertainties among their opponents. But there had been 'quite enormous progress in Iraq in spite of all the difficulties', including the restoration and improvement of medical services, the reconstruction of the educational system, and the rebuilding of the universities on different, more open, lines. 'Perhaps most remarkably of all', a lively free press, with a free exchange of opinions, had been established, which allowed for 'the often violent criticism of their liberating, occupying American Forces'.

Quite where Lewis drew his information remains a mystery, since these assertions were undocumented. Most commentators have been appalled at the collapse of services in 'liberated' Iraq, especially the hospital and educational services. If the purpose of military intervention was to ensure freedom, how genuine was that 'freedom' if many who had previously had a livelihood were now without work, if the water supply remained inadequate, and the hospital facilities were placed under insuperable difficulties by the collapse of civil order? What was the nature of a freedom imposed from outside, which left huge numbers of victims prey to kidnapping and sectarian killing? And on the main criticism of the war, its appallingly high human cost, both civilian and military, Lewis was, predictably silent. He envisaged only two difficulties. The main danger he conceived was that of excessive haste: 'democracy and democratic institutions take time to develop. If you go too fast, too far, too soon, you risk what happened in Algeria [in 1992] or worse';[39] and, secondly, there was the risk of the United Nations being given a role. In the discussion following his lecture in March 2004, Lewis made it quite clear that he thought that the UN was heading towards the fate of the League of Nations.[40]

On 12 May 2004, he returned to the theme of the inefficacy of the United Nations. There were objections to 'the record of the UN in dealing with conflicts'. 'Neither in terms of fairness, nor of efficacy' was this record encouraging, while its record on human rights was 'even worse'. For Lewis, the UN's purpose in dealing with conflicts 'seems to be conservation rather than resolution'; if let loose on Iraq, the UN would 'botch the job'.[41] Lewis's criticism of the international body was standard neo-conservative and Israeli government discourse; the real bone of contention with the UN was that the Secretary-General, Kofi Annan, had been unusually outspoken about the lack of legal justification for the war of intervention. He stated from the beginning that the invasion did not conform with the UN charter – phrasing that was seen as a diplomatic way of arguing that the war was illegal. Far from maintaining the usual diplomatic language, Annan moved in September 2004 from criticism to outright hostility, and argued that the war was indeed 'illegal'.[42]

Bernard Lewis returned to the theme of 'Freedom and Justice in the Modern Middle East' in a significant article published by *Foreign Affairs* in 2005.[43] He struck a more cautionary note than hitherto: 'creating a democratic political and social order in Iraq or elsewhere in the region will not be easy,' he reflected. 'But it is possible, and there are increasing signs that it has already begun.' He noted that while 'freedom' was not a term that resonated easily in the traditions of Islam,[44] 'justice' (*'adl*) certainly was and is. 'Consultation is a central part of the traditional Islamic order, but it is not the only element that can check the ruler's authority. The traditional system of Islamic government is both consensual and contractual.'

> Since 1940 and again after the arrival of the Soviets, the Middle East has basically imported European models of rule: Fascist, Nazi, and Communist. But to speak of dictatorship as being the immemorial way of doing things in that part of the world is simply untrue. It shows ignorance of the Arab past, contempt for the Arab present, and unconcern for the Arab future. The type of regime that was maintained by Saddam Hussein – and that continues to be maintained by some other rulers in the Muslim world – is modern, indeed recent, and very alien to the foundations of Islamic civilization. There are older rules and traditions on which the peoples of the Middle East can build.

After much historical digression and the restatement of his views on the advantages held by fundamentalists in genuinely free elections, Lewis ended with an encomium of the Iraqi assembly elections held on 30 January 2005:

> Millions of Iraqis went to polling stations, stood in line, and cast their votes, knowing that they were risking their lives at every moment of the process. It was a truly momentous achievement, and its impact can already be seen in neighbouring Arab and other countries. Arab democracy has won a battle, not a war, and still faces many dangers, both from ruthless and resolute enemies and from hesitant and unreliable friends. But it was a major battle, and the Iraqi election may prove a turning point in Middle Eastern history no less important than the arrival of General Bonaparte and the French Revolution in Egypt more than two centuries ago.

'With steadfastness and patience', Lewis concluded, 'it may now be possible at last to bring both justice and freedom to the long-tormented peoples of the Middle East.' Lewis's praise was for the process itself, not for the consequences. He was silent on the abstention rate, yet this was decisive in determining the legitimacy of the outcome. The Arab Sunni turnout, which was as low as 2 per cent in Anbar province, was a significant challenge to the outcome. Areas with mixed populations saw the vast majority of voters back Shi'ite or Kurdish parties. The largest Arab Sunni party, 'the Iraqis', won only 1.78 per cent of the vote (yet, Arab Sunnis are thought to be at least 20–30 per cent of the population). The boycott was largely a product of violence threatened both by former supporters of Saddam Hussein and jihadists.

The task faced by the Iraqi legislators elected in January 2005 was to formulate a new constitution under which full parliamentary elections could be held. The constitution was not ratified until 15 October and the new elections were not held until 15 December. Although the Sunni participation was higher than in the first election of 2005, as predicted, the Shiʿite majority emerged with a confirmed electoral mandate. Writing a column entitled 'When Sistani speaks, Bush listens' on 17 January 2004, the commentator Ehsan Ahrari noted that al-Sistani had always known what he wanted: 'the establishment of a Shiʿite-dominated moderate Islamic democracy. He envisaged the US presence as a guarantor of that eventuality. More to the point, the Americans were to safeguard the Shiʿites' right to be the dominant group, and were to protect them from the re-emergence of another form of Sunni-dominated tyranny at the end of Saddam's tyranny.'[45] The Shiʿite majority had gained power under an ambiguously drafted constitution largely suited to its interests. Although he had talked about Sunni–Shiʿite tensions after the invasion of 2003, Lewis had never identified three real possibilities: first, that Sunni resistance to the exercise of power by the Shiʿites might lead to anarchy or semi-permanent sectarian strife; secondly, that the Kurds might choose to break away in the northern region, appropriating the oil wealth based on Kirkuk; and thirdly that the Shiʿites might choose to do the same, appropriating the oil wealth based in the south. These very real obstacles to the proper functioning of democracy in Iraq because of the historical context were never considered publicly by Lewis.

In an interview at Washington DC on 27 April 2006, Bernard Lewis conceded that 'obviously the situation [in Iraq] has been getting worse over time', but he still considered it 'salvageable', while the three elections held led one 'to marvel at what has been accomplished'.[46] He recognized that Iraq had not turned out the way he had anticipated: 'I had underestimated our capacity to snatch defeat from the jaws of victory.' The way that President Ahmadinejad was talking 'shows quite clearly his contempt for the Western world in general and the United States in particular. They feel they are dealing with, as Osama bin Laden put it, an effete, degenerate, pampered enemy incapable of real resistance.[47] And they are proceeding on that assumption.' Echoing comments made by Donald Rumsfeld and others, Lewis added: 'we seem to be in the mode of Chamberlain and Munich rather than of Churchill.' The main thing we're doing wrong is psychological: 'we're showing hesitancy and weakness and fear.' Lewis returned to his theme on 16 July, in a lecture delivered on board the *Crystal Serenity* entitled 'Bring Them Freedom or They Destroy Us'.[48]

'Either we bring them freedom, or they destroy us.' No phrasing has better conveyed the Lewis Doctrine, its directness, its urgency and its contribution to the neo-conservative ideology of unilateral interventionism. Lewis accepts that trying to impose 'our kind of democracy' is foredoomed to failure. What he claims may reasonably be hoped for is that Muslim-majority countries will be able to develop some form of democratic government of their own. And yet is not the attempt to stimulate such change by military occupation not inevitably self-defeating? The reaction in the Arab world to George W. Bush's pro-democracy campaign has not been encouraging. In the meantime, the dismantling of an existing state acts as a powerful magnet to attract international terrorist activity.

Only a cynical vision, that of a Donald Rumsfeld for example, would argue that it is preferable to have chaos rather than dictatorship in order to fight a new form of 'terrorism' in Iraq rather than New York.[49] The truth is that Bernard Lewis is an old man in a hurry, an old man who admits that his mind is set in the events of 1938–40. Seminal though these events were in the struggle against Nazism, it is ultimately fatal to the search for appropriate international policies to equate the conflict against violent radicalism in Islam, which has relatively little support in the Islamic world, with the Nazi conquest of Europe. For there is no prospect of bin Laden and his criminal gang becoming the predominant ideology or political force within the Islamic world. The only risk is that because of misguided adventurism by the United States, especially the intervention in Iraq, Osama bin Laden gains a spurious credibility that he would never otherwise achieve.

It was particularly appropriate that Bernard Lewis was the recipient of the 2007 Irving Kristol award of the American Enterprise Institute, for it clearly illustrates the link between the protagonists of the 'clash of civilizations' and the neo-conservatives (the 2004 Irving Kristol award winner had been one of the most eminent neo-conservative columnists, Charles Krauthammer). Lewis's lecture – 'delivered in his ninetieth year to a hushed audience of 1,500 guests' – was on the theme of Europe and Islam and touched upon the issue of Muslims' capacity for assimilation (or more correctly, integration) into European society. He quoted the Syrian Bassam Tibi – 'will it be an Islamized Europe, or a Europeanized Islam?'[50] – and took a pessimistic view:

> The Muslims have certain clear advantages. They have fervour and conviction, which in most Western countries are either weak or lacking. They are for the most part convinced of the rightness of their cause, whereas Westerners spend much of their time in self-denigration and self-abasement. They have loyalty and discipline, and perhaps most important of all they have demography – the combination of natural increase and migration producing major population changes, which could lead within

> the foreseeable future to significant Muslim majorities in at least some European cities or even countries.

When an earlier version of his text was delivered in Israel, the *Jerusalem Post* recorded him as giving the stark warning that Muslims were 'about to take over Europe': 'Islam could soon be the dominant force in a Europe which, in the name of political correctness, has abdicated the battle for cultural and religious control', Lewis was quoted as stating at a 'special briefing' with *Jerusalem Post* editorial staff. 'The outlook for the Jewish communities of Europe is dim,' he concluded on this occasion.[51]

There was none of this in the Irving Kristol lecture, in which Lewis concluded with the hope that the idea of freedom in the Western interpretation was 'making headway in the Islamic world'. 'It is perhaps in the long run our best hope, perhaps our only hope, of surviving this latest stage – in some respects the most dangerous stage – of a fourteen-century-old struggle.'[52] It is customary for students to lavish praise on their past masters. In the case of Reuel Marc Gerecht's introductory remarks, the eulogy was excessive: he called Bernard Lewis 'the West's greatest scholar of Islam who has allowed history's two most provocative civilizations to see each other clearly, and who has allowed Muslim, Jew, and Christian to have a real dialogue of civilizations.'[53] Strange praise indeed for the scholar who single-handedly reignited the 'clash of civilizations' debate, but then is it surprising that in language of the neo-conservatives the clarity of the term 'clash' is transmuted into the obfuscation of 'real dialogue'?

How is 'real dialogue' advanced by Bernard Lewis's open support of the Likud party in Israel and the American Jewish advocacy group AIPAC (see chapter 5) in the US? (Is it an accident that Lewis's son, Dr Michael Lewis, heads AIPAC's disinformation section, keeping AIPAC's 'opposition research files' in a secure area, while making snippets of material available to interested parties in a process that former AIPAC employee Gregory D. Slabodkin described as akin to McCarthyite tactics?)[54] When, at the AIPAC conference in 2007, the former prime minister of Israel and current leader of the Knesset Opposition, Benjamin Netanyahu, described Iran as the world's first power incapable of being deterred by the doctrine of mutually assured destruction, whose view did he cite but that of Bernard Lewis, 'perhaps the greatest scholar [of Islam] living today'?[55]

> I asked Professor Bernard Lewis ... He said [that], for Ahmadinejad, mutual[ly] assured destruction is not a deterrent but a catalyst for action. This is how he gets the messianic apocalyptic age – the return of the Mahdi and the establishment of a 1,000-year old Islamic right in Israel. That's how it comes about. Millions die on both sides but the Muslim millions, the believers, go to a Muslim heaven with all the trappings ...

So much for Bernard Lewis and the claim that he sought to engage in 'real dialogue' with other religions for a peaceful world.

# Chapter Four
# Elijah's Mantle: The Inherited Struggle of Daniel Pipes

> Elijah passed by [Elisha], and cast his mantle upon him
>
> 1 Kings 19:19

> [Islamism is] the most vibrant extremist ideology in the world today, a threat to our interests not just in the Middle East but from West Africa to South-east Asia, and even here in the United States. Islamists hate us for who we are, not what we do. There is no hope of achieving a *modus vivendi* with them. You need to show them early and often that they cannot push this country around.
>
> Daniel Pipes, 'Memo to the Next President', *Middle East Insight* (November–December 2000)

> *Interviewer*: It is interesting that your son, Daniel, has followed in your tradition, and remains an 'outsider' in his profession as well – in Mideast scholarship. Like his father, he refuses to follow the favourite Party Line in academia: to toe the anti-American line and to sympathize with the tyrannical entities in his field of study. Why do so many academics who flock to their professions admire the most despotic creatures and regimes of their studies? What made the Pipes scholars different?
>
> *Richard Pipes*: I have never been able to understand the penchant of US academics for totalitarian regimes. This is a matter for psychologists and psychiatrists.
>
> Frontpage Interview with Richard Pipes (19 January 2004)[1]

Richard Edgar Pipes was born in 1923 in the town of Cieszyn (Teschen) in Polish Silesia on the Czech border. He managed to escape from Poland with his parents in September 1939. 'The main effect of the Holocaust on my psyche was to make me delight in every day of life that had been granted to me,' he writes in his memoirs.[2] 'I felt and feel to this day that I have been spared not to waste my life on self-indulgence or self-aggrandisement but to spread a moral message, using examples from history, how evil ideas lead to evil consequences.' Living under a totalitarian regime persuaded Pipes that 'one should never subordinate politics to ideology; for even if an ideology is morally sound, realising it usually requires resorting to violence because society at large may not share it.'

### *The Inheritance: Richard Pipes the Cold-War warrior*

As a distinguished scholar of old-regime Russia and the early Soviet Union at Harvard, Professor Richard Pipes became the archetype of the Cold War warrior. Throughout his career he consistently regarded the Soviet Union as an aggressive, imperial power.[3] Though he voted for Richard Nixon rather than George McGovern in 1972, Pipes was a Democrat whose political hero was the fiercely anti-Communist Senator Henry 'Scoop' Jackson (see Chapter 7). Pipes was appointed chairman of 'Team B', a counter-group of outside experts brought together in 1975 by a new team in Gerald Ford's administration – Donald Rumsfeld, Secretary of Defense, with Dick Cheney as his chief of staff, and George H. W. Bush as head of the CIA – to counter what were seen as the CIA's sanguine estimates of Soviet military strength. Pipes drew in Paul Wolfowitz, a weapons analyst recommended by Richard Perle.[4] (It is not without significance that these names reappeared in the team assembled by George W. Bush in 2000.) 'We dealt with one problem only', Pipes recalls. 'What is the Soviet strategy for nuclear weapons? Team B was appointed to look at the evidence and to see if we could conclude that the actual Soviet strategy [wa]s different from ours. It's now demonstrated totally, completely, that it was' – Pipes argues from evidence in the Polish archives that shows that the Soviets planned to use nuclear weapons in the event of war. Pipes approvingly cites the authority of George Kennan that the Russians were hostile to us 'not for what we did but for what we were … aggressiveness was embedded in their system.' 'Kennan had the uncommon ability to grasp the essential features of Communism without any of the illusions of American liberals.'

Pipes was also appointed to the National Security Council to advise Ronald Reagan's administration on its policy towards the Soviet Union. His influence peaked in 1981–2 when, as a member of the NSC, he helped steer Ronald Reagan toward the belief that the Soviet regime both could and must be 'defeated'. When, in March 1981, Richard Pipes dropped the bombshell that *détente* was dead[5] – it was, he said, 'inspired by intellectual indolence and based on ignorance of one's antagonist and therefore inherently inept' – the Reagan administration disavowed him but did not dismiss him. He briefed Reagan in the Oval Office on many occasions and considered him 'possessed to a high degree of the imponderable quality of political judgement ... to details of implementation he was indifferent, on matters of principle he was immoveable.' Reagan was 'a very successful President who contributed substantially to the collapse of the Soviet Union and the dissolution of its empire, events of world historical importance'. Pipes and his allies at the NSC and the Pentagon clashed with Reagan's Secretary of State George Schultz, whose approach to Moscow was one of willingness to 'haggle over the division of profits'. Richard Pipes was particularly dismissive of the Western European allies of the US. America's allegedly self-seeking NATO partners created 'the kind of problems we would experience later on, in the 1990s and early 2000s, after the Communist threat had vanished and the European governments began openly to resist our efforts to cope with the new global threat, Islamic terrorism'.[6]

Richard Pipes's view was that Russia's distinctive historical development ensured that it would always be an autocratic state with values fundamentally dissimilar to those of Western civilization. He was a leading advocate of the 'totalitarianism school' that saw Nazi Germany and the Soviet Union as similar regimes pursuing similar policies. He argued that the Soviet Union was an expansionist state bent on world conquest. Stephen Sestanovich, George F. Kennan Senior Fellow for Russian and Eurasian Studies at the Council of Foreign Relations, argues for a link between Richard Pipes's worldview and George W. Bush's 'war on terror':[7]

> If your view is that the problems the United States faces today are analogous to those of the Cold War, that you face an organized opponent with a radically different worldview, you can then see some similarities between a comprehensive strategy to get at that worldview that was developed by Pipes during the Cold War and the strategy the Bush administration has developed since 9/11.

## *Daniel Pipes the self-confessed 'Islamism-ophobe'*

The appropriateness of the phrase 'Elijah's mantle' became most evident when Richard Pipes's son, Daniel, pronounced in November 1994 that 'the Middle East has replaced the Soviet Union as the touchstone of politics and ideology.' He identifies similarities between the internal divisions in American politics during the two conflicts:[8]

> not only do Americans frame the discussion about Iran and Algeria much as they did the earlier one about the Soviet Union and China, but they

> also differ among themselves on the question of fundamentalist Islam roughly along the same lines as they did on the Cold War. Liberals say co-opt the radicals … Summing up, the Left is more sanguine than the Right about both Communism and fundamentalist Islam. It's hard to imagine a conservative calling the Ayatollah Khomeini 'some kind of saint', as did Jimmy Carter's ambassador to the United Nations, Andrew Young. It's about as unlikely to hear a liberal warning, along with France's Defence Minister François Leotard, that 'Islamic nationalism in its terrorist version is as dangerous today as National Socialism was in the past.'

Daniel Pipes professes himself happy to be called a neo-conservative.[9] Elsewhere he has been more prosaic, defining his political views as 'the simple politics of a truck driver, not the complex ones of an academic. My viewpoint is not congenial with institutions of higher learning.'[10]

The reality is that, since he failed to follow his father's illustrious career in academic life, he has made the universities his target. If Daniel Pipes is unacceptable to American universities, then perforce there must be something wrong with them. In his world view, the answer is simple: it is they, not he, who are biased. They are left-wing,[11] politically correct bastions of conformism, who have failed to understand his prophetic witness. Worse, the universities, and especially their centres of Middle Eastern Studies, are being undermined surreptitiously by a fifth column of professors whose political ideology is perceived by Pipes to be anti-Israel, anti-Semitic, pro-Palestinian, and pro-Islamist. In 2002, he established a website entitled Campus Watch to denounce such allegedly anti-American activities in a move criticized by his opponents as McCarthyite, an affront to academic freedom, and an attempt to silence criticism of US policies towards Israel and the Arab world.[12]

By November 2006, this campaign had brought Pipes and his supporters into direct conflict with the Academic Freedom Committee of the Middle East Studies Association of North America (MESA). This Association was founded in 1966 to promote scholarship and teaching on the Middle East and North Africa. Considering itself 'the pre-eminent organization in the field', the Association has published the *International Journal of Middle East Studies (IJMES)* since 1970 and has more than 2,600 members worldwide. Its aim is to ensure 'academic freedom and freedom of expression, both within the region and in connection with the study of the region in North America and elsewhere'.[13] Pipes had founded the rival Middle East Forum (MEF) in 1990 and is its director. MEF, which has an annual budget of $1.1 million,[14] calls itself a think tank seeking to 'define and promote American interests in the Middle East'. It defines US interests to include 'fighting radical Islam, whether terroristic or lawful;

working for Palestinian acceptance of Israel; improving the management of US democracy efforts; reducing energy dependence on the Middle East; more robustly asserting US interests vis-à-vis Saudi Arabia; and countering the Iranian threat. The Forum also works to improve Middle East studies in North America.'[15] It publishes the *Middle East Quarterly*, founded in 1994, which it claims has become 'America's most authoritative journal of Middle Eastern affairs. Policymakers, opinion-makers, academics, and journalists turn first to the Quarterly, for in-depth analysis of the rapidly-changing landscape of the world's most volatile region.'[16]

However, Daniel Pipes is contemptuous of the academic establishment in Middle Eastern studies and enthusiastically endorses the arguments of Martin Kramer in his polemic published in 2001 entitled *Ivory Towers on Sand: The Failure of Middle Eastern Studies in America*.[17] Leftist activism that 'too often passes for Middle East scholarship' must be condemned for what it is, and the various interested stakeholders must reclaim the universities 'as institutions of civilized discourse'.[18] Campuses must reclaim the 'lost ideological ground',[19] above all at Columbia University, which had provided an academic home to Pipes's lifelong ideological opponent, the late Edward Said, the most outspoken defender of the Palestinian cause in the United States.[20] The real aim of Campus Watch was not so much to 'review and critique Middle East studies in North America, with an aim to improving them' as to 'save' them; it was, in other words, an ideological crusade.[21] Those programmes of study which could not be brought into line should have their federal funding cut.[22] Celebrating five years of Campus Watch in September 2007, Pipes wrote in the *Jerusalem Post* that 'as Middle East specialists themselves acknowledge, this new accountability wrought by Campus Watch has overturned their once-insular world ... Campus Watch's highest priority is to help stimulate a diversity of opinion, so that pro-American scholars [viz: Right-wing scholars who support the policies of hardliners in Israel] – who today make up perhaps 5 per cent of Middle East specialists – reach parity with the anti-Americans.'[23] Even the publishing catalogues of academic presses were fair game for the crusader for ideological 'balance'[24] who sought to roll back the near take-over of the American universities by 'the illiberal left'.[25]

Daniel Pipes is frank about the surge in public interest in his views after the events of 9/11: 'partly, this surge is due to my specialty, what with terrorism, Islam, Iraq, the Arab-Israeli conflict, and Saudi Arabia dominating the news. Partly, it reflects a recognition that, pre-9/11, I saw the danger that militant Islam poses to the United States.'[26] It is true that on 11 April 2001 he had proclaimed in the *Jerusalem Post* that 'the time has come for Westerners ... to understand that Islamism presents a truly global threat, and to devote the mental energy and material resources required to fight it.' On 9 May, he had depicted the 'true profile' of Islamists in the same newspaper: they are 'ruthless, power-hungry operatives who cannot rightly claim the aura of piety they strenuously assert'. Rather than observant Muslims, they are political extremists.[27] 'Hating us for who we are, not what we do' places Daniel Pipes firmly as a disciple of Bernard Lewis, whom he describes as 'the leading scholar of Islam in the United States'.[28] But Pipes identifies himself as something other than a straight camp follower in the army led by Bernard Lewis and Samuel Huntington. 'Americans', he writes, 'are not involved in a battle royal between Islam and the West, or what has been called a "clash of civilizations"'. For one reason, 'violence against Americans – and against Israelis, Westerners, and non-Muslims in general – is just part of the story; Islamist enmity toward Muslims who do not share the Islamist outlook is no less vicious.'[29] He continues:

> ... if the earth-shaking clash of our time is not between two civilizations, it is and must be a clash among the members of one civilization – specifically, between Islamists and those who, for want of a better term, we may call moderate Muslims (understanding that 'moderate' does not mean liberal or democratic but only anti-Islamist). Just as the deviant Western ideologies of fascism and Communism challenged and shook and had to be expelled from the West, so it is with militant Islam and the Muslim world. The battle for the soul of Islam will undoubtedly last many years and take many lives, and is likely to be the greatest ideological battle of the post-Cold-War era ...

Pipes considers that outsiders, and the United States in particular, 'can critically help in precipitating the battle and in influencing its outcome'. They can do so both by 'weakening the militant side and by helping the moderate one'.

Most of his essays on the nature of militant Islam seek to identify both who are the militants who need to be resisted and the means by which this may be achieved. Pipes was quick to welcome George W. Bush's war on terror both as a declaration of war in itself ('by baring their teeth, Americans are far more likely to intimidate their enemies than to instigate further violence. Retaliation will reduce violence, not further increase it, providing Americans with a safety they presently do not enjoy'),[30] and also because it sought to identify the enemy who was to be confronted wherever he was found. Osama bin Laden and the Taliban in Afghanistan were therefore just the first of many opponents:[31]

> Apologists would tell us that Islamism is a distortion of Islam, or even that it has nothing to do with Islam, but that is not true; it emerges out of the religion, while taking features of it to a conclusion so extreme, so radical, and so megalomaniacal as to constitute something new. It adapts an age-old faith to the political requirements of our day, sharing some key premises of the earlier totalitarianisms, fascism and Marxism-Leninism. It is an Islamic-flavoured version of radical utopianism. Individual Islamists may appear law-abiding and reasonable, but they are part of a totalitarian movement, and as such, all must be considered potential killers.

Not until George W. Bush's speech on 6 October 2005 at the National Endowment for Democracy[32] was, in Pipes's view, the language of his administration appropriate to its real enemy in the war launched four years earlier. While distinguishing it from the religion of Islam, Bush presented this 'murderous ideology' of Islamic radicals as 'the great challenge of our new century'. He drew parallels between radical Islam and Communism (both are elitist, cold-blooded, totalitarian, disdainful of free peoples, and fatefully contradictory), then noted in how many ways the US war on radical Islam 'resembles the struggle against communism in the last century'. He described the 'violent, political vision' of radical Islam as an agenda 'to develop weapons of mass destruction, to destroy Israel, to intimidate Europe, to assault the American people, and to blackmail our government into isolation'. Its ultimate goal, the President maintained, was 'to enslave whole nations and intimidate the world'. He observed that Muslims themselves had to do the 'most vital work' to fight Islamism, but called on 'all responsible Islamic leaders to join in denouncing' this ideology and taking steps against it.[33] A less charitable view of the speech than that of Daniel Pipes called it 'a psychotic litany attempting to prove that the war on terror is just like the war on Communism. Five times [Bush] repeated: "Like the ideology of Communism, our new enemy Islamic radicalism ..."'[34]

The Pipes approach maximizes the potential number of enemies of America. In late November 2001, for example, he had estimated (without citing any evidence) that 'bin Laden enjoys the emotional support of half the Muslim world ... The wide and deep Muslim enthusiasm for bin Laden is an extremely important development that needs to be understood, not ignored.'[35] In January 2002, he noted that the idea of a 'clash of civilizations' had been supported, 'in his own diabolical way', by Osama bin Laden. In his view, the idea 'exercises an undoubted appeal': 'many Islamist elements do seek such a confrontation, out of a conviction that Islam will prevail and go on to achieve global supremacy.'[36] By October, Pipes and Jonathan Schanzer argued from the evidence of the cases of Indonesia, Bangladesh, and Nigeria that 'militant Islam and its companion violence have spread from the Middle Eastern core to the periphery of the Muslim world … It means that the enemies of the United States, moderate Islam, and of civilization itself are far more numerous and entrenched than previously thought.'[37]

Pipes considered himself vindicated by the report of the 9/11 Commission. The enemy was not just terrorism, 'some generic evil', but the more precise target of Islamic terrorism.[38] Even the President began to recognize that the 'war on terror' had been misnamed and what was being fought (still not enough for Pipes) was a war on 'ideological extremists'.[39] By November 2004, Pipes observed that 'Islamists note the urge to find moderate Muslims and are learning how to fake moderation. Over time, their camouflage will undoubtedly further improve.'[40] In April 2005, he was prepared once more to put figures on his estimates: there were '100 million Islamist enemies (not to speak of an even larger number of Muslims who wish us ill on assorted other grounds)' who could not all be incapacitated. 'Instead, the goal must be to deter and contain them … that is where the moderate Muslims come in. If roughly half the population across the Muslim world hates America, the other half does not.'[41]

Denying that he is America's 'leading Islamophobe', let alone the 'Islamophobe Incarnate', Daniel Pipes invented a new term for himself: 'what I really am is an "Islamism-ophobe".'[42] While acknowledging the use of the term 'Islamo-fascist' by President Bush and others, Pipes is wary of it, perceiving an inherent historical inaccuracy: 'few historic or philosophic connections exist between Fascism and radical Islam. Fascism glorifies the state, emphasizes racial "purity", promotes social Darwinism, denigrates reason, exalts the will, and rejects organized religion – all outlooks anathema to Islamists. In contrast, Radical Islam has many more ties, both historic and philosophic, to Marxism-Leninism …'[43]

## *Daniel Pipes and 'Sudden* Jihad *Syndrome'*

Though Pipes argues that terrorism is counter-productive to the long-term objectives of radical Islam in the Western world,[44] he remains obsessed with Islamist 'fifth-columnists', leading a persistent campaign against what he calls 'North America's leading Islamist organization, the Council on American–Islamic Relations (CAIR), for its alleged terrorist links.[45] The exclusion from the United States of prominent figures such as Tariq Ramadan and Yusuf Islam (formerly Cat Stephens), and other measures to 'profile' (that is, discriminate against) Muslims on entering American ports and airports are also justified as necessary. Indeed, for Daniel Pipes each and every curtailing of civil liberties is justified if it stops any further bomb attempt.[46] He quotes Robert S. Leiken's view that 'in Western countries *jihad* has grown mainly via Muslim immigration'.[47] And if not from immigrants, it has come from conversion. Converts to Islam are regarded with particular suspicion as potential terrorists.[48]

Pipes characterizes the apparently rapid conversion to violence of some extreme Islamists as 'sudden *jihad* syndrome':[49]

> … normal-appearing Muslims abruptly become violent. It has the awful but legitimate consequence of casting suspicion on all Muslims. Who knows whence the next *jihadi*? How can one be confident a law-abiding Muslim will not suddenly erupt in a homicidal rage? Yes, of course, their numbers are very small, but they are disproportionately much higher than among non-Muslims. This syndrome helps explain the fear of Islam and mistrust of Muslims that polls have shown on the rise since 11 September 2001. The Muslim response of denouncing these views as bias, as the 'new anti-Semitism', or 'Islamophobia' is as baseless as accusing anti-Nazis of 'Germanophobia' or anti-Communists of 'Russophobia'. Instead of presenting themselves as victims, Muslims should address this fear by developing a moderate, modern, and good-neighbourly version of Islam that rejects radical Islam, *jihad*, and the subordination of 'infidels'.

'Sudden *jihad* syndrome', Pipes claims, 'never erupts in isolation, but results from a steady diet of anti-Semitic, anti-Zionist, anti-Christian, and anti-American incitement fed by Islamist mosques, schools, voluntary associations, and media. Leftist demonizing of Israel further contributes to the problem.'[50] Pipes denies that *jihad* can ever be a peaceable phenomenon in Islam and extols those academics whose views agree with his,[51] while unfairly castigating those whose views do not.[52] Here he is caught in a trap of his own making. He wants a modern, peaceful version of Islam. Yet he both denies the capacity of Islam to change (thus either belittling, or betraying an ignorance of, the concept of *ijtihad*)[53] and at the same time asserts that the historical record of *jihad* (a largely violent phenomenon, with some exceptions) must inevitably become its future too.

The Muslim response to Pope Benedict XVI's remarks at Regensburg on 12 September 2006, and to previous incidents, such as the Danish cartoons of the Prophet, are characterized by Pipes as 'a single, prolonged campaign of intimidation, with surely more to come. The basic message – "You Westerners no longer have the privilege to say what you will about Islam, the Prophet, and the Qur'an, Islamic law rules you too" – will return again and again until Westerners either do submit or Muslims realize their effort has failed.'[54] Pipes is naturally enthusiastic about Vatican talk of reciprocity in the dealings between the West and the Islamic World.[55] He notes the (unsuccessful) 'purely unilateral American commitment' towards friendship with the Islamic world, 'a one-sided legacy [which] continues to the present'. The Bush administration 'responded to acts of unprovoked Muslim aggression [in 2001] not with hostility toward Islam but with offers of financial aid and attempts to build democracy in the Muslim world'.[56] (Whether any Muslim would agree with Pipes' viewpoint here is another matter, given the widespread perception that the 'war on terror' has become a more generalized attack on Islam.)

Daniel Pipes is particularly scathing of the attitude of certain European states, especially Britain, towards its Muslim minorities, and asserts (erroneously) the superiority of the French model over the British.[57] He is an uncritical supporter of the 'Eurabia'[58] and 'Londonistan'[59] discourse, the argument which suggests that parts of 'Old Europe' have sold out to Islamist pressure groups acting in the interests of radical rather than moderate Islam (see Chapter 10). He expresses sympathy, though not total agreement, with the views of Mark Steyn, who argues that Europe is 'too enfeebled to resist its remorseless transformation into Eurabia'. 'Islam is now the principal supplier of new Europeans,' Steyn contends. Arriving at a time of demographic, political, and cultural weakness, Muslims are profoundly changing Europe. 'Islam has youth and will, Europe has age and welfare.' Put differently, 'pre-modern Islam beats post-modern Christianity.'[60]

Pipes supports those ideologues, notably Samuel Huntington in *Who Are We? The Challenges to America's National Identity* (2004),[61] who are proponents of the drive towards the rapid assimilation of new migrants. Pipes himself decries British multiculturalism[62] and advocates a Blair-like emphasis on integration: 'as the full implications of the London terrorist attacks by domestic *jihadis* sink in, Westerners are speaking out about the problem of radical Islam with new clarity and boldness. The most profound development is the sudden need of the British and others to define the meaning of their nationality. In the face of the Islamist challenge, historic identities once taken for granted must now be codified.'[63]

### *Daniel Pipes the Neo-Zionist*

Pipes has little patience with the term 'Islamophobia', which he depicts as a case of special pleading.[64] On the other hand, he is acutely sensitive to anti-Semitism, which he claims is on the rise – chiefly because of the importance of Muslim anti-Semitism. Muslims are likely to accuse him of double standards, but he is unrepentant. The rejection of anti-Semitism (though not, apparently, the rejection of anti-Muslimism) is for Pipes the true test of a civilized society; conversely virulent Muslim anti-Semitism, which is rife in the Middle East (and according to Pipes, in much of the West as a result of the penetration of radical Islam), is a new barbarism;[65] '... as so often in the past, attitudes toward Jews serve as a vital touchstone of moderation and decency.'[66]

When President Ahmadinejad of Iran questions the Holocaust and threatens the future of Israel, he speaks for radical Islamists;[67] conversely, President Musharraf of Pakistan, speaking in the United States sympathetically about the Holocaust and rejecting anti-Semitism, is the true voice of moderation in the Islamic world.[68] Know your enemy by what they read, what they publish, and by what 'scientific' conferences they hold:[69] on this test, Pipes finds the Islamic world, with its apparent acceptance of the fraudulent *Protocols of the Elders of Zion*, its anti-Jewish cartoons, and its propensity to believe in conspiracy theories, decidedly lined up against progress and modernity. While there is some truth in his accusations, Pipes overstates his case when he claims that Muslims in Palestine would prefer to live in Israel than in their own state: 'the Hell of Israel is better than the Paradise of Arafat (or Abbas)'[70] is an unconvincing slogan, given the blockade and withdrawal of funding suffered by the Palestinians (with which Pipes wholeheartedly agrees).[71]

'... In word and deed, even anti-Zionist Palestinians acknowledge Israel as the most civilized state in the Middle East.'[72] Yet 'Israel faces the most extreme danger, surrounded as it is by enemies who in the past generation have dehumanized Jews in ways reminiscent of Nazi Germany in the 1930s.' In both cases, Pipes contends, 'governments have engaged in a systematic campaign to transform the Jewish next-door neighbour into a beast-like threat that can only be controlled through his destruction.' Pipes draws parallels, as does Bernard Lewis, to Nazi Germany. 'In Nazi Germany, this outlook culminated in the death camps; today, it could, and I stress could – I am not predicting it will – end up in a hail of nuclear bombs descending on Israel ... a second Holocaust, again of six million Jews.'[73] Pipes is particularly disingenuous in his confusion of anti-Semitism with anti-Zionism. It does not enhance his reputation to claim that any criticism of Zionism is suicidal for Jews as well as Israelis.[74] Here distinctions clearly have to be made. There are Orthodox Jews who are anti-Zionists; they can scarcely be called anti-Semites. Pipes tries to hide his colours in the current debate on the future of the polity of Israel but, within the terminology defined by historians such as Ilan Pappé, he is clearly a 'neo-Zionist'.

Traditional Zionists sought to combine ethnic segregation with an open society, but neo-Zionists do not accept that Zionism can retain its ethnocentric tenets while concluding peace with the Palestinians and 'turning Israel into a democratic, liberal entity'. Pappé defines neo-Zionism as a 'religiously inspired, ethnocentric discourse hostile to any settlement with the Palestinians and bent on sovereignty over the whole of historical Palestine'.[75] It is based on the premise that Israel's future depends on its understanding that peace with its Arab Muslim neighbours is impossible, and that, consequently, to ensure its survival, Israel must retain absolute military superiority over all the Arab armies taken together. Ultimately, the future of Israel rests on its superior technology and possession of nuclear weapons (a subject on which Pipes, predictably, is completely silent in loyalty to Israel's policy of 'strategic ambiguity'). Yet the possession of nuclear weapons by just one party in the Middle East, admitted publicly by the Israeli Prime Minister in an apparent slip on 11 December 2006,[76] serves as the spur to its rivals, first Iran and subsequently the Gulf States, to acquire nuclear capability. A spiralling arms race is thus an inevitable consequence of the neo-Zionist strategy.[77]

The virulence of Pipes's stand against any concessions to the Palestinians is well attested. In his lopsided version of the norms in international relations, all the concessions have to be made by the 'enemy', who thus implicitly or explicitly will be forced to accept the Israeli strategic gains since 1967. Once the Palestinians have, in effect, capitulated, then there can be peace. 'True acceptance, the kind Israelis dream of,' Pipes wrote in 1997, 'will come only when the Arabs are finally convinced they cannot destroy the Jewish state, today or ever. Painful as it may be for Israelis, as for many others, to acknowledge, it is the Arabs alone who will decide when a new Middle East can be born.'[78] Diplomats and strategists need to 'devise ways to induce the Palestinian Arabs to accept the existence of a sovereign Jewish state called Israel. Until that happens, no other initiatives will do any good.'[79] 'To become a normal people, one whose parents do not encourage their children to become suicide terrorists, Palestinian Arabs need to undergo the crucible of defeat.'[80] Yet the fact that Palestinian identity 'is of such recent and expedient origins' – it dates from only 1920 – suggests for Pipes 'that the Palestinian primacy is superficially rooted and that it could eventually come to an end, perhaps as quickly as it got started'.[81] Why do Muslims need a presence in Jerusalem at all, Pipes muses. They, after all, have Mecca. 'Just as Muslims rule an undivided Mecca, Jews should rule an undivided Jerusalem.'[82]

Pipes is scathing in his denunciation of 'Israel's failure to maintain the normal standards of self-preservation in 1993–2000', during the post-Oslo 'peace process'. This signalled a 'softness that rejuvenated moribund Arab ambitions about destroying the "Zionist entity"', with the second *intifada* as the direct consequence.[83] 'Interim Israeli concessions are counterproductive and must be discouraged,' Pipes pronounces: 'the only way to make progress in the Palestinian–Israeli conflict is by inducing the Palestinians to surrender their murderous intentions vis-à-vis Israel.'[84] He is scathing on the hubris of successive Israeli prime ministers who have sought a place in history by negotiating a settlement with the Palestinians, going further than they were prepared to admit to the electorate:[85]

> Two patterns have shaped Israel's history since 1992 and go far to explain Israel's predicament today. First, every elected prime minister has broken his word on how he would deal with the Arabs. Second, each one of them has adopted a[n] unexpectedly concessionary approach …
>
> Ariel Sharon won a landslide victory in January 2003 over his Labour opponent, Amram Mitzna, who called for 'evacuating the settlements from Gaza'. Mr Sharon ridiculed this approach, saying that it 'would bring the terrorism centres closer to [Israel's] population centres'. In December 2003, however, Mr Sharon adopted Mitzna's unilateral withdrawal idea …
>
> The problem is, these are undemocratic impulses that betray the electorate, undermine faith in government, and erode Israel's position. These negative trends will continue until Israelis elect a modest prime minister …

Pipes called Ariel Sharon's decision to require the withdrawal of Israeli settlers from Gaza 'an act of monumental political folly …'[86] 'Israel's mistakes', he pronounced, 'are not unique for a democracy – French appeasement of Germany in the 1930s or American incrementalism in Vietnam come to mind – but none other jeopardized the very existence of a people.'[87] As for the Iraq Study Group Report – described by Pipes as 'James Baker's terrible Iraq Report' – it calls for a Palestinian state and 'even demands' that a final settlement address the Palestinian 'right of return'. In Pipes's view, this is tantamount to 'code for dismantling the Jewish state'. Moreover, the authors of the report 'peremptorily declare that "the Israelis should return the Golan Heights", in return for a US security guarantee.'[88]

Throughout his writings, Pipes has made it clear that he regards the Palestinian refugee problem as 'manufactured', yet he acknowledges that it stands 'at the dank heart of the conflict'.[89] 'In every other instance' save the Palestinian, Pipes contends, 'the pain of dispossession, statelessness, and poverty has diminished over time. Refugees eventually … resettled, returned home or died. Their children – whether living in South Korea, Vietnam, Pakistan, Israel, Turkey, Germany or the United States – then shed the refugee status and joined the mainstream. Not so the Palestinians. For them, the refugee status continues from one generation to the next, creating an ever-larger pool of anguish and discontent.' As a riposte, Paul McCann of the United Nations Relief and Works Agency (UNRWA) writes: 'what condemns the Palestine refugees to "lives of exclusion, self-pity and nihilism" [Pipes's phrase] is not UNRWA, but rather the inability of the parties of the conflict to solve the refugee issue. Thus, dismantling UNRWA will not "solve the Palestinian refugee problem", as Pipes claims. The refugees and their plight would still exist. UNRWA itself is not mandated to solve the refugee problem, which is a political question for the parties to the conflict. In describing UNRWA as a "malign institution", and its humanitarian services as "monstrous works"', McCann argues that Pipes 'betrays the extreme bias of his views'.[90]

Why is Pipes so virulent against the refugees? It is because they are defined as the expropriated: those who lived in Palestine 'between June 1946 and May 1948, who lost both their homes and means of livelihood as a result of the 1948 Arab-Israeli conflict' and the 'descendants of persons who became refugees in 1948'. Pipes is not prepared to acknowledge the need to rectify any historical injustice since this would prejudice his neo-Zionist enterprise of creating a religiously inspired, ethnocentric state. It goes without saying that Pipes contends that a Palestinian state would be 'a nightmare' both for the Arabs and Israel.[91] Pipes is particularly scathing in his denunciation of the US and the EU for resuming the payment of subsidies to the Palestinian regime of Mahmoud Abbas on the West Bank. Writing in the *Jerusalem Post* on 19 December 2007, he cites 'innovative research' by Steven Stotsky of the Committee for Accuracy in Middle East Reporting in America, an organization seeking to promote 'fair' and 'balanced' reporting on Israel – that is, to monitor and challenge any perceived criticism of the Zionist state – supposedly demonstrating that there is a link between the budgetary support aid provided annually to the Palestinian Authority and the number of Palestinian homicides (including both criminal and terrorist activities, and both Israeli and Palestinian victims). Such a proposed link would be dismissed by most serious scholars as fatuous, but Pipes proclaims that when 'graphed together' [*sic*], 'the two [sets of] figures show an uncanny echo'. 'In brief, each $1.25 million or so of budgetary support aid translates into a death within the year. As Stotsky notes, "these statistics do not mean that foreign aid causes violence; but they do raise questions about the effectiveness of using foreign donations to promote moderation and combat terrorism."'[92]

Pipes postures as a defender of secularism: 'in an era when global *jihad* presents the major international danger, it offers a unique brake on the path to religious war. In an era of mass migration, it offers a unique method of integration.'[93] In essence, he advocates secularism as a solution to the world's problems with one exception: the state of Israel, for which no such suggestion is countenanced. For Pipes, 'the Muslim citizens of Israel, usually known in English as Israeli Arabs, constitute enemy no. 3' (that is, after the foreign states and external Palestinians). Yet for Israel itself, he argues that its alleged 'secularism' may be 'one reason for its weariness and demoralization.'[94]

What secularism is this? Jonathan Cook argues that 'when Israel demands that its "right to exist" be recognised, the subtext is that we are not speaking of recognition of Israel as a normal nation state but as the state of a specific people, the Jews ... Israel is ensuring that the Palestinians agree to Israel's character being set in stone as an exclusivist Jewish state, one that privileges the rights of Jews over all other ethnic, religious and national groups inside the same territory.' Cook maintains that the 'need to maintain Israel's Jewish character at all costs is actually the engine of its conflict with the Palestinians. No solution is possible as long as Israel insists on privileging citizenship for Jews above other groups, and on distorting the region's territorial and demographic realities to ensure that the numbers continue to weigh in the Jews' favour.' Palestinians living in Israel 'have been demanding that Israel be reformed from a Jewish state, which systematically discriminates against them and denies their Palestinian identity, into a "state of all its citizens", a liberal democracy that would give all citizens, Jews and Palestinians, equal rights.'[95] In opposition to this, Israel has been projecting the idea of an oath of loyalty to the 'Jewish and democratic state', whereby Palestinians would 'renounce their demand that Israel reform itself into a liberal democracy.'[96] Pipes considers that the 'extremism' of the report *The Future Vision of Palestinian Arabs in Israel* (December 2006) 'may well mark a turning point for Israeli Muslims. The paper rejects the Jewish nature of Israel, insisting that the country become a bi-national state in which Palestinian culture and power enjoy complete equality ... Most profoundly, the study would terminate the Zionist achievement of a sovereign Jewish state.'[97]

### *Daniel Pipes and the Long Struggle for 'Freedom' for the Peoples of the Middle East*

Pipes made his name originally as a specialist on Syria, so it was little surprise that he was brought into the ambit of the US Committee for a Free Lebanon, founded in 1997, by its founder, Ziad K. Abdelnour. In the year 2000, they co-authored a report entitled 'Ending Syria's Occupation of Lebanon: The US Role'. This argued that Syrian rule by proxy in Lebanon stood in direct opposition to American ideals, and condemned Washington's habitual willingness since 1983 to engage rather than confront the regime: Syria was the only government on the State Department's 'terrorism' list with which Washington had full diplomatic relations. The

Lebanon Study Group urged a policy of confrontation, beginning with tough economic and diplomatic sanctions that could not be waived by the president and followed up, if necessary, by military force. 'The Vietnam legacy and the sour memories of dead American Marines in Beirut notwithstanding,' the group wrote, 'the United States has entered a new era of undisputed military supremacy coupled with an appreciable drop in human losses on the battlefield.' 'This opens the door to a similar decision to act for Lebanon's endangered freedoms and pluralism,' the group argued, but the opportunity could not wait because WMD capabilities might spread, making the risks of such action much greater. In an argument which foreshadowed that of the hawks deployed prior to the Iraq invasion, the group recommended: 'if there is to be decisive action, it will have to be sooner rather than later.'[98]

Writing under his sole name on the subject, Pipes equated the struggle to that of freeing the oppressed peoples of Eastern Europe held under Soviet tutelage:[99]

> To my mind, there is really no choice: our government must stand in solidarity with the oppressed and against the oppressors. Just as we supported Estonians and Czechs through their decades of Soviet domination, even when the prospect of their independence seemed impossibly remote, so we must stand by the Lebanese people in their hour of need. Nor is this only a matter of principle: Baltic leaders all agree on the importance of the US government refusing to accept the Soviet occupation of their countries. Lebanese patriots one day will similarly thank us for standing with their people even as they faced the seemingly invincible might of the Syrian sword.

In spite of the support of such figures as Jesse Helms, Jeane Kirkpatrick, Elliot Abrams, Paula Dobriansky, and Richard Perle, the report was shelved because it was published in the last months of an outgoing presidency. Subsequently, the Bush presidency had too many other issues on its hands to take decisive action, in spite of Daniel Pipes's consistent calls for the 'liberation' of Lebanon.[100]

Pipes does not seem to have been involved in the activities of the Committee for the Liberation of Iraq, which was formed in late 2002 'to promote regional peace, political freedom, and international security by replacing the Saddam Hussein regime with a democratic government that respects the rights of the Iraqi people and ceases to threaten the community of nations.'[101] Nevertheless, Pipes's language against the Iraq dictator became increasingly aggressive. In August 2000, he announced it as 'preposterous' that Saddam was still in power ten years after the invasion of Kuwait.[102] In his memorandum to the next president written in

November–December 2000, he concluded: 'Saddam Hussein remains an aggressive tyrant intent on making his mark on the world stage through either weapons of mass destruction or his control of the oil market. We are not usually in the business of regime change; here is the exception. The best vehicle for this are the opposition groups desperate for US backing.'[103] At the beginning of December 2001, he argued with Jonathan Schanzer that 'Saddam Hussein represents the single greatest danger to the United States, not to speak of the rest of the world. Today, with Americans mobilized, is exactly the right moment to dispatch him.' The risks of doing so, they contended, 'were overrated'.[104] By March 2002, Pipes was a strong advocate of a unilateral strike by the US against Iraq.[105]

General Brent Scowcroft, who had the unique distinction of serving as National Security Adviser under two Presidents,[106] took the unusual step on 15 August 2002 of appealing to George W. Bush via the pages of the *Wall Street Journal* not to invade Iraq. There was scant evidence to tie Saddam to terrorist organizations, he argued, 'and even less to the September 11 attacks'. He further suggested that 'an attack on Iraq at this time would seriously jeopardize, if not destroy, the global counter-terrorist campaign we have undertaken'. Scowcroft's words were prescient:[107]

> … any campaign against Iraq, whatever the strategy, cost and risks, is certain to divert us for some indefinite period from our war on terrorism. Worse, there is a virtual consensus in the world against an attack on Iraq at this time. So long as that sentiment persists, it would require the US to pursue a virtual go-it-alone strategy against Iraq, making any military operations correspondingly more difficult and expensive. The most serious cost, however, would be to the war on terrorism. Ignoring that clear sentiment would result in a serious degradation in international cooperation with us against terrorism. And make no mistake, we simply cannot win that war without enthusiastic international cooperation, especially on intelligence.

Though Scowcroft had intimated that Iraq might strike against Israel in any such conflict, Pipes would have none of the former NSA's arguments. 'For the sake of America's war on terror', he contended, 'the retired general should review a primary lesson the United States was dealt by the attacks on 9/11':[108]

> America learned the hard way then that waiting to use what Scowcroft calls the 'best strategy and tactics' to remove a global threat is ill advised. Saddam Hus[sein] poses no less of a threat to American and global security than Osama bin Laden, yet for more than a decade, Washington has jockeyed and yammered for the right moment, the right place, the right opportunity to depose him. The time for prevarication has passed. The time to attack is now. Saddam must be overthrown, and soon.

When another experienced campaigner, President Mubarak of Egypt, lamented in the spring of 2003 that the consequence of the Iraq War would be the reverse of what was intended, that terrorism would be aggravated and that instead of one bin Laden there would be a hundred bin Ladens, Pipes was again dismissive. (Unusually, he recognized in September 2006 that Mubarak had been correct and he had been wrong.)[109]

Though in general Pipes was sympathetic to the neo-conservative Project for the New American Century (PNAC) lobby, he did not sign its several open letters to the President,[110] with one notable exception. This was a letter to President George W. Bush on 3 April 2002 identifying Israel as a partner of the US in the war on terror. As Secretary of Defense Donald Rumsfeld had pointed out, the group argued, 'Iran, Iraq, and Syria are all engaged in "inspiring and financing a culture of political murder and suicide bombing" against Israel, just as they have aided campaigns of terrorism against the United States over the past two decades.'[111] The signatories of the letter urged Bush to

> accelerate plans for removing Saddam Hussein from power in Iraq. As you have said, every day that Saddam Hussein remains in power brings closer the day when terrorists will have not just airplanes with which to attack us, but chemical, biological, or nuclear weapons, as well. It is now common knowledge that Saddam, along with Iran, is a funder and supporter of terrorism against Israel. Iraq has harboured terrorists such as Abu Nidal in the past, and it maintains links to the al-Qaeda network. If we do not move against Saddam Hussein and his regime, the damage our Israeli friends and we have suffered until now may someday appear but a prelude to much greater horrors. Moreover, we believe that the surest path to peace in the Middle East lies not through the appeasement of Saddam and other local tyrants, but through a renewed commitment on our part, as you suggested in your State of the Union address, to the birth of freedom and democratic government in the Islamic world.

The letter ended with a crescendo: 'Israel's fight against terrorism is our fight. Israel's victory is an important part of our victory. For reasons both moral and strategic, we need to stand with Israel in its fight against terrorism.'

There can be little doubt that Pipes's consistent support for the intervention in Iraq was predicated on the linkage with Israel's war against terror as defined in this letter. Whether Iraq was a war fought in Israel's interest as much as in (or even more than) that of the United States is a legitimate subject of debate, but remains an open question. Once it was clear no WMD were likely to be found, Pipes retreated to the rather threadbare argument that WMD were not the reason for going to war against Iraq.[112] By all means, bring on 'Iraqi Freedom', he wrote. 'But always keep in mind, as President Bush has done, that the ultimate war goal is to enhance American security.' War was not 'social work'. The obligations of the US to its defeated enemies were strictly limited.[113] Thus, Pipes criticized the Afghanistan reconstruction fund.[114] And he was equally obdurate with regard to the need to rebuild Iraq's shattered infrastructure: 'the American military machine is not an instrument for social work, nor for remaking the world. It is, rather, the primary means by which Americans protect themselves from external violent threats. The US goal cannot be a free Iraq, but an Iraq that does not endanger Americans.'[115] Thus from relatively early on in the war, he was consistent in his calls for 'Iraqification', letting Iraqis run Iraq,[116] and for handing over power to an Iraqi strongman[117] – assuming one could be found who met his stringent criteria,[118] which was not the case. In comparison with Bernard Lewis, his support for Ahmed Chalabi as a suitable leader was muted.[119]

On Iraq, Pipes found himself hoist by his own petard. In the early stages of the war, he had raised false hopes that the Middle East might be rebuilt on the model of a reconstructed Iraq.[120] For this to happen, post-Saddam Iraq had first to be stabilized and successfully remodelled. Here the Prophet Elisha would have been wise to have heeded the scepticism expressed by the Prophet Elijah. Professor Richard Pipes, when interviewed on the parallels between the remodelling of Eastern Europe and the situation in the Middle East after the occupation of Iraq was cautious: 'democracy requires, among other things, individualism – the breakdown of old clannish, tribal organizations, the individual standing face-to-face with the state. You don't have that in the Middle East. Iraq is tribally run.' 'What about the drafting of a new Iraqi constitution?', Richard Pipes was asked. 'Stalin had a wonderful constitution, the most perfect constitution in the world,' was the retort. He dismissed the policy of establishing a democratic Iraq as both naïve and over-ambitious. There was a lack of understanding of other cultures on the part of Paul Wolfowitz and others pressing for the reshaping of Iraq.[121]

In contrast, as late as 12 November 2003 Daniel Pipes endorsed President Bush's comment that 'sixty years of Western nations excusing and accommodating the lack of freedom in the Middle East did nothing to make us safe.'[122] It was only when the first fruits of that freedom were revealed, with Iraq's interim constitution in March 2004, that Daniel Pipes realized that the genie was out of the bottle:[123]

> When the interim constitution does take force, militant Islam will have blossomed in Iraq ... For their part, the occupying powers now face a monumental challenge: making sure this totalitarian ideology does not dominate Iraq and become the springboard for a new round of repression

and aggression from Baghdad. How they fare has major implications for Iraqis, their neighbours, and far beyond.

From this time on, Pipes's tone has changed. From being an advocate of action fast, provided it was in the American interest, he now cautioned against American impatience and became an advocate of slowing down the processes of change. He was less optimistic than Bernard Lewis on the nature of democracy, believing that it had to be entrenched in society. It is more than simply voting in elections.[124] The changes may take a very long time to achieve – in a debate at the Nixon Centre, Pipes suggested that in Egypt the process might take twenty-five years![125] (That the populations of the Arab countries are unwilling to wait this long, while the Arab regimes are resistant to outside interference, does not seem to be worthy of consideration for Pipes.) In March 2005, he attempted to cast a philosophical and historical gloss over his change of heart:[126] 'other than the *sui generis* Palestinian case, one main danger threatens to undo the good news: that a too-quick removal of tyranny unleashes Islamist ideologues and opens their way to power. Sadly, Islamists uniquely have what it takes to win elections: the talent to develop a compelling ideology, the energy to found parties, the devotion to win supporters, the money to spend on electoral campaigns, the honesty to appeal to voters, and the will to intimidate rivals.'

Pipes's views did not leave him without critics in the neo-conservative establishment. In answer to Pipes's slogan, 'radical Islam is the problem, moderate Islam is the solution', a fellow neo-conservative and signatory of the PINAC letter to President Bush of April 2002, Reuel Marc Gerecht, replies, 'moderate Muslims are not the answer.' His view can be summarized as 'radical Islam is both the problem and the solution.'[127] In his short study entitled *The Islamic Paradox* (2004), Gerecht pronounces: 'the Arab world is too historically and culturally different from Turkey to produce an Atatürk.'[128] The Kemalist attitude, Gerecht argues, which is focused on using a high-brow-style dictatorship to move toward secularism and subsequently to democracy, cannot be considered a viable means to introduce the Middle East to democracy. Since the end of World War II, Arab dictators have become less progressive and less liberal; the idea that a Kemalist evolution will shape the future serves only to encourage bin Ladenism. In contrast, as with Bernard Lewis, Daniel Pipes is committed to the Turkish model, 'the Muslim success story of our time. Only when Muslims turn to secularism will this terrible era of their history come to an end.'[129] Only in the course of 2007 has Pipes come out openly against the supposedly Islamist AKP government in Turkey:[130]

> Along with Japan, Turkey has shown itself to be among the most malleable of countries. In just fifteen years and almost single-handedly, Atatürk managed to move the country Westward; in just five years, Erdoğan has started moving it Eastward. The recent transformation has happened so quickly that – formal NATO relations notwithstanding – Turkey can no longer be considered a Western ally. Nor, certainly, is it an enemy. Rather, it falls into a middle status – like Russia, China, and Saudi Arabia – of rival. One day it cooperates, the next it competes. Before long, it may well threaten.

Gerecht concludes that Washington should put aside its misgivings and encourage Sunni Islamists to compete in elections. Let them come to power, discredit themselves, alienate their subject populations, and then be thrown into the dustbin of history. Against the charge of 'defeatism', Gerecht offers aphorisms such as 'bin Ladenism can only be gutted by fundamentalists' and 'moderate Muslims are not the answer. Shi'ite clerics and Sunni fundamentalists are our salvation from future 9/11s.' Pipes considers Gerecht's arguments 'hard-headed, even clever', but his principal conclusion 'fundamentally flawed'. Rather than passively reconcile itself to decades of totalitarian rule, 'Washington should actively help Muslim countries navigate from autocracy to democracy without passing through an Islamist phase. This is indeed achievable.'

Pipes lashes out at the Bush administration for its silence on the participation of Hamas, an organization that the US itself considers to be a terror group, in the Palestinian elections. He dismisses the idea of 'a moderate Islamist' as a tautology. 'Hizbu'llah and Hamas, elected or not, are unacceptable because of their goals.'[131] Once elected, Hamas had to be treated as a leper for fear of encouraging other Islamist groups.[132] (Pipes does not seem to consider the possibility that a group such as Hizbu'llah can evolve over time, though there is strong evidence that it can.)[133] He is particularly dismissive of Conflict Forum, an initiative of the British former MI6 officer, Alastair Crooke, which seeks a dialogue with peaceful Islamists.[134] Yet all the evidence of world conflicts is that a resolution only begins when the parties begin to talk to each other, understand their differences, and negotiate a common ground. Pipes's is a recipe for endless conflict without resolution since there is no avenue for dialogue. This may or may not be what Israel wants. Pipes is particularly suspicious of James Baker III's influence, since he would be willing to engage the United States in negotiations with a range of Muslim states without any participation for, and therefore much less diplomatic pressure from, Israel.[135] Baker is dismissed as too 'dictator-friendly', the personification of a failed policy in the Arab world in 1991–2.

It is in relation to Saudi Arabia that Pipes's vision of the future of the Middle East is found to be wanting because of its own contradictions. Although he claims neutrality, his basic position is one of hostility to the kingdom, on the grounds that it is linked inseparably to the Wahhabi tradition which presents a 'domestic menace' to the United States through its propagation in the mosques. This amounts to an 'insidious Saudi assault on America', which in Pipes's view 'must be made central to the (misnamed) war on terror'. The 'fantasy of Saudi friendship' must be dropped as an idea, and instead the kingdom must be viewed, 'like China, as a formidable rival whose ambitions for a very different world order must be repulsed and contained'.[136] Earlier, he had written on 'the scandal of US–Saudi relations'.[137] What would be the American position, hypothetically, were the Saudis to destroy their oil and gas infrastructure in the event of invasion, so that it was kept out of commission for decades? The effect would be catastrophic for the world economy. Pipes invites us to imagine an alternative and worse scenario:[138]

> should the monarchy be replaced by an Islamic emirate in the spirit of Afghanistan's Taliban (its main challenger for power), this ferociously anti-Western government would have at its disposal a cataclysmic suicide-bomber capacity; with one push of a button, conceivably, it could shake the world order. And it would be highly inclined to do just that.

What would be the American position, again hypothetically, once US troops had been withdrawn from Iraq, if the Saudis began arming the Sunni militias to protect them from the Shi'ite militias? Did King Abdullah of Jordan warn the US Vice-President, Dick Cheney, of this possibility in November 2006? The US administration denied the conversation had taken place or that this was Jordan's or Saudi policy.[139] In May 2004, Pipes noted that 'for Western states, the choice is an unhappy one, between the Saudi monarchy with all its faults and the still worse Ikhwan alternative'. The policy options were thus limited to 'helping the monarchy defeat the even more radical threat while pressuring it to make improvements in a range of areas, from financial corruption to funding militant Islamic organizations worldwide'.[140] By December 2007, Pipes viewed the prospect of Saudi weapons purchases from Russia with equanimity since it would tend to 'reduce or rid American politics of the noxious fumes of Saudi influence'.

The complexity of the issues means that the simple neo-conservative strategy for the Middle East (pre-emption and exporting freedom abroad)[141] has been found to be rather more difficult to implement than its theoreticians – Pipes included – maintained. In the end, as Daniel

Pipes frankly recognizes, 'the Middle East has so defined the presidency of George W. Bush that historians will … judge him primarily according to his actions there.' In July 2003, he was extolling with enthusiasm Bush's 'unapologetic and momentous break with past restraints'. First, in the area of the pre-emptive strike: 'knock out fantasist leaders (the Taliban, Saddam Hussein, Yasser Arafat) before they can do more damage.' Dismantle their polities, then 'reconstruct them along civilized lines'. 'Impose a double standard: act on the premise that the US government alone "is permitted to use force against other agents, who are not permitted to use force"' against it. 'This appeal for America to act less civilized will offend some,' Pipes acknowledged, 'but it does offer a convincing explanation for the inner logic of America's tough new foreign policy.'[142] In October 2004, he defined four areas in which Bush's foreign policy had been distinctive: he had pursued war rather than law enforcement; democracy rather than stability; pre-emption rather than deterrence; and leadership rather than reaction in setting the goals for an Arab–Israeli settlement.

Even at this date, when the signs of the Iraq intervention were all negative, Pipes praised Bush's 'exceptional willingness to take risks and shake up the malign *status quo* in the Middle East', a policy which he still thought stood 'a good chance of working'.[143] (In contrast, by December 2006, there were observers who declared without equivocation that in all areas Bush's foreign policy had made matters much worse.)[144] What was Pipes's response to the evident signs of civil war in Iraq, which appeared to be an unravelling of American policy? It was one of abject cynicism:[145]

> The bombing on 22 February [2006] of the Askariya shrine in Samarra, Iraq, was a tragedy, but it was not an American or a coalition tragedy. Iraq's plight is neither a coalition responsibility nor a particular danger to the West. Fixing Iraq is neither the coalition's responsibility, nor its burden. When Sunni terrorists target Shi'ites and vice versa, non-Muslims are less likely to be hurt. Civil war in Iraq, in short, would be a humanitarian tragedy, but not a strategic one.

In a television interview, Pipes added that the US could help the Iraqis, but 'it is not our burden to re-establish, to rehabilitate Iraq on a new basis.' He repudiated the trend since 1945, which was that reconstruction had to follow upon a military occupation of a country with which one had been at war:[146]

> I don't think the Iraqis want us there to fix Iraq. The big difference, the key difference, between the Germans and the Japanese 60 years ago and the Iraqis today is that the Germans and Japanese went through years of total war, were smashed by it. The Iraqis went through six weeks of very limited

> war, and came out liberated and feeling they are in a position to determine their destiny. I say good for them, let them do that.
>
> … the name in the US was Operation Iraqi Freedom. I bristled at that. I thought it should be 'Operation American Security'. And we don't spend American lives to win other people's freedom; we do it in order to protect ourselves. I think, again, a more modest approach [is required] where we keep an eye on our interest and hope for the best for the Iraqis and do the best we can for them, or any other peoples, but not make their welfare the reason why we go to war, why we lose lives. That's not going to work.

In such summary terms did one of America's leading neo-conservatives dismiss the human cost and infrastructural damage brought about by President Bush's 'war on terror'. What is clear is that advocates of confrontation, whether on the side of 'democracy' or Islamic radicalism, are equally callous in calculating the human cost of war. In this respect, Pipes was guilty of believing his own propaganda about the acceptable human cost of modern allegedly 'precision' warfare waged by the 'creative and humane' American and Israeli military establishments.[147] For Pipes, the 'benefits of the war have been mainly security-related and the costs mainly attitudinal … The Bush administration succeeded militarily but failed politically.'[148]

What is also clear is that Pipes, and the neo-conservative standpoint which he advocates, seeks to coerce the rest of public opinion in the West into acquiescence by gravely exaggerating the extent of the menace posed by global terrorism and extreme Islamism. Commentators who disagree with him, such as Robert Fisk or William Blum, are dismissed by Pipes as either extreme left-wingers or 'self-hating Westerners'; worse still, they are castigated as 'the Islamists' auxiliary *mujahideen*'. Pacifism represents a perceived danger for Pipes, the conviction that has already taken hold among the educated, that '"there is no military solution" to current problems, a mantra applied in every Middle East problem'. 'The absence of an impressive Islamist military machine imbues many Westerners, especially on the left, with a feeling of disdain', Pipes contends. 'Whereas conventional war – with its men in uniform, its ships, tanks, and planes, and its bloody battles for land and resources – is simple to comprehend, the asymmetric war with radical Islam is elusive.' Only the enemy within, he postulates in his end of year message for 2006, can prevent the West from defeating its Islamist opponents. 'Pacifism, self-hatred and complacency are lengthening the war against radical Islam and causing undue casualties.'[149]

## Chapter Five

# The Real American Special Relationship: Israel's Interests and the Influence of the American Jewish Lobby

> We have a special relationship with Israel. It's absolutely crucial that no-one in our country or around the world ever doubt that our number-one commitment in the Middle East is to protect the right of Israel to exist, to exist permanently, and to exist in peace. It's a special relationship.
>
> President Jimmy Carter (12 May 1977)[1]

> Your law is the law of the rich and wealthy, who hold sway in their political parties, and fund their election campaigns with their gifts. Behind them stand the Jews, who control your policies, media and economy.
>
> Osama bin Laden, 'To the Americans' (6 October 2002)[2]

> Even President Bush acknowledges that Saddam Hussein had nothing to do with 9/11. Of course there were no weapons of mass destruction ... With Iraq no threat, why invade a sovereign country? The answer: President Bush's policy to secure Israel ...
>
> Senator Ernest Hollings (Democrat, 10 May 2004)[3]

> [Tony] Blair failed to understand that America's really special relationship is with Israel, not Britain. Every time that George Bush had to choose between Blair and Ariel Sharon, he chose the latter.
>
> Professor Avi Shlaim (14 May 2007)[4]

Whether or not the Iraq invasion of 2003 was 'Israel's war' – rather than a war embarked upon solely in the strategic interests of the US – remains deeply controversial even among those who broadly share a similar (liberal) political viewpoint.[5] According to one of the pages formerly on the website of America's 'leading pro-Israel lobby', the American Israel Public

Affairs Committee (AIPAC), the United States and Israel have formed 'a unique partnership to meet the growing strategic threats in the Middle East ... This co-operative effort provides significant benefits for both the United States and Israel'.[6] The question is, is it Israel or the United States which reaps the greater benefit from the relationship? Can the closeness of the alliance remain in the longer-term American strategic interests?

In September 2007, rival books on the influence of the Jewish lobby were released in the United States. One was a study by Abraham H. Foxman, the national director of the (Jewish) Anti-Defamation League.[7] The notion that pro-Israel groups 'have anything like a uniform agenda, and that US policy on Israel and the Middle East is the result of their influence, is simply wrong,' writes George P. Shultz, US Secretary of State from 1982 to 1989, in the foreword. 'This is a conspiracy theory pure and simple, and scholars at great universities should be ashamed to promulgate it.'[8] The other – very substantial – book released in the same month was by Professors John J. Mearsheimer and Stephen M. Walt, which emphasized the contrary argument (now known as the Mearsheimer–Walt thesis), namely that while no more than a pressure group like any other in the United States, what characterizes the Jewish lobby is its particular effectiveness. American Jews who lobby on Israel's behalf are not all that different from the National Rifle Association, the anti-tax movement, AARP (formerly the American Association of Retired Persons, the movement for health care and enhancing the quality of life for people over the age of 50), or the American Petroleum Institute, they argue. 'They just happen to be really good at it.'[9]

One of the difficulties with Foxman's defence of the lobby, apart from his frequent recourse to the accusation of anti-Semitism, is that no distinction is made between Judaism and Zionism. Discussing 'the difference between Judaism and Zionism', G. Neuburger states that 'while not all Jews are Zionists, not all Zionists are Jews.'[10] 'A former president of the World Zionist Organization has stated explicitly that a Zionist owes unqualified loyalty to the Zionist state and that, in the case of a conflict, the first loyalty of a Zionist must be to the Zionist state. According to Jewish law, however, a Jew owes allegiance and loyalty to the country of which he is a citizen.'

> One of the basic aims of Zionism is *aliyah*, the immigration to the Zionist state of Jews from all countries. Nevertheless, during the past few years hundreds of thousands of Israelis have outgathered themselves from the Zionist paradise, and American Jews have 'voted with their feet' and have chosen not to be ingathered. These Jews recognize that the Zionist state is in fact nothing but a giant ghetto. Instead of being able to render

> assistance to Jewish communities in other countries, American Jews have been mobilized to concentrate on helping the Zionist state, making the US the real and major source of Zionist power and influence. The Zionists, true to the nature of their movement, rely on technical superiority and on a forbidding military deterrent – provided largely by the US – for their security. Nothing could be farther from the true ideals of the Jewish people. The Jewish people were chosen in the first place 'for you are the least of all nations'. As the Psalm says, 'they rely on vehicles and horsepower, but we invoke the name of the Eternal, our G-d.'

The Annual Survey of American Jewish Opinion has consistently reported significant support of American Jews for the establishment of a Palestinian state (53 per cent in 2001; 54 per cent in 2003; and 46 per cent in 2007) and a majority opposing the extension of the war on terrorism to Iraq (54 per cent in 2003; 66 per cent in 2004; and 67 per cent in 2007). A significant majority of American Jews believe, however, that the West and the Muslim world are engaged in a 'clash of civilizations' (64 per cent in 2006 and 63 per cent in 2007).[11] The power of the Jewish 'lobby' in the United States is all the more impressive when one realizes that it represents perhaps no more than a third of America's 6.1 million Jews. 'The dedication and single-mindedness of that one-third, however,' argues Jeff Blankfort, 'stands in stark contrast to the lack of involvement by the overwhelming majority of Americans in a system for which they long ago lost faith and respect.'[12] 'Though most American Jews favour a negotiated settlement in the Mideast,' Michael Massing argues, the 'two [most] powerful Jewish organizations have worked successfully to thwart one.'[13] Noting that 'the debate in Israel about Israeli policy is much more open and vigorous than [it is] in the United States,' the secular Jewish financier and philanthropist George Soros has added his voice to the critics, arguing that 'attitudes toward Israel are influenced by Israel's policies, and attitudes toward the Jewish community are influenced by the pro-Israel lobby's success in suppressing divergent views.'[14]

Other critics of the policies of the Jewish lobby argue from a different perspective. For Norman G. Finkelstein, the United States does not really want an Israel truly at peace with the Arabs, for such an Israel could loosen its bonds of dependence, making it a less reliable proxy. He argues that[15]

> the claim that Israel has become a liability for US 'national' interests in the Middle East misses the bigger picture. Sometimes what's most obvious escapes the eye. Israel is the only stable and secure base for projecting US power in this region. Every other country the US relies on might, for all anyone knows, fall out of US control tomorrow. The USA discovered this

> to its horror in 1979, after immense investment in the Shah. On the other hand, Israel was a creation of the West; it's in every respect – culturally, politically, economically – in thrall to the West, notably the US. This is true not just at the level of a corrupt leadership, as elsewhere in the Middle East but – what's most important – at the popular level.

## *Divergent Views of the pro-Israel Lobby in the US and its Impact on Domestic Politics*

For the prominent critic of US international policy, Noam Chomsky, the pro-Israel lobby is like any other operating in Washington DC; he disputes whether its backers have any more power than that of other pressure groups, arguing instead that they tend to succeed because Israel's interests (and those of the lobby) coincide with those of the US. Thus, for Chomsky, Israel is a tool of the US 'empire' and used as needed, though US and Israeli interests usually coincide. 'Big Oil' and the 'military-industrial complex' are, in Chomsky's view, the main forces shaping US Middle East policy and the drivers in the Iraq war and the threats to Iran and Syria. Finally, US behaviour in the Middle East is no different to that which is practised worldwide. The attractiveness of the Mearsheimer–Walt thesis concerning the power of the pro-Israeli lobby (their joint article was published in March 2006), Chomsky suggests, is that it 'leaves the US government untouched on its high pinnacle of nobility, "Wilsonian idealism", ... merely in the grip of an all-powerful force that it cannot escape' rather than the author of its own 'crimes' in foreign policy.[16] James Petras, in contrast, contests these 'dubious propositions' and considers it essential to condemn Israel's aggressive policies and the activities of what he calls the 'Zionist power configuration (ZPC)' in the US.[17]

The leaders of the ZPC, so the argument runs, are essentially out of touch with mainstream American Jewish opinion. The Editor of *Forward*, the leading Jewish weekly in the US, wrote on 8 December 2006 concerning the praise lavished on the departing John Bolton, formerly US ambassador to the United Nations, by Jewish organizations:[18]

> It's no great secret why the Jewish agencies continue to trumpet support for the discredited policies of this failed administration. They see defence of Israel as their number-one goal, trumping all other items on the agenda. That single-mindedness binds them ever closer to a White House that has made combating Islamic terrorism its signature campaign. The campaign's effects on the world have been catastrophic. But that is no concern of the Jewish agencies. Given the record, the agencies' paeans to Bolton come as no surprise. And yet, they still offend. Coming barely a month after the

midterm elections, in which Jews voted 7–1 against the Bush record, the statements show a communal representative structure working directly against the wishes and values of the community it purports to represent.

How is it that the representatives of the American Jewish community work against the wishes and values of the community they claim to represent? The principal reason, Michael Massing suggests, is the priority given to funding and the excessive influence given to successful fund-raisers. He delineates two separate, but interacting, power structures: AIPAC and the Presidents' Conference (Conference of Presidents of Major American Jewish Organizations or CoP) which 'is the main contact between the Jewish community and the executive branch' of the US Government. The first, AIPAC, is a finance-raising and lobbying organization directed at influencing the legislative branch of government, the Senate and the House of Representatives. Its board of directors is selected not according to how well they represent AIPAC's members but according to how much money they raise and donate; and within that board a 'gang of four' predominates. Steven Rosen, AIPAC's director of foreign policy issues, was the main power on the staff until he was dismissed (together with Keith Weissman, AIPAC's Iran specialist) in March 2005 after 23 years' service because of an impending prosecution:[19] up to then, he had helped shape the gang of four's pro-Likud beliefs into practical measures that AIPAC could promote in Congress.

AIPAC has 100,000 members and an annual budget of $47 million. It has been estimated that between 1990 and 2004 pro-Israel groups in the US contributed nearly $57 million for elections, as against less than a million from Arab American groups.[20] Notionally, AIPAC does not endorse candidates for election to the House of Representatives or the Senate but, when approached by pro-Israel candidates seeking financial support, it makes introductions to fund-raisers. Conversely, candidates who challenge Israel or AIPAC can find that their funds suddenly dry up. Paul Findley, who suffered a four-year campaign to remove him from Congress between 1979 and 1982 after 22 years' service, considers that AIPAC, while only part of the pro-Israel lobby, 'in terms of direct effect on public policy ... is clearly the most important ... Almost without exception, House and Senate members do its bidding, because most of them consider AIPAC to be the direct Capitol Hill representative of a political force that can make or break their chances at election time.'[21] Recent cases are difficult to document, but it is thought that AIPAC played a considerable part in defeating Illinois Senator Charles Percy in 1984 for an alleged anti-Israel stance in supporting the sale of AWACS to Saudi Arabia, while Adlai Stevenson III saw a 'critical' drop in funds when running as governor of Illinois in 1981 because of his previous record in seeking to cut US aid to Israel in the late 1970s. Even a senator of the seniority and enormous prestige of J. William Fulbright, who had promoted the passage in 1946 of legislation establishing the Fulbright Program of educational grants which now operates in 144 countries, and who was the longest-serving chair (1959–74) in the history of the Senate Foreign Relations Committee, could not withstand the ire of the lobby in 1974: it was claimed that he had been 'consistently unkind to Israel and our supporters in this country'; certainly, he had claimed that 'somewhere around 80 per cent' of the Senate were 'completely in support of Israel, anything Israel wants'. Fulbright failed to secure the Democratic nomination as the 'junior' senator of Arkansas in that year, losing the primary to Dale Bumpers who had received considerable financial support from the pro-Israel lobby.[22]

Paul Findley was a Republican representative from Illinois between 1961 until 1982, when he lost his seat to Dick Durbin. Three years later, he produced a best-seller entitled *They Dare to Speak Out: People and Institutions Confront Israel's Lobby*, in which he blamed the pro-Israel lobby for contributing to his defeat: 'in seeking gains for Israel, they rigorously stifled dissent and intimidated the entire Congress,' he argues, calling the lobby 'the 700-pound gorilla in Washington'. Unlike some of the others who suffered electoral defeat because of strong Israel lobby support for another candidate, Findley did not go without a fight. He founded the Council for the National Interest (CNI), which is run by himself and James Abourezk, a Democrat, and which even bills itself as 'the anti-AIPAC':[23]

> CNI seeks to encourage and promote a US foreign policy in the Middle East that is consistent with American values, protects our national interests, and contributes to a just solution of the Arab–Israeli conflict, as well as to restore a political environment in America in which voters and their elected officials are free from the undue influence and pressure of a foreign country, namely Israel.

More than this, included among its aims is the far-sighted and lofty ambition, to create

> a political atmosphere in which (1) a fair and objective media covers the Middle East without fear of retaliation by advertisers and pro-Israeli groups; (2) the American electorate is unafraid to debate the issues openly and frankly; and (3) our elected officials vote [according to] their conscience.

More recently, the defeat of Democratic Representative Cynthia McKinney in the Georgia primary in 2002 was secured in part by AIPAC providing funds to her opponent. She returned to Congress in 2004, but her defeat in the 2006 primary was a foregone conclusion after she introduced articles of impeachment against President Bush for manipulating intelligence and lying to justify the war in Iraq, failing to uphold accountability, and violating privacy laws with his domestic spying programme. McKinney is a particularly controversial character, but such pressure on political opponents is exerted regularly by AIPAC, which assesses voting records and public statements of candidates and provides the information to pro-Israel political action committees (PACs) which donate money to candidates. Michael Massing notes that 'the Centre for Responsive Politics, a non-partisan group that analyzes political contributions, lists a total of thirty-six pro-Israel PACs, which together contributed \$3.14 million to candidates in the 2004 election cycle,' while pro-Israel donors gave 'many millions more'. In pure fund-raising terms, it is estimated that approximately 60 per cent of Democratic party funding and 35 per cent of Republican party funding comes from pro-Israel Jewish sources.[24]

Though there is a perceptible shift in Jewish opinion, especially among younger American Jews, towards the political right,[25] centrist Republicans seeking election in 2008 were likely to be subject to what has been termed the 'Chafee effect'. Senator Lincoln Chafee of Rhode Island was a popular moderate Republican in a Democratic state, holding a 67 per cent approval rating. As the only Republican senator not to vote in 2002 in favour of authorizing the use of force in Iraq, he should have been secure against the Democratic campaign in 2006, which mainly exploited the growing unpopularity of the war in Iraq; but 'the stakes of party competition had been raised so high by the Bush approach that Democratic voters turned Chafee out of office in order to win a national party battle for Senate control.' It can scarcely have helped that Chafee was reported to have been targeted by AIPAC because of his liberal record.[26]

Contrast the position of Senator Joseph Lieberman, an Orthodox Jew who was formerly vice-presidential running mate of Al Gore in 2000, one of the Senate's most consistent supporters of Israel, and an advocate of the Iraq War. Lieberman describes himself as 'genuinely an Independent', claiming to 'agree more often than not with Democrats on domestic policy' but 'more often than not with Republicans on foreign and defence policy'. As a result of his maverick political position, Lieberman lost the Democratic primary in 2006 but stood as an 'independent Democrat' and won the Senate election, gaining considerable Republican support. The key point was that, far from losing AIPAC and other Jewish-based financial assistance, Lieberman's campaign coffers were swollen by an increase in funds following his loss of the Democratic primary. He was expected to gain $2 million, 'about one-tenth of his total projected war chest', from Jewish sources: in other words, Jewish funding follows the candidate with an unwavering track record on the issue that really counts[27] – 'Israel first' or 'Israel right or wrong'.

Publicly, 'and even more so behind the scenes', the Presidents' Conference (CoP) 'takes the lead in promoting the interests of the American-Jewish community and fostering the understanding that a safe and secure Israel will continue to be America's vital strategic ally and partner'. Representing fifty-two national Jewish organizations, the Conference claims to provide 'a common voice for affiliated American Jews from across the political and religious spectrum, forging diverse groups into a unified force for Israel's well-being, and for protecting and enhancing the security and dignity of Jews at home and abroad'.[28] According to Michael Massing, 'the organization is run largely by one man,' Malcolm Hoenlein, who was actively involved in the Jewish settlers' movement in the 1990s and has tilted CoP 'decisively to the right on critical issues involving Israel in recent years'.[29] Hoenlein was elected Executive Vice-Chairman of CoP in June 1986. 'What no-one disputes', noted Tom Carver in a BBC Newsnight interview in May 2003, 'is that, after 16 years operating behind the scenes, he has unrivalled access to the political establishment.' Hoenlein told Carver that a Palestinian right of return was 'impossible' and would amount to 'a death knell for any negotiations' with Israel.[30] For Hoenlein, 'Israel is the corporate entity that represents the Jewish people.' Those who recognize it is not acceptable to be blatantly anti-Jewish, he contends, 'have adopted the camouflage of being anti-Israel'. 'The incitement and hatred that is pouring out of Muslim media, mosques, political leaders and educational institutions, is blatantly anti-Semitic. The thin veil between anti-Zionism, anti-Israelism and anti-Semitism is quickly pierced under careful examination.'[31]

A feeling for his views can be gleaned from a number of statements made and interviews given by Hoenlein in the years 2005–7. First, commenting on the FBI investigation of the alleged secrets passed by AIPAC employees to Israel, he stated that 'the implicit references to "dual loyalty" cannot be overlooked, especially when reliable studies show that a significant percentage of Americans still believe this baseless and bigoted idea. American Jews care about Israel and advocate proudly in support of the special US–Israel relationship. So do many other Americans with historical or ethnic ties to other homelands overseas.' Secondly, he is prepared to accept that the effectiveness of pro-Israel Jewish advocacy 'has raised resentment, jealousy and wild mythologies'. There is no doubt, however, that 'the American people identify with Israel based on common values and world views …'[32] Thirdly, he contends 'the American people are essentially supportive of Israel,' but 'they like all others need to have the facts', which others call disinformation.[33] 'This is our front on Israel's battle for survival, to win the hearts and minds of the American people by our initiatives.' Fourthly, when questioned about the financial lobbying for pro-Israel candidates, Hoenlein has a clear retort: 'it is an insult to the integrity and intelligence of the American people to believe that they are somehow manipulated *en masse*.' 'The American democratic system makes one demand of us, and that is involvement. American Jews care and are involved. Their activities, like that of many other American groups, are completely consistent with our democratic system which enables citizens – even minorities – to have a say.'[34] Finally, he accuses the 'intellectual elites' of American society as having become prey to a 'cancer' which seeks to delegitimize Israel in the United States, as (in his view) has also happened in Britain. 'If you disagree with … false charges, they say you are a Zionist or lobbyist trying to squash criticism,' he claims. Hoenlein states that he is open to working with the largely supportive Evangelical Christians in the US, who have emerged as a major source of pro-Israel sentiment across the world, 'so long as there are no "ulterior motives" in the relationship'.[35]

### *Pro-Israel Think Tanks and the Lobby's Influence on the George W. Bush Administration*

The pro-Israel lobby does not maintain its position solely by direct action but also indirectly, through the influence of 'think tanks'. Since its founding in 1985, the Washington Institute, specializing in Arab–Israel relations, 'has served as a training ground for future policymakers in both Democratic and Republican administrations'.[36] Its founding director for the first eight years was Martin S. Indyk, who had previously served for three years as AIPAC's research director. He became special assistant to President Bill Clinton and senior director of Near East and South Asian Affairs at the United States National Security Council. While at the NSC, he served as principal adviser to the President and the National Security Adviser on Arab–Israeli issues, Iraq, Iran, and South Asia. He served twice as US ambassador to Israel, in 1995–7 and 2000–June 2001, and is currently a Senior Fellow and Director of the Saban Center for Middle East Policy in the Foreign Policy Studies program at the Brookings Institution.

Haim Saban exemplifies the multiple tentacles of the Jewish lobby in the United States. An Egyptian-born Israeli-American billionaire and media owner, in 2002 Saban gave the Democratic Party $12.3 million, $7.5 in one instalment. A good friend of former Israeli prime minister Ehud Barak and also of President Bill Clinton, Saban has also made large contributions to AIPAC. He also turned a formerly independent think tank into another component of the lobby[37] when, in 2002, he pledged $13 million to start a research organization at the Brookings Institution called the Saban Center for Middle East Policy.[38] ('I've heard from leaders on both sides of the aisle in the United States and leaders in Europe about what Sharon shouldn't do', he said. 'I've haven't heard one educated suggestion about what he should do.') 'I'm a one-issue guy and my issue is Israel', he told the *New York Times* in 2004.[39] On 4 April 2007, the *Jerusalem Post* reported that at a New York fund-raising dinner attended by some 1,300 individuals, Saban pledged $3.2 million towards a total of $18 million raised for improving the Israeli Defence Force's protection against Iran. The data compiled by campaignmoney.com for political donations by individuals from 1999 to the present, accessed on 6 June 2007, shows that Haim Saban was by nearly $3 million the largest individual donor: Saban had made 118 donations totalling nearly $12.9 million by that date. In contrast, George Soros was rated only fifteenth, with 99 donations totalling nearly $3 million.[40]

A second important think tank is the Jewish Institute for National Security Affairs (JINSA), a rightist Washington-based advocacy and research institution which argues that 'US–Israel strategic cooperation is a vital component in the global security equation for the United States, and has been at the heart of JINSA's mission since its inception in 1976.' The relationship is assumed to be based on shared values, technological compatibility, and the unreliability of alternative allies: 'the Middle East remains the focal point of American security policy because of the confluence of energy, money, weapons and ideology. The inherent instability in the region caused primarily by inter-Arab rivalries and the secular/religious split in many Muslim societies leaves the future of the region in doubt. Israel, with its technological capabilities and shared system of values, has a key role to play as a US ally in the region.'[41] Michael Leeden became JINSA's first executive director in 1977 and was succeeded the following year by Stephen Bryen. Later, in 1981, Bryen became deputy assistant secretary of defence (during Richard N. Perle's period as assistant secretary of defence under President Reagan). Bryen's was a controversial appointment, contends Mark H. Milstein, since he had a key 'role in choosing not only what US weaponry Israel would be allowed to purchase' with American funds, 'but also what sensitive US military technology would be made available to Israel for use in its own burgeoning arms industry'.[42]

Already well placed before 9/11, JINSA's response to these events, in a press release issued on 13 September 2001, was predictably hardline. Among its recommended list of actions to be taken by the US government were to give 'support to the Iraq National Congress, including direct American military support, to effect a regime change in Iraq'; to 'revoke the Presidential Order banning assassinations'; to 'overturn the 1995 CIA Directive limiting whom the United States can recruit to aid counter-terrorism in an effort to boost our human intelligence'; to 'demand that Egypt and Saudi Arabia sever all remaining ties with Osama bin Laden, including ties with Saudi-sponsored non-governmental organizations and groups abroad that raise money for bin Laden and other terrorist organizations'; to 're-evaluate America's security relationship with Saudi Arabia and the Gulf States unless both actually join in our war against terrorism'; and to 'take immediate steps to reduce America's dependence on foreign oil'. Osama bin Laden, Hizbu'llah, Hamas, and Islamic Jihad were declared 'only the most prominent' of the terrorist organizations. The countries harbouring and training them included not just Afghanistan – 'an easy target for blame' – 'but Iraq, Iran, Pakistan, Syria, Sudan, the Palestinian Authority, Libya, Algeria and even our presumed friends Saudi Arabia and Egypt'. The policy advocated was not quite official Israeli policy but included measures obviously favourable to Israeli interests: 'interdict the supply lines to terrorist organizations, including but not limited to those between Damascus and Beirut that permit Iran to use Lebanon as a terrorist base.'[43]

The critical point for JINSA was to ensure that America's war on terrorism was equated at all times with Israel's struggle against the Palestinians as 'the same war'. A 'report' (in effect, a press release) issued on 6 March 2003 made the point explicitly: 'Arafat had the same opportunity to make a choice that the Taliban had about support for terrorism and that Saddam had about disarming. He made the wrong choice as they did, and the consequence should be meted out to him by Israel as it is to the others by the United States. And the President should support Israel's war. It is the same war.'[44] JINSA's executive director, Thomas Neumann, delivered an address to the US–India Political Action Committee International Conference on Terrorism in India, held at Washington DC on 17 July 2003 in which the same claim was extended to India's conflict with 'terrorists' (viz. Kashmiri separatists et al.):[45]

> The countries that are number one on the terrorist hit list are Israel, India and the United States. That unfortunate commonality is what brings us together today. All three countries are democracies. All three are robust and resilient and all three are open societies. It would therefore be a wise decision for these three countries to cooperate in their struggle against terrorism. That is why JINSA, the Jewish Institute for National Security Affairs, has been fostering trilateral cooperation between these countries.

JINSA and the Center for Security Policy (CSP), with which it overlaps, are both underwritten to a large extent by Irving Moskowitz, a California-based entrepreneur known as the 'bingo king', who is committed to opposing the Israel–Palestinian peace process and has close ties to American groups sympathetic to Israel's right wing.[46] Another opponent of the peace process is Meyrav Wurmser, co-founder of the Middle East Media Research Institute (MEMRI) in February 1998 with Colonel Yigal Carmon, who for 22 years acted as an Israeli military intelligence and later counter-terrorism adviser to Israeli prime ministers Yitzhak Shamir and Yitzhak Rabin. MEMRI claims to be an independent, non-partisan and non-profit organization – and as such is tax exempt in the US – but it clearly does have a political agenda. One view of this agenda was expressed by Ibrahim Hooper of the Council on American–Islamic Relations (CAIR), who told the *Washington Times* that it was to 'find the worst possible quotes from the Muslim world and disseminate them as widely as possible'.[47] 'We must remember that everything we say is translated selectively' by MEMRI, a Saudi academic reminded Arab organizations – including the World Muslim League, the Arab League, Islamic universities, and charity funds – in December 2007. The translations of this Israeli intelligence body, which calls itself an American civil institute, serve as a source of information for congressmen, the US government, universities, and the media, the commentator observed.[48] Professor Juan Cole, a critic of MEMRI, claims that 'on more than one occasion I have seen, say, a bigoted Arabic article translated by MEMRI and when I went to the source on the Web, found that it was on the same op-ed page with other, moderate, articles arguing for tolerance. These latter were not translated.'[49] What is clear is that MEMRI favours the voice of 'secular' Muslims in the Middle East and has significant funding behind its media watch and 'reform' projects. The presence of several former Israeli intelligence officers among its personnel suggests that it forms part of Israel's public diplomacy.[50]

Meyrav Wurmser left her position as executive director of MEMRI in early 2002 to direct the Center of Middle East Policy at the Hudson Institute. Her husband David was special assistant to John Bolton at the State Department from the beginning of the George W. Bush presidency and then moved in early September 2003 to the office of Vice-President Cheney and 'Scooter' Libby, where he served as Middle East policy adviser until July 2007. David Wursmer is strongly committed to the state of Israel and is an advocate of regime change in Iraq as well of military intervention against Iran. In 1999, the American Enterprise Institute published his study *Tyranny's Ally: America's Failure to Defeat Saddam Hussein*, which lamented the failure to overthrow Saddam in 1991. He advocated support for Ahmed Chalabi and the Iraq National Congress with the aim of achieving a conservative restoration.[51] Wurmser and Michael Maloof were part of a 'Pentagon intelligence unit' appointed by Douglas Feith after 9/11 that helped produce a top-secret memorandum lamenting the lack of military targets in Afghanistan and suggesting looking elsewhere in the world, including in Iraq and Latin America, to bolster the terror target list. According to the 9/11 Commission Report, the memo pushed for 'hitting targets outside the Middle East in the initial offensive' or a 'non-al-Qaeda target like Iraq'.[52]

Significant American Jewish involvement in such think tanks as JINSA, the Washington Institute, the Saban Centre, and others (including the American Enterprise Institute), combined with the high level of political activism in the American Jewish community, has led to a distinctive feature of American political life: the disproportionate influence – disproportionate in the sense that the Jewish population is only about 2 per cent of the American population as a whole – of American Jews and advocates of the Israeli cause within the executive, particularly in the administration of George W. Bush. This is ironic, since the November 2000 exit polls indicated that approximately 79 per cent of Jews voted for the Democratic candidate, Vice-President Al Gore.[53] The ranks of the Bush Jnr administration 'have included such fervent advocates of the Israeli cause as Elliot Abrams, John Bolton, Douglas Feith, I. Lewis ('Scooter') Libby, Richard Perle, Paul Wolfowitz and David Wurmser'. Mearsheimer and Walt add that after 9/11:[54]

> within the Pentagon, the Policy Counterterrorism Evaluation Group was charged with finding links between al-Qaeda and Iraq that the intelligence community had supposedly missed. Its two key members were David Wurmser, a hard-core neo-conservative, and Michael Maloof, a Lebanese-American with close ties to Perle. Another Pentagon group, the so-called Office of Special Plans, was given the task of uncovering evidence that could be used to sell the war. It was headed by Abram Shulsky, a neo-conservative with long-standing ties to Wolfowitz, and its ranks included recruits from pro-Israel think tanks. Both these organisations were created after 9/11 and reported directly to Douglas Feith.

No figure in the George W. Bush administration has proved more controversial than Douglas Feith, who stands accused of doctoring the intelligence reports so as to strengthen the case for war against Iraq. In the early 1980s, Feith was a Middle East specialist at the National Security Council. He later transferred to the Department of Defense, where he spent two years as staff lawyer for Assistant Defense Secretary Perle. In 1984 Feith became Deputy Assistant Secretary of Defense for negotiations policy. Later in the decade, Feith and Perle emerged as leading advocates of a policy to build closer US military and diplomatic ties with Turkey and between Turkey and Israel. In a speech in October 1991, Feith argued that it was foolish for the US government and Israel to negotiate with the Palestinians over issues of land, given that contrasting principles – not differences over occupied lands – fuelled the Israeli–Arab conflict. In 1999, he wrote an essay for the book *The Dangers of a Palestinian State*, which was published by the Zionist Organization of America.[55] In 2000, Feith co-founded One Jerusalem, a private American–Israeli group, with the objective of 'saving a united Jerusalem as the undivided capital of Israel'. It actively courts the involvement of the so-called Christian Zionists.

As Under-Secretary of Defense in the Bush administration, Feith oversaw efforts to provide the type of 'strategic intelligence' needed to drive the neo-conservative policy agenda. Although he was not formally charged in connection with his work at the Pentagon, Feith's work has been repeatedly accused of bias. One investigation, by the Department of Defense's inspector general (IG), was set up to assess whether the Office of Special Plans (OSP), the specialized body set up by Feith within the Pentagon to scrutinize intelligence on Iraq (see Chapter 8), deliberately slanted information about the regime of Saddam Hussein.[56] The IG's unclassified report, released in April 2007, corroborated allegations that Feith was behind efforts erroneously to connect Saddam Hussein's Iraqi regime with al-Qaeda. The report found that despite widespread consensus among intelligence agencies, including the CIA and the Defense Intelligence Agency (DIA), there was no conclusive evidence to link the two. Feith ignored these conclusions in a September 2002 briefing delivered to Vice-President Dick Cheney and other administration officials. The report also noted that post-war debriefings of Saddam Hussein, the former Iraqi Foreign Minister Tariq Aziz, the former Iraqi Intelligence Minister Mani al-Rashid al Tikriti, and senior al-Qaeda operative Ibn al-Shaykh al-Libi, as well as document exploitation by the DIA, all confirmed that the judgement of the intelligence community was correct: Iraq and al-Qaeda did not co-operate in the key areas, including training, financing and logistics, alleged by Feith's office.[57]

Feith became embroiled in a different sort of intelligence scandal in late August 2004, when it was reported that the FBI had for the past two years been investigating intelligence leaks to Israel from the Pentagon. The Pentagon official named in the media reports was Lawrence Franklin, who was brought into the OSP from the Defense Intelligence Agency. Franklin was suspected of passing classified information about Iran to AIPAC and to Israel. His prosecution was successful and he was sentenced to 12 years and seven months' imprisonment; but the Israeli government and AIPAC denied that they had been engaged in any criminal operations involving classified Pentagon documents about Iran. Natan Sharansky, an Israeli cabinet minister (minister for Jerusalem and diaspora affairs) and One Jerusalem co-founder with Feith and its current chairman, denied there had been an attempt to involve any member of the Jewish community or any American citizens to spy for Israel against the United States. The former AIPAC employees, Steven J. Rosen and Keith Weissman, were charged with passing information that 'could be used to the injury of the United States or to the advantage of any foreign nation'.

## *Reassessing the Concept of 'Shared Values' between Israel and the US*

Grant F. Smith is one commentator, among others, who argues that 'there is ample evidence to prove beyond a reasonable doubt that the documented subterfuges of the Israel Lobby as personified by Weissman and Rosen not only endanger America, but have eroded the principles of liberty and justice upon which the US was founded.' Smith contends that 'the illicit overt and covert activities of an unregistered foreign agent committed to misleading Americans through the myth that Israeli and US interests are "exactly the same" can only be revealed and terminated through a high-profile criminal trial.'[58] (In contrast, the *Washington Post* considers the trial a 'dangerous prosecution',[59] while the Jewish lobby raises the spectre of anti-Semitism, threats to the First Amendment and free speech, and the risk of 'countless others facing trials in the future, for newly invented crimes unearthed by willing prosecutors'.)[60]

Ultimately, the conflict revolves around the concept of 'shared values' between Israel and the United States, which is continually pushed by the American Jewish lobby, and somehow is perceived to override all other considerations. The concept needs to be challenged. It is true that both states are democracies, and that Israel is the only currently functioning democracy in the Middle East. But they are very different types of state in their nature. Whether or not we accept Oren Yiftachel's characterization of Israel as an 'ethnocracy' (the Zionist project of Judaizing Israel/Palestine),[61] or Israel's self-definition from two Knesset basic laws of the 1990s as 'Jewish and democratic', it is clearly not a religiously pluralist state with a division between the state institutions and religion as occurs in the United States. It is *the* Jewish state, which through its main immigration law (the Law of Return) lays a claim to the residual loyalty of Jewish citizens of all other states: 'I see the Jewish world as one', argues Natan Sharansky, Israeli minister for Jerusalem and the diaspora; 'those who are living [in], and those who are not yet living in, Israel. It is part of the same body of people who left Egypt 3,000 years ago, and they are on their way to the land of Israel.'[62] It is realistic to perceive the United States as a secure state with a settled relationship with its neighbours, apart from what will prove to be the aberration of the years after 9/11. It is impossible to see Israel in this way because of the state of war with the Palestinians and other neighbouring states, such as Syria. Israel's attack on Syria on 6 September 2007, for example, remained secret until it was revealed by the opposition leader, Benjamin Netanyahu, on 20 September.[63]

For James Petras, the Zionist power configuration (ZPC) 'represents a basic threat' to the existence of the US 'as a sovereign state and our ability to influence whom we elect and what agendas and interests our representatives will pursue'. He continues:[64]

> no other country, abuser or not, of human rights, with or without electoral systems, has the influence over our domestic and foreign policy as does the state of Israel. No other Lobby has the kind of financial power and organizational reach as the Jewish Lobby in eroding our domestic political freedoms or our war-making powers. For those reasons alone, it stands to reason, that we Americans have a necessity to put our fight against Israel and its Lobby at the very top of our political agenda …

Three comments from Mearsheimer and Walt, the authors of the controversial publication 'The Israel Lobby and US Foreign Policy' (March 2006), in reply to their critics, are particularly worthy of quotation. 'Regrettably', they comment, 'some of our critics have tried to smear us by linking us with overt racists, thereby suggesting that we are racists or anti-semites ourselves. Michael Taylor, for example, notes that our article has been "hailed" by Ku Klux Klan leader David Duke (6 April). Alan Dershowitz implies that some of our material was taken from neo-Nazi websites and other hate literature (20 April). We have no control over who likes or dislikes our article, but we regret that Duke used it to promote his racist agenda, which we utterly reject. Furthermore, nothing in our piece is drawn from racist sources of any kind, and Dershowitz offers no evidence to support this false claim.'[65] Secondly, they note that 'the United States is in deep trouble in the Middle East, and it will not be able to develop effective policies if it is impossible to have a civilized discussion about the role of Israel in American foreign policy.' Finally, they conclude: 'the fact is that if there were no AIPAC, Americans would have a more critical view of Israel and US policy in the Middle East would look different.'[66]

In their much fuller account of the Israel lobby and US foreign policy, published in September 2007, Mearsheimer and Walt note that the two US presidents who have made the greatest contribution to Middle East peace – Jimmy Carter and George HW Bush – were able to do so 'precisely because each was willing on occasion to chart a separate course' from the Israel lobby.[67] They also paid a heavy electoral price for their chosen course, neither achieving re-election: Jimmy Carter received only 45 per cent of the Jewish vote in 1980 (whereas Kennedy had received 82 per cent twenty years earlier). Bill Clinton received 80 per cent of the Jewish vote in 1992, while GH. W. Bush received only 11 per cent (down 16 percentage points from 1988), with the third candidate, Ross Perot, receiving 9 per cent.[68] Also G. H. W. Bush increased support among Jewish voters from only 19 per cent of the Jewish vote in 2000 to 22 per cent in 2004.[69] The Republican party's attempt to attract the Jewish vote therefore seems to have stalled, and – in the words of the National Jewish Democratic Council – 'the Jewish vote has remained one of the most solidly Democratic demographics in America'.

Mearsheimer and Walt conclude that a 'new relationship' must be developed between the US and Israel, which must be treated henceforth 'as a normal state'. Treating Israel as a normal state, they continue[70]

> means no longer pretending that Israel's and America's interests are identical, or acting as if Israel deserves steadfast US support no matter what it does. When Israel acts in ways that the United States deems desirable, it should have American backing. When it does not, Israel should expect to face US opposition, just as other states do. It also implies that the United States should gradually wean Israel from the economic and military aid that it currently provides. Israel is now an advanced economy, and it will become even more so once it achieves full peace with its neighbours and reaches a final settlement with the Palestinians … there is little reason to continue the handouts that American taxpayers have provided since the early 1970s, especially when there are many countries that have greater needs. Ultimately, US aid is indirectly subsidizing activities that are not in its national interest …

Jonathan Cook proposes that 'the [US] dog and [the Israeli] tail wag each other', an ingenious middle way between the Chomsky and Mearsheimer–Walt positions with regard to the power of the American Jewish Lobby in the US. This via media suggests that the Israeli military establishment developed ambitions for the expansion of Israel in the Middle East in the 1980s and then sought a sponsor in the US, eventually finding this in the neo-conservative lobby (see chapter 7). Cook argues: 'the Israeli security establishment argued that Israel's own regional dominance and US control of oil could be assured in the same way', that is, by provoking 'a catastrophe in the Middle East in the form of a social breakdown, a series of civil wars' and the partition of rival states such as Iraq, Syria, and Lebanon and, above all, Iran. Israeli Prime Minister Ehud Olmert told a joint session of Congress in May 2006: 'it's not Israel's threat alone.' When addressing the United Jewish Communities General Assembly on 13 November 2006, Benjamin Netanyahu, the Likud leader, drew a direct comparison between Iran and Nazi Germany: 'it's 1938 and Iran is Germany', he said. 'And Iran is racing to arm itself with atomic bombs.' 'Believe him and stop him', he said of the Iranian president. 'He is preparing another Holocaust for the Jewish state.'[71] At the AIPAC conference on 11 March 2007, Pastor John Hagee of Christians United for Israel (see chapter 6) echoed Netanyahu's words to rapturous applause. The following day, Netanyahu himself denied that it was alarmist to make comparison with 1938.[72] In his press conference of 17 October 2007, George W. Bush repeated these views when he called a nuclear Iran 'a dangerous threat to world peace' which might bring about World War III. 'We['ve] got a leader in Iran who has announced that he wants to destroy Israel.'[73]

The difficulty about these remarks was that President Ahmadinejad did not threaten in 2005, as was suggested, 'another Holocaust for the Jewish state' or to 'wipe Israel off the map'. MEMRI's gloss was that 'he emphasized the need to eliminate Israel – which, he claimed, was a goal that was attainable.' In fact, Ahmadinejad restated a remark of the late Ayatollah Khomeini about the desirability of regime change in Israel.[74] The mistranslation was wilfully repeated by Olmert, Netanyahu, and others. While Israel may have been in the driving seat against Iran, the Bush administration and Congress were clearly more than willing to be driven forward. A resolution passed by the House of Representatives on 20 June 2007 requires the UN Security Council to charge President Ahmadinejad with violating the 1948 Convention on Genocide and the UN Charter because of his alleged calls for the destruction of Israel. MEMRI and the Israeli disinformation campaign achieved a notable success. As one commentator put it, 'call it MEMRI loss, the deliberate mangling of [the] media. MEMRI did this to Iranian President Mahmoud Ahmadinejad by turning a speech he delivered in 2005 into a racist and genocidal screed … He did not say Israel must be wiped off the map. But this engineered lie is repeated so constantly by the corporate media and to such a degree it is now accepted as fact'.[75] In the campaign against Iran, AIPAC was not a passive bystander. On the contrary, its role in support of Israeli policy was clarified by Netanyahu in his speech on 12 March 2007. In so doing, he stressed the effectiveness of the AIPAC and American Jewish Lobby: 'you have to win in the battlefield of public opinion', he said. 'Please carry th[e] message to your State Governors, to your Senators, to your Assemblymen, to your Representatives. Carry it yourselves personally to the State Treasurer; get this di[sin]vestment [campaign] off the ground.'

# Chapter Six
# 'Rapture', the Theo-cons, and the Christian Right in US Politics

> After 9/11, after the battles along the Euphrates and as the Jews get their full biblical lands, the Second Coming is closer every day … The hand of God is guiding American foreign policy and I rejoice in that. The turmoil in the Middle East is growing greater and I rejoice in that. The greater the turmoil, the closer the Rapture.
>
> (Bill Collins, worshipper at Kelview Baptist Church, Midland, Texas, interviewed July 2004)[1]

> George [W. Bush] is not a fanatic. He and Laura read the Bible every day and pray together in bed. That's what he tells me. He is true to his God. He tells me that, too. But that doesn't mean he asks God before deciding every bit of foreign policy. That would be stupid. And I know he's not stupid… We are proud to have a Christian President …
>
> (Sue Brannan, Republican Party Chairman in Midland, Texas, interviewed July 2004)[2]

> I think Southern Baptists overwhelmingly supported the president's action in Afghanistan and in Iraq, as they did the first President Bush's action in overturning the invasion of Kuwait. I think that if you look at polls that were done, it was clear that white evangelicals, by significant numbers, significant percentages, supported the war. Mainline Protestants actually were more supportive of the war than their leadership was, but not as supportive as the evangelical rank and file. The same thing was true with Catholic leaders. Rank-and-file Catholics tended to be more supportive of the war than the US Catholic Conference, but not as supportive as rank-and-file evangelicals. It was much higher among rank-and-file white evangelicals.
>
> (Richard Land, President of the Ethics and Religious Liberty Commission of the Southern Baptist Convention and friend and adviser to President Bush)[3]

The word 'rapture' comes from the Latin *rapere,* which means to take away or to snatch out. It is a fervent belief of many American Protestant evangelicals that they will be physically transported at the moment of the Second Coming of Christ predicted in Mark 13:26–7 ('And then shall they see the Son of man coming in the clouds with great power and glory. And then shall he send his angels, and shall gather together his elect from the four winds, from the uttermost part of the earth to the uttermost part of heaven'), 1 Thess. 4: 16–18, and 1 Corinthians 15: 51–3. At the Resthaven cemetery, on the northern edge of Midland, Texas, where George W. Bush grew up, Kylie Harris gave reporter Peter Stothard a vivid impression in July 2004 of what 'rapture' might be like in practice: 'suppose the President and his wife were to come here this afternoon and the Rapture happens. There'd be bodyguards and press people and stuff. Most of them would be left behind, especially the press people. But where the Bushes had been there'd just be piles of clothes on the ground and that pin he wears. They'd be gone – into the air. That's what we believe.'[4]

Tim LaHaye and Jerry Jenkins describe in their novel *In the Twinkling of an Eye: The Rapture* scenes much like this imagining of the physical transport of George W. and Laura Bush. 'All over the plane, people have disappeared … Their shoes, their socks, their clothes – everything was left behind. These people are gone!' A dozen children were taken. 'CNN showed via satellite the footage of a groom disappearing while slipping the ring onto his bride's finger …'[5] This particular novel is one of the sixteen titles in the Left Behind Series, a remarkable publishing feat that has achieved sales in excess of 65 million, almost exclusively in the United States.[6] The series has its critics. The Lutheran Church's Missouri Synod noted in April 2004 that 'the ideas expressed in the *Left Behind* series are in many ways contrary to the teaching of Holy Scripture. Though containing a fictional story line, the books promote a theology that is, in important respects, at odds with the biblical revelation.'[7] A less theological but more robust riposte to *Glorious Appearing,* the fifteenth of the Left Behind Series, was by Nicholas D. Kristof in the *New York Times,* also in 2004, who thought it 'disconcerting to find ethnic cleansing celebrated as the height of piety'. 'We have quite properly linked the fundamentalist religious tracts of Islam with the intolerance they nurture, and it's time to remove the motes from our own eyes.' 'People have the right to believe in a racist God, or a God who throws millions of non-evangelicals into hell', Kristof continued. 'I don't think we should ban books that say that. But we should be embarrassed when our best-selling books gleefully celebrate religious intolerance and violence against infidels. That's not what America stands for, and I doubt that it's what God stands for.'[8]

Tim LaHaye also brings his distinctive beliefs to the world of current affairs. In *Global Warning*, written with Ed Hindson, he asks the question 'whether we are on the brink of World War III?' Samuel Huntington Mark I is quoted on the threat from Islam; so too is Grant Jeffrey, who considers the 'strategic goal of Islamic terrorists' as nothing less than 'the annihilation of Judeo-Christian Western civilization'. The authors assert that 'Islamic extremism that fuels global terrorism is rooted directly in the Qur'an itself.' 'Today Iraq stands on the verge of collapse. Iran is making nuclear threats. Muslim extremists among al-Qaeda, Hamas and Hizbu'llah are running rampant on campaigns of murder, mayhem and mass destruction – all in the name of God.' In the manner of some commentators in Israel, the remarks of George W. Bush about World War III are regarded as warnings of the coming of the great battle between Gog and Magog, or the destruction of the Russo-Islamic invaders in the last *jihad*, according to LaHaye and Hindson – predicted by the prophet Ezekiel in chapters 38 and 39 of his book in the Old Testament. When President Bush remarked that a nuclear Iran would mean World War III, Israeli newscasts on channels 2 and 10 featured Gog and Magog maps of the likely alignment of nations in that potential conflict: on one side were Israel, the United States, Britain, France, and Germany; on the other were Iran, Russia, China, Syria and North Korea. LaHaye and Hindson have graphics of the end-time wars and remain confident that the invaders will be destroyed by God, which will result also in the conversion of Israel.[9] Christians need not fear, however, because 'the rapture changes everything': 'the rapture will be sudden, but not secret ...[10] This will be the most publicized event in all human history. The global media will face the challenge of covering what to many will appear to be a great tragedy. Families, friends and co-workers will be separated from each other without warning, for there are no prophetic "signs" that precede the rapture. It is an imminent event that could happen at any moment.'[11]

This belief in a 'rapture' which takes the 'elect' Christians prior to God's judgement on earth was first developed systematically by John Nelson Darby (1800–82), an Anglo-Irish evangelist, an influential figure among the original Plymouth Brethren, the founder of the Darbyites and the father of modern pre-millennial dispensationalist theology. Darby formed the view c.1826–8 that there would be a pre-Tribulation rapture of Christians, followed by a seven-year Tribulation for the others, followed by the millennium. There would be an important Jewish remnant (though they would have to undergo the Tribulation), as well as a Gentile remnant (who presumably would turn to Christ during the Tribulation). Darby stated categorically of the Christians: 'we have no need of judgement to participate in blessing under Him; we go out of the midst of all events to meet him above …'[12] 'This rapture before the appearing of Christ is a matter of express revelation,' Darby affirmed, 'as we have seen from Colossians 3:4.'[13] The Pauline text reads: 'when Christ who is your life is revealed, then you also will be revealed with him in glory.'

This event – the expected rapture – is closely associated in the modern American evangelical mind with the continued existence of the state of Israel. Alluding to Genesis 12:3, Richard Land, President of the Ethics and Religious Liberty Commission of the Southern Baptist Convention, argues that evangelicals support Israel because they believe 'God blesses those that bless the Jews and curses those who curse the Jews. Consequently, we believe America needs to bless the Jews and Israel, because if we bless the Jews and support Israel, God blesses us. And if we don't, God curses us.'[14] Most recently, on 19 July 2006, the Rev. John C. Hagee, pastor of the 18,000-member Cornerstone Church in San Antonio, Texas, and the author of *Jerusalem Countdown*, a book about a nuclear-armed Iran, inaugurated his movement Christians United for Israel (CUFI) at the Washington Hilton in front of 3,400 delegates from across the US. Hagee read greetings from President George W. Bush and Israeli Prime Minister Ehud Olmert. Bush commented: 'God bless and stand by the people of Israel and God bless the United States.'[15]

Hagee followed up this event with a virtuoso performance at the American Israel Public Affairs Committee (AIPAC) conference in March 2007. Rabbi Jonathan Biatch of Temple Beth El in Madison, Wisconsin, was among a handful of Reform Jewish rabbis opting out of the embrace of CUFI: 'the real bottom line', he commented, 'is the fact that this organization would like to exacerbate tensions in the Middle East so it will lead to Armageddon.' In a sermon to his congregation, Biach expressed concern over Hagee's anti-Muslim rhetoric, broadcast in speeches on his website and elucidated in his books.[16] Certainly, Hagee has remarked at a press conference following the inauguration of CUFI that the conflict was not with 'some big thing called terrorism'. It was with 'Islamic fascism', which was fighting a 'war against western civilization'.

The Executive Director of CUFI, David Brog, a conservative Jew, considered that working for the organization was the 'most important thing' he could do 'not only for Israel but for Judaeo-Christian civilization today, which is under threat from radical Islam'. Brog declares himself 'convinced that the evangelical Christians who support Israel today are nothing less than the theological heirs of the righteous Gentiles who sought to save Jews from the Holocaust'.[17] The CUFI website proclaims that 'Israel's time of need is now. There is a new Hitler in the Middle East – President

Ahmadinejad of Iran – who has threatened to wipe out Israel and America. And he is rapidly acquiring the nuclear technology with which to make good on his threat. If we learned anything from the Holocaust, it is that when a madman threatens genocide *we must take him seriously*.'[18] There is no sense here of the argument lucidly expressed by Vali Nasr and Ray Takeyh: 'Iran is not, in fact, seeking to create disorder in order to fulfil some scriptural promise, nor is it an expansionist power with unquenchable ambitions. Not unlike Russia and China, Iran is a growing power seeking to become a pivotal state in its region.'[19]

### *The Growth of Christian Neo-Zionism*

The development of Christian neo-Zionism is all the more remarkable, for it is a relatively recent phenomenon, in spite of Richard Land's denial that this is so.[20] Anti-Semitism remained rampant at all levels of Christian society up until the 1960s and later. Following a spate of copycat desecrations of Jewish synagogues in the US in 1960 (643 incidents in two months), the Anti-Defamation League (ADL) of B'nai B'rith commissioned research that eventually materialized as the University of California five-year study of anti-Semitism (1961–5). Based on 3,000 questionnaires returned and 1,976 interviews, this proved to be a wide-ranging survey of Christian attitudes across the denominations. Christians 'seem constrained to view Jews with suspicion and contempt', the authors concluded. Among the Protestant groups, the proportion holding both anti-Semitic beliefs and feelings ('the hatred of persons because they are Jews') was as high as 50 per cent among the more conservative groups.

The research suggested that 'religious outlooks and religious images of the modern Jew seem to lie at the root of the anti-Semitism of millions of American adults.' Religion was considered to be 'an extremely important force in maintaining the endemic level of American prejudice against Jews'. What was needed, the researchers concluded, was a systematic reappraisal of Christian education, both the teaching of history and doctrines and particularly the way in which questions of anti-Semitism were dealt with. Between 20 and 30 per cent of American Christians (within the study, taken to mean members of church congregations) accepted images of the Jew as 'soft on Communism', a potential draft-dodger, and 'more loyal to Israel than America'.[21]

Such were the basic attitudes of American Christians in 1960, a year in which the Southern Baptist evangelical leader Billy Graham acted with courtesy and tact during a visit to Israel, during which Prime Minister Golda Meir presented him with a Bible inscribed 'to a great teacher in all the important matters to humanity and a true friend of Israel'.[22] Yet the Nixon tapes reveal a different Billy Graham twelve years later. During a conversation with Richard Nixon and White House Chief of Staff H.R. Haldeman in 1972, Graham agreed with the President that the best Jews were the Israelis. The American Jews were too liberal, however. 'I go and see friends of Mr Rosenthal at the *New York Times*, and people of that sort. And, I don't mean all the Jews, but a lot of the Jews are great friends of mine. They swarm around me and are friendly to me, because they know I am friendly to Israel and so forth. They don't know how I really feel about what they're doing to this country.' After Graham left the Oval Office, Nixon remarked to Haldeman: 'you know, it was good we got this point about the Jews across ... The Jews are [an] irreligious, atheistic, immoral bunch of bastards.'[23]

How it was that Nixon continued to dupe Graham about his true attitude towards the Jews throughout his presidency remains a mystery. Nearly twenty years after Watergate, one of Graham's close associates confided that, 'for the life of me, I honestly believe that after all these years, Billy still has no idea of how badly Nixon snookered him'. Richard Land comments that 'if Billy Graham's words weren't captured on tape saying those things, I simply wouldn't have believed he had said them' because the Graham he remembers was the evangelical leader who very early in his ministry 'confronted the demons of racial prejudice and segregation, refusing to allow segregated seating at his evangelistic crusades from the late 1940s onward'. These Oval Office conversations, however, not only reveal 'anti-semitic sentiments, but also some intent to act on them, as well as hypocritical behaviour in concealing these feelings from Jewish "friends" and acquaintances'.

Anti-Semitism, Richard Land declares, is 'the most irrational of prejudices for a Christian ... since Jesus, the one who we follow as Saviour and Lord, was Jewish. Evangelical Christians across the denominational spectrum support the state of Israel by overwhelming margins and love and respect the Jewish people.'[24] It was not Israel's alleged weakness, not the fear of a 'second Holocaust', 'but rather its proven strength and strategic alliance with the United States that led Jewish elites to gear up the Holocaust industry' after the Six Day War in June 1967.[25] Israel occupied the ancient Jewish lands of Samaria and Judea in the West Bank along with the Gaza Strip and the Sinai desert to the South, the Golan Heights in the north and all of the city of Jerusalem. The Six Day War led to the emergence of the Christian neo-Zionist movement, which believes that the return of the Jews to the Holy Land (that is, the foundation of the state of Israel in 1948) is in accordance with biblical prophecy. With the Israeli gains in 1967, it seemed that for the first time since the period of King Solomon Jews had sovereignty over most of the land that God had promised them. Richard Land explains the connection between evangelical support of Israel because of the Abrahamic covenant, and the biblical prophecies on the need for Jews to be physically present in the Holy Land:[26]

> Once Israel was established, there were a lot of people who said, 'Wait a minute now. Isn't that what the Book of Revelation says?' [cf. Rev. 3:9] People say that because the state of Israel was established, that proves the end-times are coming and that is why keeping the Abrahamic covenant, keeping Israel strong, is so important – because it's a sign of the end-times. I think it is a sign of the end-times. But that's not the reason to bless Israel. The reason to do it is because God commanded it. Yes, we're one step closer to the end-times than we were before Israel came back into the land, because my understanding of biblical prophecy is that Israel is established in the land at the time that the events of the Second Coming take place. But the Bible tells us no man knows the hour or the day of [Jesus' second] coming ...

Whereas, in 1948, only about 34 per cent of Americans sympathized with the Jews in their struggle against the Arabs, for the forty years since the Six Day War, Americans have consistently sided with Israel, with the figure rising from 45 per cent in 1967 to a record 64 per cent at the time of the first Gulf War. The lowest figure recorded, 32 per cent, was at the time of the Israeli invasion of Lebanon in 1982, when American support for the Palestinians rose to a record 28 per cent.[27] The shrewd Menachem Begin, who had recently been awarded the Nobel Peace Price for his work with President Sadat in negotiating the Israel–Egypt peace of 1978, saw his opportunity to garner a new type of political support in the US when he invited the Rev. Jerry Falwell for his first official visit to Israel, and the following year, 1979, his government gave Falwell a gift – a Lear Jet.

Begin's timing was impeccable: he began working seriously with Christian Zionists at the precise moment that Christian fundamentalists in America were discovering their political voice. A firm friendship was forged between Begin and Falwell that lasted until Begin's death in 1992. Falwell was the leader of a deeply conservative church that had resisted integration until 1968; it was not until 1971 that the first African American members were baptized.[28] The same year that Falwell received his Lear Jet from Begin – 1979 – he formed the Moral Majority, an organization that changed the political landscape in the United States for a decade (it was dissolved officially in 1989). The official biography on the website of the University Falwell founded – Liberty University, Lynchburg, Virginia – states:[29]

> During the first two years of its existence, the Moral Majority attracted over 100,000 pastors, priests, and rabbis and nearly seven million religious conservatives who mobilized as a pro-life, pro-family, pro-Israel, and pro-strong national defence lobbying organization. The Moral Majority chose California Governor Ronald Reagan as 'their candidate' for President in 1980, registered millions of new voters, and set about to inform and activate a sleeping giant – 80 million Americans committed to faith, family, and Judaeo-Christian values.

In November 2004, Falwell revived the Moral Majority name for a new organization, the Moral Majority Coalition. The intent of the organization is to continue the 'evangelical revolution' to help conservative politicians get elected. Referring to the Coalition as a '21st century resurrection of the Moral Majority', Falwell committed himself to leading the organization for four years, but died on 15 May 2007. His son Jonathan has taken over the leadership since his death.[30] In his encomium of Falwell, John Hagee noted that with his death 'we in the Christian Zionist world lost one of our pioneers and leading lights'.[31] Asked why he supported Israel so strongly, Falwell

> often mentioned Israel's democracy and the fact that Israel was a strong American ally in both the Cold War and the War against Terror. Dr Falwell was also fond of quoting Genesis 12:3. As he once correctly noted: 'I firmly believe God has blessed America because America has blessed the Jew ...'

When interviewed in 2002 concerning the top challenges facing Christians, Falwell declared: 'there's nothing that would bring the wrath of the Christian public in this country down on this government like abandoning or opposing Israel in a critical matter.' Falwell was strongly supported by many Jewish groups, but even they baulked at some of his more controversial statements. In October 2002, the Anti-Defamation League (ADL) strongly condemned his statement that the Prophet Muhammad 'was a terrorist' and called on him to apologize to the followers of Islam. The ADL's national director noted that Falwell 'has once again demonstrated his intolerance by his outrageous charge about the Prophet Mohammed. He owes an apology to the millions of good people who follow the Muslim faith. As a man of the cloth, he should be working toward bringing faith communities closer together, not driving wedges through them.'[32]

Though an adviser to three Republican presidents – Nixon, Ford, and Reagan – and a campaigner for the Republican nomination for the presidency twice, in 1992 and 1996, Patrick J. ('Pat') Buchanan never succeeded in establishing his credentials as leader of the Christian Right after the dissolution of the Moral Majority in 1989 because he alienated too many important groups. He vowed to 'take back' the conservative movement from the 'neo-con cabal'.[33] As a pre-Vatican II Catholic, Buchanan called Pope John Paul II 'the most politically incorrect man on Earth', and praised his views on abortion, homosexuality, and extra-marital sex. He has continued the praise for Benedict XVI because of his uncompromising stand on Catholic doctrines, including divorce, contraception, and women's ordination. Buchanan has been accused of anti-Semitism: Norman Podhoretz called him 'soft on Hitler' and claimed that he had a 'habit of championing the cause of almost anyone accused of participating actively in Hitler's genocidal campaign against the Jews'.

Nor is Buchanan a Christian Zionist. Although he considers that 'the Israeli people are America's friends and have a right to peace and secure borders', and that the United States has a 'moral commitment' to recognize Israel's right to defend itself, 'US and Israeli interests are not identical. They often collide, and when they do, US interests must prevail.' In 1990, he referred to Capitol Hill as 'Israeli-occupied territory', while the following year he wrote that Congress had become 'a Parliament of Whores incapable of standing up for US national interests if AIPAC is on the other end of the line'.[34] In March 2003, he wrote an *American Conservative* cover story arguing that neo-conservatives want 'to ensnare our country in a series of wars that are not in America's interest'. Buchanan continued:[35]

> This is a time for truth. For America is about to make a momentous decision: whether to launch a series of wars in the Middle East that could ignite the Clash of Civilizations against which Harvard professor Samuel Huntington has warned, a war we believe would be a tragedy and a disaster for this Republic ... Who would benefit from a war of civilizations between the West and Islam? Answer: one nation, one leader, one party. Israel, Sharon, Likud ...
>
> The neocons seek American empire, and Sharonites seek hegemony over the Middle East. The two agendas coincide precisely. And though neocons insist that it was 11 September that made the case for war on Iraq and militant Islam, the origins of their war plans go back far before ...

By such outspoken pronouncements, and earlier versions of the same, Buchanan made himself unacceptable to the Christian Zionists and lost any prospect of leadership of the Christian Right. Instead, that role went to the Southern Baptist 'televangelist' Marion Gordon 'Pat' Robertson, who campaigned unsuccessfully for the Republican party's presidential nomination in 1988. Robertson used the remnants of his campaign organization to start the Christian Coalition, which became a 1.7-million-member Christian Right organization that lobbied for conservative candidates. Though Robertson is a Christian Zionist, his value to the pro-Israel lobby has been damaged by his capacity for ill-judged statements. He announced, for example, that Ariel Sharon's incapacity through a stroke in January 2006 was in effect a punishment from God: 'God has enmity against those who, quote, "divide my land". And I would say, Woe unto any prime minister of Israel who takes a similar course to appease the EU, the United Nations or the United States of America. God says, "This land belongs to me. You['d] better leave it alone."'[36]

When, in June 1994 the ADL released a report entitled *The Religious Right: the Assault on Tolerance and Pluralism in America*, which singled out Falwell and Robertson, among others, for attack, Robertson found a surprising defender in Norman Podhoretz. 'By this time, it seems clear,' comments Murray Friedman, 'neo-cons seemed more at home with Christian conservatives than with liberal Jews. They believed that the spread of secularism and relativism was far more dangerous than [the] occasionally outrageous statements of the religious right.'[37]

Robertson's capacity for alienating his friends resulted in the day-to-day leadership of his movement being assumed by Ralph E. Reed Jnr as executive director of the Christian Coalition for eight years until April 1997. In the wake of the ADL report on the Religious Right, Reed played the role of healer, speaking mollifying words to ADL and AIPAC respectively in April and May 1995. He projected a 'softer' public face of Christian conservatism. By the time of the mid-term elections in 1994, the Christian Coalition had distributed 40 million copies of the 'Family Values Voter's Guide' in more than 100,000 churches nationwide. *Time Magazine*, in May 1995, called Ralph Reed 'the Right Hand of God' and credited the Christian Coalition with critical assistance in the Republican victories the previous year: of 45 new members in the House of Representatives and nine in the Senate, roughly half were Christian Coalition candidates. The Christian Coalition had campaigned on their behalf exclusively in fundamentalist, Pentecostal, and Charismatic churches. Its claim is to 'protect and defend the Judaeo-Christian values that made this the greatest country in history'.[38] The Catholic conservative writer, Richard Neuhaus called Reed's book, *Active Faith: How Christians Are Changing the Soul of American Politics* (1996), 'a kind of populist manifesto' which 'eschews populist stridency'.[39] In 1996, 45 million voter guides were distributed, while in 2000, 75 million voter guides were sent out to support George W. Bush in the presidential election, though by this time Reed had moved on to become co-chairman with Rabbi Yechiel Eckstein of Stand for Israel, a sort of Christian AIPAC, 'an effort strategically to mobilize leadership and grassroots support in the Christian community for the State of Israel'.[40]

With Reed's departure, the Christian Coalition 'became a skeleton of its former self'.[41] Robertson resigned from the Christian Coalition in 2001, but Reed re-emerged in 2004 as a senior member of the team campaigning for the re-election of George W. Bush and Dick Cheney.[42]

### *George W. Bush as the Effective Leader of the Evangelical Right*

Evangelical groups are the fastest-growing of the Christian denominations in the US as in the UK, and their success arises from a particular formula described by Christian Smith as balancing 'high tension with, and high integration into, mainstream American society simultaneously'. Whereas the mainstream 'liberal' Protestant churches seek to reduce tension between themselves and the surrounding cultures 'and so integrate comfortably into mainstream society', and the fundamentalist groups seek to withdraw from extensive participation in mainstream society, religious vitality is fostered in the evangelical community by 'a situation of sustained dissonance, if not outright conflict, between evangelical believers and the (majority) non-evangelical world with which they – with tension – engage'. For Christian Smith, 'it is precisely evangelicalism's heavy exposure to, and engagement with, modern pluralism – and the attendant distinctions, tensions and conflicts that necessarily arise – which reinforces evangelical boundaries, identity, solidarity, mobilization, and membership retention'.[43]

Though some commentators, such as Steve Bruce (writing before 9/11), are unimpressed by the longer-term achievements of 'zealot politics',[44] the Christian Right is strong in certain regions, such as the South, and in its veto power in the Republican Party.[45] Its largest constituent element is the Southern Baptist Convention (SBC), whose membership in 2005 was estimated at 16.3 million persons based in some 43,000 churches, the largest body of Christians in the US after the Roman Catholics. Richard Land, president of the Ethics and Religious Liberty Commission of the Southern Baptists, states openly that the evangelical vote was critical to the re-election of Bush and Cheney: according to 'some estimates, 40 per cent of their raw vote came from evangelicals. Mr Bush carried every state in which there was a significant Southern Baptist presence.' Bush is considered by Land much more identifiably 'one of us' than any president since Eisenhower, arising from his upbringing in Midland, Texas.

'This president not only thinks we're important; he shares our concerns …' Land contends that Southern Baptists should not be endorsing candidates: 'we should be looking for candidates who endorse us.' With George W. Bush, to be pro-life 'is a settled faith conviction'. 'The president comes out of that evangelical faith. It's part of the warp and woof of his being. He is offended at very basic levels that we have a society that kills approximately one out every three babies conceived.' In the 2000 presidential elections, Land contends that two-thirds of the voters who 'went to church or synagogue or mosque at least once a week' voted for George W. Bush: 'that was the single most reliable predictor of how a person voted', apart from the 'anomaly' of 91 per cent of African–Americans voting for Al Gore. Bush's chief speech writer in 2005–6, Michael J. Gerson, is an evangelical, but Land dismisses the idea that Bush's speeches carry specific messages to an evangelical audience: 'one of the reasons that this president is so effective as a speaker is that he says what he thinks, and he thinks what he says.'[46]

Land argues that the Iraq intervention is a 'just war', an argument that has led to the charge that he has become 'a court priest for a pro-war denomination.'[47]

> George Bush and most of George Bush's supporters believe God has a side, and we believe that side is freedom. We believe that side is democracy. We believe that side is respect for basic human rights. We don't see the world starkly in terms of black and white. But we do see that there is a good and there is an evil, and that there is no moral equivalence between Saddam Hussein and the United States of America.
>
> There is no moral equivalence between the radical Islamic jihadists and the United States of America. As Tony Blair said, this is a struggle for civilization. It's a struggle between the force of civilization and the force of barbarism …

Commentators such Robert Parham, executive director of the Baptist Center for Ethics in Nashville, Tennessee, and a frequent critic of the SBC leadership, argue that in his support for the Iraq war, Land continuously mis-states the rules of just war; either Land 'doesn't understand the rules or he misuses them because he is more politically loyal to President Bush than morally faithful to the biblical call for the prophetic voice'. 'From my perspective,' Parham states, 'Land's most grievous accomplishment is helping hard-wire fundamentalism to the Republican Party, fusing agendas and signalling that "GOP" stands for "God's Only Party".'[48] But then, no doubt, Parham – an opponent of the Iraq war before it was declared, and a supporter of Jimmy Carter and Bill Clinton's call for a reformed Baptist union that is more inclusive[49] – would be regarded by Land as virtually an apostate.

The religious conservatives in the United States have so embraced George W. Bush that an event such as the resignation of Pat Robertson as head of the Christian Coalition in December 2001 created little stir. As the *Washington Post* put it: 'for the first time since religious conservatives became a modern political movement, the president of the United States has become the movement's *de facto* leader – a status even Ronald Reagan, though admired by religious conservatives, never earned.'[50] That status as effective leader has been nurtured and deepened by Bush's pronouncements, particularly in the aftermath of the 11 September 2001 attacks, which emphasized relatively simple dichotomies, playing on the 'justice of our cause', the good/evil conflict in the world, the security/peril challenge for the United States, the sense of mission contrasted with the abdication of responsibilities ('history will judge harshly those who saw this coming danger but failed to act ... the only path to peace and security is the path of action'), the unity/dissent contrast to isolate and damage critics at home, and finally the proclamation of the universal gospel of freedom and liberty in order to confront dictatorship and repression. In all this, what could be more reassuring than the ways of divine providence?[51]

> We can ... be confident [George W. Bush pronounced at the fifty-first National Prayer Breakfast, held in February 2003 in Washington DC] in the ways of providence, even when they are far from our understanding. Events aren't moved by blind change and chance. Behind all of life and all of history, there's a dedication and purpose, set by the hand of a just and faithful God. And that hope will never be shaken.

The response to 9/11 was the epitome of 'muscular Christianity', with the statements issued by the White House uncritically reproduced by the American electronic and print media. During the 2004 re-election campaign, the chief presidential strategist, Karl Rove, held a weekly conference call from the White House with religious leaders, and evangelical churches handed over membership directories to the Bush campaign for voter-registration drives. Sidney Blumenthal notes that 'the religious right is not a majority, but it was indispensable to Bush's victory. Across the country, it has become the most energetic, reliable and productive part of the Republican organization. The worth of its values-based politics is power ...'[52] In 2006, Karl Rove infuriated the Democrats when he accused them of being weak and timid in the face of terror. He stated: 'conservatives saw the savagery of 9/11 in the attacks and prepared for war. Liberals saw the savagery of the 9/11 attacks and wanted to prepare indictments and offer therapy for our attackers.'[53] David Domke calls this 'moral stance underpinned by threat, fear and paranoia' as well as connotations of the apocalypse 'political fundamentalism'.[54] It was precisely that alleged contrast – between Republican action/strength and Democrat inaction/weakness – which the voters overwhelmingly rejected in the 2006 mid-term elections by giving the Democrats control of both houses of Congress for the first time since 1994.

One of the interesting features of the new Baptist Covenant proposed by former presidents Jimmy Carter and Bill Clinton and their supporters among the liberal wing of the Baptist movement is the phrase it contains committing Baptists to their 'obligation as Christians to promote peace with justice'.[55] Carter has made himself *persona non grata* with the Jewish establishment in the United States because of his commitment to peace with justice for the Palestinians and his denunciation of 'apartheid' in Israel and 'the extraordinary lobbying efforts of the American–Israel Political Action Committee and the absence of any significant contrary voices'.[56] Carter's aim is to undermine the uncritical conservative evangelical support for Israel without naming it specifically. At its most extreme, in the formulations of the Christian Zionist Congress of February 1996, the movement affirms that, 'because of the sovereign purposes of God for the city, Jerusalem must remain undivided, under Israeli sovereignty, open to all peoples, the capital of Israel only' and that it would be 'error for the nations to recognize a Palestinian state in any part of Eretz Israel'. The Congress condemns the 'radical view now ascendant within Islam which, by its own tenets, advocates violence and *jihad* as 'a legitimate means to spread the Islamic faith and advance the Islamic world view'. It expresses 'deep concern' with and seeks to address 'the increasing threat posed by radical Islam to Israel, to Christian minorities in the Middle East and to the world, while offering compassionate prayer for those millions of people now in the Islamic faith'.[57]

A decade later, the Christian leaders in Palestine in turn condemned the Christian Zionist programme as providing a worldview according to which 'the Gospel is identified with the ideology of empire, colonialism and militarism'. 'In its extreme form, it places an emphasis on apocalyptic events leading to the end of history – here the leaders refer to predictions such as in Ezekiel chapters 38 and 39[58] – rather than living Christ's love and justice today.' The leaders continued[59]

> We categorically reject Christian Zionist doctrines as false teaching that corrupts the biblical message of love, justice and reconciliation. We further reject the contemporary alliance of Christian Zionist leaders and organizations with elements in the governments of Israel and the United States that are presently imposing their unilateral pre-emptive borders and domination over Palestine. This inevitably leads to unending cycles of violence that undermine the security of all peoples of the Middle East and the rest of the world ... Rather than condemn the world to the doom of Armageddon we call upon everyone to liberate themselves from the

> ideologies of militarism and occupation ... With urgency we warn that Christian Zionism and its alliances are justifying colonization, apartheid and empire-building ...

## *'God is Not a Democrat':*[60] *Conservative Catholicism and the 'Theo-cons'*

The concept of 'Rapture' is not just a religious idea but has clear political implications. The website Rapture Ready, 'your prophecy resource for the end times' provides much up-to-date material for devotees. A recently posted article contends that 'the Lord would certainly not be a Democrat.'[61] 'The Democratic Party continues to be led by those who believe pacifism is the easiest pathway to world peace,' the author argues. 'They constantly do all within their power to support legislative action designed to disarm the military of the US and the American public. Again, that woolly-minded leadership violates basic biblical precepts. Jesus spoke about being vigilant and prepared to defend one's home: "Or else how can one enter into a strong man's house, and spoil his goods, except he first bind the strong man and then he will spoil his house" (Matt. 12:29).' Perhaps surprisingly, the author asserts 'with equal certainty that Jesus would not be a card-carrying member of the Republican Party. The Grand Old Party may share many values that can be traced back to the Bible, but it is still the GOP, not the GOD party.'

> When it gets down to the bare facts, the only advantage the Republican Party offers is that it is the lesser of two evils. Even so, the Republican Party brings to the legislative table in America a much safer, [sounder] course of governing, in our view. The GOP, for the most part, opposes abortion, legitimizing homosexuality as equal to heterosexual relationships, and huge ... social programs (welfare in nature, based upon the definition of welfare given above). Th[e Republican] party is, by and large, in favour of a strong national defence, national sovereignty, and keeping God's name at the heart of our national character.

When and why did the alienation of the religious Right from the Democratic party take place? Mark Stricherz argues that it is long-standing, and a defensive reaction to changes which took place in the Democratic party in 1972, when George McGovern became the presidential candidate under new party rules and was defeated ignominiously by Richard M. Nixon (though his campaign aides committed the Watergate burglary to steal Democratic party information during the election). In 1968, 13 per cent of the delegates to the Democratic convention were women. In 1972, the number had jumped to 40 per cent. 'In adding women and feminists, most of whom supported legal abortion', the McGovern commission (which had been responsible for changing the party's rules) 'loosened other groups' ties to the party. One such group would be the so-called Reagan Democrats, 'typically Midwestern Catholics disheartened by the party's embrace of social liberalism. When the economy is strong ... these voters tend to vote Republican.'[62]

As a result of the party changes, at the 1972 party convention secularist delegates suddenly constituted the largest bloc among Democratic delegates. The Democrats became the first mainstream party in American history, in Ross Douthat's expression, 'to pander to a sizable bloc of aggressively secular voters'. If the Republican party became 'more religious', this was because the Democrats 'became self-consciously secular, and the turning point wasn't the 1992 or the 2000 elections but the *putsch* of 1972'.[63] The Democrats made a conscious decision to jettison blue-collar voters in favour of what a 1969 memorandum had called 'a different political and social group with rising educational levels, affluence, and ... greater cultural sophistication'. It meant the loss of their former heartland in the southern states. Ironically, after this the black vote and the blue-collar vote in the north firmed up for the Democrats and has continued to increase at every election subsequently. The result is that the Democrats have become increasingly the party of the ethnic minorities and economically disenfranchised,[64] while the Republicans have been the party of the conservative religious, whether Catholic or Protestant, and the economically prosperous. Religion and class have gone hand in hand.

Against the cries of 'theocracy, theocracy, theocracy' – the name given to a campaign against religion said to be associated with the *New York Times* by a number of conservative commentators – William Rusher argues that far from being 'theocrats' seeking to mount a takeover, the religious Right is a movement of self-defence: 'they are simply trying to preserve, and where necessary restore, the politico-religious balance that has been traditional in this country. It is the intellectuals, with the critical support of the courts, and above all the Supreme Court, that have successfully eroded that balance, seeking to marginalize religion and convert the entire civic framework of the nation into a purely secular arena.'[65] This is not the view of Representative Christopher Shays (Republican, Connecticut), who argued in the *New York Times* on 23 March 2005: 'this Republican Party of Lincoln has become a party of theocracy.' Nor is it the view of theocracywatch.org a public information project of the Center for Religion, Ethics and Social Policy at Cornell University, which cites Shays's view in its introduction to 'the rise of the religious Right in the Republican Party'.[66]

Two ecumenical documents, entitled 'Evangelicals and Catholics Together' (29 March 1994) and 'Evangelicals and Catholics Together II' (December 1997), were of fundamental importance in sealing a political alliance which, given the number of doctrinal issues frankly acknowledged and left outstanding in the first document, might have seemed improbable. ECT I hoped for 'mutually respectful conversation' between Muslims and Christians, but it acknowledged that 'in many instances' Islam 'denies the freedom to witness to the Gospel', a fact which 'must be of increasing concern to those who care about religious freedom and the Christian mission'. Together, evangelicals and Catholics 'contend for the truth that politics, law, and culture must be secured by moral truth' as a bastion against 'influential sectors' of both elite and popular culture which are 'laid waste by relativism, anti-intellectualism and nihilism ...' They sought together to defend religious freedom and to strive 'for a renewal of the constituting vision of the place of religion in the American experiment'. If religion were to be excluded from the public arena, this would constitute 'an assault upon the most elementary principles of democratic governance'.

'The pattern of convergence and cooperation between Evangelicals and Catholics' was declared 'in large part, a result of common effort to protect human life, especially the lives of the most vulnerable among us.' Abortion was declared 'the leading edge of an encroaching culture of death ... We will do all in our power to resist proposals for euthanasia, eugenics, and population control that exploit the vulnerable, corrupt the integrity of medicine, deprave our culture, and betray the moral truths of our constitutional order.' 'Our cultural heritage', the representatives of the two denominations contended, 'is inseparable from the formative influence of religion, especially Judaism and Christianity.' Laws and social policies should be designed with particular care for the stability and flourishing of families. Foreign policy should reflect a concern for the defence of democracy and, 'wherever prudent and possible', the protection and advancement of human rights, including religious freedom. The parties rejected any suggestion that their document constituted a partisan 'religious agenda' in American politics: 'rather, this is a set of directions oriented to the common good and discussable on the basis of public reason.'[67]

David Martin contends that 'America's recent venturesome foreign policy is not driven by conservative Protestantism [alone] ... conservative Catholics are too easily discounted in analyses of American elections.'[68] There are, it is claimed, 61 million baptized Roman Catholics in the United States, which makes that denomination considerably more numerous than the combined evangelicals, though the total adherents of the Protestant denominations outnumber the Catholics.[69] Sidney Blumenthal notes that 'more than 40 conservative bishops' – out of a total of 176 Roman Catholic bishops in the US – 'worked with the Bush campaign against John Kerry' in 2004, and that Kerry, though a Catholic, received 2 per cent less of the Catholic vote than had the Southern Baptist Al Gore four years earlier. Bush won 52 per cent of the Catholic total and 79 per cent of the white evangelicals, which 'gave him his critical margin nationally and in the swing states'.[70]

The leader of the Catholic 'theo-conservative' movement is a former Lutheran, Father Richard John Neuhaus. In the pages of his monthly magazine *First Things*, published by the neo-conservative Institute on Religion and Public Life (IRPL) of which he is president,[71] Neuhaus and his ideological allies set the 'theo-con agenda' on a range of policies. *First Things* has now become 'the country's leading scholarly, conservative publication dealing with religion and society ...'[72] The principal ideologue of the movement, and certainly its most brilliant mind, is George Weigel, Senior Fellow at the Ethics and Public Policy Center (EPPC) in Washington, which was established in 1976 'to clarify and reinforce the bond between the Judaeo-Christian moral tradition and the public debate over domestic and foreign policy issues'. EPPC and its scholars work to influence policy-makers and to transform the culture through the world of ideas: 'our Protestant, Catholic, and Jewish scholars probe the riches of their own traditions, forge alliances within their communities, and work together to promote a shared understanding of the common good.' 'From the Cold War to the war on terrorism, from disputes over the role of religion in public life to battles over the nature of the family, EPPC and its scholars have consistently sought to defend the great Western ethical imperatives – respect for the inherent dignity of the human person, individual freedom and responsibility, justice, the rule of law, and limited government.'[73]

Neuhaus and Weigel et al. provide an intellectual edge to the writings of the Christian Right which is, on the whole, lacking within the evangelical tradition. And these writings are put to the service of George W. Bush's foreign policy. In October 2005, Neuhaus commented on Bush's second inaugural speech as president that it was 'a statement of national purpose in international affairs'.[74] Neuhaus continued:

> George W. Bush has provided a fresh conceptual framework for America's role in the world, and has acted upon it with remarkable energy. Whether the energy is matched by wisdom is debatable and is, in fact, hotly debated. He believes, and urges us to believe, that idealism is realism. We do not have to choose between national interests (such as oil) or national commitments (such as the security of Israel) and our moral responsibility in world affairs;

> they are all of a piece. It is a bold and comprehensive proposal, and it may well be vindicated. It may be unfair that such a proposal will stand or fall upon the outcome in Iraq, but so it probably is …

Arguing the pros and cons of the Iraq war in 2003, Neuhaus made it clear that he considered the war to be just: 'whether it turns out to have been wise depends upon contingencies that are known to none but God. There are great risks in such actions. There are, it can be reasonably argued, greater risks in inaction.' 'War may sometimes be a moral duty in order to overturn injustice and protect the innocent,' Neuhaus contended. 'The cause must be just, and the just cause in this case is the disarmament of Iraq.' Dismissing the United Nations as on the way towards the fate of the League of Nations, he further contended:[75]

> in the judgment of the US and many other governments, Saddam posed a grave and imminent threat to America, to world peace, and to the lives of innumerable innocents. If that judgment is correct … the use of military force to remove that threat is, in the absence of plausible alternatives, both justified and necessary …

In retrospect, the fact that Neuhaus was on easy personal terms with George W. Bush, who calls him 'Father Richard',[76] may have led him to follow the White House line naïvely. The Anglo-American bombing tactics against Baghdad ('shock and awe') were certain to cause unwanted and unwarranted civilian casualties, as indeed they did. Writing on the theme of religious freedom in a time of war in January 2002, Neuhaus noted that 'a vibrant expansion of Christianity need not mean "a global war of religions",' but that 'Islam is the great question for this century, and perhaps beyond.' 'The aim of the current war', he declared, 'is to demonstrate decisively that the murderous global ambition of the political ideology called Islamism has no future whatsoever.' Muslim leaders needed to reassess the past of their faith in order to create a 'more sustainable future'. In the meantime, 'the United States must be, and must be seen to be, the uncompromising champion of human rights, including the first and the font of all rights, which is religious freedom.'[77]

Neuhaus is firmly in the camp of the war on terror as a war for civilization, directed 'against those within Islam who have no doubt that they are at war with the rest of the world, including most of the Islamic world (which they view as the pseudo-Islamic world)'. There is 'no doubt that millions of people possessed of lucidly lethal intentions in obedience to what they believe to be the commands of God have declared war on us, and therefore we are, not by our choice, at war'.[78]

The intellectual and moral justification for the 'war on terror' in its second application, the invasion of Iraq in 2003, was provided by George Weigel's 'Moral Clarity in a Time of War' (see Chapter 8). Weigel contends that both contemporary international law and much recent Catholic commentary seem to have come to the settled view that the first use of armed force is always bad, while the second use of armed force (in response to that always bad first use) may be morally justifiable. Weigel argues that this is not the traditional Catholic teaching and that the definition of, and response to, 'aggression underway' (which bears on the classic just war criteria of 'just cause' and 'last resort') has become critically important.[79] (We may add that there still needs to be consideration of the 'supreme emergency exemption', according to which the victim resorts to immoral measures to stave off disaster and death; 'we can excuse the victim's actions, but never justify them.')[80] Weigel argued that a revitalization of Catholic international relations theory would be 'good for the Church and good for the world'.

Another area on which George Weigel concentrates his intellectual energy is the presumed moral collapse of Europe. He argues that the United States must draw lessons from what he perceives as the European historical amnesia about cultural and civilizational roots: 'Americans ought not to want that to happen in America.' He joins the camp of those who predict a doomsday scenario for Europe with its Muslim immigrant population and an alleged 'appeasement mentality towards radical Islam':

> Europe's current demographic trendlines could eventually produce a Europe in which Sobieski's victory at Vienna in 1683 is reversed, such that the Europe of the twenty-second century, or even the late twenty-first, is a Europe increasingly influenced, and perhaps even dominated, by radicalized Islamic populations, convinced that their long-delayed triumph in the European heartland is at hand.

Weigel concludes that the long-term answer to the demise of Europe will only be found in a 'revitalization of Europe's Christian roots and the rebirth of Christian conviction in Christianity's historic heartland'. He argues that 'generously funded trans-Atlantic initiatives that seek to challenge the hegemony of "exclusive secularism" in European intellectual life and its impact on public policy' are as imperative in the contemporary era as were initiatives such as the CIA-funded and sponsored Congress for Cultural Freedom and its journal *Encounter*, which flourished respectively from 1950 to 1967 and 1953 to 1990.

### *The Theo-cons' Re-Definition of the War on Terror as a War of Religion*

The story of the 'theo-con' movement led by Neuhaus, Weigel, Michael Novak, and others, is told in more detail than is possible here in Damon Linker's *The Theocons: Secular America under Siege* (2006), a work that is the more valuable because Linker worked for the movement between May 2001 and February 2005. Linker recalls that the staff of *First Things* gathered in early October 2001 to discuss how the magazine might respond to the traumatic events of 11 September. 'Neuhaus explained to his staff in a tone of grave authority', Linker notes, 'that Samuel Huntington's controversial thesis about an impending "clash of civilizations" was America's surest guide to the coming years and decades of violent conflict with militant Islam.' Neuhaus continued:[81]

> The United States was the most powerful nation in the Christian West and the only one with sufficient self-confidence to lead a potentially victorious campaign against its enemies in the Muslim world – which was what the so-called 'war on terror' was all about. Even if diplomatic considerations prevented the president from speaking truthfully about the civilizational scope of the struggle that awaited us, it was imperative that someone do so with intelligence and force. That … would be a task for *First Things*.

Damon Linker states that it was Neuhaus who went on to pen an unsigned editorial for *First Things* published in December 2001 which made it clear that 'the theo-cons considered Bush's open-ended "war on terror" to be an obvious example of a "just war".'[82] The editorial is remarkable for the ferocity of its attack on a number of simultaneous targets. First, it was an attack on the United Nations and alliance systems such as NATO: proclaiming 'the rule of justice' that it is the first duty of the state to protect its citizens, Neuhaus stated that there were 'no credible instruments of international force that can fulfil that duty or see that justice is done. The United States must lead, in the hope that those who understand that "an attack on us is an attack on them" will follow.' Secondly, it was an attack on Europe, a subject on which Neuhaus endorsed Weigel's predictions about the demographic decline of Christians and the inevitability of an 'appeasement mentality towards radical Islam':

> If the current fertility level continues, Europe's population of 727 million will plummet to 556 million by the year 2050, requiring more than three million immigrants per year for the next fifty years if Europe is to remain economically viable. Such immigration will be, for the most part, from Islamic countries, thus profoundly transforming a continent that has been almost entirely Christian.

While 9/11 may not have changed everything, Neuhaus thundered, 'it did reconfigure world politics. That reconfiguration has already happened, and there is now no undoing of it. At the centre of that reconfiguration is the world-historical role of Islam.' For ten years, 'a few prescient scholars have been warning about the coming conflict, now commonly referred to by Samuel Huntington's phrase "the clash of civilizations".' Muslim organizations had attacked *First Things* for drawing attention to that warning. 'Samuel Huntington does not exaggerate when, surveying conflicts all over the world, he speaks of "the bloody borders of Islam". (Bernard Lewis is also praised for his 'eerily prescient' article on 'The Roots of Muslim Rage'.) 'We cannot ask "Who are they?" without also asking "Who are we?" More and more, as this war continues, we may come to recognize that we are, however ambiguously, who they think we are, namely, the Christian West.' Neuhaus dismisses the concept of a clash of rival fundamentalisms and welcomes as a likely consequence of the war 'the collapse of the [concept of] multiculturalism that has dominated the academy in recent years':[83]

> Like it or not, and we decidedly do not like it, we are engaged in a war that can be defined in many ways, but is also and inescapably a war of religion ... The memory of wars of religion, and the fear of their revival, make some commentators understandably hesitant to emphasize the religious dimension of the contest in which we are engaged. A few acknowledge that the contest is most importantly about religion, but then go on to trivialize that reality by saying we are at war with all forms of 'fundamentalism', including the 'religious right' in this country ... Bin Laden and his like are not fundamentalists. Scholars urge upon us the distinction between Islam and Islamism, the latter denoting the militant faith and theocratic aspirations now arrayed against us. Call them militant Muslims, radical Muslims, monistic Muslims, or even fanatical Muslims. They call themselves faithful Muslims ... The terrorists have now unmistakably underscored their otherness, and with it the otherness of Islam.

With this extraordinary attack on a world religion with 1.2 billion adherents and the lack of realism in expecting that the fanatics can be split off from the majority of Muslims if it is the 'otherness of Islam' itself which is stressed, we end this account of the theo-cons and their influence. Theo-cons such as Richard Neuhaus purport to know something about the faith of Islam that they denounce but they are, in reality, profoundly ignorant. They enthusiastically endorse the statements of Pope Benedict XVI, but he, too, has shown himself to be insensitive to the faith of Islam. One of his first actions as pope was to merge the Pontifical Council for Inter-Religious Dialogue with the Pontifical Council for Culture and export the most knowledgeable expert on Islam far away from Rome – to Cairo, where he would have no influence on the Pope himself or the Roman Curia. Less well reported than the *faux pas* of his speech at Regensburg on 12 September 2006 is the fact that Benedict XVI has recanted to an extent, by reinstating the independent status of the Pontifical Council for Inter-Religious Dialogue. In his Christmas 2006 address to the Roman Curia he spoke of 'a dialogue to be intensified with Islam.'[84] In October 2007, 138 Muslim scholars signed a letter to Christian leaders calling for high-level dialogue 'on the common essentials of our religions'. At first the response from the Vatican appeared to be negative; but at the end of November, it agreed that 'we can and therefore should look at what unites us'. The joint working group would include officials from the Pontifical Council for Inter-Religious Dialogue.[85] Friends of Roman Catholicism can only hope and trust that the Catholic theo-conservatives in the United States will learn from the Pope's mistakes and reconsider their vilification of the faith of Islam (rather than the correct target, the ideological programme of violent jihadists such as Osama bin Laden and Ayman al-Zawahiri). If they do not, then they should be called to account by the Roman Catholic hierarchy in the United States.

They should also bear some of the responsibility for the damage that they have done to ecumenical relations with the mainstream Protestant churches in the United States. Richard Neuhaus wrote the founding document for the Washington-based Institute on Religion and Democracy (IRD) in 1981 and has been a central figure from its inception. Damon Linker describes it as an 'ecumenical non-profit organization that works to discredit theological and political liberals within the Protestant main[stream], as well as to encourage the main[stream]'s few remaining traditionalists to advance a conservative theological and political agenda.'[86] IRD has received substantial benefactions – between 1985 and 2005 right-wing patrons donated at least $4,764,000 to IRD – but 'not a penny has been spent nor staff member assigned to attempt to change anything about the Catholic Church'. (As a leading architect of the theo-con movement, Neuhaus and his IRPL have benefited from funding by the same benefactors who backed IRD to the tune of $8,387,500 from 1989 to the end of 2005.) The website of IRD denounces the United Methodist Church for its liturgical materials for the sixth anniversary of 9/11: 'pacifism, moral equivalence, anti-US stereotypes continue to characterize official UM Resources for the 9/11 Anniversary.'[87] This sustained attack on the United Methodist Church and other mainline Protestant leaders and their denominations, it has been said, 'constitutes the single greatest breach in ecumenical good will between Roman Catholics and Protestants since Vatican II.'[88]

Both the evangelicals and the 'theo-cons' seem indifferent to the fate of other Christian denominations in the Middle East and especially Iraq. Before the outbreak of war in 2003, it is thought that the Assyrian or Chaldean Christians (together with a smaller number of Armenians and Catholics) in Iraq numbered between 600,000 and one million, or 4 per cent of the population. 'Christians live in constant fear of being attacked, kidnapped and killed by radical Islamic groups,' an Iraqi Catholic nun was quoted as stating in October 2004. 'Armed groups of Islamic fundamentalists break into homes of Christians to kill and steal. In some mosques Imams are now teaching that it is not a crime to kill a Christian.' Fr Nizar Semaan, a parish priest in Iraq, noted that 'fundamentalist criminals' were continuing to attack the churches. 'There are two options for Christians. Either we leave our country', he said, 'or we stay and are massacred.' Appealing to Christians around the world, he asked: 'even if you are watching at a distance, do you feel solidarity or only pity? Couldn't you do something more?' Through the Vatican Secretary for Relations with States, Archbishop Giovanni Lajolo, the late Pope John Paul II warned that the war against terror had had as one of its side-effects the spread of 'Christianophobia' in 'vast areas of the globe where, wrongly, Western civilization or certain political strategies of Western countries are considered to be determined by Christianity or at least not separated from it'. The Vatican asked the UN Commission of Human Rights in Geneva in December 2004 to condemn 'Christianophobia', along with 'Islamophobia' and anti-Semitism on which it had already held hearings.[89]

There have been some voices in the United States calling for help to be given to Iraq's Christians. *The National Review*, an influential neo-conservative publication, appealed to the Bush administration in October 2004 to create a 'safe haven' within Iraq specifically for Iraq's Christians. 'The community needs American help to create a district which should encompass the traditional community villages located near Mosul, in the Nineveh Plains', wrote Nina Shea, formerly the director of Freedom House's Center for Religious Freedom. Describing the Chaldean community as 'the canaries in the coal mine for the Great Middle East', Shea noted that the treatment of Christians in the new Iraq was 'being watched closely by the Maronites of Lebanon, the Copts of Egypt, and other non-Muslim populations in the region'.

By January 2007, the United Nations reported that half the Iraqi Christian population had moved, either into exile abroad or to the relatively peaceful Kurdish region. Nina Shea wrote in the *Washington Post* in August 2007: 'the United States has no policies designed to protect or rescue them. Worse, it has carried out policies heedless of their effect on Iraq's most vulnerable.' 'Today, a handful of Jews remain. Unless Washington acts, the same fate awaits Iraq's million or so Christians and other minorities. They are not simply caught in the crossfire of a Muslim power struggle; they are being targeted in a ruthless cleansing campaign by Sunni, Shi'ite and Kurdish militants.'[90] In a first positive step, on 12 June 2007, the US House Appropriations Subcommittee on State and Foreign Operations passed a budget amendment that directs $10 million for internally displaced religious minorities in the Nineveh Plain. The amendment represents the first formal allocation of funding and acknowledgement of the crisis facing Iraq's indigenous Assyrian–Chaldean–Syriac Christian population. The risk is that it may be too little, too late.[91]

One of the least surprising consequences of the controversial years of George W. Bush in the White House has been the difficulty of the Republican Party in finding a successor for the presidential election in 2008. To what extent is Bush's legacy enduring, both in foreign and domestic policy? Can a single candidate match his capacity to satisfy the combination of lobbies in order to capture the party nomination and, eventually, the White House itself? Mitt Romney appeared to have established an early lead in two small, but key, states – Iowa and New Hampshire – but encountered a great deal of resistance from the evangelical lobby because he is a Mormon – and also because of his close association with the notorious Blackwater Worldwide military outsourcing company. Since then he has made a strong pitch to the religious Right, seeking 'to convince evangelical Protestant and conservative Catholic voters that [he] shares their ideology, the ideology of theo-conservatism.'[92] John McCain had alienated the evangelicals by his remarks in the 2000 campaign. As the former mayor of New York at the time of the 9/11 catastrophe, Rudolph ('Rudy') W. Giuliani – 'George W. Bush with brains' in Michael Tomasky's phrase – benefited from instant name recognition, but evangelicals were split on his candidature. Pat Robertson was prepared to endorse him as the best-placed candidate to take on the threat from 'Islamo-fascism': 'to me, the overriding issue before the American people is the defence of our population from the bloodlust of Islamic terrorists', Robertson stated on the occasion of his endorsement. 'Rudy Giuliani took a city that was in decline and considered ungovernable and reduced its violent crime, revitalized its core, dramatically lowered its taxes, cut through a welter of bureaucratic regulations, and did so in the spirit of bipartisanship which is so urgently needed in Washington today,' he added. Others, such as Ralph Reed, were unconvinced, while Mitt Romney doubted that the Republican party would choose a 'pro-choice, pro-gay civil union candidate to lead' it. Norman Podhoretz stated in an interview in the *New York Observer* that he had met Giuliani to discuss his book on World War IV, in which he advocates bombing Iran as part of a larger struggle against 'Islamo-fascism', and concluded that 'there is very little difference in how he sees the war and I see it'. Other neo-conservatives advising Giuliani on foreign policy included neo-Zionists Daniel Pipes and Martin Kramer. Pipes names three other advisers – Peter Berkowitz, Nile Gardiner, Robert Kasten – while others mention also Michael Rubin, a scholar at the American Enterprise Institute who has written in favour of revoking the United States' ban on assassination and Charles Hill, a career diplomat and former deputy to Secretary of State George P. Schultz in the Reagan administration. Some of the former members of the George W. Bush administration had shifted to John McCain, including Richard L. Armitage and the neo-conservatives William Kristol, Gary Schmitt, and Robert Kagan, in what the *Washington Post* called the 'war over the wonks'.[93] The surprise candidate in terms of his apparent popularity, Mike Huckabee, campaigned without any high-profile foreign policy advisers. Kevin Zeese commented that 'if nominated Huckabee better be taken seriously because a minister as commander-in-chief at this critical moment could produce a very long-term war against Islam.'[94]

The most obvious conclusion to draw was that the evangelical Right was divided in a way that had not been seen since the 1990s. Richard Land, president of the Southern Baptist Convention's Ethics and Religious Liberty Commission, argued that Robertson's endorsement probably reflected a belief by the TV evangelist that Giuliani was the candidate most likely to beat the Democratic nominee. 'Pat Robertson may have decided that Rudy Giuliani is the best way to keep Hillary Clinton out of the White House,' Land commented, but added that he was 'not going to vote for Rudy under any circumstances'. When Giuliani was asked in an interview if he could be viewed as an even-handed broker when it came to Israeli–Palestinian issues, he questioned the premise of the question. 'America shouldn't be even-handed in dealing with the difference between an elected democracy that's a government ruled by law, and a group of terrorists,' he said. 'I think that was part of the mistake of the 1990s that led to the debacle that we saw in the Middle East in the way Clinton was handling it.'[95]

### *Divisions in Our World are Not the Result of Religion or Religious Difference – but 'Faith-Based Leadership' Carries Risks*

'The divisions in our world are not the result of religion or of culture, but are politically based,' Karen Armstrong proclaims. 'There is an imbalance of power in the world, and the powerless are beginning to challenge the hegemony of the Great Powers, declaring their independence of them – often using religious language to do so.'[96] Former President Jimmy Carter, in a publication in 2005 entitled *Our Endangered Values: America's Moral Crisis*, castigates the neo-conservatives' 'rigid, dominating and exclusive policies', which he considers are threatening 'the fundamental political and religious values of the United States'. According to Carter's definition, fundamentalists believe that 'they are absolutely aligned with God and anyone who disagrees with them is inherently wrong and therefore inferior'. It is against their principles to admit that they are in error; to compromise with anyone is a violation of their principles.[97]

The fundamentalist takeover of evangelical Christianity – particularly the Southern Baptist Convention – is a relatively recent development of the previous twenty-five years (i.e. since 1980), that is, beginning towards the end of Carter's presidency (1977–81). He was shocked when the President of the Southern Baptist Convention closed a visit to the White House with the comment: 'we are praying, Mr President, that you will abandon secular humanism as your religion'[98] – this to the first president of the United States who was avowedly an evangelical Christian and who still teaches Sunday school at his Baptist Church in Plains, Georgia.[99] This was, in effect, a criticism of Carter for not trying to force his private religious beliefs onto the American public using the authority of the presidency. The statistical analysis of religious terms used in presidential speeches undertaken by David Domke and Kevin Coe demonstrates conclusively that 'the God strategy' – the deliberate and partisan use of faith as a political weapon – 'moved to the centre of American politics' in the 1980 presidential election campaign. Whereas Carter had avoided overtly religious language, it was Ronald Reagan who became the first modern president to act as 'political priest' to the nation by speaking the language of the faithful; to fuse God and the country by linking America with the divine will; to embrace important religious symbols, practices, and rituals; and finally to engage in morality politics. Since 1980, the Republicans have advocated the key policy goals of religious conservatives, while the Democrats have not. It is much harder for the Democrats to employ the 'God strategy' since their religious base in the electorate is less clear, while the political signals sent out by the politician have to be consistent with the evidence of his personal life – a test which Bill Clinton singularly failed.[100]

Pat Robertson is one of those named by Carter for disavowing or challenging the traditional Christian and American constitutional separation between church and state. George W. Bush has gone further with his 'faith-based initiative' since 2001 in undermining the constitutional separation between church and state than might be imagined. As Bill

Berkowitz puts it, the White House Office of Faith-Based and Community Initiatives (OFBCI) issued executive orders: 'Centers for Faith-Based and Community Initiatives were established at seven federal agencies, web sites were created, technical assistance to religious organizations was given at seminars and conferences, guidebooks helping religious groups apply for government funds were published, and billions were earmarked for faith-based institutions.'[101] 'Rallying the armies of compassion'[102] cost US taxpayers more than $2.2 billion in fiscal year 2005 – or, as Carter puts it, 'taxpayers' money is distributed to churches and other religious institutions that will comply with the basic principles of the present ... administration.'

Yet Jimmy Carter's critique goes deeper. In his version of evangelical Christianity, 'we worship the prince of peace, not war'; and, for Carter, Jesus Christ was 'committed to compassion for the most destitute, poor, needy, and forgotten people in our society'. In a chapter of his book entitled, 'Worshipping the Prince of Peace, or Pre-emptive War?', Carter contends that 'the most tell-tale distinction between Republicans and Democrats is their preference between ways of resolving controversial international issues – [whether by] reliance on force, or diplomacy.' Carter denies that size and military capacity are the only attributes of a superpower. They should also include 'a demonstrable commitment to truth, justice, peace, freedom, humility, human rights, generosity and the upholding of other moral values'. 'I've got more in common with Pope John Paul II than I do with Jimmy Carter or Bill Clinton,' Richard Land, president of the Ethics and Religious Liberty Commission of the Southern Baptist Convention, claimed in the January 2005 edition of *Atlantic Monthly*. Such a statement suggests, his opponents retorted, that politics are more important to Land – and the constituency he represents – than theology, 'since only in partisan terms could he make such a remark.'[103]

Carter depicts preventive war as a catalyst for a cycle of escalating violence. It is illegal under international law and a blatant rejection of the American tradition of resort to war only when its security is directly threatened, as against perhaps being threatened at 'some time in the distant future'. War may sometimes be necessary, he argues, but it must meet just-war criteria: last resort after other options have been exhausted; a clear discrimination between combatants and non-combatants; violence proportionate to the injury suffered; the attackers must have a legitimate moral authority; and the peace to be established at the end of the military intervention must mark a clear improvement over the pre-war situation. Carter does not consider that the Iraq war meets these standards and, as a result he is concerned at the loss of America's moral authority in the international community. The violation of human rights, and the death of at least 28 prisoners in US custody abroad, he considers 'inconceivable' under previous administrations. The publication of the *Camp Delta Standard Operating Procedures* of 28 March 2003 occurred as a result of a leak in November 2007. The procedures outline the 'Behaviour Management Plan', which is meant to isolate the captive and 'enhance and exploit the disorientation and disorganization felt by a newly arrived detainee'. Sleep deprivation is one of the key tactics: 'hanging [a] towel in [the] cell to block [the] sun or light at night when sleeping' is denied to all prisoners.[104]

Carter considers that the religious Right's views towards the state of Israel has been influenced by the crude theology of Tim LaHaye's Left Behind series which – when interviewed – Carter called 'a completely foolish and erroneous interpretation of the Scriptures' which has resulted in a 'terrible, very costly and bloody deterioration in the relation between Israel and its neighbours'. He calls this theology 'very disturbing', while acknowledging that it has been 'amazingly influential in shaping our own government's policy'.[105] No one, Carter claims, 'can challenge me on my commitment to Israel and its right to live in peace with its neighbours'. Interviewed by Ayelish McGarvey on 5 April 2004, Carter noted that

> it's nearly the 25th anniversary of my consummation of a treaty between Israel and Egypt [the Camp David accords of 17 September 1978 were followed by the treaty of March 1979] – not a word of which has ever been violated. But this administration, maybe strongly influenced by ill-advised theologians of the extreme Religious Right, has pretty well abandoned any real effort that could lead to a resolution of the problems between Israel and the Palestinians ... there has to be a negotiated settlement; you can't just ordain the destruction of the Palestinian people, and their community and their political entity, in favour of the Israelis.

Carter has elucidated the issues of making a just peace in the Middle East – just that is, for Palestinians and not just for a hegemonic state of Israel – in his *Palestine: Peace not Apartheid* (2006). This book brought down upon Carter the rage of the American Jewish and pro-Israel lobby and, predictably, the epithet 'anti-Semitic'. It is true that one of his most prominent critics, Abraham Foxman of the Anti-Defamation League, denied that he called Carter an anti-Semite. 'But you said he was bigoted', pressed his interviewer, James Traub. 'Isn't that the same thing?' 'No. "Bigoted" is you have preconceived notions about things.' The argument that the Israel lobby constricted debate was itself bigoted, he said.[106] In his book Carter makes a telling point about the security wall constructed by the government of Israel, which 'ravages many places along its devious route that are important to Christians'. He notes 'one of its notable intrusions' at Bethlehem, but the 'especially heart-breaking division' on the southern slope of the Mount of Olives, where Israel's thirty-foot wall cuts through the property of Santa Martha Monastery. 'The house of worship is now on the Jerusalem side, and its parishioners are separated from it because they cannot get permits to enter Jerusalem.' For nine hundred years under different regimes no one previously had ever stopped people from coming to pray until the wall was built. Father Claudio comments on the wall that it does not separate 'Palestinians from Jews'; rather, he says, it separates 'Palestinians from Palestinians'.[107]

Anders Strindberg comments that 'Christians find themselves under the hammer of the Israeli occupation to no less an extent than Muslims, yet America – supposedly a Christian country – stands idly by because its most politically influential Christians have decided that Palestinian Christians are acceptable collateral damage in their apocalyptic quest.' As the now retired Anglican bishop of Jerusalem, the Right Reverend Riah Abu el-Assal has explained, 'the Arab Palestinian Christians are part and parcel of the Arab Palestinian nation. We have the same history, the same culture, the same habits and the same hopes.' Of the 750,000 Palestinians who were forced from their homes in 1948, some 50,000 were Christians – 7 per cent of the total number of refugees and 35 per cent of the total number of Christians living in Palestine at the time. Today it is believed that the number of Christians in Israel and occupied Palestine number some 175,000, just over 2 per cent of the entire population, but the numbers are rapidly dwindling owing to mass emigration.[108] In Bishop Riah's estimation, by 2015 on present trends, the land that saw the birth of Christianity will become no more than a set of archaeological sites visited by Christian tourists: it will have no Christians living there any longer. Only the old remain. The younger Christian families have been forced out by an unholy alliance of the oppressive policies of the state of Israel and the campaigning and fundraising of the neo-Zionist Christian groups chiefly – though not exclusively – in the US. The neo-Zionist Christian movement helps fund new Jewish settlements in the occupied lands, and refuses any help to the beleaguered Christians of Palestine because they are Arabs and thus dispensable. As Bishop Riah states in his autobiography, on the plight of the Palestinians in general: 'we have yet to discover who will be our Good Samaritan.'[109]

In his more general critique of the George W. Bush administration, Jimmy Carter emphasizes the decline in trust in the American government, and public scepticism that the administration has told, and is telling, the truth as a central aspect of the crisis in moral values that he describes.

In a remarkable quotation from a presidential aide in the summer of 2002, Ron Suskind presents the contrast between the faith-based presidency of George W. Bush and the 'reality-based community':[110]

> The aide said that guys like me were 'in what we call the reality-based community', which he defined as people who 'believe that solutions emerge from your judicious study of discernible reality' ... 'That's not the way the world really works anymore,' he continued. 'We're an empire now, and when we act, we create our own reality. And while you're studying that reality – judiciously, as you will – we'll act again, creating other new realities, which you can study too, and that's how things will sort out. We're history's actors ... and you, all of you, will be left to just study what we do.

The 'reality-based community' is only slowly coming to terms with the Republicans' use of language to create a docile and submissive electorate. Frank Luntz, one of their polling specialists, in *The 14 Words Never to Use*, urges conservatives to restrict themselves to phrases from his *New American Lexicon*. Thus, a smart Republican, in Luntz's view, never advocates 'drilling for oil'; he 'explores for energy'. He should never criticize the 'government', which cleans our streets and pays our firemen; he should attack 'Washington', with its ceaseless thirst for taxes and regulations. 'We should never use the word outsourcing', Luntz writes, 'because we will then be asked to defend or end the practice of allowing companies to ship American jobs overseas. Rather, we should talk about the "root cause" why any company would not want to hire "the best workers in the world". And the answer: "over-taxation, over-regulation, too much litigation, and not enough innovation or quality education". Because it rhymes, it will be remembered.'[111] Such 'political framing', as the parlance now goes, is rapidly being picked up by Democrats, too, but they have difficulty in replacing the four Republican themes that are easily remembered even by political illiterates: lower taxes, less government, strong defence, and family values.[112] 'Language is clearly important in politics, but the message remains more important than the messaging,' Jim Wallis of *Sojourners* magazine – a progressive Christian commentary on faith, politics, and culture, which seeks to build a movement of spirituality and social change – argues. He continues: '... until Democrats are willing to be honest about the need for [a] new social policy and compelling political vision, they will never get the message right. Find the vision first, and the language will follow.'[113]

'God gave us this president to be the man to protect the nation at this time ... I believe he's an instrument of God ...' Thus confided Hardy Billington, a Bush supporter from Poplar Bluff, Missouri, to Ron Suskind in the 2004 presidential election campaign. The frequent appeal to God keeps Bush in touch with his electoral base. But there is more to his faith-based presidency than the continual appeal to God. 'Mr President, how can you be so sure when you don't know the facts?', Senator Joseph Biden asked Bush. 'My instincts, my instincts', he replied. As Ron Suskind argues, 'faith-based presidency is a "with us" or "against us" model.' Jim Wallis argues that Bush has transmogrified from 'a self-help Methodist' to a 'messianic American Calvinist. He doesn't want to hear from anyone who doubts him.' He suggested to the President that 'unless we drain the swamp of injustice in which the mosquitoes of terrorism breed, we'll never defeat the threat of terrorism.' That was the last conversation he had with George W. Bush (Wallis went on to write a piece entitled 'Dangerous Religion: George W. Bush's Theology of Empire' for *Sojourners* magazine).[114] For the Bush regime, the swamp metaphor was to be used exclusively for a quite different purpose. As Donald Rumsfeld stated on 18 September 2001, 'the best way to get at the terrorist networks is to "drain the swamp they live in", referring to action against countries that harbour terrorist activities' – meaning in the first instance, Afghanistan.[115]

Bruce Bartlett, who had served as a domestic policy adviser to Ronald Reagan and a Treasury official to George H. W. Bush, noted to Ron Suskind that George W. Bush 'dispenses with people who confront him with inconvenient facts'. He continues:

> This is why George W. Bush is so clear-eyed about al-Qaeda and the Islamic fundamentalist enemy. He believes you have to kill them all. They can't be persuaded [because] they're extremists, driven by a dark vision. He understands them, because he's just like them ... Absolute faith like that overwhelms a need for analysis. The whole thing about faith is to believe things for which there is no empirical evidence. But you can't run the world on faith.

As Jim Wallis puts it, 'the Bush theology deserves to be examined on biblical grounds. Is it really Christian, or merely American? Does it take a global view of God's world or just assert American nationalism in the latest update of "manifest destiny"? ... Bush seems to make this mistake over and over again – confusing nation, church, and God. The resulting theology is more American civil religion than Christian faith.'[116]

Lieutenant-General William 'Jerry' Boykin, the Deputy Under-Secretary of Defense for Intelligence, caused a furore with his remarks on Islam, made while wearing army uniform, in 2003. He described the United States as a 'Christian nation' and stated that he knew he would capture a Muslim Somali warlord because 'I knew my God was bigger than his God. I knew that my God was a real God and his was an idol.' In addition, he called the 'war on terror' a 'spiritual battle': 'Satan wants to destroy this nation,' Boykin claimed, 'he wants to destroy us as a nation, and he wants to destroy us as a Christian army.' Senator Dianne Feinstein urged Secretary of Defense Donald Rumsfeld to take action on Boykin's speech in a letter sent on 21 October 2003. Boykin's remarks, she noted, 'do not represent the values of the United States Government or the United States Army'. Al-Qaeda and others seek a 'clash of civilizations': 'remarks such as those by General Boykin can only serve to give impetus to those who would seek to recruit and brainwash disaffected Muslim youth to carry out acts of terror against Americans and our friends and allies.' If the United States is to succeed in the war on terror, the Senator added, 'both the actions and rhetoric of America's leaders must accurately reflect our mission – and not contribute to an atmosphere of hatred, intolerance and mistrust that can only serve to undermine our national security interests'.[117] Donald Rumsfeld defended Boykin, describing him as 'an officer that has an outstanding record in the United States armed forces', and noting that the 'War on Terror' was 'not a war against a religion'. He also spoke about the right of freedom of speech.[118]

Boykin's talk was videotaped and broadcast on NBC News on 15 October 2003. But it was not an isolated incident – Boykin had discussed his involvement in the war on terrorism at 23 religious-oriented events after January 2002 and had worn his uniform while speaking at all but two. He had spoken mostly at Baptist or Pentecostal churches.[119] Boykin commented on 9/11: 'now ask yourself this: why is this man in the White House? The majority of Americans did not vote for him. Why is he there? And I tell you this morning he's in the White House because God put him there for such a time as this. God put him there to lead not only this nation but to lead the world, in such a time as this.' Esther Kaplan notes that 'such a time as this' is a Biblical phrase, a theme to which Boykin refers again and again in his speech.[120]

Kaplan observes that the Christian Coalition alone distributed 30 million voter guides in the 2004 presidential election, and adds: 'the atmosphere in the final months was electric. To the party's base, the election was more than a chance to re-elect a president who'd kept faith with them on their core agenda; it was a referendum on God.' At a Christian Coalition gathering in late September 2004, Jerry Falwell told the cheering crowd that he wanted 'an overwhelming landslide' so that 'the nation, including the Republican Party, will know that Christ did it'.[121] In the event, Bush did win a majority (50.7 per cent) of the votes cast (62 million to 59 million), unlike the election of 2000, when he had won only 47.9 per cent of the vote. In the year 2000 presidential election, the Bush campaign had spent $6.84 for each vote gained (50.4 million in all, as against 51 million won by Gore). Al Gore 'lost' the election, but then he had only spent $4.25 for each vote gained. In the 2004 election, Bush spent $5.92 for each vote cast in his favour, as against Kerry's expenditure of $5.52 for each vote gained. At least on a cost-benefit analysis, being a president at war with God supposedly on his side had made a difference in 2004.

# Chapter Seven
# Regime Change? Assertive Nationalism Captures the White House Post-9/11

> Wolfowitz saw very early that the fundamental choice was American leadership, or increasing chaos and danger ... I think Wolfowitz is now vindicated by history, but it took a long time to get vindicated ... It really wasn't until 9/11 that Wolfowitz's paper – which by that time was, what, nine years old – came to be seen as perhaps prophetic.
>
> (William Kristol, 14 January 2003)[1]

> ... Barring extraordinary events, the United States will always feel obliged to defend, if possible, a democratic nation under attack from non-democratic forces, external or internal. That is why it was in our national interest to come to the defence of France and Britain in World War II. That is why we feel it necessary to defend Israel today, when its survival is threatened. No complicated geopolitical calculations of national interest are necessary.
>
> (Irving Kristol, 25 August 2003)[2]

> Neo-conservatism... was hijacked by elite American supporters of the Likud [party in Israel], both Jewish and non-Jewish, and their Christian allies, long before the neo-cons, temporarily, perhaps, hijacked US foreign policy under the second Bush. I can attest that there are neo-conservatives, including Jewish neo-conservatives, who don't share a love affair with the Likud, but if they said so in public their careers in the movement would end. (Michael Lind, February 2004)[3]

The influence of the American pro-Israel lobby and the Christian Right on foreign policy would have been much less significant but for a third movement – the neo-conservative pundits who, during the 1990s, became increasingly organized and drew up specific policy proposals to give substance to what up to then had been only a set of broad ideas. Many of the prominent neo-conservatives are pupils of the conservative political philosopher Leo Strauss (1899–1973), and became involved in common projects. Several – William Kristol, Robert Kagan, Gary Schmitt,and Paul Wolfowitz – were involved in the Project for the New American Century. Wolfowitz and Abram Shulsky served together in the Pentagon's Office of Special Plans.

Strauss wrote that 'to make the world safe for the Western democracies, one must make the whole globe democratic, each country in itself as well as the society of nations,' which sounds quite like a neo-conservative maxim; yet the political philosopher Gregory Bruce Smith declared in 1997 that 'there can be no such thing as Straussianism'.[4] While some of the Straussians, such as Fukuyama and Wolfowitz, dismissed the emphasis on Strauss and the Straussians (let alone the 'Leo-cons'),[5] Abram Shulsky, together with Gary Schmitt, wrote an article in 1999 entitled 'Leo Strauss and the World of Intelligence (by which we do not mean nous)' on the advantages of Strauss's teaching for intelligence work.[6] The CIA's analysts, Shulsky and Schmitt argue, 'were generally reluctant throughout the Cold War to believe that they could be deceived about any critical question by the Soviet Union or other Communist states. History has shown this view to have been extremely naïve.' They suggested that political philosophy, with its emphasis on the variety of regimes, could provide an 'antidote' to the CIA's failings, and would help in understanding Islamic leaders, 'whose intellectual world was so different from our own'. Strauss's idea of hidden meaning, Shulsky and Schmitt added, 'alerts one to the possibility that political life may be closely linked to deception. Indeed, it suggests that deception is the norm in political life …'[7] Elsewhere, in *Silent Warfare*, they wrote that in intelligence work 'truth is not the goal, but only a means toward victory'.[8]

Shadia B. Drury, a scholar of Leo Strauss's writings, argues that Straussians believe that 'peace leads to decadence. Perpetual war, not perpetual peace, is what Straussians believe in.' Such views naturally lead to an 'aggressive, belligerent foreign policy', she contends.[9] 'Because mankind is intrinsically wicked', Strauss once wrote, 'he has to be governed. Such governance can only be established, however, when men are united – and they can only be united against other people.' Shadia Drury adds that this means: 'if no external threat exists then one has to be manufactured.' Whenever he discussed contemporary international relations, Strauss was fond of repeating the story of Gulliver and the Lilliputians. 'When Lilliput was on fire, Gulliver urinated over the city, including the palace. In so doing, he saved all of Lilliput from catastrophe, but the Lilliputians were outraged and appalled by such a show of disrespect.' 'An apt image, then, for an American Gulliver today', John G. Mason adds, 'who shows strong exhibitionist tendencies and whose militarist urges push him to play the *pompier pyromane* around the world while "Old Europe" looks on in disbelief.'[10]

Consistency is no requirement for neo-conservative affiliation. According to Shadia Drury, 'Irving Kristol, the father of neo-conservatism and a Strauss disciple, denounced nationalism in a 1973 essay; but in another essay written in 1983, he declared that the foreign policy of neo-conservatism must reflect its nationalist proclivities. A decade on, in a 1993 essay, he claimed that "religion, nationalism, and economic growth are the pillars of neo-conservatism".'[11] 'There is no set of neo-conservative beliefs concerning foreign policy,' affirms Irving Kristol – the author of *Neo-Conservatism: The Autobiography of an Idea* (1995) – 'only a set of attitudes derived from historical experience'. He identifies four so-called 'attitudes': patriotism is a natural and healthy sentiment and should be encouraged by both private and public institutions; world government is a terrible idea since it can lead to world tyranny; statesmen should have the ability to distinguish friends from enemies; and, finally, a great power has more extensive interests than small ones: 'it is a fact that if you have the kind of power we now have, either you will find opportunities to use it, or the world will discover them for you.'[12]

## *The Influence of Think Tanks post-9/11*

Irving Kristol's influence on the development of the neo-conservative thinking on foreign policy has been, and continues to be, considerable. Since 1988, Kristol has been the John M. Olin Distinguished Fellow at the American Enterprise Institute (AEI). An annual public lecture is now held there in his honour, which in 2007 was delivered by none other than Bernard Lewis. When President George W. Bush visited and spoke at AEI on 15 February 2007, he stated: 'I admire AEI a lot – I'm sure you know that. After all, I have been consistently borrowing some of your best people. More than 20 AEI scholars have worked in my administration.'[13] As a key right-wing think tank, AEI has had few difficulties in securing funding. Between 1985 and 2005, AEI received more than $44.5 million in grants from right-wing foundations including the John M. Olin Foundation (the institution which funded the Fukuyama–Huntington debate).[14] Its annual budget is $24.4 million, an enormous figure – but such is the scale of the budgets for think tanks in the United States that it rates only ninth in budget size.

All the other think tanks are dwarfed by the RAND Corporation, with its budget of $227.2 million, and the Carter Center ($82 million).

Then there follow another eight think tanks, with budgets above $20 million – the Brookings Institution ($47.7 million), the East-West Center ($37.6 million), the Heritage Foundation ($34.6 million), the Council on Foreign Relations ($29.3 million), the Hoover Institution on War, Revolution and Peace ($25 million), the Center for Strategic and International Studies (CSIS, $25 million), AEI ($24.4 million), and Stanford's Institute for International Studies ($20 million). There are a further three think tanks with budgets between $14 million and $19.4 million, and a further eleven with budgets between $1.1 million and $8.5 million.[15]

However, budget size does not necessarily guarantee access to politicians and the shaping of policy. Few think tanks have devoted more time and resources – in 2003, $6.6 million, or 19.3 per cent of its budget – on media and government relations than has the Heritage Foundation. In the same year, Brookings devoted only $1 million to communications – yet it claimed to have the highest Washington think tank ratings for press citations. Brookings claimed 845 television and radio interviews in 2003, while Heritage reported 1,100 television and 1,418 radio appearances.[16] In terms of print media coverage for the period January 2001 to January 2005, Abelson's figures suggest that Brookings ranked first, receiving over 4,045 citations out of a total of 20,776 or 19.5 per cent, almost twice the share generated by AEI, Heritage, and RAND. In terms of television coverage between the same dates, his figures suggest that again Brookings fared much better than other think tanks, receiving 40.2 per cent of all broadcast media citations, twice that of the Council on Foreign Relations. The exception was CBS, which relied equally on RAND and Brookings, both receiving about a quarter of the network's coverage.

Such media visibility does not necessarily translate into political influence. Abelson's figures for testimony before the US Senate and House of Representatives committees between January 2001 and January 2005 demonstrate that the most frequent testimony – 33 testimonies out of a total of 120, or 27.5 per cent – were given by CSIS, a think tank that has a relatively slight media presence. Brookings came second, with 22 testimonies, or 18.3 per cent; AEI was third with 14 testimonies, or 11.7 per cent; while RAND, for all its fabulous income, fared less well than it had in either print or electronic media (10 testimonies or 8.3 per cent of the total).

The Project for the New American Century (PNAC), which many observers have credited with the primary role in the change of direction of George W. Bush's foreign policy, fared badly under all three criteria – 1 per cent of print media citations, less than 1 per cent of electronic media citations and only 2.5 per cent of testimonies before Congress (a total of three in all).[17] Gary Schmitt was executive director of PNAC from 1998 to 2005 and then moved to AEI, where in 2007 he remained a resident scholar and director of its programme on Advanced Strategic Studies. Schmitt states: 'we would love to take credit for the Bush doctrine, but in all honesty we can't.' PNAC 'set the terms' about 'how to think about the world'. 'It's perfectly obvious that Bush's war on terror was not something we articulated before 9/11 ... Bush pulled together a strategic vision based on the advice he received from Cheney, Wolfowitz and Rumsfeld.' It was not PNAC itself which had the clout: it was that several members of the Bush administration happened to have had an affiliation with this group.[18] And it was Bush himself who had the final decision on foreign policy.

Unlike Ronald Reagan, George W. Bush has demonstrated a marked reluctance to solicit the advice of non-governmental policy experts, preferring instead to surround himself with a small circle of advisers whom he has trusted to execute his foreign policy. In the words of Daalder and Lindsay (of the Brookings Institution), 'George W. Bush led his own revolution.'[19] They contend that neo-conservatives ('who might be better called democratic imperialists') were more prominent outside the administration, particularly on the pages of *Commentary* (Norman Podhoretz) and the *Weekly Standard* (William Kristol) and in the television studios of Fox News than they were inside it. Bush, Cheney, and Rumsfeld were not neo-conservatives but 'assertive nationalists': 'traditional hard-line conservatives willing to use American military power to defeat threats to US security but reluctant as a general rule to use American primacy to remake the world in its image.'[20] Assertive nationalists and the neo-conservatives formed 'a marriage of convenience' in that they both placed their faith not in diplomacy and treaties but 'in power and resolve'.

### *It's All in the Genes: Prominent Second-Generation Neo-Conservatives*

The influential neo-conservative Richard Perle admitted in 2003 that he was still a registered Democrat, out of 'nostalgia' for Henry 'Scoop' Jackson, in whose entourage a number of like-minded future neo-cons had worked.[21] For Jackson (1912–83), the Soviet invasion of Afghanistan revealed the true intentions of the regime: it showed 'that détente for us was an illusion, and Soviet "restraint" merely the absence of opportunity. And the political, economic and military policies developed to fit the theory that we have moved from confrontation with the Soviets to co-operation now lies in ruins ...'[22]

Jackson was awarded the Presidential Medal of Freedom posthumously in 1984 by Ronald Reagan, who called him 'one of the greatest lawmakers of our century', and praised his bi-partisanship in foreign and defence policy. Jackson used to say, 'in matters of national security, the best politics is no politics.' Reagan pronounced himself 'deeply proud, as he would have been, to have Jackson Democrats serve in my administration'. In June 2007, when he presented the Truman–Reagan Medal of Freedom posthumously, Senator Joe Lieberman recalled that Jackson had 'helped change history' during the Cold War and had not been afraid 'to challenge conventional wisdom and take on the enemies of freedom': 'that's why we call ourselves Scoop Jackson Democrats, Scoop Jackson Republicans, and in my case a Scoop Jackson Independent.'[23] Paul Wolfowitz had researched the anti-ballistic missile (ABM) system for Jackson: 'he spoke with such authority ... when he really believed something on a defence issue', Wolfowitz recalls, that 'few members of the Senate were comfortable challenging him.'[24]

Murray Friedman notes that, in the shaping of the policies of the Reagan administration, first-generation neo-conservatives such as Jeane Kirkpatrick, Eugene V. Rostow, Norman Podhoretz, Richard Pipes, and Richard Perle 'played a critical role'. By the latter part of the 1980s, 'the very force of Perle's ideas, and the fierce energy he exerted in advancing them, made him perhaps the central figure here, save Reagan himself.' And yet, Perle was a Scoop Jackson Democrat, not a Republican. Out of government in 1992, Perle published a novel, *Hard Line*, in which the narrator, broadly the author himself, denounces the claim of the 'liberals of the period' that the Soviet Union 'never really threatened the Free World' and that the Pentagon had 'overstated Soviet military power to justify huge military budgets'. Perle clearly felt that his advocacy of Reagan's Strategic Defense Initiative (SDI or 'Star Wars'), though derided by critics as mere fantasy, had been justified in the longer term. In Perle's view, it was Reagan's hardline policy – the deployment of missiles in Western Europe, along with the commitment to SDI – that had forced the Soviet Union under Gorbachev to adopt a more conciliatory position and sign the Intermediate Nuclear Force Treaty in Europe.[25]

Neo-conservative apologist Michael Novak recalls the left-leaning tendencies of the first generation of neo-cons:[26]

> It is worth remembering that the first so-called neo-cons were a tiny band, indeed, usually quickly named as Irving Kristol and Gertrude Himmelfarb, the two Daniels, Bell and Moynihan, Norman Podhoretz and Midge Decter, and a very few of their intellectual friends. Virtually all in this company had a history as men and women of the left, indeed to the left of the Democratic party, maybe in the most leftward two or three per cent of Americans, in some cases socialist in economics, in others social democratic in politics.

Michael Harrington coined the term 'neo-conservative' in the early 1970s to describe a group of his old socialist allies who had turned away from the true political faith and become 'socialists for Nixon' – because in their view, the alternative, McGovern for president, was infinitely worse. He clearly intended the term as an insult,[27] but it stuck because the new converts came to regard themselves as new conservatives.

Unlike their predecessors, most of the younger neo-conservatives have never experienced being left of centre. Jim Lobe notes 'just how small and incestuous the neo-conservative elite is, what with the Kristol-Himmelfarbs, the Podhoretz-Decter-Abrams, the Kagans, the Gaffneys (Frank and Devon) siblings, and the Ledeens (Michael, Barbara, and Simone), to the most prominent. It's no wonder that they are so susceptible to groupthink.'[28] Daniel Pipes professes not to know quite which views define a neo-conservative but since 'some of my oldest friends and closest allies are called neo-conservative, I happily accept this appellation. Indeed, it has a certain cachet, given that no more than 50 Americans have been called neo-conservative, yet we allegedly drive American foreign policy.'[29]

The marriage of Irving Kristol, the conservative intellectual organizer, to Gertrude Himmelfarb, a scholar whose work has focused on issues of virtue, morality, Victorian society, and modern values, provided a leader for the neo-conservative movement in the person of their son, William Kristol. Kristol Jnr was Chief of Staff and Counsellor to the Secretary of Education, William Bennett (1985–8) under President Reagan; then Chief of Staff to Vice-President Dan Quayle (1989–92) under President Bush Snr; and Chairman and Founder of the Project for the Republican Future (1990–3), the latter an organization that was credited with helping shape the strategy that produced the 1994 Republican congressional victory. Using money from Rupert Murdoch, Kristol established (along with fellow neo-conservative offspring, John Podhoretz, son of the commentator Norman Podhoretz) *The Weekly Standard* (its first published edition was on 18 November 1995), which rapidly became the most forthright neo-conservative publication outlet.

The following summer, Kristol co-authored with Robert Kagan an influential *Foreign Affairs* article entitled 'Towards a Neo-Reaganite Foreign Policy', in which they argued that the United States should establish a 'benevolent global hegemony' based on military supremacy and moral confidence: having defeated the 'evil empire' of the Soviet Union, 'the first objective of US foreign policy should be to preserve and enhance that predominance by strengthening America's security, supporting its friends, advancing its interests and standing up for its principles around the world.' Without 'moral clarity', such hegemony would serve no purpose; with it, the moral goals and fundamental national interests would 'almost always' be in harmony. They envisaged the active pursuit of policies in Iran, Cuba, and China ('for instance' – the list was not necessarily exhaustive) 'ultimately intended to bring about a change of regime'.[30] 'Regime change', the famous practice of George W. Bush's presidency, was thus on the agenda of the neo-conservatives from at least 1996.

The idea had its origins in the reaction of a number of neo-conservatives to the disappointing ending to the First Gulf War, particularly the US failure to support the rebellions against Saddam Hussein after he was left in power. William Kristol noted in 2003 that 'people like Charles Krauthammer, myself [and] Paul Wolfowitz ... thought right then [in 1991] that we probably had made a mistake when we failed to aid the rebels against Saddam.' Wolfowitz's Defense Planning Guidance of 1992 (the 'Wolfowitz Doctrine') was one response although, after being leaked to the *New York Times,* it was considerably diluted. The original wording by Wolfowitz asserted the right of the US to intervene pre-emptively when and where it believed necessary: 'we will retain the pre-eminent responsibility for addressing selectively those wrongs which threaten not only our interests, but those of our allies or friends, or which could seriously unsettle international relations.' 'Wolfowitz saw very early that the fundamental choice was American leadership, or increasing chaos and danger,' William Kristol recalled in 2003. But President George H. W. Bush 'didn't really want to think about that in 1992. He had a very difficult re-election coming up.'

There were questions in 1996 whether, as Kristol and Kagan claimed, a neo-Reaganite foreign policy would be 'good for conservatives, good for America and good for the world'. Walter A. McDougall of the Foreign Policy Research Institute (FPRI) questioned their contention that history showed that 'the American people can be summoned to meet the challenges of global leadership if statesmen make the case loudly, cogently, and persuasively'. The two cases they cited – how Harry Truman and the Congress resisted the arms build-up needed to wage the Cold War until the Korean war broke out, and how the Carter administration refused to increase the defence budget until the Soviets invaded Afghanistan – showed the reverse, he suggested. 'Americans tend not to rally until a loud, cogent disaster persuades them to do so': McDougall assumed that Kristol and Kagan were not hoping for another Korean war or comparable disaster – no one could conceive of a 9/11 in the late 1990s – to whet Americans' appetite for hegemony.[31]

The 'present danger', Kristol and Kagan argued in the preface to *Present Dangers: Crisis and Opportunity in American Foreign Policy* (2000), 'lies in America's hesitancy in maintaining its global hegemony against the many emerging challenges'. The contributors to *Present Dangers* – Richard Perle wrote on Iraq, Reuel Marc Gerecht on Iran, Elliott Abrams on Israel, Frederick W. Kagan on the decline of America's armed forces, and Paul Wolfowitz on statesmanship in the new century – were all 'conservative internationalists ... true heirs to a tradition in American foreign policy that runs at least from Theodore Roosevelt through Ronald Reagan'. Both the first Roosevelt and Reagan 'made Americans proud of their leading role in world affairs', Kristol and Kagan had argued in 1996. Without the support of such an 'elevated patriotism', conservatives would fail in their effort to govern America and Americans would fail in their responsibility to lead the world.

Paul Wolfowitz's contribution on statesmanship to *Present Dangers* deserves a fuller treatment than it has usually received.[32] He noted the need for Kennan's prescience in the post-Cold War era. Though 'many have aspired to play the role of the next George Kennan by defining American strategy for this new era that does not yet have a name, no-one has so far succeeded'[33] – by definition, not Huntington with his 'clash of civilizations' thesis which had been proposed seven years earlier. On the contrary, in *Present Dangers* as a whole there was only one reference to Huntington – and that was by Aaron L. Friedberg, in relation to the possibility of an expansionist and militaristic China.[34] Wolfowitz referred to his draft memorandum of 1992 and its key phrase – subsequently retained by Defense Secretary Dick Cheney in the Regional Defense Strategy document – that a 'dominant consideration' in US defence strategy should be 'to prevent any hostile power from dominating a region whose resources would, under consolidated control, be sufficient to generate global power'.[35] One obvious application of this principle, though not mentioned in the 2000 chapter on statesmanship, was oil in the Middle East.

Much of Wolfowitz's chapter was devoted to the case of China, 'in the opinion of many, the most serious policy issue facing us in the immediate future'. He alluded, however, to Fukuyama's argument that most of the struggles of the twentieth century had had an ideological basis, but contended that 'the absence of ideological competition does not guarantee peace'. 'It is only in the Muslim world', Wolfowitz wrote, 'that a revolutionary notion of societal organization has philosophical roots, and that notion, at least for now, is very much on the defensive in Iran, its own home base.' There was no mention of Osama bin Laden. Only Reuel Marc Gerecht, in his chapter on Iran, mentioned him at all in *Present Dangers*.[36]

The need for democracy promotion was one of the lessons Wolfowitz drew from the Cold War. In essence, it was a means of weakening one's enemies and strengthening one's friends. There were limits, however, to how far the United States could go in promoting democracy or nation-building. 'We must proceed by interaction and [indirect control], not imposition. In this respect, post-World War II experiences with Germany and Japan offer misleading guides to what is possible now, even in a period of American primacy' (see Chapter 9). Deterrence works, and coalitions count, Wolfowitz proclaimed. Conflicts cause arms competition, not vice versa. 'It is far better to equip others to fight for their country than to send Americans to fight for them ... refusing to arm our friends... is a strategic as well as a moral mistake ...' Force, when it has to be used, should be used decisively. 'Statesmanship requires ... not only a moral vision', Wolfowitz declared, 'but a willingness and ability to take a hard-headed and clear-eyed view of the world'. To avoid a war, four actions were required: a strengthening of the liberal democratic–free market consensus; the maintenance and strengthening of the alliance structure with liberal democratic states, including NATO and other bilateral alliances; dealing effectively with rogue states and disturbers of the international order; and finally, and most important of all, preserving the US leadership role, including its military pre-eminence, 'a necessary underpinning of the global democratic consensus'.[37]

### *The Project for the New American Century as Think Tank, Lobby, and Israel's Stalking Horse*

In 1997 William Kristol co-founded with Robert Kagan the Project for the New American Century (PNAC), which was clearly an institutional extension of the arguments projected in their article the previous year: the 'fundamental propositions' were that 'American leadership is good both for America and for the world; and that such leadership requires military strength, diplomatic energy and commitment to moral principle'. PNAC's statement of principles of 3 June 1997 proclaimed a 'Reaganite policy of military strength and moral clarity' with four immediate consequences:[38]

> We need to increase defense spending significantly if we are to carry out our global responsibilities today and modernize our armed forces for the future; we need to strengthen our ties to democratic allies and to challenge regimes hostile to our interests and values; we need to promote the cause of political and economic freedom abroad; [and] we need to accept responsibility for America's unique role in preserving and extending an international order friendly to our security, our prosperity, and our principles.

The signatories of the statement of principles are of considerable interest. There is little surprise in finding several prominent intellectuals of the neo-conservative movement – names such as Norman Podhoretz,

Francis Fukuyama, Eliot A. Cohen, and George Weigel. A former vice-president, though an undistinguished one – Dan Quayle – and a future vice-president – Richard Cheney were also there, as well as the brother of a future president – Jeb Bush, for whose support as governor in Florida in 2000, George W. Bush would come to owe a great debt. Some of the names were associated with funders: Stephen P. Rosen had been associate director of the John M. Olin Institute for Strategic Studies between 1990 and 1996. What is really striking is just how many of the signatories were either past members of Republican administrations or future members of the George W. Bush administration (and sometimes both), often in senior positions concerned in the making of security policy and foreign policy, names such as Elliott Abrams, Zalmay Khalilzad, I. Lewis 'Scooter' Libby, Donald Rumsfeld, and Paul Wolfowitz.

Almost the only significant absentee from this neo-conservative hall of fame – although he signed other PNAC statements – was Richard Perle, the so-called 'prince of darkness' or 'neo-conservative high priest', whose role in, and influence over, the George W. Bush administration may in any case have been exaggerated since he resigned from it in February 2004. Perle was Chairman of the Defense Policy Board between 2001 and 2003 and had served on it for 17 years under both Democrat and Republican administrations. In 1996, Perle had co-authored with Douglas Feith, David Wurmser, and Meyrav Wurmser a report for the incoming government of Benjamin Netanyahu in Israel which proposed, among other controversial measures, that 'removing Saddam Hussein from power in Iraq [was] an important Israeli strategic objective in its own right'.[39]

The most important output of PNAC was the report released in September 2000, before the US presidential elections in November, entitled *Rebuilding America's Defenses: Strategy, Forces and Resources for a New Century*.[40] Signed by Donald Kagan and Gary Schmitt as project co-chairmen, with Thomas Donnelly as principal author, the report established four 'core missions' for US forces: to defend the American homeland; to have the capacity to fight and decisively win multiple, simultaneous major theatre wars ('anything less than a clear two-war capacity threatens to devolve into a no-war strategy'); to perform the 'constabulary' duties associated with shaping the security environment in critical regions; and transform US forces to exploit the 'revolution in military affairs' to ensure the long-term superiority of US conventional forces. They dismissed the 1990s as a 'decade of defense neglect'. They considered that the 'need for a substantial American force presence in the Gulf transcends the issue of the regime of Saddam Hussein' since 'for decades' the United States had 'sought to play a more permanent role in Gulf regional security'. Nevertheless, the authors affirmed:

> The current American peace will be short-lived if the United States becomes vulnerable to rogue powers with small, inexpensive arsenals of ballistic missiles and nuclear warheads or other weapons of mass destruction. We cannot allow North Korea, Iran, Iraq or similar states to undermine American leadership, intimidate American allies or threaten the American homeland itself. The blessings of the American peace, purchased at fearful cost and a century of effort [*sic*], should not be so trivially squandered.

Whether or not the authors had checked their historical facts (there was no *permanent* US commitment abroad before 1942, so the effort was one of less than sixty years' duration continuously, or sixty years in total if the intervention in Europe in 1917–18 is included because of its scale), the allusion to 'rogue powers' was sufficient to indicate the intentions of the PNAC leadership. In this respect, *Rebuilding America's Defenses* has to be read in conjunction with the two PNAC letters of 1998 calling for regime change in Iraq ('that now needs to become the aim of American foreign policy', PNAC had informed President Clinton in January 1998).[41]

The PNAC/AEI lobby anticipated that the election of George W. Bush would bring them to the pinnacle of influence and their hopes were not disappointed. Yet few of them could have anticipated the enormous opportunity with which they were presented by the events of 9/11. William Kristol, interviewed in January 2003, contended that the basic elements of 'all foreign policy doctrines, or governing agendas ... are always around beforehand. Very few people come into government and invent something out of whole cloth. I think we at *The Weekly Standard* and the Project for the New American Century – and many other people, Wolfowitz way back in 1992 – had articulated ... parts of what later became the Bush Doctrine [of 2002]: the focus on regime change, the focus on democracy promotion, possibly the pre-emption, in this new post-Cold War world, of the proliferation of weapons of mass destruction.' Even so, Kristol confessed that he had been 'amazed by the speed and decisiveness with which the Bush administration, post-9/11, moved to pull these different arguments together and to construct arguments into a pretty coherent document' – that is, *NSS-2002, The National Security Strategy of the United States of America*, issued in September 2002. The Bush administration's view, as stated in the strategy paper, is that 'military pre-emption' is legitimate when the threat is 'emerging' or 'sufficient', 'even if uncertainty remains as to the time and place of the enemy's attack'.

The American Enterprise Institute had in its wings an adjunct fellow, Laurie Mylroie ('the neo-cons' favourite conspiracy theorist'),[42] to provide the arguments needed to bolster the case for a preventive war against Iraq on the grounds that al-Qaeda was 'a front for Iraqi intelligence'. Two days after 9/11, she argued in the *Wall Street Journal* that 'whether Osama bin Laden was involved ... remains to be seen. Yet if that proves to be so, it is extremely unlikely that he acted on his own. It is far more likely that he operated in conjunction with a state – the state with which the US remains at war, namely Iraq.'[43] She subsequently published *Bush vs the Beltway* in 2003, which was promoted by Danielle Pletka and Richard Perle at the AEI, and attacked the CIA and other federal agencies for failing to demonstrate a connection between al-Qaeda and Iraq. At the time, she was far from alone in her contentions, although all aspects of the Iraq conspiracy theory have been found to be unsubstantiated.[44]

Within nine days of the attack on 9/11, PNAC had drafted and obtained signatories for its first letter to the president on the war on terrorism, which included expanding the war beyond Afghanistan to Iraq, regardless of whether Saddam's complicity in the events of 9/11 could be proved. The 'failure to undertake such an effort will constitute an early and perhaps decisive surrender in the war on international terrorism,' the signatories claimed. 'The United States must therefore provide full military and financial support to the Iraqi opposition. American military force should be used to provide a "safe zone" in Iraq from which the opposition can operate. And American forces must be prepared to back up our commitment to the Iraqi opposition by all necessary means.'[45]

The first aim was to reverse the 'paper tiger' image of America portrayed by bin Laden. This would be done in Afghanistan, which would be hit very hard: 'daisy-cutter bombs, B-52s and American soldiers in Afghanistan have certainly helped change Middle Eastern views. The Bush administration has demonstrated a tenacity toward al-Qaeda and the Taliban that bin Laden and Mullah Omar probably didn't expect.' 'Winning the war in Afghanistan will not do it alone. Nor will a war against al-Qaeda's networks elsewhere,' Reuel Marc Gerecht pointed out in the *Wall Street Journal* on 19 December 2001. 'Only a war against Saddam Hussein will decisively restore the awe that protects American interests abroad and citizens at home. We've been running from this fight for 10 years. In the Middle East, everybody knows it. We're the only ones deluding ourselves.'[46]

A second, equally significant, aim was to identify on a permanent basis in the minds of the Bush administration the struggle of the United States against 'terror' with the long-standing Israeli struggle against its Arab enemies, especially the Palestinians. This was the purpose of the PNAC letter sent to George W. Bush on 3 April 2002, which thanked the president for his 'courageous leadership in the war on terrorism' and commended him for his support of Israel, 'a fellow victim of terrorist violence'.

Israel, the signatories of the letter proclaimed, 'is fighting the same war' against the 'Axis of Evil'. It was, though, a different Axis of Evil from that identified by Bush: Israel's enemies, Iran, Iraq, and Syria were named, rather than Iran, Iraq, and North Korea which had been identified by Bush in his speech on 29 January – an example of PNAC's sleight of hand. (It was only subsequently, on 6 May 2002, that Under-Secretary of State John R. Bolton gave a speech entitled 'Beyond the Axis of Evil' in which three more states – Libya, Syria, and Cuba – were named along with the other three 'rogue states'.)

The PNAC letter argued that the Israeli government should no more be pressurized into negotiating with Yasser Arafat than the US into accepting negotiations with Osama bin Laden or Mullah Omar. It was declared 'common knowledge' that Saddam, along with Iran, was a funder and supporter of terrorism against Israel. 'Iraq has harboured terrorists such as Abu Nidal in the past, and it maintains links to the al-Qaeda network.' 'The surest path to peace in the Middle East', it was contended, 'lies not through the appeasement of Saddam and other local tyrants, but through a renewed commitment on our part, as you suggested in your State of the Union address, to the birth of freedom and democratic government in the Islamic world.'[47]

Not surprisingly, a number of Jewish intellectuals and political activists – including William Kristol, Elliot Cohen, Midge Decter, Martin Peretz, Richard Perle, Daniel Pipes, and Norman Podhoretz – signed this PINAC letter, though they were not the only signatories. In his study on *The Neo-conservative Revolution: Jewish Intellectuals and the Shaping of Public Policy* (2005), the American Jewish historian Murray Friedman (1926–2005) confirms the distinctively Jewish contribution towards the neo-conservative movement. The PNAC letter of 3 April 2002 was perhaps the clearest moment when the neo-conservatives projected the arguments for US policy being aligned with Israel's, and for not pressurizing the Israeli government into making concessions for the sake of a peace agreement with the Palestinians.

The signatories were significantly different, and more representative of neo-conservative thinking as a whole, in the two PNAC letters of 19 March and 28 March 2003 on post-war Iraq. In the first, the removal of the Iraqi regime was said to create the opportunity for achieving three vital goals: 'disarming Iraq of all its weapons of mass destruction stocks and production capabilities; establishing a peaceful, stable, democratic government in Iraq; and contributing to the democratic development of the wider Middle East'. 'Any early fixation on exit strategies and departure deadlines' was considered likely to 'undercut American credibility and greatly diminish the prospects for success'. As soon as the security situation permitted, authority should be transferred 'to civilian agencies, and to representatives of the Iraqi people themselves'. Much of the long-term security presence, as well as the resources for reconstruction, would have to come from 'our allies in Europe and elsewhere – suggesting the importance of involving the NATO Alliance and other international institutions early in any planning and implementation of the post-conflict stage'. Clearly the PNAC signatories had not appreciated the depth of international opposition to the US–UK pre-emptive strike against Iraq.

The second letter was written in support of Tony Blair's attempt to 'get America and Europe working again together as partners and not as rivals' and argued that, 'given NATO's capabilities and expertise, it should become [integrated] as soon as possible in the post-war effort'. The Atlantic Alliance had already pledged to confront the new threats of the twenty-first century. In the view of the signatories, 'no current challenge is more important than that of building a peaceful, unified and democratic Iraq without weapons of mass destruction on NATO's own borders.'[48] This wish was not to be fulfilled, though in 2004, in response to a request of the Iraqi Interim Government, NATO agreed to help Iraq provide for its own security by training Iraqi military personnel, supporting the development of the country's security institutions, and co-ordinating the delivery of equipment.[49]

## *End of the Neo-Con Dream?*[50] *The Limited 'Surge' and Outsourcing of the Iraq Campaign*

By January 2003, the increased commitments posed by the likely intervention in Iraq had made it clear to the PNAC neo-conservatives that one of the pre-requisites of *Rebuilding America's Defenses* for the new American century was not being fulfilled: a sustained increase in expenditure on the military as a proportion of GDP.[51]

> By every measure, current defence spending is inadequate for a military with global responsibilities. Ten years ago, America's defence burden was 4.8 per cent of GDP. Although the decline in defence spending has been halted, we have not done nearly enough to make up for this decade of neglect. The modest increase planned for next year will still leave Pentagon spending at about 3.4 per cent of GDP, and Congressional Budget Office projections are that the proportion will decline to approximately 3 per cent by 2007. Inadequate funding results in an inadequate force. Today's military is simply too small for the missions it must perform.

Recognizing the increased pressures on the military resulting from the insurgency in Iraq, PNAC returned to the theme in January 2005. 'We can afford the military we need. As a nation, we are spending a smaller percentage of our GDP on the military than at any time during the Cold War', a letter drafted to the Congress proclaimed. 'It is our judgment that we should aim for an increase in the active duty Army and Marine Corps, together, of at least 25,000 troops each year over the next several years.' 'Our national security, global peace and stability, and the defense and promotion of freedom in the post-9/11 world require a larger military force than we have today.'[52]

The neo-conservative lobby has faced two ways on the size of the intervention force required for the Iraq war. The initial, 'gut' reaction was to go with Rumsfeld's view that what was needed was a relatively small, mobile army. According to Danielle Pletka of AEI, writing in September 2003, the demand for more American troops 'rests on a false premise – that the additional troops would be used to battle resurgent Ba'athists and patch over the gaps in security that exist throughout Iraq'. Instead, she contended, 'more Americans will end up doing jobs they ought to hand off, like guarding electrical lines and schools, policing neighbourhoods and directing traffic in downtown Baghdad.' 'Making the transition to an Iraqi security force', Pletka pronounced, 'is an imperative for the liberation of the country.'[53] As the military position deteriorated, support for Rumsfeld's 'less is better' approach collapsed in the AEI. Frederick W. Kagan published an article in *Foreign Affairs* on the 'crisis' in American military manpower in July 2006,[54] and after Rumsfeld's resignation following the sweeping Democratic gains in the mid-term elections, denounced his period in office: 'the problem with Rumsfeld was not his flawed managerial style, but his flawed understanding of war ... his stubbornness has destroyed the ground forces. The Army and Marines have worn out their equipment and their troops ... Rumsfeld leaves behind him a military far weaker and less capable than the one he took charge of in 2001.'[55] Though the neo-conservatives advocated privatization in other areas – even with regard to the CIA[56] – they do not seem to have advocated (or even perceived until relatively late on) the rapid 'outsourcing' of the war in Iraq that took place under Rumsfeld, a process which made it quite different from previous conflicts in which the United States was involved. In its commitment to outsourcing the war if in no other area, the Bush administration appears to have *exceeded* the neo-conservative agenda (see Chapter 9).

Between 1994 and 2005, 66 grants to a value of almost $3.6 million were made by conservative funding bodies – the Lynde and Harry Bradley Foundation, the John M. Olin Foundation, the Sarah Scaife Foundation, and the Scaife Family Foundations – to the New Citizenship Project, Inc., the sponsor of the Project for the New American Century.[57] Then quite suddenly, with increasing criticism of Donald Rumsfeld and other figures in the Bush administration for incompetence in their handling of the Iraq intervention, the PNAC project ended with a whimper[58] and was merged with the general neo-conservative agenda of the American Enterprise Institute.

In testimony given to the House Committee on Armed Services on 7 April 2005, Richard Perle drew four broad lessons from Iraq: the need to align political and military objectives; the need for support from a significant segment of the local population (missing in Iraq, but not in Afghanistan where the Americans enabled a Northern Alliance victory, which itself was problematic); the inadequacy of American intelligence on matters such as the state of the Iraqi infrastructure; and finally, the need to avoid becoming an occupying power: 'the image on Iraqi television of an American pro-consul informing the Iraqi people of the rules we made for them and the arrangement of their lives for which we assumed responsibility, contributed significantly to the difficulties we have had in Iraq.'[59] This was not necessarily the consensus, since Perle is notoriously his own man. In a startling break with the official White House and Downing Street lines on the legality of the Iraq war, he told an audience in London in November 2003: 'I think in this case international law stood in the way of doing the right thing'; 'international law ... would have required us to leave Saddam Hussein alone,' and this would have been morally unacceptable.[60]

When the criticism of US policy in Iraq seemed to have reached its apogee with the publication of the report of the Iraq Study Group, and the policy had been repudiated by American voters in the mid-term elections of 2006, the Bush administration once more turned to the familiar narrow coterie of advisers for the idea of a 'limited surge', the short-term addition of a further 21,500 US troops in Iraq. In spite of some earlier comments in respectable academic journals such as *Foreign Affairs*,[61] the chief propagandist for the 'surge' was none other than Frederick W. Kagan, the brother of Robert Kagan, whose writings had helped set the Bush administration on the path towards 'benevolent hegemony'.

Frederick W. Kagan is a resident scholar at the American Enterprise Institute, and a former professor of military history at the US Military Academy at West Point. He authored the so-called 'real Iraq Study Group' report as the AEI's 'hawkish' rival to the ISG report of James Baker and Lee H. Hamilton in December 2006. The AEI report, entitled *Choosing Victory: A Plan for Success in Iraq*, was released on 5 January 2007, after which Kagan is said to have convinced President Bush, strongly influencing his subsequent 'surge' plan for changing the course of the Iraq war.[62] Nothing seems to have been learned by an administration which seeks to confront an 'evil ideology' of militant Islamism and yet is itself in tutelage to another ideology, that of neo-conservatism, which has resulted in untold devastation in Afghanistan and Iraq and a loss in confidence in the legitimacy of American foreign policy.[63] At a time when the consensus of sixteen US intelligence agencies was that the Iraq war in effect could no longer be 'won',[64] Robert Kagan was still asking in February 2007 'what better cause is there today, at the beginning of this new century of danger and challenge, than support for victory in a just war? The consequences of defeat would be ghastly. The prospect of victory is difficult but real.'[65] In September, Kagan pronounced that 'American and Iraqi successes in pursuing our joint and individual vital interests over the past nine months have been nothing short of staggering'; the achievements of the 'surge' were 'incredible' and in many cases 'unexpected'.[66]

### *If the Policy Fails, Blame Another 'Enemy': Iran*

Another group was furiously at work in January and February 2007, seeking to promote a US surgical strike against Iran's nuclear facilities, advocating regime change, and threatening a new rift with Europe.[67] Richard Perle had famously advocated invading Iraq with as few as 40,000 troops, in expectation of the support of native Kurdish and Shi'ite rebels on the model of the US deal with the Northern Alliance in Afghanistan. However, the situation was not comparable: the Northern Alliance had not been abandoned by the US, as had the Kurds and Shi'ites, in 1991. Speaking as a senior fellow at the American Enterprise Institute in January 2007, Perle expressed his confidence that President Bush 'would order the necessary military action' against Iran.[68]

In July the previous year Perle had asked why the Bush administration was not supporting Iranian dissidents, especially the student leadership under Amir Abbas Fakhravar, in their struggle for regime change.[69] In January 2007, Fakhravar was playing the role of Ahmed Chalabi in the run-up to the intervention in Iraq: 'when the United States strikes Iran,' Fakhravar stated, 'the ruling mullahs will run.' He believed that Iranian leaders would demonstrate less resistance than did the Saddam Hussein regime in neighbouring Iraq. 'They don't know how to fight,' Fakhravar said. 'When they feel a true threat, they escape. Look at the Shi'ite mullahs in Iraq during Saddam's regime. None of them fought.' He claimed to have 12,000 students in his opposition movement;[70] but what use would they be in any conflict with the

Iranian Revolutionary Guards? And what of the fanatical resistance to the Iraqi invasion displayed by Iran in the war of 1980–8? Bernard Lewis never mentioned it in his interview to the *Jerusalem Post* on 29 January. On the contrary, 'all the evidence is that the regime is extremely unpopular with their own people,' he said. 'I am told that the Israeli daily [radio] program in Persian is widely listened to all over Iran with rapt attention.' The objection was not so much to Iran having nuclear weapons 'but to the regime that governs Iran having' them, Lewis asserted.[71]

More realistic, and chastened, commentators such as Francis Fukuyama argued instead that 'an air campaign is much more likely to build support for the regime than to topple it, and will stimulate terrorism and attacks on US facilities and friends around the globe. The US would be even more isolated in such a war than during the Iraq campaign,' Fukuyama concluded, 'with only Israel as a certain ally.'[72] Indeed, Israel was reported in late February 2007 to be pressing the US to let it go ahead alone with air strikes against Iran if the Americans would not take the lead.[73] Ali Ansari added that it was the 'very international crisis that may serve to save Ahmadinejad's presidency, a reality that the president undoubtedly understood all too well. As domestic difficulties mount, the emerging international crisis could at best serve as a rallying point, or at worst persuade Iran's elite that a change of guard would convey weakness to the outside world.'[74] As the *New York Times* put it, 'the response from Congressional and other critics' spoke 'volumes about the current state of American credibility, four years after the intelligence controversy leading up to the Iraq war'. The Bush administration suffered from its previous lack of transparency when dealing with intelligence reports.[75]

In June 2007, after more than two years of appeals from Israel, the Bush administration appeared to place its plans to attack Iran on hold. 'The United States has decided that Iran's cooperation was needed for a withdrawal from Iraq,' an administration source said. 'There won't be a situation where there will be cooperation and then war with Iran.' The subtext of the announcement was a twofold one. Israel would not be allowed to undertake what the US itself had decided not to do; and the administration accepted intelligence assessments that air strikes were unlikely to destroy all or even most of Iran's alleged nuclear facilities. It seemed a clear rebuff for Richard Perle, the so-called Iranian 'opposition' – in spite of talks about unity in Paris the same month – and the American Enterprise Institute lobby. Troop withdrawals from Iraq, excluding those needed for the new American bases, were to be achieved by December 2008, and Iran could not be antagonized to the extent that it would have an interest in preventing this timetable from being fulfilled.

Yet a setback for the AEI is not necessarily what it seems, since the multi-faceted neo-conservative network has a proven capacity to regroup and launch a new strike. While Frederick W. Kagan and the Iraq Planning Group at AEI were busy challenging the Center for a New American Security (CNAS) report published in June 2007 with their own riposte entitled *No Middle Way: the Challenge of Exit Strategies from Iraq*,[76] the *Weekly Standard* obligingly published a 30-page report by Kimberly Kagan, his wife and director of an entity called the Institute for the Study of War, entitled 'Iran's Proxy War Against the United States and the Iraqi Government'.[77] The report seemed intended to back up a series of assertions by the President in his American Legion speech in Reno on 28 August 2007 about alleged Iranian support for, and arming of, 'Shia extremists'.[78] The coincidence of the speech and the report suggests a degree of co-ordination between the White House and the *Weekly Standard* since, if the report had been officially sanctioned, it would normally have been released by either the State Department or the Pentagon.

Kimberly Kagan's conclusions imply that diplomatic engagement with Iran is counter-productive: '... negotiations with Iran, including the establishment of a tripartite sub-ambassadorial level coordinating committee on security in Iraq, have coincided with a significant increase in Iranian support for violence in Iraq,' she asserts.

> The Coalition has stepped up its efforts to combat Iranian intervention in Iraq in recent months both because the Iranians have increased their support for violence in Iraq since the start of the surge and because Coalition successes against al-Qaeda in Iraq and the larger Sunni insurgency have permitted the re-allocation of resources and effort against a problem that has plagued attempts to establish a stable government in Iraq from the outset. With those problems increasingly under control, Iranian intervention is the next major problem the Coalition must tackle.

The top US commander in Iraq, General David Petraeus, confirmed in September 2007 that he had hard evidence of Iranian involvement in attacks on US soldiers and accused Iran of fighting a 'proxy war' in Iraq through the covert operations unit of its elite Revolutionary Guards. Iran vehemently denied the accusation, but the temperature was raised considerably when the supreme leader, Ayatollah Ali Khamenei, stated in a sermon on Friday 14 September at the beginning of Ramadan that George W. Bush and his advisers should be prosecuted in an impartial 'international court for the atrocities committed in Iraq'. 'They have to be held accountable,' he added. The United States could not 'ignore its responsibility' for the devastation caused by the war.[79] Not until late December 2007 was it categorically admitted by the American authorities that Iran had moved 'at the most senior levels' to restrain the operation of Shi'ite militas in Iraq.[80]

The former US ambassador to the United Nations as well as adviser to the presidential campaigns of John Kerry in 2004 and Hillary Clinton in 2008, Richard C. Holbrooke, spoke in Toronto in November 2007 about the prospects of war with Iran. He called Iran the most pressing problem for the United States and the 'most dangerous country in the region'. He accused the president of Iran of being 'the world's most virulent anti-Semite' and a 'Holocaust denier', and he cited the Iranian Revolution as a central cause for the rise of fundamentalist Islam in the region. He further accused the Iranian government of fomenting terror worldwide and of providing IEDs (improvised explosive devices) 'that are killing Americans in Iraq'. Yet notwithstanding these considerations, Holbrooke – the only person to have been Assistant Secretary of State for two different regions of the world (Asia and Europe) and thus well placed to become Secretary of State if Hillary Clinton is elected in 2008 ('Hillary Clinton is a classic national-security Democrat,' he says)[81] – chose to downplay the prospects of 'the Bush Administration' bombing Iran. The nuclear installations are dispersed and built deep underground and so would not be sufficiently damaged to be put out of commission this way; much of the US military is diametrically – even vehemently – opposed to embarking on a third 'adventure' when the first two are far from over; such an attack might well serve to unite the people of Iran behind Ahmadinejad and thereby make the nation of Iran even more of a 'destabilizing force in the region'; finally the US would further isolate itself from the international community, since none of its allies would support such an attack.[82]

What Holbrooke did not admit to is that Russia's support of Iran is a further powerful disincentive to the United States. (Fear of a 'grand bargain' between the United States and Iran sent even Saudi Arabia's Prince Sultan bin Abdul Aziz to Moscow to buy Russian weapons for the first time in its history.)[83] Nor did Holbrooke declare such a unilateral strike against Iran as in any way illegal – the Bush Doctrine, therefore, in essence, seems to be accepted by the triumvirate advising Hillary Clinton on foreign policy matters (Holbrooke, Madeleine Albright, and Sandy Berger, President Clinton's national security adviser from 1997 to 2001). Holbrooke's views were also diametrically opposed to those of Zbigniew Brzezinski, Jimmy Carter's national security adviser, for whom – contrary to the image projected by its ruling mullahs – 'Iran stands the best chance, of all the countries in the region, of embarking on the path traced earlier by Turkey'. Iran, in his view, could 'be on the way toward successful modernization and democratization'. The future relationship between the United States and Iran, in Brzezinski's view, 'should not be addressed in a manner reminiscent of the earlier US exaggerations of the alleged Iraqi WMD threat'.[84] 'The method to [the madness of] all the mad threats of war coming out of the White House', Frank Rich suggests, may well 'be less to intimidate Iranians than to frighten Americans. Fear, the only remaining card this administration still knows how to play, may once more give a seemingly spent GOP a crack at the White House in 2008 ...' George W. Bush 'has nothing to lose by once again using the spectre of war to pillory the Democrats as soft on national security. The question for the Democrats is whether they'll walk once more into this trap.'[85]

Well-informed commentators on Iran's nuclear programme conclude that a military strike by the United States is 'not an option'. Destroying the facilities without the equipment and materials present 'would not set back the enrichment part of the program significantly'. Moreover, 'rather than possibly delaying or making it impossible for Tehran to carry out a final decision to make nuclear weapons, an attack might force the Iranian leadership's hand. Iran would almost certainly ... accelerate any weaponization efforts, launching a Manhattan Project-style undertaking in defence of the homeland.' The result would be 'a long, costly war against Iran'.[86] Bruce Riedel comments that the implications of the 6 September 2007 Israeli attack on a nuclear facility in Syria serves notice that 'Israel will use force to prevent the creation of a second nuclear weapons state in the Middle East ... it is prepared to fight a war to stop Iran from crossing the nuclear threshold.'[87]

Sixteen US intelligence agencies pooled their expertise to produce a national intelligence estimate (NIE) on Iran's nuclear intentions and capabilities in November 2007 (published on 3 December) which, surprisingly, provided a clear statement that Iran had halted its programme in 2003 'primarily in response to international pressure' and was unlikely to be technically capable of producing and reprocessing sufficient plutonium for a weapon before 'about 2015'. Hardliners such as Daniel Pipes argued nevertheless that the NIE made war against Iran more, not less likely: 'thus have short-sighted, small-minded, blatantly partisan intelligence bureaucrats, trying to hide unpleasant realities, helped engineer their own nightmare.'[88] 'The NIE is internally contradictory and insufficiently supported,' claimed John Bolton, formerly US ambassador to the United Nations, who called it 'politics disguised as intelligence'. 'National Intelligence Estimates contain the coordinated judgements of the Intelligence Community regarding the likely course of future events and the implications for US policy,' stated Donald Kerr, Deputy Director of National Intelligence, on 8 December in response to critics such as Bolton. 'The task of the Intelligence Community is to produce objective, ground truth analysis. We feel confident in our analytic tradecraft and resulting analysis in this estimate.' In a deeply polarized US political establishment on the eve of an election year, there was no agreement that a NIE on Iran could be 'objective'.[89]

### *If the Policy Fails, Blame an Ally: Pakistan*

In September 2007, William Kristol told Fox News the neo-cons wanted military action taken against Pakistan 'over the next few weeks or months …' President Bush had to disrupt the alleged sanctuary for al-Qaeda and the Taliban in the tribal regions (Federally Administered Tribal Areas or FATA) of Pakistan. In fact, according to Kristol, 'we won't even tell Musharraf … We'll do what we have to do in Western Pakistan and Musharraf can say, "Hey, they didn't tell me."'[90] He had earlier written in the *Washington Post*:[91]

> Western Pakistan, where President Pervez Musharraf's deals with the Taliban are apparently creating something like havens for terrorists, is an increasing problem. That's why our intelligence agencies are worried about a resurgent al-Qaeda – because al-Qaeda may once again have a place where it can plan, organize and train. These Waziristan havens may well have to be dealt with in the near future. I assume Bush will deal with them, using some combination of air strikes and special operations.

William Kristol displays his lack of historical consciousness by such remarks. In the aftermath of the attacks against the World Trade Center and the Pentagon, the Deputy Secretary of State (and former PNAC signatory) Richard Armitage allegedly threatened – according to Pakistan's President, Pervez Musharraf – to 'bomb Pakistan into the stone age'[92] if it did not join the 'coalition of the willing'. This specific threat has been denied by Richard Armitage but the Pakistan ambassador to the US (and subsequently the UK), Dr Maleeha Lodhi, confirms that he stated 'we're asking people whether they're with us or against us.'[93] Whether acting under coercion or not, there can be no doubt that Pakistan immediately withdrew its support from the Taliban regime in Afghanistan after 9/11, and has been an active ally of the United States since then. Pakistan has lost more troops in combat than any other ally of the United States in the 'war on terror'. Notwithstanding these facts, the *Washington Post* adopted the neo-conservative viewpoint on 29 August 2007, asserting that 'while professing commitment to the war against terrorism, Mr Musharraf has allowed al-Qaeda and the Taliban to re-establish themselves in Pakistan's unruly tribal areas bordering Afghanistan. He has been an unfaithful and at times meretricious ally of the United States, even while accepting some $10 billion in American aid.'[94]

Rarely has the neo-conservative lobby received such a well-informed and cogent riposte as it did on this occasion, in General Anthony Zinni's response to this editorial. Zinni was in a position to know the reality, both as a former commander of US Central Command (CENTCOM) and one who, in his retirement from the military, had recently visited Pakistan and met Musharraf. His article demonstrated both the ill-informed nature of the neo-conservative analysis and also the danger to longer-term US interests posed by sudden shifts in policy at the behest of the neo-cons:[95]

> [after 9/11] the United States was fortunate to have a leader in Pakistan who was willing to take on the fight against terrorism. We may criticize some of his undemocratic governing decisions and his failure to prevent al-Qaeda's leadership from gaining a foothold in the volatile border area with Afghanistan. But we should acknowledge the price the Pakistani military has paid in this battle and recognize the political courage it took for Musharraf to wage it at all, despite its unpopularity with the many Pakistanis who think that the fight against terrorism is not their struggle and despite the vast array of political, social and security problems his government faces ...
>
> Allies are supposed to be partners, not paragons. We will find ourselves in trouble if we insist that our allies do everything we ask, measure up totally to our concepts of how their societies should function and make no demands of us ... Careless, irresponsible statements can damage fragile alliances and erode cooperation and trust ... Unless we do better, we will continue to lose allies as a result of reckless, alienating comments that amount to short-term domestic political posturing and hurt US security interests in the long run.

Bin Laden's call to Pakistanis to rise up in *jihad* against the 'infidel' Musharraf on 20 September 2007 because of his support for the war on terror and his crushing of the Islamist rebellion at the Red Mosque in Islamabad served to reinforce General Zinni's arguments.[96]

Subsequently, the waters have been muddied considerably by the return of former prime ministers Benazir Bhutto and Nawaz Sharif (under very different circumstances), the imposition of a state of emergency, the calling of parliamentary elections for 8 January 2008, and Musharraf's resignation from the army and assumption of a civilian presidency. Frederick W. Kagan, resident scholar at AEI and the author of the 'limited surge' strategy in Iraq, and Michael O'Hanlon of the Brookings Institution posted a summary of an earlier paper in the *New York Times* in November 2007, entitled 'Pakistan's Collapse, Our Problem'. When summarized by the foreign press, this 'thinking aloud' paper sounded more extreme than was probably intended: 'Bush handed blueprint to seize Pakistan's nuclear arsenal.'[97]

'As the government of Pakistan totters', Kagan and O'Hanlon wrote that

> one possible plan would be a Special Forces operation with the limited goal of preventing Pakistan's nuclear materials and warheads from getting into the wrong hands. Given the degree to which Pakistani nationalists cherish these assets, it is unlikely the United States would get permission to destroy them. Somehow, American forces would have to team [up] with Pakistanis to secure critical sites and possibly to move the material to a safer place.
>
> For the United States, the safest bet would be shipping the material to someplace like New Mexico; but even pro-American Pakistanis would be unlikely to cooperate. More likely, we would have to settle for establishing a remote redoubt within Pakistan, with the nuclear technology guarded by elite Pakistani forces backed up (and watched over) by crack international troops. It is realistic to think that such a mission might be undertaken within days of a decision to act. The price for rapid action and secrecy, however, would probably be a very small international coalition.

Kagan is an advocate of the Bush administration spending 'whatever it takes on the war on terror'. He argues that 'victory in Iraq and Afghanistan is vital to US national security', and that America must spend whatever is necessary in both countries. The $190 billion requested for fiscal year 2008 is still less than 1.5 per cent of GDP, 'a small burden given the enormity of the stakes'. Though ceding either Iraq or Afghanistan would be 'a tragic mistake', if a choice is to be made, the preference must be for retaining Iraq. 'Iraq is a potentially wealthy country in the heart of the Middle East; Afghanistan is an isolated land with few resources and central to nothing. Al-Qaeda would happily trade Afghanistan for Iraq – indeed, it has done so, funnelling its own resources into Iraq to fight us where we are strongest.' Frederick Kagan admits that trying to use 'American forces to defeat al-Qaeda in Pakistan would be extremely difficult and dangerous'.[98] The implication is that the untried Musharraf-Kyani-civilian prime ministerial regime has to be supported at all costs in its counter-insurgency efforts against the neo-Taliban and those al-Qaeda elements that have joined the movement in the tribal areas. The assassination of Benazir Bhutto on 27 December 2007 threw the entire Pakistan election process – and with it, US foreign policy objectives in Pakistan – into chaos.

India's former external affairs minister, Jaswant Singh, did not hesitate to call US policy towards Pakistan and Afghanistan 'disastrous'. '[The] US has absolutely no options left in Pakistan, but to continue to support the regime of President Musharraf', he concluded. '[The] verbal statements [the] US makes on democracy … have failed to carry conviction', Singh claimed. The statement of the former Indian minister was akin to the sweeping headline in *The Economist* (3 January 2008), which called Pakistan 'the world's most dangerous place'. The disparaging subtitle in the article was that 'nothing else has worked: it is time for Pakistan to try democracy'. The reality is that elections had to be rescheduled because of the chaos in certain areas after Benazir Bhutto's assassination, but were still to be held on 18 February in the presence of an enlarged number of more than 200 election monitors from the European Union to ensure that they were 'free, fair, and secure'. As Musharraf told a news conference in Brussels on 21 January, the West's obsession with its version of democracy and human rights made no allowances for the special problems of a country such as Pakistan, which was seeking simultaneously to return to democracy while confronting a Taliban-led insurgency. He rebuffed the Bush administration's proposals to expand any American combat presence in Pakistan, either through unilateral covert CIA missions or by joint operations with Pakistani security forces. Musharraf was willing to accept training, equipment, and technical help but insisted that Americans should not become involved in ground operations. As for international fears about the safety of Pakistan's nuclear weapons, Lieutenant-General Kidwai, director-general of the Strategic Planning Division, gave a presentation to foreign media on 26 January seeking to demonstrate that the command and control structures and the security presence of 10,000 troops around Pakistan's nuclear facilities were 'capable of thwarting all types of threat ..., whether insider, outsider, or a combination' of the two. 'There is no conceivable scenario, political or violent, in which Pakistan will fall to the extremists of the al-Qaeda or Taliban type', Kidwai stated. 'The fears [expressed abroad] are based on a lack of objective understanding of Pakistan's ground situation and [a] lack of information.' In spite of the simplistic neo-conservative lobbying for a US strike, the ground realities in Pakistan remained intractable, with direct US intervention in Pakistan likely to prove counter-productive as well as extremely dangerous.[99]

# Chapter Eight
# 'Making the World Safer and Better'? Iraq and the Moral Arguments Concerning Preventive War

> If a war is initiated when the threat is not imminent and grave, but rather undertaken against a possible future threat, then the war is preventive and hence unjust.
>
> (Neta C. Crawford)[1]

> Suppose the Security Council were to adopt a resolution recognizing that the following set of conditions would constitute a threat to the peace sufficient to justify the use of force: (1) possession of weapons of mass destruction or clear and convincing evidence of attempts to gain such weapons; (2) grave and systematic human rights abuses sufficient to demonstrate the absence of any internal constraints on government behaviour; and (3) evidence of aggressive intent with regard to other nations. This cluster sets a very high threshold for the use of force ...
>
> (Anne-Marie Slaughter, 13 April 2003)[2]

'We will not hesitate to act alone, if necessary, to exercise our right of self-defense by acting pre-emptively against such terrorists ...', George W. Bush pronounced in his address at the National Cathedral on 14 September 2001 just three days after the terrorist atrocities of 9/11. 'We will also wage a war of ideas to win the battle against international terrorism,' adding that this meant 'supporting moderate and modern government, especially in the Muslim world, to ensure that the conditions and ideologies that promote terrorism do not find fertile ground in any nation ...'[3] He returned to the theme of terrorism in ten subsequent radio addresses between 15 September and 24 November.[4] In an address at West Point in June 2002, Bush reaffirmed and extended the principles of the 'Wolfowitz Doctrine' of 1992 (Chapter 7) in what has come to be known as the 'Bush Doctrine':[5]

> the United States has long maintained the option of pre-emptive actions to counter a sufficient threat to our national security. The greater the threat, the greater is the risk of inaction – and the more compelling the case for taking anticipatory action to defend ourselves, even if uncertainty remains as to the time and place of the enemy's attack. To forestall or prevent such hostile acts by our adversaries, the United States will, if necessary, act pre-emptively.

'The US national security strategy', Bush affirmed at West Point, 'will be based on a distinctly American internationalism that reflects the union of our values and our national interests. The aim of this strategy is to help make the world not just safer but better.'[6] *The National Security Strategy of the United States of America* published on 17 September 2002 *(NSS-2002)*[7] represented the viewpoint championed by Vice-President Dick Cheney, Secretary of Defence Donald Rumsfeld and a number of influential Department of Defense policy-makers such as Paul Wolfowitz and Richard Perle. Whereas in the past pre-emptive actions have been justified on the basis that the threat was imminent, the Bush administration argued in the strategy paper – repeating the wording of the President's speech at West Point – that 'military pre-emption' is legitimate when the threat is 'emerging' or 'sufficient', even if the timing is unclear.

The difference between pre-emption and prevention in warfare is deliberately obfuscated in *NSS-2002*. 'Pre-emptive military action', Neta C. Crawford suggests, 'is undertaken to eliminate an immediate and credible threat of grievous harm'; in contrast, a preventive war is undertaken 'when a state believes that war with a potential adversary is possible or likely at some future date ... the threat is not imminent or even certain to materialize in the near future.' Though Condoleezza Rice, among others, has argued that 'new technology requires new thinking about when a threat actually becomes "imminent",' there is much to suggest that *NSS-2002* was inappropriately labelled pre-emptive and that the strategy created in essence a doctrine justifying preventive war (and *ipso facto*, unjust war).[8]

### *Christian Just War Theory and its Application Prior to 2001*

Mark Evans has provided a useful 'representative statement' of Christian just war theory, divided into its three sections: prior to the outbreak of war (*jus ad bellum*), during the war itself (*jus in bello*), and at the end of the war in order to secure a just peace (*jus post bellum*).[9] In order to have the moral right to wage war, the cause must be just (*jus ad bellum*). The justice of the cause must be sufficiently great as to warrant warfare. There must be reasonable confidence in achieving the just objective without bringing about longer-term consequences which would be worse than leaving matters alone. The recourse to warfare must be genuinely in the last resort, all other peaceful alternatives having been exhausted. The moral standing of the primary actor waging the war must not have been compromised and the resort to war must be motivated by the just cause and not by some other hidden reason. The power waging the war must have the authority and legitimate competence to do so. In addition, the power declaring war must be prepared to account for its conduct of the war and its making of peace in accordance with *jus in bello* and *jus post bellum* principles.

The second stage of just war theory is fighting the war justly (*jus in bello*). Here the most important aspects are discrimination in the selection of targets (though in a supreme emergency this clause may be suspended); proportionality in the use of force; the just treatment of all non-combatants; and the observance of national and international laws governing the conduct of war which do not conflict with the theory's other requirements. The final stage of just war theory is to secure the justice sought through the recourse to war, by helping to make a just peace (*jus post bellum*); by taking full share of the material burdens of the conflict's aftermath; and by participating actively in the process of forgiveness and reconciliation that will create a just and stable peace.

To ensure that the peace is truly just, Patrick Hayden argues that 'financial restitution may be mandated, subject to proportionality and discrimination, and the reform and reconstruction of an aggressive, rights-violating regime may be permissible',[10] while Andrew Rigby suggests that to become truly durable, the peace settlement must pass tests such as inclusiveness, security, strengthening of the state, economic reconstruction, and socio-cultural repair work.[11] Clearly no peace can be truly worthy of that name that does not pass the supreme test, that of providing human security: human security, Mary Kaldor argues persuasively, cannot be found without there being a legitimate political authority. 'The wars in Iraq and Afghanistan have not created legitimate political authorities – they have speeded up the process of state failure, contributing to an environment in which various armed groups can operate.'[12]

After 9/11, what should have been the 'just conduct of war against radical Islamic terror and insurgencies'?[13] The terrorists are not bound by Western just war considerations of proportionality and discrimination. 'How many innocent people, elderly men and children have been killed and displaced under the al-Qaeda banner?', asked a former Saudi dissident of bin Laden in September 2007. 'Would you be happy to meet God carrying the burden (of their death) on your shoulders?'[14] The apparent answer would be 'yes'. 'What good is it if you destroy one of your enemy's buildings, and he destroys one of your countries?', asks Sayyed Imam al-Sharif, an important figure in the global *jihad* movement, who calls in his *Document of Right Guidance for Jihad Activity in Egypt and the World* for a stop to *jihad* activities in the West. 'What good is it if you kill one of his people, and he kills a thousand of your people? ... That, in short, is my evaluation of 9/11.' Bin Laden and al-Zawahiri should be put on trial for their crimes, if necessary *in absentia*, he concludes.[15]

As Terrence K. Kelly argues, if the Huntington prediction of a clash of civilizations is to be avoided, it is necessary to win the hearts and minds of Muslims who do not agree with the position of the violent extremists. In such circumstances, what level of force is acceptable? Against whom should it be applied? What level of force will lead to success? What else beside force is needed? Indiscriminate and disproportionate force will be regarded as such and will be counter-productive in the struggle for hearts and minds. Beyond these considerations, however, Kelly argues that there will be no victory 'unless there is the vision of a just peace and the will and capabilities to achieve it': 'stability and reconstruction' are needed as 'part of a more holistic effort to defeat enemy insurgents while bettering the lives of the innocent people among whom they live and fight'. Both stability and reconstruction and the resources to pay for them should be 'essential elements of just wars against insurgents',[16] not relatively late afterthoughts as in the Afghanistan and Iraq interventions.

### *George Weigel and the 'Moral Imperative' of a Revised Christian Just War Theory to Contend with 'Rogue States'*

In the immediate aftermath of 9/11, George Weigel, Senior Fellow of the Ethics and Public Policy Center in Washington DC, called for 'moral clarity in time of war'. In a public lecture delivered in 2002 he declared: 'to suggest that the just war tradition is obsolete is to suggest that politics – the organization of human life into purposeful political communities – is obsolete ... What we must do, in this generation, is to retrieve and develop the just war tradition to take account of the new political and technological realities of the twenty–first century.' The events of 11 September 2001, what has followed, and what lies ahead, 'have demonstrated just how urgent that task is'.[17] What Weigel seeks to do is to redefine the just war tradition to serve the cause of hardline Christian fundamentalist advisers to the White House. This approach seems to deny the right of the Church in a democratic society to make a judgement – one which is in principle no better and no worse than that of the politicians – about whether the just war criteria appear to be met. In particular, Weigel and those who follow his reasoning and dominate policy-making in the US try to modify three areas of the Christian just war tradition to take account of new circumstances since 11 September 2001. These are 'just cause', 'last resort', and 'competent authority'.[18]

First, just cause. Weigel is critical of the American Catholic bishops' understanding of the just war tradition, stated in 1983, as based on a 'presumption against violence'. For him in the case of 'rogue states developing or deploying weapons of mass destruction, a developed just war tradition would recognize that here … last resort cannot be understood mathematically, as the terminal point of a lengthy series of non-military alternatives. Can we not say that last resort has been satisfied in those cases when a rogue state has made plain, by its conduct, that it holds international law in contempt and that no diplomatic solution to the threat it poses is likely, and when it can be demonstrated that the threat the rogue state poses is intensifying?' Here Weigel concludes: 'I think we can. Indeed, I think we must.'

Secondly, last resort. For Weigel, 'some states, because of the regime's aggressive intent and the lack of effective internal political controls on giving lethal effect to that intent, cannot be permitted to acquire weapons of mass destruction. Denying them those weapons through proportionate and discriminate armed force – even displacing those regimes – can be an exercise in the defence of peace, within the boundaries of a developed just war tradition. Until such point as the international political community has evolved to the degree that international organizations can effectively disarm such regimes, the responsibility for the defence of order in these extreme circumstances will lie elsewhere' – for elsewhere, of course, read the US.

Weigel contends that 'if you are under attack, according to the [United Nations] Charter, you don't have to wait for the permission of China, France, Russia, or others of the veto-wielding powers to defend yourself.' But in what ways was the United States 'under attack' from Iraq in 2002–3? A decade of sanctions after the First Iraq War in 1991 had rendered Iraq more or less powerless, and further US air strikes since 1996 had confirmed overwhelming American air supremacy. Weigel further argues:

> it makes little moral sense to suggest that the United States must wait until a North Korea or Iraq or Iran actually launches a ballistic missile tipped with a nuclear, biological or chemical weapon of mass destruction before we can legitimately do something about it. Can we not say that, in the hands of certain kinds of states, the mere possession of weapons of mass destruction constitutes an aggression – or, at the very least, an aggression-waiting-to-happen? The 'regime factor' is crucial in the moral analysis.

Thirdly, competent authority. It is clear that Weigel, and the US decision-makers who follow his logic, are dismissive of the present structure of the United Nations Security Council. He castigates 'the manifest inability of the UN to handle large-scale international security questions', which suggests to him that assigning a moral veto over US military action on these fronts to the Security Council would be a mistake. Then there is the question of what Weigel calls 'the "neighbourhood" of the Security Council: what kind of moral logic is it to claim that the US government must assuage the interests of the French foreign ministry and the strategic aims of the repressive Chinese government – both of which are in full play in the Security Council – in order to gain international moral authority for the war against terrorism and the defense of world order against outlaw states with weapons of mass destruction?' Weigel dismisses this as 'a very peculiar moral logic indeed'.

Weigel essentially argues that defence against aggression does not require the authority of the Security Council of the UN. It may be prudent to seek it, but it is not for him 'a moral imperative'. George Weigel has returned to the fray to justify *NSS-2002,* contending that it reflects 'a serious reception of the just war way of thinking in American public life'. Weigel maintains that *NSS-2002* 'spends far more time discussing co-operative diplomatic, economic and political activity in support of the peace of order than it does discussing pre-emptive military action'. There are nevertheless plenty of statements in *NSS-2002* to provide fodder to critics of US foreign policy, such as the remark that the US 'will not use force in all cases to pre-empt emerging threats' but it 'will, if necessary, act pre-emptively'. Weigel rephrases a number of passages, altering the wording to 'the first use of armed force'. 'Phrased this way, *NSS-2002* emerges more clearly as what I expect its authors intended: an effort to describe a morally serious and politically feasible national-security strategy in which the use of armed force, as one necessary instrument of statecraft, is understood according to the canons of a developed just war tradition.'[19]

John Langan rejects Weigel's attempts to rewrite *NSS-2002,* which, he asserts, 'gives much greater importance to adversarial situations and possible hostilities than it does the concept of democratic peace …' 'Contrary to Weigel's analysis', Langan concludes, 'it is … difficult to show the world in general that the goals that the *NSS-2002* proposes can be derived from a universalist moral theory or from the principles of Christianity. The world is to be made safe for American democracy. The international common good is determined by one pre-eminent power, and it consists very largely in maintaining the security of that same power.'[20] In questioning the traditional just war requirement of last resort, *NSS-2002* 'is likely to make peace less stable and to undercut the negotiating processes in critical situations'. Because of the preponderance of American power, proponents of intervention can make claims that enormous good can be achieved through the use of military force 'and that devastating evils can be averted, at least for the Americans and their allies, though not for their adversaries'. Langan concludes from this that 'judgements about proportionality in the use of force by the manifestly superior power are systematically skewed in favour of active reliance on force'.[21] An escalation of the use of force and an expansion of the political agenda tend to follow, whereas prudent realism combined with a sense of moral responsibility should dictate the pursuit of limited and specific objectives.

In order to counter the attempted reworking of Christian just war theory, Darrin W. Belousek reformulates current American policy as six propositions. The first is that 'you are either with us or against us,' an argument used to force Pakistan into the 'coalition of the willing' in 2001 (Chapter 7). In contrast with just war tradition, 'our' presumed unassailable righteousness constitutes sufficient 'legitimate authority' to wage war against evildoers: precisely because 'we' are good, 'we' have an unqualified right to judge evildoers. The second proposition is that 'we can either do nothing or seek to destroy the evildoers.' Any response to evil other than war is thus the same as inaction. Furthermore, because there is no neutral ground, to be inactive is to side with evil. Hence, non-violence, and even questioning a violent response to evil, is doing nothing and thus siding with evil. The third element of the paradigm is the notion that 'if we do nothing, nothing will be done to prevent the evildoers from seeking to destroy us,' an argument championed by Bernard Lewis among others (Chapter 3). It is linked to a fourth proposition, that 'if the evildoers succeed in destroying us, evil will triumph, all good will perish (including us), and peace will be destroyed.' The paradigm assumes that 'evildoers have virtually unlimited power to accomplish their will and that they will be successful if left unopposed.' The fifth proposition is that 'if, on the other hand, we seek to destroy the evildoers before they seek to destroy us, the evildoers will be vanquished.' This is the particularly dangerous element in the paradigm. 'All "just war" limits on the use of violent force are thus irrelevant,' Belousek argues. 'The only discrimination necessary is between "us" and "them", and in fighting evildoers no amount of force can be disproportionate to an unqualified righteous cause.' The sixth and final proposition is that 'if the evildoers are vanquished, good will be saved (including us), and peace will reign.' The implication here is that our violence, because it intends only good, accomplishes only good – otherwise, if our actions could harm the innocent, then there would be moral ambiguity and no distinction between what we do and what the evildoers do to us. 'Because we are good and our cause is righteous, our violence leaves us unsullied by evil; none of the blood we shed is on our hands.'[22]

### *The Manipulation of Intelligence Reports by the Supporters of George W. Bush and Tony Blair*

The invasion of Iraq in 2003 was 'sold' on the basis that Saddam Hussein, its ruler, possessed an arsenal of weapons of mass destruction (WMD) and was co-operating actively with terrorists. Yet other reasons for the invasion are clear, as revealed by the former US National Coordinator for Security and Counterterrorism, Richard A. Clarke, in his account of discussions in the days following 9/11. Defense Secretary Donald Rumsfeld complained that 'there were no decent targets for bombing in Afghanistan and that we should consider bombing Iraq'. President Bush retorted: 'what we needed to do with Iraq was to change the Government, not just hit it with more cruise missiles,' as Rumsfeld had implied.[23]

Other issues influenced the decision to go to invade Iraq though they are interconnected.[24] Arguing that terrorism had its roots in the undemocratic nature of the Middle East regimes – a controversial proposition arising from Bernard Lewis's analysis (Chapter 3) – the Bush administration declared that its goal was to fight terror by bringing democracy to the Middle East, starting with Afghanistan and Iraq. Mearsheimer and Walt continue to maintain (see Chapter 5) that the war would 'almost certainly not have occurred' were it not for the influence of the pro-Israel lobby.[25] The former chairman of the Federal Reserve, Alan Greenspan, who worked alongside six successive presidents of the US, revealed in his memoirs and accompanying interviews in September 2007 that Saddam's alleged WMD were 'utterly beside the point'. 'Whatever their publicized angst over Saddam Hussein's "weapons of mass destruction", American and British authorities were also concerned about violence in the area that harbours a resource indispensable for the functioning of the world economy. I am saddened that it is politically inconvenient to acknowledge what everyone knows: the Iraq war is largely about oil.' Had Saddam been able to close the Straits of Hormuz and so control Middle East oil shipments through the vital route out of the Gulf, his actions would have been 'devastating to the West'. Preventing the export of 5 million barrels a day would have brought 'the industrial world to its knees'.[26]

From the outset, the propaganda campaign seeking to link Saddam Hussein's regime with al-Qaeda lacked credibility: as Richard A. Clarke puts it, 'any Iraqi "link" to al-Qaeda is a minor footnote when compared to the link with other regimes such as Afghanistan, and none of the possible "links" between Iraq and al-Qaeda rise to the level of noteworthy assistance and support.' For the US to go after Iraq in response to an attack by al-Qaeda, was, in Clarke's view, akin to 'our invading Mexico after the Japanese attacked us at Pearl Harbor' in 1941.[27] The British intelligence officers understood that there was no link between al-Qaeda and Saddam, an assertion made against all the evidence by Dick Cheney and his circle. On 12 September 2001, the day after al-Qaeda's attacks on America, George Tenet, then CIA director, met three British guests – Sir David Manning, then Tony Blair's foreign policy adviser; Richard Dearlove, then head of MI6; and Eliza Manningham-Buller, then head of MI5. 'I hope we can all agree that we should concentrate on Afghanistan and not be tempted to launch any attacks on Iraq', Manning, the leader of the British delegation, told Tenet, who appeared to agree.[28]

Carne Ross, a well-placed British diplomat who resigned in protest at the drift to war, has stated categorically that Iraq's capacity to engage in a first strike against its enemies was gravely exaggerated by those seeking to justify war in 2003. There was no suggestion, Ross asserts, 'that Iraq had any intention to launch an attack against its neighbours or the UK or US'. He had many conversations with diplomats representing Iraq's neighbours; except for the Israelis, none expressed any belief that they might be attacked. Instead, 'their concern was that sanctions, which they and we viewed as an effective means to contain Iraq, were being de-legitimized by evidence of their damaging humanitarian effect.' With the exception of some unaccounted-for Scud missiles, Carne Ross maintains that there was no intelligence evidence of significant holdings of chemical weapons, biological weapons, or nuclear material: 'Iraq's ability to launch a WMD or any form of attack was very limited.'[29]

The British government exaggerated the threat posed by Saddam Hussein's alleged weapons of mass destruction, its own leading expert, Dr David Kelly, contended.[30] The claim that Saddam could deploy chemical or biological weapons within 45 minutes – though based on a single piece of unverified intelligence – was highlighted in Tony Blair's preface to the dossier issued by the British government in September 2002 in the run-up to the Iraq war.[31] It was also at the heart of the row between Downing Street and the BBC, after doubt was cast on its accuracy by the government weapons scientist, David Kelly. The 45-minute claim, included four times in the dossier, was perhaps the most eye-catching item and was extensively used by the media to warn of the imminence of an attack on the West. The claim was finally admitted to be incorrect by Jack Straw over two years later, on 12 October 2004, although Geoff Hoon had already dismissed the claim as 'insignificant' in February 2004. (In fact the claim referred only to Iraqi short-range battlefield weapons, and not long-range missiles as was widely assumed at the time.)[32] Carne Ross was dismissive of the argument, as he subsequently revealed:[33]

> ... I knew that the evidence they were presenting for WMD was totally implausible. I'd read the intelligence on WMD for four and a half years, and there's no way that it could sustain the case that the government was presenting. All of my colleagues knew that, too. We all believed the Iraqis had something, but that is very different from saying they had that much. The intelligence indicated that they'd failed to account for what they had in the past. They hadn't given us a complete account of the disposal of their past stocks, so we thought there was something, but there was no way that the claim of an imminent threat was sustainable. The 45-minute stuff was ridiculous.

The most important revelation on the shortcomings in interpreting intelligence reports came on 23 April 2006, when Tyler Drumheller, the former CIA chief of clandestine operations for Europe, was interviewed for CBS television. Drumheller disclosed that the agency had received documentary intelligence from Naji Sabri, Saddam's foreign minister, that Saddam did not possess WMD. 'We continued to validate him the whole way through,' said Drumheller, but 'the policy was set. The war in Iraq was coming, and they were looking for intelligence to fit into the policy, to justify the policy.' Sidney Blumenthal notes that Drumheller's account is consistent with the so-called 'Downing Street memorandum', which records Tony Blair's conference with top national security and intelligence advisers on 23 July 2002. The memorandum stated that 'Bush wanted to remove Saddam through military action justified by the conjunction of terrorism and WMD. But the intelligence and facts were being fixed around the policy.'[34]

In September 2007, Blumenthal confirmed Drumheller's account from the evidence of two former senior CIA officers who provided him with the background to the story of 'how the information that might have stopped the invasion of Iraq was twisted in order to justify it'.[35] Both the French intelligence service and the CIA paid Sabri hundreds of thousands of dollars (at least $200,000 in the case of the CIA) to give them documents on Saddam's WMD programmes. 'The information detailed that Saddam may have wished to have a program, that his engineers had told him they could build a nuclear weapon within two years if they had fissile material, which they didn't, and that they had no chemical or biological weapons,' one of the former CIA officers told Blumenthal. On 18 September 2002, Tenet briefed George W. Bush on Sabri. 'Tenet told me he briefed the president personally', said one of the former CIA officers. According to Tenet, Bush's response was to call the information 'the same old thing'. Bush insisted it was simply what Saddam wanted him to think. Yet French intelligence eavesdropped on Sabri's telephone conversations and shared them with the CIA. These wiretaps 'validated' Sabri's claims, according to one of the CIA officers.

The CIA officers submitted a report on Sabri which they believed would halt the march to war. Instead, they later learned that a new report had been written. They were unclear by whom it was written, 'it was so tightly controlled'. The new report stated the things the President wanted to hear. 'They knew what would please the White House. They knew what the king wanted.' It contained a false preamble stating that Saddam was 'aggressively and covertly developing' nuclear weapons and that he already possessed chemical and biological weapons. The report with the misleading introduction was passed on to Richard Dearlove of MI6, who briefed the British prime minister. 'They were given a scaled-down version of the report,' one of the CIA officers stated. 'It was a summary given for liaison, with the sourcing taken out. They showed the British the statement [that] Saddam was pursuing an aggressive program, and rewrote the report to attempt to support that statement. It was insidious. Blair bought it.' 'Blair was duped,' the other CIA officer stated. 'He was shown the altered report.' Coates and Krieger ask whether Blair was 'bushwhacked [and] bamboozled by the overselling of the data by the Bush team?' They conclude that 'the UK went to war when it should not have done so, led by a prime minister who was either misleading us or being misled himself.'[36] Later, when Blair admitted that the evidence for war 'had turned out to be wrong', he still refused to apologize for removing Saddam: 'I don't think we were wrong to go in.'[37] However, the moral case for a war of intervention on human rights considerations was immeasurably stronger in 1988, when Saddam was in the process of gassing the Kurds, or in 1991 when he was slaughtering the Shi'ite rebellion. Blair himself had accepted 'entirely [that] the legal basis for action was through weapons of mass destruction'.[38] And the intelligence upon which the war was based was subsequently proven to have been 'flawed' (Lord Falconer's expression), that is, erroneous. Blair's qualified apology to the House of Commons was to take responsibility for 'any information given in good faith that has subsequently turned out to be wrong'.[39]

The information provided by Sabri was considered so sensitive that it was never shown to those who assembled the National Intelligence Estimate on Iraqi WMD. Later revealed to be utterly wrong, the NIE read: 'we judge that Iraq has continued its weapons of mass destruction

(WMD) programs in defiance of UN resolutions and restrictions. Baghdad has chemical and biological weapons as well as missiles with ranges in excess of UN restrictions; if left unchecked, it probably will have a nuclear weapon during this decade.' While one Iraqi source told the CIA that there were no WMD, the lies of another Iraqi source were eagerly embraced. (CIA deputy director, John McLaughlin, was 'excited' about Sabri, but stated that his information was at odds with 'our best source', who was code-named 'Curveball'. This 'best source', who provided over 100 reports between January 2000 and September 2001, was later exposed as a liar, an alcoholic, a thief posing as a chemical engineer seeking asylum in Germany, and the brother of a top aide of Ahmed Chalabi. German intelligence had passed on the reports but had warned the Americans that Curveball's information was not credible.)[40] 'The real tragedy is that they had a good source that they misused,' one of the former CIA officers told Blumenthal. 'The fact is there was nothing there, no threat. But Bush wanted to hear what he wanted to hear.' George Tenet fails to mention Sabri in his memoirs, *At the Center of the Storm* (2006); nor did he brief Colin Powell on Sabri before the Secretary of State delivered his speech to the United Nations on Iraq's WMD. Tellingly, Sabri's picture was never put on the deck of playing cards of former Saddam officials to be hunted down by American troops in Iraq, a tacit acknowledgement of his covert relationship with the CIA. At the time this book was going to press, Sabri was living in exile in Qatar.

### *The Rift within the American Administration: Cheney and Rumsfeld versus Powell*

In 1992, reflecting on first-hand experience in the Gulf War, General Colin L. Powell – then chairman of the Joint Chiefs of Staff – stated that there were a number of questions policy-makers should ask, and obtain answers on, before committing American troops to war. 'Is the political objective we seek to achieve important, clearly defined and understood? Have all other non-violent policy means failed? Will military force achieve the objective? At what cost? Have the gains and risks been analyzed? How might the situation that we seek to alter, once it is altered by force, develop further and what might be the consequences?' Powell was hostile to the idea of a set of rules before the use of force could be triggered because this would send too obvious a signal to an enemy: 'it destroys the ambiguity we might want to exist in our enemy's mind regarding our intentions.' But he clearly expected the questions to be asked. Regrettably, there is no evidence that they were asked effectively in 2002 before the drift to war became irresistible. In contrast to the standard neo-conservative criticism, Powell praised President George H.W. Bush's decision not to oust Saddam Hussein in 1991:[41]

> … even if we had been able to capture him, what purpose would it have served? And would serving that purpose have been worth the many more casualties that would have occurred? Would it have been worth the inevitable follow-up: major occupation forces in Iraq for years to come and a very expensive and complex American pro-consulship in Baghdad? Fortunately for America, reasonable people at the time thought not. They still do.

Mark Danner, writing on 'a doctrine left behind' for the *New York Times* following Powell's resignation as secretary of state, remarked that 'these lines carry with them the whiff of far-off times, a lost world of pragmatism that pre-dated the religious trappings of the war on terrorism.'[42] The first presidential term of George W. Bush was marked by a strong and deepening rift between Powell as secretary of state, who advocated realism and regarded Saddam Hussein as a 'kidney stone that will eventually pass'[43] and the zeal of Donald Rumsfeld and Paul Wolfowitz at the Department of Defense, who favoured a more aggressive stance on Iraq. Powell correctly recognized that the pursuit of regime change in Iraq would undermine the coalition of support enjoyed by the US after 9/11, but ironically the task of explaining the evidence for the existence of WMDs in Iraq to the United Nations Security Council in February 2003 fell to him. Subsequently, in September 2005, Powell described this as a 'blot' on his record in public service.[44] As Fred Kaplan observed a year after the UN presentation, 'from the start of this presidency, and to a degree that no-one would have predicted … Powell has found himself almost consistently muzzled, outflanked, and humiliated by the true powers – Vice-President Dick Cheney and Secretary of Defense Donald Rumsfeld.'[45]

Yet Powell deserved better. The National Security Council (NSC) should have played a significant role in mediating the disputes and providing a single set of proposals to the President. Under President Bill Clinton's Presidential Decision Directive 62, signed in May 1998, the NSC was tasked with 'continuity of operations' in counter-terrorist operations.[46] The role of Dr Condoleezza Rice as National Security Adviser before replacing Powell as Secretary of State is therefore crucial. Called the 'warrior princess' – after an American TV show *Xena: the warrior princess* – Rice sensed where power lay and opted for fierce support of the Iraq intervention: 'instead of a commitment to disarm, Iraq has a high-level political commitment to maintain and conceal its weapons, led by Saddam Hussein and his son Qusay, who controls the Special Security Organization, which runs Iraq's concealment activities,' she wrote in the *New York Times* on 23 January 2003.[47] Subsequently, in the 2004 presidential election campaign, Rice gave active assistance to Bush and claimed that while 'Saddam Hussein had nothing to do with the actual attacks on America, Saddam Hussein's Iraq was a part of the Middle East that was festering and unstable, [and] was part of the circumstances that created the problem on 11 September.'[48] Stefan Halper and Jonathan Clarke contend that the NSC failed to fulfil its responsibilities under Rice, in particular to 'rationalize the differing perspectives of the State and Defense Departments and to contain special interest agenda such as those of the neo-conservatives'. They conclude that 'the President was left to choose among options, at times bitterly disputed, to the detriment of the administration'.[49]

Not only did Powell receive no support from parts of the administration where he was entitled to expect it, he was undermined by a campaign of disinformation. This was managed from the Office of Special Plans (OSP) set up by Douglas Feith (see Chapter 5), whose director was the Straussian scholar and guru of disinformation ('truth is not the goal'), Abram Shulsky. If Special Plans was going to search for new intelligence on Iraq, the most obvious source was defectors with first-hand knowledge. The office inevitably turned to Ahmed Chalabi's Iraqi National Congress (INC). Seymour M. Hersh reports on the close ties between Chalabi and Rumsfeld, Wolfowitz and Perle, and also Douglas Feith and I. Lewis 'Scooter' Libby. Of course, Chalabi and the INC were not neutral: rather, they were an opposition political unit, not an intelligence agency, and even among the exiles Chalabi's credibility was suspect.[50] Chalabi and the INC managed to bring over a number of Iraqi defectors, but as Shulsky had noted in his 1991 textbook on intelligence, there is a strong incentive for defectors to tell interviewers what they want to hear.[51]

The campaign of disinformation was fed directly into newspaper reports. The reporter Judith Miller of the *New York Times* had preferential access both to Chalabi and the INC and also to Richard Perle, Paul Wolfowitz, and the Office of Special Plans. Miller's over-reliance on Chalabi, his Iraqi defectors, and his Pentagon champions, especially Under-Secretary of Defense Douglas Feith, became clear subsequently.[52] On 26 May 2003, when it seemed clear that the United States would find no WMD in Iraq, the *New York Times*'s editorial on 'Reviewing the Intelligence on Iraq' noted that

> numerous questions need to be explored. Some are narrow issues, like how the administration came to rely on forged documents to make the case

> that Iraq was trying to import uranium for its presumed nuclear weapons program. Others are broader, like the role played by a new special office in the Pentagon that applied its own interpretations to the information and analyses generated by the traditional intelligence agencies. A critical question is what information was presented to the president in the run-up to war.

What the editorial did not comment on was the newspaper's own shortcomings in failing to verify the basis for Judith Miller's over-credulous reports. Judith Miller's relationship with the *New York Times* ended on 9 November 2005 after she was jailed for 85 days for contempt of court for refusing to testify before a federal grand jury investigating a leak naming Valerie Plame as a covert CIA agent. According to a subpoena, Miller met an unnamed government official – later revealed to be 'Scooter' Libby, Vice-President Cheney's Chief of Staff – on 8 July 2003, two days after Plame's husband, former ambassador Joseph Wilson, published an article in the *New York Times* criticizing the Bush administration for 'twisting' intelligence to justify war in Iraq. (Plame's CIA identity was – illegally – leaked by the conservative political commentator Robert D. Novak on 14 July 2003 in his syndicated column in the *Washington Post*.) Miller testified as a witness on 30 January 2007 at the trial of 'Scooter' Libby, which ended with Libby's conviction on 6 March 2007 and a sentence of thirty months in jail for perjury and obstruction of justice (subsequently commuted by George W. Bush on 2 July).[53] Valerie Plame did not go quietly: finally, in March 2007 she testified to Congress, then she gave an interview to the CBS television channel, and in October she published her autobiography entitled *Fair Game: My Life as a Spy. My Betrayal by the White House*. The critical point was not only that Plame was a covert CIA operative: she had been working for the CIA on the (weak) evidence for the existence of alleged Iraqi WMD.[54]

Libby was not charged with leaking Valerie Plame's name: Novak's sources were later revealed to be Richard L. Armitage, a former deputy secretary of state, and Karl Rove, George W. Bush's senior political adviser in the White House, neither of whom was charged with violating the law prohibiting the disclosure of the identities of CIA officers. Writing for the *New Yorker*, George Packer claimed that 'the Rove approach to governing helped lose Iraq. That may be the most enduring legacy of this supposed political genius.'[55] Rove's 'strategic communications' task force within the White House Iraq Group (WHIG) helped write and co-ordinate speeches by senior Bush administration officials, emphasizing in September 2002 the theme of Iraq's purported nuclear threat. James Dobbins, Bush's first envoy to Afghanistan, commented on the terminology of the global war on terror:[56]

> I never liked the term *war*. This is a campaign conducted primarily, [as it] should be, by law-enforcement, diplomatic and intelligence means. The militarization of the concept is a theme that mobilizes the American public effectively, but it's not a theme that resonates well in the Middle East or with our allies elsewhere in the world. I think some re-conceptualization would be helpful. But the White House probably doesn't. Karl Rove doesn't spend a lot of time worrying about the impact of his strategies in the Muslim world.

### *Jus in Bello: the Principles of Discrimination, Proportionality, and Respect for Human Rights*

The first principle of warfare is that of discrimination. Soldiers are only entitled to target those who are 'engaged in harm'. Thus, when they take aim, soldiers must discriminate between the civilian population, which is morally immune from direct and intentional attack, and those legitimate military, political, and industrial targets involved in 'rights-violating harm'. While some collateral civilian casualties are excusable, it is wrong to take deliberate aim at civilian targets. An example would be the saturation bombing of residential areas which occurred in World War II, which given the advances in guidance systems, would now be regarded as unacceptable. In the Second Iraq War, the treatment of the civilian populations of Baghdad and Basra through air strikes or other military action was an extremely important indicator of how much genuine concern (as against lip service) was being paid to *jus in bello* principles.

President Bush's speech announcing the outbreak of war contained these words: 'in this conflict, America faces an enemy that has no regard for conventions of war or rules of morality. Saddam Hussein has placed Iraqi troops and equipment in civilian areas, attempting to use innocent men, women and children as shields for his own military – a final atrocity against his people. I want America and all the world to know that coalition forces will make every effort to spare innocent civilians from harm.'[57] Thus, the principle of discrimination was asserted at the outset of hostilities. But it is not always possible to distinguish between combatant and non-combatant in modern warfare, and non-combatants inevitably are killed, thus weakening the moral argument for going to war. It is also the case that once war has begun, the important thing, both politically and in the sense of defending one's own troops, is to win quickly. Moral rules that limit the nature of the conflict, especially if the other side flouts them, are therefore potentially a hindrance to the main military endeavour, which is a short war and conclusive victory.

Set against this is the traditional distinction made between those who contribute directly to the war effort and the rest of society. The war was not a war against the Iraqi people. By definition, therefore, civilian casualties were more serious than something called 'collateral damage'. President Bush stated: 'we come to Iraq with respect for its citizens, for their great civilization and for the religious faith they practice. We have no ambition in Iraq except to remove a threat and restore control of that country to its own people.'[58] The paper published by the US and the UK Governments entitled 'A Vision for Iraq and the Iraqi People' talked of the military alliance 'working to ensure any military campaign is as swift and carefully targeted as possible'.[59]

A second and related issue is that of proportionality. In this context, proportionality means that the damage to be inflicted and the costs incurred by war must be proportionate to the good expected by taking up arms. The pastoral letter of the American Catholic Bishops in 1983 has relevant words: 'when confronting choices among specific military options, the question asked by proportionality is: once we take into account not only the military advantages that will be achieved by using this means but also all the harms reasonably expected to follow from using it, can its use still be justified? We know, of course, that no end can justify means evil in themselves, such as the execution of hostages or the targeting of non-combatants.' (We would also add mass rape campaigns; genocide or ethnic cleansing; torturing captured enemy soldiers; and using weapons whose effects cannot be controlled, such as chemical or biological agents.)

Factors to be taken into account include the military importance of the target, the density of the civilian population in the target area, the likely collateral effects of the attack, including the possible release of hazardous substances, the types of weapon available and their accuracy, whether the defenders are deliberately exposing civilians to risk, the mode of attack, and the timing of the attack. For instance, during the First Iraq War, allied attacks on so-called 'dual-use facilities' were normally scheduled at night because fewer people would be inside or on the streets. Much more was expected during the Second Iraq War, since the weapons were said to be more accurate still; the television news reports which have been broadcast throughout the world suggest that, as Tony Blair has contended, civilian casualties have been low in comparison with the scale of the military effort or under the previous regime.[60] There have nevertheless been some serious errors of judgement apart from regrettable instances of 'friendly fire' on coalition forces.[61]

The philosopher Jan Narveson argues that in certain circumstances the appalling human rights record of a regime may be sufficient to justify military intervention to secure regime change, and that this argument could be applied to the circumstances of Iraq in 2003. Narveson considers that five conditions are necessary to justify a humanitarian intervention and regime change against tyranny: the new regime that is intended is better than the old one, a good deal better; the costs imposed on the invaded state must be acceptable to its people; the costs to the invading state must be acceptable, in turn, to its people; the objective must be 'worth it' to the invading state and 'to a just world'; and finally, there must be a reasonable prospect of success for the new regime. Narveson argues that simply introducing a democratic regime is insufficient: in view of the demographic balance between the majority Shi'is and the minority Sunnis and Kurds in Iraq, giving everyone the vote without further constitutional safeguards would be 'equivalent to fomenting civil war'.[62]

In his statement to the House of Commons on 18 March 2003, Tony Blair referred to 'the future of the Iraqi people, for so long brutalized by Saddam' before giving a long historical disquisition on the regime's attempted acquisition of WMD. Towards the conclusion of the statement, Blair noted that many of those opposed to the war shared his detestation of Saddam:[63]

> Four million people out of a population of just over 20 million[64] are in exile. The brutality of the repression – the death and torture camps, the barbaric prisons for political opponents, the routine beatings for anyone or their families suspected of disloyalty – are well documented. Just last week, someone slandering Saddam was tied to a lamp post in a street in Baghdad, his tongue cut out, mutilated and left to bleed to death, as a warning to others ... That is how the Iraqi people live. Leave Saddam in place and that is how they will continue to live...

It is probable that Tony Blair exaggerated the number of Iraqi exiles abroad; in any case, the prolongation of the war has added to, rather than diminished, the number of exiles from Iraq. The UN refugee agency, the UNHCR, has reported that Iraqis continue to flee abroad since the invasion, while the numbers of internally displaced continue to grow. In early June 2007, more than 2 million Iraqis were thought to be displaced inside the country, with another 2.2 million sheltering in neighbouring states.[65] On 17 September, the BBC reported that the United States had admitted 1521 Iraqis refugees since the invasion in 2003.

At 31 July 2007, Iraqbodycount put the number of civilians killed as between 68,009 and 74,403. Yet Iraqbodycount is one of the more conservative sources for civilian casualties of the war.[66] The Iraq household survey of 2006 concluded that an estimated 600,000 people had died from violence since the invasion in 2003.[67] The methodology used was consistent with survey methodology that has long been standard practice in estimating mortality in populations affected by war.[68] (On 14 September 2007, Opinion Research Business estimated the number of violent deaths in Iraq since the invasion as even higher: 1.2 million.)[69] The true cost of preventive war is a human cost, about which both the US and British governments are in a state of denial. The overall post-invasion violent death rate (March 2003–June 2006) was estimated at 7.2 deaths per thousand per annum. What is really striking, however, is that the rate of excess deaths increased significantly the longer the military occupation lasted. In terms of the most fundamentally important issue of all – saving human lives – the conclusion is inescapable. Only a prompt withdrawal of foreign troops, with an orderly transfer of power, was likely to bring the rate of violent death among civilians back to its pre-war level.[70]

To this heavy mortality rate can be added the continuing dereliction of the infrastructure and the massive social implications of the ongoing violence. 'Nearly a third of Iraqis need immediate emergency help', an Oxfam press release on 30 July 2007 stated, 'as conflict masks humanitarian crisis.' Eight million Iraqis, nearly one in three, are in need of emergency aid, while 70 per cent of the population remained without adequate water supplies. 'Basic indicators of humanitarian need in Iraq show that the slide into poverty and deprivation since the coalition forces entered the country in 2003 has been dramatic, and a deep trauma for the Iraqi people. The number of refugees and displaced persons is now massive by any modern standards.' The Oxfam-NCCI report *Rising to the Humanitarian Challenge in Iraq*[71] was in itself compelling evidence to suggest that the price of intervention for human liberation, even if in principle acceptable at the outset, had proven far too high four years after the invasion. As John Gray has commented, 'liberal interventionists who supported regime change as part of a global crusade for human rights overlooked the fact that the result of toppling tyranny in divided countries is usually civil war and ethnic cleansing. Equally they failed to perceive the rapidly dwindling leverage on events of the western powers that led the crusade … The result of these delusions is what we see today: a world of rising authoritarian regimes and collapsed states no one knows how to govern.'[72]

# Chapter Nine
# 'We Don't Do Nation-Building' Towards a *Jus Post Bellum* for Iraq and Other Cases of Intervention

> Our goal would be an Iraq that has territorial integrity, a government that is democratic and pluralistic, a nation where the human rights of every ethnic and religious group are recognized and protected.
>
> (Vice-President Richard Cheney, 26 August 2002)[1]

> ... what the United States can do and indeed [has] an obligation to do in our own interest is to help contribute to peace and stability in the world in a way that allows others to build their nations ... there's a subtle difference between that and nation-building but it is a critically important difference ... [We] ought not to be trying to do things we're not capable of doing like nation-building, telling other people how they should live their lives ... We should learn that we need to avoid being so heavy-handed that we create ... a dependency and a weakness as opposed to a strength.
>
> (Donald H. Rumsfeld, Secretary of Defense, 8 September 2003)[2]

> Building a free and democratic Iraq is going to be a huge victory in the war on terrorism, and the terrorists realize that. And that's why they're in there trying their best to defeat it.
>
> (Paul Wolfowitz, Deputy Secretary of Defense, interview with the *Jerusalem Post*, 22 September 2003)[3]

It is frequently stated that there was no planning for a post-war Iraq immediately after the overthrow of Saddam Hussein. In an important respect the claim is completely untrue. The State Department began planning for post-regime-change Iraq less than a month after the 11 September attacks. Under the direction of a former State Department official, Thomas S. Warrick, the Department brought together over 200 Iraqi engineers, lawyers, businesspeople, doctors, and other experts into 17 working groups to formulate strategies on public health and humanitarian needs; transparency and anti-corruption; oil and energy; defence policy and institutions; transitional justice; democratic principles and procedures; local government; civil society capacity building; education; free media; water, agriculture, and the environment; and the economy and the infrastructure.

'The people of Iraq are being promised a new future and they will expect immediate results. The credibility of the new regime and the United States will depend on how quickly these promises are translated to reality,' the Working Group on Transparency and Anti-Corruption declared. The State Department's mammoth 13-volume study, *The Future of Iraq Project* (posted online on 1 September 2006 by the National Security Archive) was one of the most comprehensive US government planning efforts of all time.[4] Yet it was entirely ignored because of Defense Department–State Department rivalry and because it did not fit the neo-conservatives' 'template for intervention'.[5] Instead, L. Paul Bremer III, the American proconsul appointed through Rumsfeld's influence, learnt of *The Future of Iraq Project* through the media after his arrival in Baghdad.[6] Subsequently, in September 2007, the British military commander, General Sir Michael Jackson, commented that 'all the planning carried out by the State Department went to waste'. He called the approach taken by Donald Rumsfeld 'intellectually bankrupt', and dismissed his claim that US forces 'don't do nation-building' as 'nonsensical'.[7] Nora Bensahel maintains that *The Future of Iraq Project* was not an actionable plan: 'it contained general information rather than specific tasks; it did not prioritize reconstruction of certain areas over others, and it did not address the question of resource allocation at all.' However, it was intended as 'a collaborative effort that would encourage Iraqi exiles to think about some of the challenges that a post-war Iraqi government, not the United States, would have to address'.[8]

The State Department's Working Group on Transitional Justice in Iraq predicted that 'the period immediately after regime change might offer … criminals an opportunity to engage in acts of killing, plunder, looting, etc.' Thomas E. Ricks comments that 'as US forces triumphed, Iraqis rose up and expressed their hatred for Saddam Hussein's regime in an extraordinary act of vandalism.'[9] Peter Galbraith recounts how the Saddam Fedayeen files – the names and addresses of the people attacking US troops and later the backbone of the insurgency – were burnt or looted. On 11 April, two days after the regime fell and the US became legally responsible for Baghdad, looters attacked the Iraq National Museum; the museum library, and many of its records were destroyed, while some of the most valuable artefacts were stolen. Not until 15 April were Marines finally deployed to protect the building. The Foreign Ministry was looted, as was the Ministry of Irrigation. The Oil Ministry was given protection, on Rumsfeld's specific orders, but this was wholly exceptional. As Galbraith comments, 'oil was a priority but the water on which millions of Iraqis depended was not.' He considers it no exaggeration to say that the US may have lost the war 'on the very day that it took Baghdad, 9 April 2003'. Iraqis were bound to conclude that the US was 'either too incompetent to keep order or so evil as to desire the country's physical destruction. Either view made resistance a logical response.'[10] Fred Ikle, Under- Secretary of Defense for Policy at the Pentagon during the Reagan administration, concurs: 'America lost most of its prestige and respect in that episode. To pacify a conquered country, the victor's prestige and dignity is absolutely critical.'[11]

### *Early Mistakes of the American Interim Regime in Iraq*

The American forces were unable to maintain law and order in the early days of the occupation in 2003 because they were fully stretched on other duties such as guarding supply routes and enemy prisoners of war. One of the key decisions had been made before the invasion of Iraq: the army to be deployed was of sufficient size to win the war, but insufficient to maintain law and order afterwards. It was a matter of principle to the neo-conservatives that the invasion would be a 'cakewalk' because of the technical superiority of the US forces and thus the war could be undertaken at minimal financial and human cost.[12] In reality, all the prior military planning for such an eventuality by Central Command (CENTCOM) under General Tony Zinni before 2000 was that an Iraq occupation force of very considerable size, with inter-government agency support, would be needed. A retired infantry colonel (anonymous) recalls that in 1996 the CENTCOM assessment of the complex society of Iraq was that Saddam Hussein was 'the glue that held Iraq together'. If Saddam was to be removed, 'there was a great chance that Iraq would come apart at the seams.' 'General Zinni fully understood the complexities in Iraq and the role that Saddam played.' If Saddam died in his sleep or was assassinated, the US might 'be left to go into Iraq to quell the ensuing chaos'.[13] But a large occupation force was unacceptable to those in power in the US and so Zinni's contingency plans were ignored by the Pentagon planners prior to the 2003 invasion.

Army Chief of Staff General Eric Shinseki told the Senate Armed Forces Committee on 25 February 2003 that an army of several hundred thousand troops – Thomas E. Ricks suggests that he was thinking of 260,000 men[14] – would be needed to sustain security in Iraq after the war was over; but Wolfowitz dismissed his estimate as 'widely off the mark'.[15] Before leaving for Iraq in May 2003, Presidential Envoy to Iraq L. Paul Bremer III sent the Defense Secretary a copy of a RAND report estimating that 500,000 troops would be needed to stabilize post-war Iraq – more than three times the number of troops then deployed.[16] Predictably, since the estimate diverged from the neo-conservative planning template, Bremer received no answer from Rumsfeld.

The first two decisions taken by L. Paul Bremer in Iraq compounded the crisis caused by the already inadequate American troop strength. Coalition Provisional Authority order 1 issued on 16 May 2003 eliminated in its entirety the Ba'ath party's structures and removed former senior members from positions of authority in the 'new' Iraq. The State Department's Democratic Principles working group had endorsed de-Ba'athification 'of all facets of Iraqi life', it is true, but had done so with the caveat that such a programme should 'not consist of the total abolition of the current administration, since, in addition to its role of social control, that structure does provide a framework for social order'. Moreover, those former Ba'athists who were not reintegrated into society, most notably members of the Iraqi army, the group recognized, might 'present a destabilizing element, especially if they are left without work or ability to get work'. Bremer's thinking was that his de-Ba'athification order was akin to the extirpation of Nazism from Germany after 1945, and was closely aligned to neo-conservative thinking even if not specifically authorized as he claimed. It was regarded as a necessary process prior to the implantation of democracy.

A number of Bremer's colleagues, including his predecessor Jay Garner, and David Nummy, a former Assistant Secretary to the Treasury, whose role was in effect that of acting Minister of Finance, were appalled. Nummy cited the examples of the Ukraine, Bosnia, and Kosovo: 'there was absolutely no [recent] experience in any country that said that being a member of the dominant political party meant that you were a bad guy.' Nummy subsequently noted that 'obviously you needed to be extremely careful about who you worked with. You needed to try to utilize whatever way you could to try to evaluate whether the people you were dealing with had been professional civil servants just trying to do their job or whether they had been instruments of the regime.' He concluded that 'there were probably fewer than 50 people in the entire Iraqi government who were part of the Saddam Hussein inner circle,' a much smaller proportion than eastern European experience might have suggested. Nummy considered the de-Ba'athification order 'incredibly self-destructive and inappropriate' and covertly ignored it in order to get the government ministries working and their civil servants paid.[17] Nevertheless, significant numbers of Ba'athists – perhaps between 15,000 and 40,000 – were construed as 'senior members' in terms of Bremer's first order and were driven into the arms of what became an insurgency against American occupation.

The second Coalition Provisional Authority Order signed by Bremer, this time on 23 May 2003, was to disband Iraq's army, air force, navy, secret police, intelligence service, the Republican Guards, the Ba'ath Party militia, and the Ministry of Defence. In Galbraith's words, 'for eighty years, Sunni Arabs were the guardians of Iraqi unity, keeping the country together by force.' With a few strokes of the pen, Bremer destroyed the pillars on which Sunni Arabs had established their control of Iraq. Galbraith considers that by this action 'Bremer ... sealed Iraq's fate as a unitary nation.'[18] Again, Nummy 'strongly objected' to the disbanding of the Iraqi military. Soldiers were not politicians pursuing a political agenda. 'They were generally the poorest and least educated of the country and were in the military because they needed a job and income.' If the country was to be stabilized it was essential to avoiding alienating a potentially hostile group by denying them both employment and a pension.

In contrast to these orders, in 2002, *The Future of Iraq Project*'s Defense Policy and Institutions group had instead advocated gradually halving the army's size and transforming it as an 'important tool for supporting democracy', with additional long-term tasks like fighting terrorism and drug smuggling. Jay Garner had worked on the assumption that members of the Iraqi army could be used for lower-level expertise reconstruction work. Instead, the Iraqi armed forces of 385,000 men were disbanded together with the police and domestic security forces (285,0000) and the 50,000 men comprising the presidential security units. Not only did the abrupt termination of this group of over half a million men create a vast pool of the 'humiliated, antagonized and politicized', many of whom were armed, it served to aggravate the fundamental security problem of Iraq, which was the lack of safety for ordinary Iraqis. 'We snatched defeat from the jaws of victory and created an insurgency,' a military liaison officer told Bremer.[19]

## *The Wrong Paradigm: the Inapplicability of the 1945 Example to Iraq*

As the Coalition forces were being assembled, Zalmay Khalilzad, the US President's special assistant for Near East affairs (among others), presented a plan modelled on the post-war occupation of Japan, to install an American-led military government once Saddam was toppled. David E. Sanger and Eric Schmitt covered the story for the *New York Times* on 11 October 2002, stressing the parallelism with MacArthur in 1945 and the need for military control to prevent anarchy:[20]

> Administration officials said they were moving away from the model used in Afghanistan: establishing a provisional government right away that would be run by Iraqis … Instead … the administration is studying the military occupations of Japan and Germany. But they stressed a commitment to keeping Iraq unified, as Japan was, and avoiding the kind of partition that Germany underwent when Soviet troops stayed in the eastern sector, which set the stage for the cold war. The military government in Germany stayed in power for four years; in Japan it lasted six and a half years …

Like MacArthur in Japan in 1945, L. Paul Bremer III did not have an entirely free hand in Iraq. But unlike MacArthur in Japan, Bremer knew nothing about Iraq. He had never been there, did not speak Arabic, had no experience in dealing with a country emerging from war, and had never been involved in 'nation-building'. During the two weeks he was given to get ready, he recruited senior staff including several retired ambassadors, a former assistant secretary of state for administration, and a high-powered Republican Washington lobbyist. Only one of his recruits had any background in the region. Crucially, when he flew into Baghdad on 12 May 2003, the capital had been without police or government for over a month and had been left largely in the hands of the looters. Though the neo-conservative mentality was not to worry about historical precedent or historical accuracy, even a cursory reflection on the experience of the US military administration of defeated Japan ought to have prompted the advisers of the President to appreciate that the differences between Japan in 1945 and Iraq in 2003 were so overwhelming as to vitiate any comparison except in the most superficial respects. Post-invasion Iraq in 2003–5 diverged from the Japanese experience in at least six important respects.

First, Japan had been at war since 1941 against the United States and was exhausted and traumatized after two atomic bombs had been dropped at Hiroshima and Nagasaki. There was no prospect of any military resistance, formal or informal, to the American presence. Although Saddam's forces were quickly dispersed by a rapid Coalition military victory, following upon the complete air supremacy enjoyed by the Coalition which preceded the intervention, this did not imply that they had been defeated. George W. Bush declared the 'end of major combat operations' while aboard the USS *Abraham Lincoln* off Iraq on 1 May 2003. In retrospect, this statement seems premature. Even as the Ba'ath party organization disintegrated, elements of the secret police and army began forming guerrilla units, since in many cases they had simply gone home rather than openly fight the invading forces. These units began to focus their attacks around Mosul, Tikrit, and Fallujah. In the autumn the *jihadis* began using ambush tactics, suicide bombings, and improvised explosive devices, targeting coalition forces and checkpoints. Saddam Hussein himself was captured on 14 December, but in the spring of 2004 there were fierce uprisings based on Fallujah and Najaf. The insurgency has continued since, varying in severity. None of this is comparable to the acquiescence of the Japanese with US occupation following the surrender in 1945.[21] There is little doubt that the strength of the insurgency, and the fact that at various times it has comprised both Sunni and Sh'ia elements, took the Coalition by surprise. Bremer admitted 'the insurgents have proven better organized and more difficult to penetrate than we had expected.' The difficulty here, as in other aspects of the post-war planning, was that a single set of assumptions drove US government efforts; 'no contingency plans were developed in case that one scenario did not occur.'[22]

Secondly, Japan in 1945 was united under Emperor Hirohito. Regime change there might be for the Japanese, but they were absolutely determined to retain their ruler in some form or other. The fate of the emperor was the central issue for Japanese politicians and led directly to a far-reaching discussion of Japanese national identity and the all-important question of where sovereignty would reside. Though regime change was relatively swiftly accomplished in Iraq, in the sense that the Ba'athist regime was swept aside, this did not confer legitimacy on the Coalition Provisional Authority (CPA) or the Iraq Interim Governing Council it appointed. In Japan in 1945, Emperor Hirohito was retained, but his powers curtailed; this had secured Japanese compliance. In contrast, the whole purpose of the Iraq intervention was to oust Saddam Hussein and his dynasty: his two sons were killed in July 2003. In all, over 200 top leaders of the former regime were killed or captured, as well as numerous lesser functionaries and military personnel. A pre-invasion Iraqi intelligence document had called for a strategy of organized resistance to be put into effect if and when Saddam's regime collapsed. In his memoirs of his fourteen months in power,[23] Bremer argues that the former Iraqi army had disbanded and could not be other than formally dissolved: 'when Iraqi draftees had seen which way the war was going in 2003, they simply deserted and went home to their farms and families.' Bremer left the de-Ba'athification policy to Iraqis on the Governing Council such as the former exile and Pentagon favourite Ahmed Chalabi. 'Our de-Ba'athification policy had targeted only the top 1 percent of the party's members,' he writes, 'but under Chalabi's direction, the Iraqi De-Ba'athification Council had broadened the policy, for example, depriving thousands of teachers of their jobs.' In retrospect, Bremer adds, he 'had been wrong to give a political body like the Governing Council responsibility for overseeing the de-Ba'athification policy'. The unwarranted extension of de-Ba'athification not only deprived the interim governing regime of administrative experience; it also unnecessarily created grievances among Iraqis against the new administration.

Thirdly, the Japanese politicians in 1945 were in ethnic and cultural terms united, as was the society which they sought to govern. Because of this, they were able to evade awkward or bizarre American proposals, such as MacArthur's wish to have the emperor convert to Christianity. It is still the case today that Japan remains a relatively monocultural society unaffected by mass immigration in a way which is quite different from Western Europe or the United States. There was no ethnic or cultural coherence in the Iraq ruled by the Coalition Provisional Authority in 2003. It was hopelessly split between Shi'ites and Kurds seeking revenge for their treatment under Saddam, and the Sunni minority, largely left out in the cold during the American administration and pursuing an insurgency which amounted to a continuing war of attrition. The old Iraqi army had been a Sunni Arab army. To reconstitute it would, as Bremer argued, have provoked strong reactions from Iraq's Shi'ite and Kurds; and it was in any case unlikely to have been loyal to Iraq's new Shi'ite-dominated political order. But since the Ba'athist army had already dispersed, Bremer's decree dissolving it was quite unnecessary; to Sunni Arabs – including former officers who had no intention of returning to military service – it was an added, and gratuitous, humiliation. This sense of having no stake in the new regime was accelerated by the perception that the provisional authority was not even-handed: such rebuilding of Iraq as has taken place – and this much less than was expected, with American budget resources coming to an end[24] – has been overwhelmingly in Shi'ite areas, not in the Sunni triangle. The Americans, says Zaid Saleem, a young man who works at a market in Baghdad, 'are the best [at] destroying things but they are the worst [at] rebuilding'.

Fourthly, the Japanese politicians in 1945 accepted a degree of accountability for the aggressive militarization of the 1930s. This consensus with the occupying power meant that the pacifist provisions within Article 9 of the Constitution were of secondary importance. The debates on this issue were not as contentious as might have been expected. There was a degree of optimism in a future world created by negotiation and alliance systems rather than the naked exercise of force. In contrast, in Iraq, there has been no prospect of achieving a governing consensus of all Iraqis, regardless of ethnic and religious loyalty. A memorandum of Stephen J. Hadley, the US National Security Adviser, from November 2006, leaked to the *New York Times*, raised serious doubts about Iraqi Prime Minister Maliki's capacity to rise above the sectarian challenges facing his government.[25] Commenting on the formation in August 2007 of a new government under Maliki, based on Shi'ites and Kurds but without Sunni participation, Guido Steinberg observes that the 'federalists' are the only force in Iraqi politics that can be expected to make any headway when it comes to stabilizing the country. 'This does nothing to change the observation that they are less interested in a functioning federal system than autonomy motivated by the desire for political power.' The only realistic objective was to establish a minimum of stability, even if this was to be achieved by a Shi'ite dictatorship in the Arab part of Iraq. The previous participation of Sunnis in the 'government of national unity' had failed to bring about reconciliation between the warring groups but had, predictably, paralysed the government.[26]

Fifthly, and unexpectedly, MacArthur did not have the free hand in Japan in 1945 for which he had wished. The United States agreed to share ultimate decision-making responsibility with other Allied powers in the Far Eastern Commission (FEC), which included France, Britain, and the USSR in addition to the United States. Each of these had a veto power, and the FEC itself was charged with setting policy for the post-war occupation of Japan. Thus, while MacArthur had a free hand on the ground, he ultimately had to answer to the FEC. These limitations compelled MacArthur to move as quickly as possible to establish a Japanese constitution that suited the United States. MacArthur and his staff used a degree of duplicity that enabled them to present the FEC with a constitutional *fait accompli*.

In Iraq, the original timescale envisaged by Jay Garner, the head of the civilian Office for Reconstruction and Humanitarian Assistance, was to stay only until June 2003, with a permanent, elected, government to be in place by August. Surprisingly, and perhaps in the hope of providing greater unity of effort, the Department of Defense rather than the State Department was placed in charge of civilian reconstruction, but it lacked expertise in this area.[27] Bremer reversed the policy of his predecessor and sought, with the help of right-wing Americans, to appoint Iraqis to draw up a new constitution which would be a model for the Middle East. His plan was blocked by Ali al-Sistani, the most senior Shi'ite cleric and leader of the Shi'ite coalition, an Iranian citizen who became the arbiter of Iraq's future while stubbornly refusing to meet Bremer. On 26 November 2003, under the headline 'How Cleric Trumped US Plan for Iraq', the *Washington Post* recorded that 'the unravelling of the Bush administration's script for political transition in Iraq began with a *fatwa*.' The wording of the *fatwa* was simple. It declared: 'there is no guarantee that the council would create a constitution conforming [to] the greater interests of the Iraqi people and expressing the national identity, whose basis is Islam, and its noble social values.'[28] With no way to get around the *fatwa*, and with escalating

American casualties creating pressure on the Bush administration, Bremer dumped his original plan in favour of an arrangement that would bestow sovereignty on a provisional government before a constitution was drafted.

Finally, the conclusion to be drawn from the drafting of the Japanese constitution in 1946 is deeply ambiguous. One response might be triumphalism: according to this view, Americans, following the providential victory of their armed forces, brought democracy to Asia. As Moore and Robinson express this response, American power might be said to have served the cause of universal democratization. But as the two authors recognize, the constitution imposed in 1946 was drafted largely by American military officers: 'virtually everyone in Tokyo suspected' this in 1946. 'It has also been generally known ever since. The Japanese people have had to live with this embarrassing reality. It has made their constitution vulnerable to right-wing fulminations, and it has left a sour taste.'[29] Moreover, institutional arrangements 'cannot be transported from one culture or country to another with predictable effects'. It was thus by no means inevitable that the commitment to parliamentary government would have 'the effect in Japan desired by the American framers'.[30] Though Japan has lacked a competitive two-party system for most of the last half-century, the democratic system itself has survived well: 'that this transformation of ideas was ultimately accomplished was a major achievement, and it was profoundly a joint achievement. Neither side could have produced this constitutional revolution alone.'[31]

Japanese politicians in 1945 had acted with a degree of consensus with the occupying power over the aims of the new constitution. In contrast, the American-dominated administration in Iraq found it very difficult to achieve agreement with the Shi'ite and Kurdish leadership, while for the most part the Sunnis remained outside the political process. Which of the many possible federal models does the Iraqi constitution mandate?, asks Gareth Stansfield, writing in *Prospect* in May 2006:[32]

> The imprecise nature of the document – adopted by referendum in October 2005 – makes it hard to say. It describes Iraq as being democratic, federal and representative. But it is difficult to pin down exactly how these ideals will be achieved. Kurdistan was 'approbated' in the constitution and recognised as existing within the boundaries of the 1991 entity – which did not include any of the disputed territories, including Kirkuk.[33] In addition, provision is made in section 5 of the constitution for new regions to establish themselves. The regional governments are held responsible for all domestic affairs that lie outside those assigned to the federal government, including the organization of internal security forces, and regional guards (known as

> militias, or *peshmerga* in Kurdistan). The ownership of oil and gas reserves is vague, but the emphasis of article 109 upon the federal government's management of oil and gas from 'current fields' has encouraged both the Kurds and Shi'as to believe that new fields would be the property of the region rather than the centre. Furthermore, the fact that article 117 places regional law above federal law (at least for those matters not designated as exclusively federal) again emphasises the extent of possible decentralization. However, all of these federal provisions remain in question, and the constitution is flanked by several supplementary deals, such as the famous 'Kurd veto', which remain shrouded in mystery and ambiguity.

## *The Implications of Shi'ite Majoritarianism*

If the story is correct (we have the testimony of the former US ambassador to Croatia, Peter Galbraith, that it is), President George W. Bush only discovered that there was a non-Sunni (viz. Shi'ite) majority in Iraq two months before the invasion of March 2003.[34] In an interview in August 2006, Ambassador Galbraith recounted this anecdote from his book to exemplify the 'culture of arrogance that pervaded the whole administration'. He added:[35]

> From the president and the vice-president down through the neoconservatives at the Pentagon, there was a belief that Iraq was a blank slate on which the United States could impose its vision of a pluralistic democratic society. The arrogance came in the form of a belief that this could be accomplished with minimal effort and planning by the United States and that it was not important to know something about Iraq.

Writing a column on 17 January 2004, the commentator Ehsan Ahrari noted that Grand Ayatollah Sistani had always known what he wanted: 'the establishment of a Shi'ite-dominated moderate Islamic democracy. He envisaged the US presence as a guarantor of that eventuality. More to the point, the Americans were to safeguard the Shi'ites' right to be the dominant group, and were to protect them from the re-emergence of another form of Sunni-dominated tyranny at the end of Saddam's tyranny.'[36]

The promise to support Iraq's reintegration into the region and the wider international community looks increasingly problematic in view of fears expressed in some quarters in the Middle East as to the emergence of a 'Shi'ite crescent', which provides Iran with a potential coalition of international allies and threatens a more general Sunni–Shi'ite conflict.[37] As *Le Monde* pointed out in an editorial on 19 July 2005, normalization of relations between Iraq and Iran was imposed on the American occupation regime by al-Sistani.[38] Though former president Khatami of Iran has denied the existence of a 'Shi'ite crescent',[39] the potential danger of such a realignment of forces has been raised by King Abdullah of Jordan. Abdullah told the *Washington Post* that the creation of a new Shi'ite crescent would particularly destabilize Gulf countries with Shi'ite populations. 'Even Saudi Arabia is not immune from this. It would be a major problem. And then that would propel the possibility of a Shi'ite–Sunni conflict even more, as you're taking it [beyond] the borders of Iraq', the king argued.[40]

There is no doubt that, although al-Zarqawi's ferocious jihadist assault on Shi'ites accelerated the breakdown of community relations between Sunnis and Shi'ites in Iraq, the advent of majoritarian democracy has been a destabilizing factor. Political leaders played upon ethnic and sectarian identities to gain election in Iraq. As the Indian sub-continent discovered in the 1930s and 1940s, once this particular genie is unleashed, it cannot be put back in the bottle. Contrary to Egyptian President Hosni Mubarak's comments in April 2006, most experts consider that Shi'ite Arabs remain more loyal to the country in which they live than to Iran.[41]

One of the saddening, maddening, and ultimately catastrophic verdicts on the Iraq intervention in 2003 was given in a little-noticed news story in the *New York Times* published on 17 July 2006. 'In an about-face', the headline reads for the story covering sectarian strife in Iraq, 'Sunnis want [the] US to remain in Iraq.'[42] The article argued that the pleas from Sunni Arab leaders had been growing in intensity since the eruption of sectarian violence in February. The Sunni Arab leaders still sympathized with the anti-US insurgency and considered that the Americans had helped strengthen the power of Iran, which backs the ruling Shi'ite parties; but they considered American military power in Iraq a 'bulwark' against Iranian intervention. Put another way, the news story virtually admitted that the American-led intervention in Iraq had made matters so bad that, although everyone wanted American troops to leave, there was simply no prospect of an early withdrawal without either sectarian civil war breaking out, or the partition of Iraq, or both.

In late July 2006, the Iraqi Prime Minister, Nuri al-Maliki, visited London and Washington and made it clear that there had been a failure to contain the spiralling violence in Baghdad, which was claiming approximately 100 fatalities a day: 2669 civilians had been killed in May and 3149 in June 2006 alone. President Bush acknowledged that the 'violence in Baghdad is still terrible' and that more troops were needed, which would be moved from other, more peaceful, areas of Iraq. Analysts talked freely of 'chaos' in Baghdad, with a battle needed to retake the city neighbourhood by neighbourhood. Former Democratic presidential candidate John

Kerry called the revised security plan for Baghdad 'a stunning sign that the administration still isn't being candid about Iraq's escalating civil war and the failure of Iraqi security forces to stand up on schedule'. The Iraqi Prime Minister closed his address with the acknowledgement that he was most concerned about continuing sectarian violence but that 'God willing, there will be no civil war in Iraq.'[43]

Beginning in February 2007, the White House sent an additional 28,000 US troops to Baghdad in an effort (called 'a limited surge') to quell the violence there. Securing the capital with overwhelming force was a key component of the anti-insurgency plan developed by General David Petraeus, the top American commander in Iraq and the military's foremost expert on counter-insurgency tactics. It took until June for all the forces to be put in place, but by August 2007 most American commentators (including a majority of conservative commentators) concluded that the 'surge' was too little too late. A bipartisan majority of experts, 68 per cent, favoured redeploying US forces from Iraq during the following 18 months.[44] Neo-conservative commentators, most notably the author of the 'limited surge' scheme, Frederick W. Kagan of AEI, maintain that the increase in troop levels has had a significant effect.[45] If so, this only serves to demonstrate that many of the problems faced by the occupying troops in Iraq would have been much less serious had troop levels been set at a more realistic level at the outset.

Unlike analysts in the West, some Arab commentators deny that the Americans and British have made 'mistakes' in Iraq. On the contrary, they argue that the intervening powers have been relatively successful in achieving their long-term aim, which was to 'divide and rule' and then partition the country. In the short term, sectarian tensions escalated to such a degree following the invasion that the Americans could justify their continuing presence on the grounds of acting as impartial arbiters. According to Ahmed Janabi, Hasan Nasr Allah, the leader of Hizbu'llah in Lebanon, has stated:

> the US has driven the situation in Iraq to a state where they offer themselves to Shi'a as a guarantee [of protection] against Sunni, and offer themselves to Sunni as a guarantee against Shi'a. They present themselves to Arabs as a guarantee against Kurds, and present themselves to Kurds as a guarantee against Arabs. Their plot is doing just fine. Look at the situation in Iraq nowadays: what could possibly happen that is more appropriate for separatists to say [than] that they have to split from Iraq to protect their community?[46]

Some commentators, such as Gareth Stansfield, go further and argue that partition, or 'radical decentralization', should not be seen as a problem.

'It is centralized Iraq – starting with Britain's creation of the modern state in 1921–23 and reaching its nadir in nearly three decades of Saddam Hussein's dictatorship – that has failed and should be allowed to die.'[47]

Within a year of the Iraq intervention, Samuel Berger, the National Security Adviser to President Bill Clinton from 1997 to 2001, argued that[48]

> Iraq ... will require a generational commitment by the international community. Regardless of whether the war was justified, everyone now has a profound stake in Iraq's success. The disintegration of that country along ethnic and religious fault lines would destabilize the Middle East and energize radical movements that threaten the world. A stable and democratic Iraq, on the other hand, would stimulate reform throughout the region. Attaining the latter outcome will require continuous involvement in Iraq's reconstruction and political development, as well as a proactive military posture that does not leave foreign troops hunkered down in bases and barracks, delegating security to an ill-prepared Iraqi security force. But that level of involvement will be unsustainable – and will be considered illegitimate by ordinary Iraqis – unless it is viewed as a truly international, rather than exclusively American, effort.

There has been little sign of that 'truly international effort' coming about to prevent the discomfiture of the United States. The Gulf States, in particular, have sought to prevent the Middle East peace conference from assisting the United States out of its 'Iraqi *impasse*'.[49]

### *'Balance of Consequences': the Tension between Privatizing Security and Reconstruction and Delivering on the Promises Made in 2003*

Tony Blair stated that 'we will help Iraq rebuild and not rebuild because of the problems of conflict ... but rebuild Iraq because of the appalling legacy that the rule of Saddam has left the Iraqi people.' The 'pledge to the people of Iraq' seems disingenuous. Tony Blair lacked the authority to prevent the abuses in the award of contracts, which placed Halliburton and other US companies with which prominent members of the Bush administration had long-standing financial interests in the driving seat for Iraq reconstruction. In a speech on 8 August 2003, President Bush claimed that 'in a lot of places, the infrastructure is as good as it was at pre-war levels, which is satisfactory, but it's not the ultimate aim. The ultimate aim is for the infrastructure to be the best in the region.'

US officials at the time promised a steady supply of 6,000 megawatts of electricity and a return to oil production output of 2.5 million barrels a day. However, 'the US never intended to rebuild Iraq completely,' Brigadier General William McCoy, the Army Corps of Engineers commander overseeing the work, told reporters. 'This was just supposed to be a jump-start.' The *Washington Post* reported on 2 January 2006 that oil production remained at 2 million barrels a day, still below the pre-invasion figure, while the national electrical grid had an average daily output of 4,000 megawatts, about 400 megawatts less than its pre-war level. Iraqis nationwide received on average less than 12 hours of power a day. For residents of Baghdad, it was six hours a day in December 2005, according to a US estimate, which residents claimed was an exaggeration. There was talk of a 'reconstruction gap', the difference between what Iraqis and Americans expected from the reconstruction effort at first and what was visible by 2006. Significant budget reallocations had occurred, including additional projects costs of nearly 25 per cent to provide for security. At least $1 billion earmarked for electricity was shifted to the budget to build up Iraq's army and police.[50]

Finally, in August 2007, the Iraq Finance Minister, Bayan Jabor, announced in Amman, Jordan, the reality that had been suspected for a long time, that his country remains devastated. 'We are in need of at least $100 billion to $150 billion to restore [the] infrastructure – from sewerage to water, to electricity, to bridges and [the] basic needs of the country,' he announced. He stated that about $4 billion had been spent on infrastructure projects thus far in 2007, more than in the whole of 2006, when internal violence and the limited capacity of the Iraqi private sector had resulted in only about 40 per cent of the $6 billion budget allocation being used. Iraq's 2007 budget allocation for capital investment was $14 billion and the government had withdrawn $7.4 billion from the Development Fund for Iraq (DFI), where Iraq's oil income is deposited and audited by the United Nations.[51]

The difficulty in rebuilding Iraq has resulted in part from political divisions within the Iraqi government; in part from the scale of the devastation; and in part because of the continuing problem in maintaining law and order. There is nothing magic about the calculation of successful troop levels for post-conflict stabilization: Bosnia and Kosovo suggest a ratio of 20 troops per thousand inhabitants. James T. Quinlivan of RAND calls the arithmetic 'painful'; but no one, he observes, 'has discovered successful stabilization strategies that avoid large troop commitments while trying to bring order to large populations'. In Afghanistan, the estimated population is 32 million, but the NATO force level is only 32,000 and the US force level is even less, at 10,000; the army/population level is less than one soldier per thousand inhabitants. In Iraq, on the assumption that the population is 27.5 million, the CIA estimate for 2007, then a post-conflict stabilization force in the region of 550,000 men would be needed (writing in 2003, and assuming a population of 25 million, Quinlivan considered that the Iraq intervention would require more than 500,000 foreign troops on the ground to meet a standard of 20 troops per thousand residents, the force used in Kosovo).[52]

James Dobbins, writing also for RAND in 2003, observed that

> [the] figures of 500,000 troops or $36 billion in aid [required for Iraq] are beyond the capacity of even the world's only superpower to generate or sustain. Even half those levels will require the United States to broaden participation in Iraq's post-conflict stabilization and reconstruction well beyond the comparatively narrow coalition that fought the war, thereby mounting a broader international effort on the Balkan models. According to the lessons learned, the ultimate consequences for Iraq of a failure to generate adequate international manpower and money are likely to be lower levels of security, higher casualties sustained and inflicted, lower economic growth rates, and slower, less thoroughgoing political transformation.

Short departure deadlines are incompatible with nation-building, in Dobbins's view. 'The United States will succeed only if it makes a long-term commitment to establishing strong democratic institutions and does not beat a hasty retreat tied to artificial deadlines.' Setting premature dates for early national elections can also be counter-productive: the Iraq experience shows a considerable hardening of the sectarian divide once religious parties received democratic endorsement. Internal fragmentation (along political, ethnic, or sectarian lines) and a lack of external support from neighbouring states are further hindrances to nation-building. Dobbins predicted that the United States was 'unlikely to be able to generate adequate levels of troops, money, or endurance as long as it relies principally upon the limited coalition with which it fought the war'.[53]

The true scale of the nation-building exercise in Iraq can only be estimated by adding together the official military figures and the unofficial civilian presence. In September 2007, there were 169,000 US troops in Iraq, up from 130,000 before Bush announced a 'surge' of US forces in January. The scale of outsourcing in Iraq is staggering. During the first Gulf war in 1991, there was one contractor for every 100 soldiers. At the start of the 2003 Iraq invasion, the ratio was one contractor for every 10 soldiers. Three years into the US occupation, the ratio had reached 1:3. Less than a year later, with the occupation approaching its fourth year, there was one contractor for every 1.4 US soldiers.[54] As Peter W. Singer commented in his *Foreign Affairs* article on the subject in 2005, 'by privatizing parts of the US mission, the Bush administration has dramatically lowered the political price for its Iraq policies,' since it has not had to make the painful choice of either increasing the number of serving American troops or bringing in combatants from allied countries.[55]

A census of contractors carried out by CENTCOM in February 2007, and notified to the *Los Angeles Times* four months later,[56] revealed that there were more private contractors than troops in Iraq. More than 180,000 civilians – including Americans, foreigners, and Iraqis, who formed the majority by far (118,000) – were working in Iraq under US contracts, according to State and Defense department figures. However, even if the numbers of troops and civilian contractors are added together, the total force for stabilization and reconstruction – 349,000 – is still well below the number suggested in the RAND report of 2003.

On 18 September 2007, the Iraqi government ordered the private contracting firm Blackwater USA – the firm that guards the US Ambassador, Ryan C. Crocker – out of the country following a shooting leaving eight dead and 13 wounded. The interior minister pronounced on television that foreign contractors 'must respect Iraqi laws and the right of Iraqis to independence in their land'. The legal difficulty with his comment was that before the United States handed over sovereignty to the Iraqis in 2004, a law was passed (Order No. 17) which gave private companies immunity from Iraqi law.[57] The Americans suggested a joint commission to look at the facts of the case, but reports in the *New York Times* accepted that armed guards in Iraq operated in a 'legal limbo'.[58] Michael Rubin had earlier observed in August 2005 that 'local workers can do without the private security people whom foreign contractors employ and whose recklessness Iraqis despise.' 'Iraqi civilians and politicians both identify the security contractors as the biggest impediment to the battle for hearts and minds. Nor would Iraqis spend aid money on unnecessary foreign personnel.'[59]

The Report of the UN High-Level Panel on Threats, Challenges and Change in December 2004, entitled *A More Secure World: Our Shared Responsibility* argued (para. 207) that 'in considering whether to authorize or endorse the use of military force, the Security Council should always address – whatever other considerations it may take into account – *at least* the following five basic criteria of legitimacy: seriousness of threat; proper purpose; last resort; proportional means; and balance of consequences.' The last criterion was defined thus: is there a reasonable chance of the military action being successful in meeting the threat in question, with the consequences of action not likely to be worse than the consequences of inaction?[60] A true *jus post bellum*, it has been argued,[61] needs to include the *principle of repentance*, requiring a sense of humility and remorse by the victors for the suffering and death that was brought about even in a just struggle; the *principle of honourable surrender* (not demeaning the vanquished or being punitive in intent); the *principle of restoration* (the removal of the instruments of war from the fields of battle, and assistance to the losing nation in repairing the basic infrastructure of the society); finally, the *need to re-establish civil society* (extending the principle of restoration to encompass not merely the basic infrastructure but also the human infrastructure for peaceful communal life).

Even those formerly close to the regime, whether in Washington DC or in Iraq,[62] have been unsparing in their criticism. Henry Kissinger stated before the war: 'I am viscerally opposed to a prolonged occupation of a Muslim country at the heart of the Muslim world by Western nations who proclaim the right to re-educate that country.'[63] In a speech in Orlando, Florida, former White House counter-terrorism chief Richard A. Clarke stated on 26 June 2004 that the invasion of Iraq was an 'enormous mistake' that was costing untold lives, strengthening al-Qaeda, and breeding a new generation of terrorists. 'We did exactly what al-Qaeda said we would do: invade and occupy an oil-rich Arab country that wasn't threatening us in any way,' Clarke commented, adding that 'the hatred that has been engendered by this invasion will last for generations …'[64]

In his collection of essays entitled *Arguing about War,* Michael Walzer argues that 'we need criteria for a *jus post bellum* that are distinct from (though not wholly independent of) those that we use to judge the war and its conduct.' Discussing the intervention in Iraq more specifically, he argues that having fought the war 'we are now responsible for the well-being of the Iraqi people; we have to provide the resources – soldiers and dollars – necessary to guarantee their security and begin the political and economic reconstruction of their country.'[65] In constructing a *jus post bellum,* David E. Kellogg has stressed the importance of war crimes trials;[66] in contrast, Kenneth R. Himes in essence argues for reconciliation and mutual forgiveness,[67] both of which are extremely difficult to achieve when there have been substantial civilian casualties and the normal ordering of society has been permanently disrupted. Writing in 2000, Brian Orend discusses the application of the concept of the *jus post bellum* to a specific situation, the aftermath of the first Gulf war of 1991.[68] However, the difference between the first and the second Gulf Wars centres on the question of regime change and the consequences which flow from this; on this point, understandably, Orend is silent.

Recently, Dr Timothy L. Challans of the US School of Advanced Military Studies has taken up the issue precisely in the area of regime change.[69] He argues that 'political and military leaders share moral agency in both the political and military realms at all stages of a regime change operation. Following this state of affairs, it may be time to address the issue of also assigning them moral responsibility …' The analysis is penetrating, but no solutions are offered by Challans. Instead we have to turn to the discussion by Rear Admiral Louis V. Iasiello, who specifically addresses the moral responsibilities of victors in war and provides the most thorough discussion of the dimensions of post-war needs to date. He notes the need for a healing mindset; a just restoration; safeguarding the innocent; respect for the environment; *post-bellum* justice; warrior transition; and learning the lessons.[70] Had this analysis been taken seriously by the military planners in 2002 and early 2003, many of the mistakes in Iraq would have been avoided.

Given the deeply pessimistic conclusions of former Secretary of State Henry Kissinger ('Americans must accept the reality that their country can never make a total political withdrawal, though the size and location of the military presence [in Iraq] will vary'),[71] James Dobbins's conclusion comes almost as a relief: 'there is no quick fix for nation-building. None of our cases was successfully completed in less than seven years.' The American-led stabilization and reconstruction program for Iraq, Dobbins correctly observes, has 'not gone as smoothly as might be expected, given abundant, recent, and relevant American experience. This is, after all, the sixth major nation-building enterprise the United States has mounted in eleven years, and the fifth in a Muslim nation or province.'[72] Post-conflict stabilization and reconstruction with the objective of promoting a transition to democracy 'appear to be the inescapable responsibility of the world's only superpower':[73]

> Nation-building has been a controversial mission over the past decade, and the extent of this controversy has undoubtedly curtailed the investments needed to do these tasks better. So has institutional resistance in both the state and defence departments, neither of which regards nation-building among its core missions. As a result, successive administrations tend to treat each new such mission as if it were the first and, more importantly, the last …

On this occasion, however, they will be unable to do so, because of the signature by George W. Bush and Prime Minister al-Maliki of a 'declaration of principles' in November 2007, whereby Iraq's government will 'embrace a long-term US troop presence in return for US security guarantees as part of a strategic partnership … an enduring relationship in military, economic and political terms'. Allegedly, the Iraq government representatives who negotiated the declaration of principles foresee a long-term presence of 'about 50,000 US troops' at the American bases in Iraq as well as 'preferential treatment for American investments'.[74] In these circumstances, the outcome of the Iraq intervention would be much like the PNAC report of 2000 had envisaged, and would survive any transition to a Democrat-led executive under Hillary Clinton or Barack Obama in January 2009.

# Chapter Ten
# Towards 'Eurabia' or the Co-Habitation of Civilizations?

> While I maintain that the future of Europe – whether continuing in its historic Christian identity or becoming an adjunct of Muslim North Africa – is still an open question, the behaviour of the British public, that weakest link in the Western chain, suggests that it, at least, may be too confused to resist its Londonistan destiny.
>
> (Daniel Pipes, 'Piggybacking on Terror in Britain', *New York Sun*, 29 August 2006)

> Euro-Islam is the very same religion as Islam, although culturally adjusted to the civic culture of modernity. In European civil societies, an 'open Islam' could be as at home as, for instance Afro-Islam, having been adjusted to domestic African cultures ... the politics of Euro-Islam would not allow complete assimilation of Muslims. Yet it could enable the adoption of forms of civil society leading to an enlightened, open-minded Islamic identity compatible with European civic culture.
>
> (Bassam Tibi, 2002)[1]

In 1995, during a two-year tenure as NATO Secretary-General, the Belgian politician Willy Claes claimed that, since the collapse of communism, the new threat to the alliance was Islam. He contended that NATO was much more than a military alliance, but was committed to 'defending basic principles of civilization that bind North America and Western Europe'.[2] What he meant, and should have said, Bassam Tibi correctly argued, was that a potential threat to the countries of the alliance arises from Islamic fundamentalism. Tibi quoted the retort of King Hassan II of Morocco, which is that if Islamic fundamentalism is to be engaged, it cannot be with tanks and other weapons by means of a defensive alliance such as NATO. Islamic fundamentalism is a political challenge and has to be met on its own terms and in the struggle of ideas.[3]

Timothy M. Savage contends that Huntington's *Clash of Civilizations* has had 'and continues to have a far greater resonance in Europe than it does in the United States'. He notes that 'many inside and outside Europe will consider the failure to address and avert the looming crisis arising from the clash of cultures within European borders as confirmation of Huntington's thesis'. Conversely, success in dealing with the potential clash of cultures and identities, 'which results in a shift of both Muslim and non-Muslim European mindsets, and crafts a societal framework that encourages integration and respects individual as well as national identities would negate Huntington's thesis of the inevitable incompatibility of Islam and the West'.[4] Savage at least regards the outcome as far from predetermined. George Joffé is ambivalent,[5] while others are much more alarmist, and it is to these commentators that we turn first to understand the 'Eurabian' discourse.

### *Burgeoning Muslim Demographic Advance and 'Eurabian' Civil War: the Alarmist Scenario*

In one of his long ruminations in 2003, Donald Rumsfeld noted that there are 'unknown unknowns – the ones we don't know we don't know'. A chronic insecurity pervades the writing of many American commentators since 9/11, arising perhaps from Thomas Friedman's remark that the failure to prevent those events was not so much a failure of intelligence – though the intelligence failings are clear[6] – as a failure of imagination.[7] Bernard Lewis has added to these fears by his contrast between the certainties of besieged Britain in 1940 and the uncertainties of the West in the twenty-first century: 'in 1940, we knew who we were, we knew who the enemy was, we knew the dangers and the issues … It is different today. We don't know who we are, we don't know the issues, and we still do not understand the nature of the enemy.'[8] (In fact, Lewis has made his predictions clear in *ex cathedra* statements that the Muslims will take over Europe, which in turn 'will be[come] part of the Arabic west, of the Maghreb'.)[9]

When such statements are made by the West's supposed 'pre-eminent scholar of Islam', it is likely that others will become fearful and indulge their fantasies in elaborate scenarios of collapse. The US National Intelligence Council joined the trend in December 2004, according to the controversial journalist Mark Steyn, predicting the 'collapse' of the European Union by 2020; while for his part Steyn considers this prediction over cautious![10] In reality, the 2004 report of the US NIC did nothing of the sort. It gave three possible estimates for the Muslim population in Europe in 2020 (low: below 25 million; medium: under 30 million; high:

under 40 million) and talked of 'economic stasis' unless the growing immigrant – chiefly Muslim – population was accommodated. It noted that the current total birth-rate (existing Europeans plus new immigrants) of 1.4 was well below the level of 2.1 needed to secure a replacement of, rather than a decline in, the overall population level.[11]

The term 'Eurabia' was popularized by the Geneva-based historian Bat Ye'or ('Daughter of the Nile', the pseudonym of Gisèle Litmann). She maintains that the Euro–Arab Dialogue between the European Union and the Arab League has been 'a means of spreading the economic and cultural *jihads* from the Middle East to Europe'. 'Eurabia's destiny was sealed when it decided, willingly, to become a covert partner with the Arab global *jihad* against America and Israel,' Ye'or argues.[12] For Bat Ye'or, not only is Islam a global threat to Western civilization, it has already begun to create the 'dhimmitude of the West' – that is, to reduce the West to the subordinate status of the *dhimmis* or protected religious minorities under Islamic suzerainty. (Her websites are devoted to the concepts of *dhimmi* and dhimmitude.)[13] She creates a vision of Islam as an evil, infiltrating force, incapable of changing its 'innate character of *jihad* and dhimmitude'.[14]

Subsequently the term 'Eurabia' has been given a much wider meaning. Instead of being confined to Euro–Arab relations, the emphasis is now more on changes within Europe itself, resulting from immigration and Muslim demographics – in Mark Steyn's expression, 'Islam is now the principal supplier of new Europeans.'[15] The same author declares Eurabia to be 'in the early stages of an undeclared civil war', with every 'Western' woman in the EU producing an average of 1.4 children, while every 'Muslim' (= 'Eastern') woman – in Steyn's mindset, by definition there can be no 'Western' Islam or Western Muslims – is producing 3.5 children. Whereas America's population growth is 'secure', Europe's is in 'precipitous decline'.[16] Paul Weston claims that it is 'inevitable' that by 2025 Europe will find itself engaged in civil war because of a rapidly increased Muslim population. He suggests that a Muslim/non-Muslim ratio of 1:9 among males aged between 20 and 40 is 'not hypothetical' by 2025. If 28 million immigrants arrive, and 70 per cent are Muslims, the figure might rise to 1:5. By 2025 there will be 'some 12 million Turkish males of fighting age' (*sic*); if Turkey joins the EU by then, the ratio could become 1:2.[17]

Such extrapolations from the existing demographic evidence are highly controversial, indeed tendentious. Other, less hectoring, neo-conservative commentators draw similar conclusions. Thus, George Weigel asked in 2004, 'why is Europe systematically depopulating itself? Why is Europe committing demographic suicide? Why does no Western European country have a replacement-level birth-rate? Why will Spain's population [in all likelihood] decline from 40 million to 31.3 million by the middle of the century? Why will 42 per cent of Italians be over age sixty by 2050?' These phenomena, he concludes, are 'the expression of a profound, longstanding crisis of civilizational morale'.[18] Daniel Pipes's projection is characteristically blunt. 'Demographic collapse also points to Europe being Islamized.' The existing rate is just two-thirds of what it needs to be: 'one-third of the requisite population is simply not being born.' For Pipes, Europe faces three options: assimilation (his terminology) of the Muslim minority; the expulsion of the Muslim minority; or an Islamic takeover.[19]

It is possible to arrive at more conservative estimates of Muslim population growth in Europe, but first we need to start from an agreed baseline figure and define what we mean by Europe. Philip Jenkins notes that the sharpest 'Islamic challenge' is in fact to be found in Russia, which many exclude from the category of 'Europe'. Its Muslim population is largely concentrated in regions far removed from the heartland, yet the numbers are significant: 15 to 20 million Muslims out of a national population of 143 million, or between 10 per cent and 14 per cent of the total. The other problematic country is Turkey, with an almost entirely Muslim population of 70 million. Turkish admission to the European Union is fiercely contested by conservative politicians in some EU countries and while in principle it is likely that it will gain admission at some future date, it would be a brave person who would predict when this will happen.

Leaving Russia and Turkey aside, there are three categories of states in or under negotiation for the European Union.[20] First, the older member states of the EU, whose total Muslim population is thought to be a mere 15.3 million out of a total of 358.1 million (or 4.3 per cent). The second category are the newer member states and those which joined in 2007–8. This would add another 135.8 million to the total population of Europe but only 1.45 million extra Muslims. Finally, there are those states which are candidate countries or whose membership is under negotiation, excluding Turkey. This comprises a much higher proportion of Muslims (28.2 per cent) but a relatively small number – only 7.1 million – out of a total population of 25.1 million. Taking these figures as whole (and assuming successful accession negotiations), Jenkins estimates the EU population at 521 million, with 23.8 million Muslims or 4.6 per cent of the total. Given that the EU population is expected to stagnate while the Muslim population is still increasing through immigration and in some cases higher birth-rates (though birth-rates in some countries with Muslim majorities are also falling),[21] it is realistic to envisage a Muslim population of 40 million in 2025 out of a total EU population of 500 million, or 8 per cent, perhaps increasing to 15 per cent by 2050.[22] Even if we accept a rival estimate of

20 per cent by 2050,[23] such numbers are potentially manageable under certain conditions – conditions which we will consider below.

In large areas of continental Europe – Poland, Portugal, Greece, the Czech Republic, Hungary, Slovakia, Finland, Ireland, and the Baltic states – there is either no Muslim presence at all, or only a minimal Muslim presence. Eighty per cent of the mosques and 55 per cent of the total Muslim presence in Europe apart from Russia and Turkey are to be found in just six countries: France, Germany, the UK, Italy, Spain, and the Netherlands. Even within those states, the Muslim population is again geographically confined in certain urban centres. Members of the alarmist school such as Bruce Bawer denounce these 'Muslim enclaves' as places ruled by theocracy rather than democracy, 'ruled by *imams* and elders' who preach 'contempt for the host society and its values'.[24] Even serious scholars talk of Muslim 'ghettos' and the phenomenon of 'ghettoization'. Here important distinctions need to be made between types of housing, and educational and employment opportunities for the residents within predominately Muslim areas. Where educational and economic self-advancement occurs, the detailed evidence suggests that Muslims move away from cramped housing conditions into the suburbs much as prosperous white residents have done in previous generations.[25]

However, the converse is also true: where there are large conglomerations of Muslims in poor housing, with low educational and employment opportunities, then the problems of urban management become most acute. The situation is compounded in circumstances when anti-Muslim sentiment has been mobilized and exploited by extreme right-wing political groups for their own purposes and with the aim of stimulating religious, racial, and inter-community tension. The riots in the Paris *bidonvilles* in November 2005 are the clearest example of the resentment that can arise among the Muslim population at social exclusion and high rates of unemployment. The protest was at once political, social, cultural, and economic. Contrary to some of the alarmist reporting at the time, which made reference to the discourse of Eurabia, the Paris riots provided little evidence of a domestically based *jihad* against European values as such.[26]

In contrast, the London bombers of 7 July 2005 were apparently reasonably well 'integrated' into British society, but the difference was that they had not accepted that they owed their primary responsibility and loyalty to British society in which they lived. Instead, they had pledged a higher loyalty to the Muslim *ummah* and the supposed *jihad* against British foreign policy in Iraq and Afghanistan. The London bombers exemplify the reality that al-Qaeda's current campaign is 'less a product of Islamic fundamentalism than of a simple strategic goal' – to obtain the withdrawal of Western combat forces from Muslim-majority countries where they are stationed.[27] None of this condones or justifies the action of the London bombers; but we do need to understand their mental world view in order to address the key issue facing both the Muslim and non-Muslim populations of Europe: that of integration.

### *What is to be Done? Integration and Learning the Art of Reciprocity*

With his customary assertiveness, the journalist Mark Steyn contends that when his Belgian grandparents emigrated to Canada, 'the idea was that the immigrants assimilated with the host country. As Kofi [Annan] and Co. see it, today the host country has to assimilate with the immigrants.'[28] For immigrants, of course, read Muslims. They, the same author contends, have rapidly 'mastered the language of victimhood' in appropriating the name of 'Islamophobia' for anti-Muslim prejudice and action. Steyn claims that Muslims use 'politically correct self-indulgent victimology as a cover'; 'Islamophobia' is an invented psychosis of the progressive mind, while the phenomenon it purports to describe is 'bogus'.[29] Unsurprisingly, Daniel Pipes joins the chorus of those who argue against the term and consider that the phenomenon it describes is exaggerated.[30]

Writing in March 2006, Salman Rushdie – and eleven other writers united against Islamist 'totalitarianism' – called 'Islamophobia' 'a wretched concept that confuses criticism of Islam as a religion and stigmatization of those who believe in it'.[31] Whether we like it or not, the concept is with us. Its proponents argue that it has eight features. Islam is seen as a monolithic bloc, static and unresponsive to change. It is considered as separate and 'other'. Islam is perceived not to have values in common with other cultures, not to be affected by them, and not to influence them. It is seen as inferior to 'the West', barbaric, irrational, primitive, and sexist. It believed to be violent, aggressive, threatening, supportive of terrorism, and engaged in a Clash of Civilizations. It is viewed as a political ideology, used for political or military advantage. Criticisms made of 'the West' by Islam are rejected out of hand. Hostility towards Islam is used to justify discriminatory practices towards Muslims and the exclusion of Muslims from mainstream society. Finally, anti-Muslim hostility is seen as natural and normal.[32] Islamophobia has replaced anti-Semitism as the focus of the European Far Right, according to Glyn Ford, a British member of the European Parliament and author of a book on neo-Fascism in Europe. 'Europe is in danger of seeing its extreme-Right parties move into the mainstream', he claims. 'Islamophobia has become the prejudice of the day, but the threat from the extreme Right is real and it is found across the European Union.'[33]

American commentators invariably use the term 'assimilation' to describe the phenomenon of merging new immigrants into European societies. Yet in so doing, they fail to recognize the different understanding of the term in the UK and the US. In the US, 'assimilation' is perceived as a virtue. In Robert Park's definition in 1930, it is a process, or set of processes by which people of diverse racial origins and different cultural heritages occupy a common territory, and achieve a cultural solidarity sufficient 'at least to sustain a national existence'. Milton Gordon in 1964 suggested that the components of the process were legitimacy (each group must believe that the other has a legitimate right to be in the US), effective functioning in the workplace and other social settings; exercise of civic responsibility; and finally, immigrants must identify themselves as Americans first, ahead of any residual association with their birthplace or ethnic homeland. Peter D. Salins argued in 1997 that the reason assimilation has been successful in the US is that Americans have been predisposed to make it work, since they were 'instilled with the assimilationist ethos': 'Americans, through their faith in individual achievement, have given immigrants the chance to prove themselves.' Surprisingly, Salins contends that 'the great hallmark of assimilation, American style, is that immigrants are free to retain or discard as much or as little of their homeland cultures as they wish without compromising their assimilation.' He does not demonstrate how this is achieved. When assimilation fails, he distinguishes between assimilation and acculturation. Timothy J. McVeigh, the perpetrator of the bombing of the Oklahoma City federal office building in April 1995 was acculturated – in Salins's definition – but not truly assimilated since he rejected America's ethnic diversity and civic assimilation.[34]

In contrast to the broad support for the term 'assimilation' in the US, it is viewed pejoratively in the UK. 'Assimilation', the former Commission for Racial Equality (CRE) defines as 'absorbing minorities into the ways of the majority – requiring them to adopt the majority's language, customs and "values". Broadly speaking, it means creating a loyalty to the majority and a reduction of differences with it on the part of minority groups.' 'One of the problems with assimilation policy', the CRE continues, 'is that it presupposes a unitary pattern of views and practices among the majority which does not in fact exist.' It has tended to have the negative connotation of 'enforced uniformity and disregard for minorities'. In contrast, integration[35]

> requires acceptance of a country's laws, of human rights such as freedom of speech, and of basic democratic rights, but does not require the eradication of all cultural differences or group-identities; it is conceived of as a two-way process, through which both the majority and the minorities influence

> and change one another, and in which differences can be peacefully accommodated as long is there a common commitment to living together. 'Mutual tolerance' was the aim expressed by Roy Jenkins, Home Secretary in 1967. The term, 'integration' was much used in the late 1960s and 70s to defend minority rights, but fell out of favour when its use was felt to disguise what was really assimilation. More recently it has been rehabilitated as an explicit aim of policy, and the CRE has defined its conditions as being the equality, interaction and participation of all groups in society ...

For Bassam Tibi, 'integration does not demand cultural surrender of the self through total conformity, but merely ... participation in ... civil society's system of civic values. Unlike assimilation, integration limits itself to the adoption of a citizen identity within civil society; it focuses on the rights and duties of the *citoyen*.'[36] Tibi asserts that 'Islamists often willingly confuse assimilation with political integration in order to rebuff the latter.'[37]

How might such integration of Muslims work in practice? How might the competing demands of the faith – especially the concept of a world-wide community of believers (*ummah*) – be reconciled with the requirement of European governments that the primary allegiance should be to the country of residence and the European Union rather than to a residual loyalty overseas? Well, not in the way that Gulam Rasool Khan from Lahore, Pakistan, suggests in a posting on the BBC website. For Khan, 'Muslims in non-Islamic lands must, and will, eventually exist as a separate nation bound to the *Ummah*, and not to the non-Islamic laws of the host country. Muslims have a supreme constitution, the Qur'an, that supersedes any earthly constitution.'[38] This is exactly the way to make matters worse very fast indeed! Olivier Roy terms this approach 'neo-fundamentalism', which he argues is not tied to a particular nation or national identity, but is a product of contemporary globalization.[39]

For Bassam Tibi, Islam and Europe need to be harmonized through what he calls 'Euro-Islam', which is something more than Tariq Ramadan's being a European Muslim ('Tariq Ramadan presents orthodox Islam as Euro-Islam presumably with the intent to deceive').[40] Euro-Islam, Tibi suggests, 'is the opposite of Ghetto-Islam or fundamentalist Islam. It is the Muslim migrants in Europe who need to choose, for themselves and for their children, whether to continue to be alien or to join the changed "club" of Europe, i.e. to be integrated without being assimilated.'[41] Tibi arrived at his viewpoint from observing the African experience in the 1980s:

> The concept of Euro-Islam derives from observations that I had made a decade earlier in West Africa ... In Senegal I was able to identify an Africanization of Islam. Having seen how Islam had been adopted in West

> Africa despite its Arab origins, how it had become part of the autochthonous culture, I asked whether it would not be possible to attempt to make Islam indigenous to Europe along similar lines. In Europe, the Islam of immigrants remains utterly alien because it is not European ... how can we make Islam European in Europe, in the way that it has become African in Senegal and South-East Asian in Indonesia?

In Indonesia, Abdurrahman Wahid has noted that 'the indigenization of Islam is part of the history of Islam', though he contends that 'what is being "indigenized" is only the manifestation of Islam.' Munawir Syadzali for his part emphasizes the need through independent reasoning (*ijtihad*) to make Islam more responsive to the needs of Indonesia's local and temporal circumstances.[42]

John Kelsay has described European Islamic communities as forming 'a sort of sectarian enclave in ... Western culture', of being 'in the West, but not of it'. The most extreme example, according to Dominique Thomas, Melanie Phillips, and others, is London, which they claim has become 'the European hub for the promotion, recruitment and financing of Islamist terror and extremism – so much so that it has been mockingly dubbed "Londonistan".'[43] The complex interplay of identities – French, Algerian, Kabyle, Muslim, and secular – that unites Algeria and France into a single post-colonial and trans-political space is most clearly described by Paul A. Silverstein's chosen title – *Algeria in France*.[44] But these are only some of the Muslim identities in France. (A similarly diverse picture is to be found of Muslim identities in the UK.) Laurence and Vaisse try to dispel the common perception that French Muslims form a 'homogeneous and mobilized community' set on 'creat[ing] a society separate from the mainstream'. The reality, they point out, is that France's five million Muslims are divided along ethnic, socio-economic, ideological, and even religious lines.

Three-quarters of French Muslims originally came from the Maghreb; half are Arab. The largest group is the Algerians (1.55 million), with the Moroccans not far behind (about 1 million), and the Tunisians, Turks, and Black Africans some way off in numerical importance (350,000, 315,000 and 250,000 respectively).[45] About half are French citizens, and half of those are of voting age. Foreign policy is not a high priority for French Muslims. Even if it were, there would be no Muslim voting bloc to influence it effectively; France's Muslim population is simply too diverse. 'France's position on foreign affairs', the authors conclude, 'would not look much different even if there were no Muslim minority in France.' Though serious problems exist, Laurence and Vaisse foresee the emergence of a religion and a population that feels at home in, and at peace with, French society – a 'French Islam' to replace 'Islam in France'.[46] Jocelyne Cesari is broadly in agreement with this prognosis.[47] After a historical discussion of Islamophobia in France and the Algerian 'problem', Neil MacMaster also concludes positively on the deep 'level of change toward integration and adaptation' and the 'growing awareness of the rich and positive diversity of an Islam in and of France'.[48]

'Integration is our objective', comments Nadia Chekrouni, the minister for Moroccans living abroad (about one-third of all Moroccans living abroad live in France), 'but that need not constitute a rupture with the mother country ... Political representation is one of our priorities, because our strategy is centred on citizenship.'[49] More controversially, the French example demonstrates the active role of the government in trying to create a 'wise, reasonable Islam, which would not pose any danger, and with which one could have a dialogue'. The intention has been and remains to draw a line between an Islam 'which we can organize and administer, to give [it] respectability and visibility ...' and a fundamentalist Islam which 'we cannot accept' and must be contained and marginalized.[50]

It is no surprise that the battleground between fundamentalist and progressive Islam in the West, especially in Europe, has been the position of women. 'The Islamist version of Islam', Nikki R. Keddie correctly observes, 'includes a return to universal veiling, however changed the endorsed costume may be, and to various degrees of sex segregation. In addition, Islamist pressure or rule in various Muslim countries has resulted in reverses in legal gains for women and greater tolerance for various forms of violence against, and mistreatment of, women.' Keddie argues that women and gender issues are both 'core-central to Islamist ideologies and practices' and to opposition to Islamism.[51] Olivier Roy agrees that 'the status of women is at the core of the crisis,'[52] while Ronald Inglehart and Pippa Norris contend that 'Samuel Huntington was only half-right': 'the real fault line between the West and Islam, which Huntington's theory completely overlooks, concerns gender equality and sexual liberalization.'[53]

Caught between the traditional patriarchal family model and an egalitarian nuclear model, today's Muslim families have been called 'neo-patriarchal'. They continue to display traits of intra-familial gender-based inequality. Priscilla Offenhauer talks in terms of a 'wish list' of conservatives and Islamists.[54] Islamic family law, with gender relations at its core, has become 'the preferential symbol' of Islamist or fundamentalist identity. Unusually, the two Islamic countries to the east and west of the European Union, Turkey and Tunisia, by eliminating dual legal systems and opting for a unitary secular law, have realized many of the individual items of family law reform that have been sought elsewhere. Turkey, after the establishment of the republic in 1923, and Tunisia, after gaining independence in 1956, outlawed polygamy, raised the minimum age of marriage for females and required their consent, outlawed a husband's unilateral right to divorce by giving both spouses the right to seek legal divorce, and granted the mother the guardianship of minor children in the case of the father's death. In January 2004, the Moroccan senate unanimously adopted a far more liberal family code. The code requires that divorce be granted only in court, thus curtailing men's privilege to divorce their wives verbally.

In contrast, under Khomeini, Iranian law was changed to stipulate that girls might marry at the age of nine. While this provision might have produced some instances of early marriage, it has not prevented Iran's current average marriage age from soaring well into the 20s, as people make decisions on marriage in the light of a set of socio-economic factors and changes, regardless of what the law permits. Remarkably, the Islamic Republic of Iran experienced the fastest fertility transition ever recorded in history, with a drop from 6.4 children per woman in 1986, to a below-replacement level of 2.06 in 1998. The figure for 2005 is reported to be 2 children per woman for Iran, 2.2 for Turkey, 2.4 for Algeria, 2.5 for Morocco and 2 for Tunisia. Delayed marriage, wider acceptance of – and access to – family planning services, and increased education of girls and young women have brought about these changes,[55] which seem to be largely independent of type of regime, Islamist or otherwise. (It should be noted that the figure for Israel is higher – 2.8 children per woman.) These actual figures provide a definitive answer to the alarmist projections of the supporters of the 'Eurabia' myth cited earlier.

By delaying marriage and having fewer children, Muslim women are rapidly reducing or eliminating the distinction between their marriage and childbearing patterns and those seen in non-Muslim societies at comparable levels of development. Muslim women also are closing the gap between their rates of participation in the work force and those of non-Muslim women. All of this augurs well for the integration of Muslims in Europe: the alarmist demographic projections may well be found to be untrue, particularly if the Muslim rate of reproduction continues to decline in line with European trends, while the evidence suggests that a high participation of Muslim women in employment is possible provided that they have the necessary education and language skills. The key to integration is therefore social inclusion, above all immediate and full access to primary, secondary, and higher education for Muslims, both male and female.

A change of attitudes is required for integration to work, which leads us back to Bassam Tibi's agenda for a European Islam (or, preferably we would argue, an Islam firmly rooted in each of the different European societies, since the complexion of the Muslim religio-cultural traditions varies in each case). 'Either Islam gets Europeanized, or Europe gets Islamized', Tibi wrote in *Welt am Sonntag*. 'The problem is not whether the majority of Europeans is Islamic', he adds, 'but rather which Islam – *sharia* Islam or Euro-Islam – is to dominate in Europe.' Tibi is categorical in his assertion that

> only an Islam that is in tune with the fundamentals of cultural modernity (democracy, individual human rights, civil society) and embraces pluralism deserves to be defined as Euro-Islam. And furthermore, the concept of Euro-Islam applies only to Europe, in other words unlike the earlier universal vision of Westernising the world – the world of Islam included – it is not universalism.

The Muslim presence in Europe is made up of migrants from all over the world, but three large blocs predominate: the Maghrebis – more than 5 million of them in all; the Turks and Kurds – more than 3.5 million; and the South Asians – principally in Britain, but in lesser numbers in most European countries. Tibi argues that the identity of Muslims is that of 'culturally different people who nevertheless share the same faith'. If it is possible to talk about Afro-Islam for African Muslims or Indo-Islam for Indian Muslims, he asks, 'why should it not be possible to talk about Euro-Islam in the context of Muslims who have migrated to Western Europe?' 'Islam will always be an ever-changing cultural system designed by Muslims themselves', he contends.

'Euro-Islam' seeks to make Islam part of Europe and share its identity, and not the other way around. Bassam Tibi contends that Muslims have to give up three things if they want to become Europeans. 'They have to bid farewell to the idea of converting others, and renounce the *jihad*. The *jihad* is not just a way of testing yourself but also means using violence to spread Islam. The third thing they need to give up is the *Shariah*, which is the Islamic legal system.' In addition, however, Muslims need to redefine their understanding of the twin pillars of modern society, pluralism and tolerance. In an interview with Spiegel Online on 2 October 2006, he continued:[56]

> pluralism doesn't just mean diversity. It means that we share the same rules and values, and are still nevertheless different. Islam doesn't have this idea. And Islam also has no tradition of tolerance. In Islam tolerance means that Christians and Jews are allowed to live under the protection of Muslims but never as citizens with the same rights. What Muslims call tolerance is nothing other than discrimination.

As with other commentators, Tibi is prepared to argue that there is an ongoing 'ideological war' between the Western world and Islamists. 'People politicize their cultural backgrounds,' he argues. 'In Germany representatives of the Islamic communities try to hijack children who are born here, along with the entire Islamic community, to prevent them from being influenced by the society which has taken them in. Children born here are like blank sheets on which you can write European or Islamic texts. Muslim representatives want to raise their children as if they don't even live in Europe.' Sounding almost like Cardinal Ratzinger – now Pope Benedict XVI – Tibi affirms: 'Europeans have stopped defending the values of their civilization. They confuse tolerance with relativism.' 'Islamists know that as soon as you accuse someone of demonizing Islam, then the European side backs down.' What is clear is that a peaceful future for Europe depends on success in dealing with the potential clash of cultures and identities. It will need a shift of both Muslim and non-Muslim European mindsets, and a framework for society that encourages integration and respects individual as well as national identities. The prize is substantial. If these things are achieved, then Huntington's thesis of the inevitable incompatibility of Islam and the West will be negated where it matters most, in the living reality of people engaged in a future of co-operation not conflict. In any case, it is important to remember that many of the arguments directed against Muslims in the present generation could have been said about the spread of Christianity overseas – and there are also parallels with attitudes in the Jewish community, in the distinctions between conservatives and liberals. The integration of Muslims will be a gradual process; but the speed of the immigration has been faster, and the extent of the immigration greater, than in earlier generations.

## *The Alliance of Civilizations Report*

Commentators have expended considerable efforts and ingenuity in trying to explain the timing of the 9/11 attacks. Were they, for example, organized to coincide with the anniversary of the last great military strike against the West, the second siege of Vienna by the Ottoman army (the siege was lifted on 11 September 1683)? Queen Noor of Jordan provides a much more plausible explanation of the timing of 9/11. She writes:[57]

> 11 September 2001 was supposed to mark the celebration of the International Day of Peace at the UN, a highlight of the Year of Dialogue among Civilizations. Instead, history itself was highjacked by the forces of intolerance. The fanaticism of a few destroyed the lives of thousands – citizens of 70 nations, including more than 200 Muslims. When the voices

> of extremism and hatred drown those of moderation, everyone suffers, not any one culture or creed.

In fact, we know that bin Laden attempted to bring the date of the attacks forward, so the precise timing may have had no significance. 'How can we challenge the despair and gloom engendered by the idea of an unending night of clash and conflict?' In the aftermath of 9/11, Akbar Ahmed and Brian Forst, in answer to this question, managed to persuade even Bernard Lewis, the false prophet of the clash thesis, to talk the language of dialogue of cultures, even if only very briefly.[58] The contribution of Kofi Annan, then Secretary-General of the United Nations, was much more pertinent. In what sense is the dialogue among civilizations a useful concept, he asked. His reply was that it 'is an appropriate and necessary answer to the notion of an inevitable clash of civilizations'. As such, it provides an important vehicle for advancing cooperation. But dialogue also 'can help us distinguish lies from facts, and propaganda from sound analysis'. This, Kofi Annan continued, 'can be especially helpful in uncovering the real grievances that lie at the heart of conflict'. If anyone ever doubted the need for dialogue among civilizations, he concluded, 9/11 'made the need for such dialogue crystal clear'.[59] Ironically, almost exactly a year earlier, on 5 September 2000, Kofi Annan had welcomed at New York President Khatami of Iran's initiative for Dialogue among Civilizations and declared the year 2001 the United Nations Year of Dialogue among Civilizations: 'without this dialogue taking place every day among all nations, within and between civilizations, cultures and groups, no peace can be lasting and no prosperity can be secure. That is the lesson of the United Nations' first half-century. It is a lesson that we ignore at our peril.'[60]

Shortly after the events of 9/11, Hans van Ginkel and Ramesh Thakur, respectively rector and vice-rector of the United Nations University in Tokyo, Japan, reflected on the impact of what had happened on the work of those committed to dialogue. They concluded: 'the need of the hour is for discourse among the civilized, not a dialogue of the uncivilized deafened by the drumbeats of war.'[61] It was to continue this discourse among the civilized that the United Nations commissioned the report of the High-Level Group on the Alliance of Civilizations (13 November 2006), the fruit of the deliberations of a cross-civilization group of experienced individuals under the co-sponsorship of the prime ministers of Spain and Turkey. Predictably, there were neo-conservatives who were prepared to argue that the United Status should 'oppose' the proposed UN Alliance of Civilizations, but such views carried little weight by 2007.[62]

The authors of the Alliance of Civilizations Report comment (para 1.3):[63]

> The anxiety and confusion caused by the 'clash of civilizations' theory regrettably has distorted the terms of the discourse on the real nature of the predicament the world is facing. The history of relations between cultures is not only one of wars and confrontation. It is also based on centuries of constructive exchanges, cross-fertilization, and peaceful co-existence. Moreover, classifying internally fluid and diverse societies along hard-and-fast lines of civilizations interferes with more illuminating ways of understanding questions of identity, motivation and behavior. Rifts between the powerful and the powerless or the rich and the poor or between different political groups, classes, occupations and nationalities have greater explanatory power than such cultural categories. Indeed, the latter stereotypes only serve to entrench already polarized opinions. Worse, by promoting the misguided view that cultures are set on an unavoidable collision course, they help turn negotiable disputes into seemingly intractable identity-based conflicts that take hold of the popular imagination. It is essential, therefore, to counter the stereotypes and misconceptions that entrench patterns of hostility and mistrust among societies.

In refutation of the 'conflict of civilizations model', the report continues (para 2.4):

> Diversity of civilizations and cultures is a basic feature of human society and a driving force of human progress. Civilizations and cultures reflect the great wealth and heritage of humankind; their nature is to overlap, interact and evolve in relationship to one another. There is no hierarchy among cultures, as each has contributed to the evolution of humanity. The history of civilizations is in fact a history of mutual borrowing and constant cross-fertilization.

The view that conflicts between the world's religions are the cause of international tension or conflict is vigorously rejected (para 3.8):

> The exploitation of religion by ideologues intent on swaying people to their causes has led to the misguided perception that religion itself is a root cause of intercultural conflict. It is therefore essential to dispel misapprehensions and to give an objective and informed appraisal of the role of religion in modern-day politics. Indeed, a symbiotic relationship may be emerging between religion and politics in our time, each influencing the other. As an example from the past, the seemingly secular colonial enterprise of the 'civilizing mission' or the nineteenth-century conviction of 'manifest destiny' in reality had deep religious roots. Conversely, the overtly religious platforms of some contemporary movements conceal political ambitions that appropriate religion for ideological ends.[64]

The Alliance of Civilizations seeks to 'address widening rifts between societies by reaffirming a paradigm of mutual respect among peoples of different cultural and religious traditions and by helping to mobilize concerted action toward this end.' 'This effort', the authors of the November 2006 report contend, 'reflects the will of the vast majority of peoples to reject extremism in any society and support respect for religious and cultural diversity'. They recommend 'a practicable program of action for states (at national, regional, and local levels), international organizations, and civil society', which they hope 'will assist in diminishing hostility and in promoting harmony among the nations and cultures of the world'.

In order to achieve such a desirable outcome for the world, certain prior changes are required which will take a long time to bring about. These include, first and foremost, a renewed commitment to multilateralism. Regardless of the failed neo-conservative ideology, many of the problems facing the international community can only be addressed effectively within a multilateral framework. The authors of the Alliance of Civilizations Report argue (para 5.11) that 'it is ... incumbent upon states to reinforce multilateral institutions – particularly the United Nations – and to support efforts at reform that will strengthen the capacity and performance of these institutions'. Secondly, there must be a rejection of preventive war and a recourse to war only in much more carefully defined circumstances than those operational in 2003.

There is broad agreement, to use the phrasing of the Report, that 'democratic governance that is representative of citizens and responsive to their needs and aspirations provides the most effective means for individuals to achieve their full potential.' But, *pace* the 'exporting democracy' programme of the neo-conservatives in the United States, as the report continues (para 2.7), 'to be successful, democratic systems must emerge organically from within each society's culture, reflecting its shared values and adapted to the needs and interests of its citizens. This is only possible when people are free and feel in control of their destiny.'

Regime change imposed from outside, followed by the assertion of the democratic credentials of the governing system imposed by the intervening powers, is no recipe for the successful enlargement of the number of democratic states in the world. Moreover, as the Alliance of Civilizations Report contends (para 5.10), 'it is in the interest of Muslim and Western societies alike that ruling parties in the Muslim world provide the space for the full participation of non-violent political parties, whether religious or secular in nature.' 'To this end', the authors continue, 'foreign governments should be consistent in their support for democratic processes and not interfere when the results do not fit their political agenda.' This call for expanded political pluralism – and we would add for religious pluralism as well[65] – 'applies not only to countries in the Middle East or in the larger Muslim world, but to all nations.' The authors of the Report note (para 4.9) that 'while Western military operations are widely condemned by Muslims, this is not the case with intra-Muslim conflicts. Sectarian violence between Shi'as and Sunnis in certain Muslim countries and the atrocities committed against civilians in Darfur, for instance, has not led to widespread condemnation in the Muslim world.'

A report such as this is easily consigned to the margins of international political action. Unusually, an individual has been charged with continuing the work of lobbying and dialogue: Jorge Sampaio, formerly president of Portugal, was appointed High Representative for the Alliance of Civilizations on 26 April 2007. On 11 May, Sampaio gave an opening statement at the Informal Thematic Debate of the UN General Assembly on 'Civilizations and the Challenge for Peace: Obstacles and Opportunities'. He urged the world to challenge the idea that civilizations were doomed to confrontation and war and stated that an action-oriented strategy was currently being developed to promote better understanding and interaction in the world of politics and religion, and to ensure that such understanding was reflected in global diplomatic efforts and political decisions.[66]

At the end of 2006, the BBC World Service commissioned, via the Program on International Policy Attitudes (PIPA) at the University of Maryland and GlobeScan, the most comprehensive poll to date on the possibility of a 'conflict of civilizations' between the Islamic world and the West, seeking to assess public opinion in twenty-seven countries.[67] The quality of reporting on the poll world-wide varied considerably. The message given out by the poll organizers was predictably upbeat. Steven Kull, director of PIPA at the University of Maryland, commented: 'most people around the world clearly reject the idea that Islam and the West are caught in an inevitable clash of civilizations.' Doug Miller, president of GlobeScan, added: 'perhaps the strongest finding is that so many people across the world blame intolerant minorities on both sides for the tensions between Islam and the West.'[68] The *Times of India* professed that Indians were uncertain: 'Indians are more pessimistic than the rest of the world about finding common ground between Islam and the West even as they remain marginally more optimistic than everyone else that violence will be avoided in the clash of civilizations ...'[69] Only 35 per cent of Indians reject the idea of a 'clash of civilizations', *The Hindu* reported.[70] The *Daily Telegraph* (UK) was concerned to stress the main negative results: 'the sharp division in the attitudes of Muslim and non-Muslim nations was laid bare by new research published yesterday. An international survey conducted for the BBC World Service also indicated that a global majority believes tensions between the West and Islam are rooted in politics rather than religion. A majority of respondents in Indonesia, the world's most populous Muslim nation, stated that a clash of civilizations with Islam was inevitable, while India, the country with the biggest Islamic minority, returned the lowest support for peaceful co-existence.'[71]

The first question concerned the relationship between Muslim and Western cultures: 'do you think that violent conflict is inevitable or that it is possible to find common ground?' Overall, 52 per cent of the 5,000 Muslims surveyed considered it possible to find common ground, including majorities in Lebanon (68 per cent) and Egypt (54 per cent) as well as substantial minorities in Turkey (49 per cent) and the United Arab Emirates (47 per cent). Even in religiously divided Nigeria, a large majority of Muslims (63 per cent) believe it is possible to find common ground, while Christians are divided on the question. Only in Indonesia does a slim majority (51 per cent) of Muslims take the view that violent conflict is inevitable, while 40 per cent considers it possible for the two sides to find common ground.

Only 42 per cent of Filipinos believe that it is possible for Muslim and Western cultures to find areas of agreement, while 39 per cent think that violent conflict is inevitable. India has weaker support for the idea of common ground (only 35 per cent), but fewer people than in the Philippines thought that violent conflict between the cultures was inevitable (only 24 per cent). Among the main Western countries, Britain and Italy are strongly supportive (77 and 78 per cent respectively, the one-point difference being clearly within the margin for error). The idea of common ground also finds significantly more support in France and the US than in Germany.

The second question considered tensions between Islam and the West: 'do you think they arise more from differences of religion and culture or from conflicts about political power and interests?' In all but three countries among those polled, citizens were more likely to think that tensions between Islam and the West arise from 'conflicts about political power and interests' than from 'differences of religion and culture'. For example, a majority (56 per cent) in Nigeria – a country that has suffered clashes between its Muslim and Christian communities – consider that tensions primarily arise from religion and culture. World-wide, Muslims (55 per cent) are somewhat more certain than Christians (51 per cent) that the problem mostly derives from political conflict. This is a widely held view in Lebanon (78 per cent), Egypt (57 per cent), Indonesia (56 per cent), and Turkey (55 per cent) as well as in the United Arab Emirates (48 per cent). The survey found that 52 per cent of people overall considered that tensions between Muslims and Westerners were caused by political power and interests, compared with 29 per cent who thought religion and culture were to blame.

What of the role of 'intolerant minorities on both sides' in bringing about the conflict? Seven in ten (70 per cent) in Britain contend that 'intolerant minorities on both sides' are the primary cause of current tensions – the highest response recorded among the study's twenty-seven countries. Another 8 per cent blame an intolerant Muslim minority, and 1 per cent an intolerant Western minority. Only 9 per cent of Britons polled consider that fundamental cultural differences are responsible for the current global tensions between Islam and the West. In this respect, Britain and France are considerably in advance of the Muslim-majority countries, which (with the notable exception of Turkey) tend to consider that the fundamental differences between the cultures are of more importance than 'intolerant minorities on both sides'. Of the countries polled, Nigeria displays the greatest readiness to view the differences between the cultures as critical, while the average of all countries polled shows that this question (which provided the largest number of options of the three main questions) most divided people: on average, 39 per cent blamed 'intolerant minorities on both sides', while 26 per cent considered that current global tensions between Islam and the West were caused by fundamental differences between the two cultures.

### *Towards Inter-Cultural Understanding: the Real Need of Our Times*

Amartya Sen, the Nobel Prize winner for Economics in 1998, charges both the 'conflict of civilizations' and 'alliance of civilizations' projects with a particular type of reductionism which he terms 'singular affiliation'. This takes the form of 'assuming that any person pre-eminently belongs ... to one collectivity only'. The reality is that individuals have many identities. 'The illusion of unique identity is much more divisive', Sen contends, 'than the universe of plural and diverse classifications that characterize the world in which we actually live.' Our shared humanity 'gets savagely challenged when our differences are narrowed into one devised system of uniquely powerful categorization'. Sectarian activists want us to ignore all other links that could moderate our loyalty to 'the specially marked herd'.[72] A unique or singular identity has the advantage for violent purposes of eclipsing other associations and affiliations which might lead to moderation: 'how could you possibly talk about these other things when our people are being killed and our women raped?'[73] For Amartya Sen, 'the main hope of harmony in our troubled world lies in the plurality of our identities, which cut across each other and work against sharp divisions around one single hardened line of vehement division that allegedly cannot be resisted.'[74]

The year 2008 has been proclaimed the European Year for Inter-Cultural Dialogue.[75] In spite of one's inherent misgivings about such initiatives from the 'top down' in Europe, there is no doubt that the great need of our time is for improved intercultural understanding. Amartya Sen makes the distinction between multiculturalism and what he calls 'plural monoculturalism'. Much of the vocal defence of multiculturalism, he contends, is in fact a plea for plural monoculturalism: the importance of honouring traditional cultures is stressed, as if cultures can somehow be sequestered and remain in secluded boxes. 'There would be serious problems with the moral and social claims of multiculturalism if it were taken to insist that a person's identity must be defined by his or her community or religion, overlooking all the other affiliations a person has … and through giving automatic priority to inherited religion or tradition over reflection and choice.' And in a criticism of British government policy encouraging faith schools for Muslim, Hindu, and Sikh children (in addition to those for Christian and Jewish children), he notes that 'the important goal' for education 'is not some formulaic "parity" in relation to old Brits with their old faith schools but what would best enhance the capability of the children to live "examined lives" as they grow up in an integrated country.' Immersion in an 'old, inherited ethos' is not the solution, any more than the assumption that a culture is somehow 'fixed in time'. Rather, young citizens need to develop the capacity to reason about the decisions they make as grown ups.[76] And they need to know something about the 'other' through direct knowledge – an intercultural activity at the grass roots of society which segmented schooling may actually inhibit.

Instead of fixed traditions to be jealously preserved and defended, cultures need to be seen as dynamic rather than static; as relative, not absolute; as complex and varying from person to person, from group to group, and over time; cultural identities need to be seen as multi-layered and often based on assumptions that are not immediately evident, though we can gain insight into our cultural identities through an exploration of our own ways of behaving, thinking, valuing, and acting. In turn, intercultural understanding can be facilitated by exploring one's own cultural influences, and opening up a dialogue about the cultural influences affecting others.

Clearly faith can be seen as one of the factors in making one's identity, but no one should be categorized simply on the basis of religion, any more than 'simply' on ethnicity, gender, class, politics, profession, tastes, social choices, and so on – the power of competing identities needs to be recognized in any intercultural meeting which is more than just dialogue but which leads to greater understanding. Thus, for example, Bassam Tibi, who stresses the need for intercultural understanding, talks of his triple identity as an Arab Muslim migrant: 'religio-culturally, I am a Euro-Muslim; ethnically, I am a Damascene Arab; and politically, I am a German citizen.' Tibi considers that a 'combination of these identities is feasible within the framework of a cultural pluralism and political integration.'[77] Let us trust that he is correct and that cultural pluralism and political integration, rather than the monoculturalism proposed by Samuel Huntington in *Who are We?*, become the norm in European society in the twenty-first century.

# Conclusion
## Demise of the False Prophets?

> ... Western intervention in the affairs of other civilizations is probably the single most dangerous source of instability and potential global conflict in a multi-civilizational world.
>
> Samuel P. Huntington (1996)[1]

> And let us have an American foreign policy that reflects American character. The modesty of true strength. The humility of real greatness.
>
> George W. Bush (campaign speech, 19 November 1999)[2]

> ... To invade an Islamic country to force it to adopt democratic reforms is democratic imperialism. If we practise it, we must expect that some of those we are reforming will resort to the time-honoured weapon of anti-imperialists – terrorism, the one effective weapon the weak have against the strong.
>
> Patrick J. Buchanan (27 December 2004)[3]

> Partial truths or half-truths are often more insidious than total falsehoods.
>
> Samuel P. Huntington[4]

'There is no war on terror.'[5] The outspoken speech of the UK's Director of Public Prosecutions, Sir Ken MacDonald, to the Criminal Bar Association on 23 January 2007, put him at odds with Tony Blair, the Prime Minister and the Home Secretary. How seriously is the threat to the security of the West to be taken? Sir Ken stated: 'London is not a battlefield. Those innocents who were murdered on 7 July 2005 were not victims of war. And the men who killed them were not, as in their vanity they claimed on their ludicrous videos, "soldiers".' Instead, Sir Ken affirmed 'they were criminals. They were fantasists. We need to be very clear about this. On the streets of London, there is no such thing as a "war on terror", just as there can be no such thing as a "war on drugs".' While acknowledging the seriousness of a threat that contained 'all the disturbing elements of a death cult psychology', the head of the Crown Prosecution Service insisted that it must remain an article of faith that crimes of terrorism are dealt with by the criminal justice system and that a 'culture of legislative restraint in the area of terrorist crime is central to the existence of an efficient and human rights-compatible process'. He continued: 'it is critical that we understand that this new form of terrorism carries another more subtle, perhaps equally pernicious, risk … It might encourage a fear-driven and inappropriate response. By that I mean it can tempt us to abandon our values. I think it important to understand that this is one of its primary purposes.' There was a significant contrast between Sir Ken MacDonald's attitude and the posture of successive Attorneys-General of the United States in the administration of George W. Bush: neither John Ashcroft nor Alberto Gonzales left office without having aroused significant controversy.

Democratic principles, in other words, need not be an impediment to prosecuting terrorists. On the contrary they are, the security specialist Louise Richardson asserts, 'among the strongest weapons in [our] arsenal'.[6] The Director of Public Prosecutions is therefore correct to state that it is essential not to erode these principles in a panic over-reaction to the threat posed by terrorism. The neo-conservative agenda, however, is that it is perfectly legitimate to erode the civil rights of alleged terrorists since it is only by means of information gained as a result of torture that human intelligence is improved. Norman Podhoretz, among commentators, has argued this point; Daniel Rumsfeld as Secretary of State for Defense implemented it as policy; the scandal of the 'extraordinary rendition' of prisoners abroad ('torture by proxy'),[7] the abuses at Abu Ghraib, and the long periods of detention without trial suffered by prisoners at Guantánamo Bay have been the inevitable consequence.

### *Avoiding Making the Mistake of Falling into the Terrorists' Trap*

In September 2007, bin Laden issued a long video to coincide with the sixth anniversary of 9/11 which referred to the 'deception and blatant lies' of the White House before the Iraq war. Because of the video's length, it may be understandable that the popular media extracted only certain sections, though this is much less excusable in the case of supposedly specialist media outlets such as MEMRI, whose objectivity has been questioned (see Chapter 5).[8] What is clear is that bin Laden, and those in his circle, are well informed about the public debate in the United States and the arguments of critics of American policy such as Noam Chomsky[9] and the intelligence specialist Michael Scheuer, as well as recent media reports.[10]

It has been suggested this is because that part of bin Laden's address was drafted by 'Azzam the American' (Adam Gadahn), an American member of al-Qaeda and the first American charged with treason since 1952.[11]

Bin Laden's verdict on George W. Bush's speech to the Veterans of Foreign Wars National Convention on 22 August 2007 was that in Iraq Bush is repeating the mistakes made in the past by Brezhnev in Afghanistan: 'refusal to acknowledge defeat' does not 'change the facts for thinking people' but 'exacerbates the problem and increases the losses'. George W. Bush referred in his speech to learning the lessons from the US intervention in Vietnam and not abandoning former allies. Bin Laden retorts that John F. Kennedy was assassinated because he had wanted to stop that 'unjust war' – an unlikely verdict, but one which finds its supporters among the bloggers in cyberspace.[12] Bin Laden refers to the 'arrogance and indifference ... for the lives of humans outside America' and – in an allusion to the Iraq household survey of 2006 – to the 'American statistics' that speak of the death of 'more than 650,000 of the people of Iraq as a result of the war and its repercussions' (see Chapter 8).

Bin Laden castigates Richard Perle, who (with David Frum) states in *An End to Evil: How to Win the War on Terror* (2004) that 'there is no middle way for Americans: it is victory or holocaust.' 'The morality and culture of the holocaust is your culture,' he replies, 'not our culture. The holocaust of the Jews was carried out by your brethren in the middle of Europe.' Had the Jews lived closer to the Muslim-majority lands, 'most of the Jews would have been saved by taking refuge with us,' as was the case with the expulsion of the Jews from the Spanish and Portuguese territories in the early modern period. No doubt the observation drawn from an earlier period of history was not one likely to influence American Jewish opinion about al-Qaeda's current intentions.

But by far the most interesting comment made by bin Laden was missed by all the commentators. This was that al-Qaeda's interests overlap 'with the interests of the major corporations and also with those of the neo-conservatives, despite the[ir] differing intentions'. In this surprising admission, bin Laden acknowledges that through their policy decisions, President Bush, Vice-President Cheney, and their neo-conservative supporters and allies in the military-industrial complex have played, and are continuing to play, into al-Qaeda's hands. In the potential or actual 'Clash of Civilizations', it requires two sides to participate. George W. Bush stated after 9/11 that 'every nation, in every region, now has a decision to make. Either you are with us, or you are with the terrorists ...' For his part, bin Laden described the struggle in similar terms after 9/11: 'these events have divided the world into sides – the side of believers and the side of infidels.'[13]

On the sixth anniversary of those tragic events, it is a matter of profound regret that so little seems to have changed in the intervening period.

Terrorists must be regarded as 'sub-state actors', not states. To refer to them by name, let alone to give credence to their definition of the conflict, as President Bush has done, is to elevate a terrorist to the status of a foreign leader and to legitimize his definition of the 'war'.[14] In his speech at Fort Bragg, North Carolina, on 28 June 2005, George W. Bush stated: 'some wonder whether Iraq is a central front in the war on terror. Among the terrorists, there is no debate. Hear the words of Osama bin Laden: "This third world war is raging" in Iraq. "The whole world is watching this war." He says it will end in "victory and glory or misery and humiliation".' It would have been preferable for the Bush administration simply to have targeted the 'terrorist entity' responsible for the attacks of 9/11, 'those who supported actively such entities, and those who continue to plan future such attacks'. This would have avoided the open-ended formulation of the 'war on terror'.[15]

'A policy informed by the work of the terrorism studies community', Louise Richardson contends, 'would never have declared a global war on terrorism, because we know that such a war can never be won ... [it] would have sought, instead, the more modest and attainable goal of containing terrorist recruitment and constraining resort to the tactic of terrorism.'[16] Paul Pillar, another counter-terrorist specialist, agrees that 'terrorism can be reduced and controlled, not defeated'.[17] 'Governments are invariably placed under enormous pressure to react forcibly and fast in the wake of a terrorist attack,' Richardson writes. 'This response is not likely to be most conducive to long-term success against terrorists.' Instead of a war without end which cannot be won, and which concedes 'far too much to one's adversary to allow them to demonstrate that you have not won the war',[18] Louise Richardson advocates 'six rules' for countering terrorism: have a defensible and achievable goal, such as stopping the spread of Islamist militancy; live by your principles (no more Abu Ghraibs); know your enemy; separate the terrorists from their communities; engage others in countering terrorists with you; finally, have patience and keep your perspective.[19]

Have a defensible and achievable goal: though President Bush declared that 'our war on terror' would not end with al-Qaeda, but only when 'every terrorist group of global reach has been found, stopped and defeated', there was no reason for the US Congress to follow this maxim. It was the wording of the authorization by the US Congress on 18 September 2001 for the President to 'use all necessary and appropriate force' which extended the scope of retaliation not just to 'those nations, organizations or persons' judged to have planned the attacks, but also those who 'harboured such organizations or persons'[20] – this implicitly extended the conflict to Afghanistan and beyond in what critics argue is potentially a war without limits to 'remake the world'.[21]

'Anonymous', the former senior US intelligence official Michael Scheuer[22] with nearly two decades of experience in national security issues related to Afghanistan and South Asia, argues in *Imperial Hubris* that 'bin Laden is out to [alter drastically] US and Western policies towards the Islamic world, not necessarily to destroy America, much less its freedoms and liberties. He is a practical warrior, not an apocalyptic terrorist in search of Armageddon. Should US policies not change, the war between America and the [militant] Islamists will go on for the foreseeable future.'[23]

Halper and Clarke maintain that 'the fatal error of neo-conservatism is its lack of a coherent and accurate [sense of] history'.[24] The wrong historical parallels are invariably cited for the task in hand – for example, Germany and Japan in 1945 as the precedent for nation rebuilding as in Iraq in 2003. The idea of a complete victory and the overthrow of the jihadist ideology, in the way that fascism was overthrown in 1945, is a chimera. There was an overwhelming coalition against Germany and Japan in that exceptionally bloody conflict which ultimately was a war between states. In an asymmetrical war, one in which the enemy observes no state boundary and there is no clear conflict between distinct states, ultimate victory is impossible. And, with the exceptions of 1815, 1918, and 1945, it is worth remembering just how rarely in human history one side in a conflict has completely defeated the other and the peace settlement resulted in a draconian treaty imposed by the victor powers. The 'victory' of the West in the Cold War in 1989 is irrelevant, because the Soviet system imploded without a shot being fired. The Russian defeat in Afghanistan merely started a process of unravelling the Soviet system, the collapse of which might have been averted under better leadership in the years before Gorbachev came to power.

Mocking President Bush's plans to send a further 21,500 US troops to Iraq, Ayman al-Zawahiri addressed the American public in January 2007, stating they must 'accept the facts of what is happening on the ground, and reject the fantasies with which Bush tries to deceive you'. 'You must honestly try to reach a mutual understanding with the Muslims, for then, and only then, you might enjoy security,' he argued. 'Security is a shared destiny, if we are secure, you might be secure, and if we are safe, you might be safe. And if we are struck and killed, you will definitely – with Allah's permission – be struck and killed. This is the correct equation.'[25]

If it is unlikely that the enemy can be completely defeated this raises the question at what point, if at all, a political dialogue with al-Qaeda should begin. Commentators such as Bernard Lewis and Daniel Pipes suggest that negotiations with the terrorist 'enemy' amount to a new form of appeasement as in the years 1936–8. The comparison obscures the nature of the problem. In the case of appeasement, the delay was sufficient to allow the remilitarization of Germany: this gave it a military edge in Continental Europe which was not reversed until 1944. With regard to the terrorist threat posed by al-Qaeda and such-like groups, the Western states have overwhelming forces at their disposal and cannot be defeated militarily. But, like the British in Northern Ireland, such overwhelming military superiority cannot result in victory, because the problem is in its nature not military, but political. Terrorists cannot survive if they cannot replace their cadre and train new recruits; this is where latching onto an insurgency, as in Iraq and Afghanistan, is so vital to their cause. The first principle of counter-insurgency warfare is 'the primacy of the political': it is this principle which the United States government has failed to acknowledge since 2001.[26]

In a debate at Doha on 5 September 2007, chaired by Tim Sebastian and subsequently broadcast by the BBC World Service, a majority of participants (63 per cent) thought that the time had already come for such a dialogue to begin. Opposing the motion, Laith Kubba stated that al-Qaeda was different from other extremist organizations. 'Talking to al-Qaeda is an illusion. It is a group of Muslims with twisted theological and ideological perceptions. Al-Qaeda is a death machine and a cancer that can destroy the entire Islamic society. Any attempt to give legitimacy to this group will be dangerous.' Those who supported the motion argued that it is time to give dialogue a chance since military action had failed to contain al-Qaeda. Terrorism is a symptom of more deep-rooted issues and it manifests itself as an extreme reaction to the mistakes committed by the West in the Islamic world. It is important to address the root causes rather than treating the symptoms.[27] Bin Laden and al-Zawahiri seek to project the struggle as the very 'clash of civilizations' that the United States and its coalition partners have tried to disclaim and prevent.[28] If there are military operations, they must be sensitive military operations to avoid creating a further groundswell of support for the terrorists. Every time a mosque is destroyed in Iraq – and numerous mosques were destroyed in the Fallujah offensive of November 2004 and elsewhere[29] – Arab opinion, and opinion in the Muslim world more generally, becomes convinced of the 'truth' of the al-Qaeda propaganda that the 'war on terrorism' is a misnomer for 'crusade'.[30]

These arguments coincide well with Robert A. Pape's analysis of the political objectives of suicide bombers – namely, that there are real political objectives underlying their extremist ideology – and that the priority is to remove the chief grievance, which is the presence of US troops on Arab soil and the soil of Muslim-majority countries. (Bin Laden reminds his world-wide audience that 'helping the Infidel to take the land of Muslims and control them is one of the ten acts contradictory to Islam'.)[31] Pape calls for a return to the traditional, pre-1990, US policy towards the Gulf region. 'A return to off-shore balancing', as Pape terms this policy, would 'send an unmistakable signal that the United States is not in the business of empire, and will thus suck the oxygen out of the atmosphere that breeds anti-American suicide terrorism.'

Pape's recipe for American policy in the region is to have the friendliest possible relations with Saudi Arabia, Iraq, and Iran, 'or at least with two of them, if their behaviour toward one another makes cooperative relations with all three impossible'. This means refraining from military coercion unless one of these countries attacks another, or otherwise 'immediately threatens the balance of power in the Persian Gulf'. Better still than off-shore balancing would be for the United States to achieve energy independence, for this would halt al-Qaeda propaganda that the reason for the US presence is oil theft ('the biggest reason for our enemies' control over our lands is to steal our oil');[32] but on the assumption that this is unlikely to happen, off-shore balancing remains the second-best option. 'By assuring the local populations in the Persian Gulf that the United States has no imperial designs, it reduces al-Qaeda's power to mobilize popular support, while safeguarding America's core interests in the region.'

Daniel Byman suggests that the war on global *jihad* should be fought on five fronts. The first task is to rethink the role of the military, which will require changes to their procurement practices, recruitment, training, and doctrine. Instead of the US fighting insurgencies itself, it should offer its expertise to allied governments, which will fight them directly. The war of ideas is being lost: instead of trying to justify unpopular US policies, 'we should go negative and remind people of the jihadists' unpopular deeds and theology', making the debate 'about them, not about us'. The other elements required for successful prosecution of the 'war on terror' are improvements in counter-intelligence (though analysts are agreed on the difficulty in penetrating the jihadists' network and the insufficiency of linguists with the right profiles in the West);[33] in homeland defence; and finally in sponsoring democratic reform abroad. Where reforms are occurring in allied countries, these should be backed; but the limits of reform in time of war must be recognized. You have to go to war with the allies you have in the real world, not those you would like to have in an ideal world, the aim being to improve their effectiveness in the medium term.[34]

Effective allies are the key to successful counter-terrorism efforts. With allied help, terrorism can be contained and, in the long term, the many potential divisions between the terrorist networks will rise to the fore. This is where the Bush–Cheney lurch to unilateralism has been a disastrous *fausse démarche* in international relations. Dramatic dual approaches such as 'crushing the terrorists unilaterally through overwhelming force and transforming terrorist breeding grounds via democratization' are likely to fail and are tremendously expensive – 'a prohibitive combination'.[35] 'Public diplomacy is not a magic wand', Byman concedes. The United States and allies may toil for years and make only limited progress towards improving the image of the US in the Islamic world. Yet a 'supreme effort is essential. Our goal is not to be loved; it is to make the jihadists hated.' Failure to engage in this effort seriously is tantamount to surrendering the quest for legitimacy to the jihadists. Bin Laden's propaganda success rests on precarious foundations:[36]

> He has managed to convince sizable parts of the Muslim world that the killing of innocents is acceptable and that his own noxious agenda should be supported as the alternative to US dominance. By changing such perceptions, we can isolate the most extreme jihadists. We cannot change their violent ends, but we can render them, over time, a far less dangerous fringe movement.

### *Preventive War, Nation Rebuilding, and the Failure of 'Benevolent Hegemony'*

The United States continues to be willing to spend more than all the other countries of the world combined on its armed forces and to perceive dangers from a range of countries which others do not. In the words of the chair of the US joint chiefs-of-staff, 'you can take a lap around the globe. Start with Pakistan, Afghanistan, Iran, Iraq, Syria, Lebanon, Yemen, Somalia, Sudan, Colombia, Venezuela, the Philippines, Indonesia, Malaysia, North Korea, and back around to Pakistan. And I'm sure I missed a few ...'[37] For an analysis of what went wrong in the leadership and direction of American policy, it is useful to turn to the arguments of an erstwhile neo-conservative, Francis Fukuyama, whose work, it has been said with some exaggeration, has had more influence on the Bush administration than that of 'any other living thinker'.[38] The distinctive neo-conservative contribution to American foreign policy, according to Fukuyama, is the belief that democratic states are by nature friendly and unthreatening, and therefore America ought to go around the world promoting democracy and human rights wherever possible; the belief that American power can serve moral purposes; the distrust of ambitious nation-building (or 'social engineering') projects; and finally scepticism about the legitimacy and effectiveness of international law and institutions to achieve either security or justice.[39] An interesting feature of the neo-conservative mindset is that there is far from unanimity about the enterprise. Joshua Muravchik, for example, offers a four-point prescription that differs from Fukuyama's.[40] William Kristol and Robert Kagan suggested in *Present Dangers* that the United States would use its margin of power to exert a kind of 'benevolent hegemony' over the rest of the world and concluded: 'it is precisely because American foreign policy is infused with an unusually high degree of morality that other nations find they have less to fear from its otherwise daunting power.'[41]

In his verdict on 'the failure of benevolent hegemony', Fukuyama correctly stresses that 'the Bush administration and its neo-conservative supporters did not simply underestimate the difficulty of bringing about [desirable] political outcomes in places like Iraq; they also misunderstood the way the world would react to the use of American power.' When President Bush talked about 'being for us or against us' in the global war on terrorism, it was aimed at countries such as Pakistan and Yemen. 'The problem was that the phrase was heard in Europe as a challenge to get with the Bush administration's agenda in a take-it-or-leave-it fashion, which they naturally resented'. The 'axis of evil' (Iraq, Iran, and North Korea) reference in the State of the Union Address in 2002 could be interpreted in the sense that the US was planning 'a series of three preventive wars'.[42] But there were more basic flaws in the assumptions underlying 'benevolent hegemony'.[43]

> In the first place, it was premised on American exceptionalism, the idea that America could use its power in instances where others could not because it was more virtuous than other countries. The doctrine of pre-emption against terrorist threats contained in the 2002 National Security Strategy was one that could not safely be generalized through the international system; America would be the first country to object if Russia, China, India or France declared a similar right of unilateral action. The United States was seeking to pass judgment on others while being unwilling to have its own conduct questioned in places like the International Criminal Court.

Not only did most non-Americans find the belief in American exceptionalism lacking in credibility;[44] they also criticized 'benevolent hegemony' on more prosaic grounds of a lack of competence (did the US administration understand the issues at stake in invading Iraq and then restructuring a defeated state?). Fukuyama spares no blushes to the administration he formerly supported in his criticism of 'the most basic misjudgement':[45]

> The most basic misjudgement was an overestimation of the threat facing the United States from radical Islamism ... [The] intelligence community never took nearly as alarmist a view of the terrorist/WMD threat as the war's supporters did. Overestimation of this threat was then used to justify the elevation of preventive war to the centrepiece of a new security strategy, as well as a whole series of measures that infringed on civil liberties, from detention policy to domestic eavesdropping.

This is a realistic verdict on the policies advocated by those whom we have termed in this study the *False Prophets*. The American administration made mistakes; but the mistakes were predictable because it turned to a limited set of people for guidance, people whose priority was not just counter-terrorism but, as Louise Richardson terms it, both 'counter-terrorism policy and American power'.[46] Following a lead from President Bush himself in the aftermath of the 9/11 attacks, they sought to conflate 'two very distinct security issues: the threat from al-Qaeda and the threat from Saddam Hussein'. Hardliners such as Paul Wolfowitz, in a memorandum of 17 September 2001, pushed for an immediate attack on Iraq even if there was only a 10 per cent chance that Saddam was behind the 9/11 attacks.[47] The Iraq war was a diversion of attention and resources away from Afghanistan, where bin Laden and the al-Qaeda leadership had not been caught and the threat of a resurgent Taliban remained real. In October 2004, an erstwhile rival of bin Laden and one of the leaders of the Iraq insurgency, al-Zarqawi, pledged his allegiance and that of his terrorist group to bin Laden as 'Sheikh of the *Mujihadeen*'.[48] For Fukuyama, 'Iraq has now replaced Afghanistan as a magnet, a training ground and an operational base for jihadist terrorists, with plenty of American targets to shoot at.'[49]

The US seeks to impose its distinctive vision on the world. It does not ask, 'why is the world not like us?' or 'what right have we to impose our vision on the rest of the world?' As Clifford Longley commented in September 2003, 'the unexamined neo-con assumption [is] that these values are absolutes, independent of culture and history. In fact they are deeply historically conditioned, moulded out of seventeenth-century settler Puritanism and inspired by European Enlightenment ideals to find solutions to late-eighteenth century constitutional difficulties with Britain.' Comparing the American assumptions with Iraq, the country invaded in 2003, Longley commented 'there is nothing parallel to American history in the story of the people of Mesopotamia, now modern Iraq ... Their idea of freedom is more associated with freedom to obey the will of Allah than with Yankee get-up-and-go individualism ... Above all, Arab and Muslim cultures do not have that distinctive American habit of mind, the belief in Progress ... countries with a different history and culture cannot be presumed to be destined to cover the same historical trajectory.'[50]

This means that the nation-rebuilding (or 'social work') side of regime change – a process that is anathema to the neo-conservative mindset[51] – looms much larger than was ever considered by the US administration prior to the intervention in Iraq. As Fukuyama is now prepared to recognize, 'excessively optimistic assumptions about post-Saddam Iraq set the stage for the failure to think through the requirements of post-conflict security and nation-building. Regime change was conceived not as a matter of the slow and painstaking construction of liberal and democratic institutions but simply as the negative task of getting rid of the old regime.'[52] In modern circumstances, with the almost instantaneous reporting of the situation on the ground in Afghanistan and Iraq, those who debate the principles of *jus ad bellum* but fail to take the lead from their military in considering the issues of *jus post bellum* (see Chapters 8 and 9) are open to serious criticism on grounds of their lack of competence as well as their lack of sympathy for the plight of the civilian casualties of war.

Under Gordon Brown, the British government's new emphasis on reconstruction after state collapse comes as a welcome change. It is suggested that the international community in future 'should be ready to act with a standby civilian force including police and judiciary who can be deployed to rebuild civilian societies' and that local development agencies be sponsored to rebuild societies.[53] The price tag for the wars being waged by the US military in Iraq and Afghanistan will reach nearly $1.6 trillion (£771bn) during fiscal year 2008, according to a report released by the Democratic staff of Congress's Joint Economic Committee in November 2007, estimated as equivalent in the years 2002–8 to $20,900 for an average American family of four, possibly rising to $46,400 by 2017.[54] If a significant proportion of this expenditure was redirected to rebuilding destroyed societies, then the commitment to Iraq and Afghanistan would have some meaning and chance of success. However, since the Joint Economic Committee notes that the 'total economic costs of the wars in Iraq and Afghanistan so far have been approximately double the total amounts directly requested by the Administration to fight these wars', the chances of such a shift in expenditure are slim.

*The Increased Danger of Intra-Civilizational Conflict Following the Iraq Intervention*

There are neo-conservative critics of the Bush administration's policy – Daniel Pipes among them – who argue that the old regime should have been removed in Iraq and so too should the American forces immediately after the task was completed. And what if, as has proved to be the case, civil war resulted? This would be considered, in Pipes's dictum quoted in Chapter 4, 'a humanitarian tragedy but not a strategic one'. It is still very difficult for the neo-conservative pundits to accept responsibility for the outcome in Iraq. When Fareed Zakaria, the editor of *Newsweek*, asserts that 'we did not give them a republic. We gave them a civil war', Charles Krauthammer contends that the Iraqis 'chose civil war' themselves; 'we midwifed their freedom'; in spite of the American 'mistakes in Iraq', any assertion to the contrary is deemed 'stupid' and 'pernicious'.[55]

If Vali Nasr is correct that 'conflicts within Islam will shape the future' perhaps more than any alleged conflicts between civilizations, intra-civilizational conflict should not become a plaything of Western powers seeking to maintain their hegemony. An invasion embarked upon without sufficient consideration of the long-term issues at stake – and the potential for the implosion of the Ba'athist state into sectarian civil war – has not made the world safe from terrorism. Quite the reverse, there has been a profound impact of the Iraq civil war in extremist circles. There, Vali Nasr suggests,[56]

> the Shi'a revival in Iraq is seen as a calamity, a monumental reversal in the fortunes of Islam. It is also further evidence of sinister US intentions towards Islam after the events of 11 September – the grand conspiracy to weaken and subjugate the faith. This has served as a new call to arms, expanding the scope of the confrontation with the United States ... The conflict that mattered ... was not the one against oppression but rather the age-old battle of the two halves of Islam, Shi'as and Sunnis. This was the conflict that Iraq has rekindled and this is the conflict that will shape the future.

'The Middle East that will emerge from the crucible of the Iraq war may not be more democratic', Vali Nasr contends, 'but it will definitely be more Shi'ite. It may also be more fractious ... The Shi'ites' rise to power in Iraq sets an example for Shi'ites elsewhere in the Middle East, and as the model is adopted or tested it is likely to exacerbate Shi'ite–Sunni tensions.'[57] This is one reason why Saudi Arabia is so concerned about the regional intentions of Iran. With the heartland of Islam being ripped apart by Muslim violence against Muslim, the need for Muslims of Sunni and

Sh'ia backgrounds to come together to declare their shared humanity and reject violence has never been more urgent.

With the war rhetoric of the US being directed against Iran by the Bush administration, the oldest division in Islam is being exploited to rally support against Iran. Talk of an 'arc of moderation' (allegedly the Sunni states of Saudi Arabia, Egypt, Jordan, and Turkey) confronting the 'Shi'a crescent' (centred on Iran and stretching from Pakistan to the Lebanon) forewarns us that a potential new front in the 'war on terror' could be opening up. Already anti-Shi'a *fatawa* have been issued by some Saudi scholars. Yet important work has been done by prominent *ulama* of both traditions to emphasize unity and tolerance in three major declarations issued in Amman, Mecca, and Doha in 2005–7.[58] The danger arises that the bloody sectarianism of Iraq may be spread around the Middle East and further afield with disastrous consequences for all. As Vali Nasr concludes:[59]

> those forces that are most dangerous to Western interests and to the peace of the region are likely to thrive during this [violent] transition. It is in the interests of Shi'as, Sunnis and the West to minimize the pains of transition and hasten its end. This means contending with the reality of sectarian rivalries and understanding what motivates them and how they play out socially and politically. As in all wars of religion and conflicts over identity, in the end, peace, like war, is a function first and foremost of recognizing the fact of differences, and only then going beyond them in the pursuit of common goals. It is not possible to tell how the sectarian struggle in Iraq will turn out, or when and where the next battle between Shi'as and Sunnis will be joined, or how many sectarian battles the Middle East must endure and for how long. What is clear is that the future for the Middle East will not be brighter than the past so long as the shadow of sectarian conflict hangs over it. This is the conflict that will shape the future.

Even if Vali Nasr's prediction is too gloomy, it serves as a useful corrective to the 'clumsy and provocative debates' on the relationship between the West and the Islamic world in the fifteen years since Huntington originally proposed his thesis, debates which, in Orla Lynch's view, have often failed to 'understand the deeply variegated nature of Islam and the Muslim world'.[60] As Willfried Spohn has suggested, we need to go beyond the Huntington clash of civilizations thesis, which 'concentrates one-sidedly on the religious and nationalist tensions and contradictions between civilizations', and instead consider the 'religious and secular conflicts within civilizations as well as the religious-ecumenical and secular-cosmopolitan forms of co-operation and bridging between civilizations'. We need also to go beyond 'a simple evolutionary assumption that the religious bases of collective identities are replaced or dissolved by processes of modernization or globalization'. Instead Spohn's concept of 'multiple modernities', which draws on the work of Shmuel Eisenstadt, suggests that 'trans-national and trans-civilizational interactions are taking place in varying competitive, co-operative and conflictive forms at the same time'. The 'multiple modernities' approach highlights the internal dynamics and contradictions *within* civilizations as well as the interactions *between* civilizations.[61]

### *Cautioning against the Urge to Redraw Maps and Reaffirming the Issue of Trust in International Relations*

The clash of civilizations thesis, especially in Huntington's model of eight main civilizations which can be mapped, illustrates two persistent themes in international relations: the tendency to think aloud and redraw maps, which creates the impression that the West is still operating in its former colonial mode, when the maps of Africa and the Middle East were redrawn at will; and the issue of trust in the making of peace or the breakdown which leads to war. Since 1954 an elite coterie of Western thinkers and power-brokers known as the Bilderberg has been meeting on a regular basis to discuss world issues. (The name 'Bilderberg' comes from the Hotel de Bilderberg in Oosterbeek near Arnhem in the Netherlands where the first meeting took place.) In 1979, Bernard Lewis presented the Bilderberg group with a plan for redrawing the borders of the larger Middle East into a mosaic of competing mini-states, thereby weakening the power of the existing republics and kingdoms. The 'Bernard Lewis Project', as it has come to be known, proposed the fragmentation and balkanization of Iran along regional, ethnic, and linguistic lines especially among the Arabs of Khuzestan (the Al-Ahwaz project), the Baluchis and Pashtuns (the Baluchistan–Pakhtunistan project), the Kurds (the Greater Kurdistan project), and the Azerbaijanis (the Greater Azerbaijan Project). Independence movements led by separatist Kurds, Azeris, Baluchis, Pashtuns, and Arabs would represent dire threats to Turkey, Iraq, Pakistan, and other neighbouring states. 'Herein lays the tragedy', writes Kaveh Farrokh. 'Lewis wields his treasure trove of knowledge as an engine of destruction.'[62]

The continued urge to redraw maps is illustrated by Thomas P. M. Barnett's recent study entitled *The Pentagon's New Map*.[63] Barnett, a research professor at the Naval War College, previewed his thesis just prior to the invasion of Iraq in an article of the same title in March 2003.[64] Barnett proposes two types of state, the 'Functioning Core' of developed states, and a second group, the 'Non-Integrating Gap', of failed or failing states, 'plagued by politically repressive regimes, widespread poverty and disease, routine mass murder, and – most important – the chronic conflicts that incubate the next generation of global terrorists'. Barnett argues that bin Laden and al-Qaeda are 'pure products of the Gap'. 9/11 represented an attempt by bin Laden to create a 'systems perturbation' in the Core so that he would be able to take the Islamic world 'off line' from globalization and return it to some seventh-century definition of the good life. For Barnett, the proper strategic response to 9/11 is to create a 'countervailing systems perturbation' in the Gap – which is exactly what the Bush administration did by striking Afghanistan and Iraq.[65] Simon Dalby argues of Barnett's interpretation that 'the "enlargement" of the sphere of democratic states, the Clinton administration's reversal of the US Cold War policy of "containment", has now been militarized. Imperial ambition is tied to a geography of violence with both security and moral rationalizations ... Extending civilization into the wild lands of the frontier is a task that US military power can facilitate – indeed, one that Barnett argues is an essential task for the protection of civilization.'[66] Subsequently, Thomas Barnett produced a second study, entitled *Blueprint for Action: a Future Worth Creating* (2005), which details how the non-integrating 'gap' is to be shrunk and the wild zones that spread danger, terrorism, violence, and instability are to be eradicated. Barnett contends that the Pentagon for too long has refused to invest in 'an effective nation-building response, which naturally remains manpower-intensive'. For Simon Dalby, this argument is no longer 'about managing an empire ... it's about forcibly expanding it'. The 'enforced expansion of the zone of economic freedom is part and parcel of the National Security Strategy of the United States'.[67]

Another example of thinking aloud is provided by the online article of Ralph Peters in June 2006 entitled 'Blood Borders: How a Better Middle East Would Look', which argues that without 'major boundary revisions, we shall never see a more peaceful Middle East'.[68] The author is correct to argue that the borders of Africa and the Middle East are 'the most arbitrary and distorted borders in the world', drawn up for the most part by 'self-interested Europeans'. 'We are dealing with colossal, man-made deformities that will not stop generating hatred and violence until they are corrected', Peters contends. An independent Kurdish state should be created out of part of present-day Turkey and Iraq; Afghanistan would lose out to Iran in the west, but would gain at the expense of Pakistan by a correction of the Durand Line.[69] And so on. It has been suggested that the revised map of Iran and the so-called 'Middle East' proposed by Ralph Peters, and apparently endorsed by some within the Pentagon, is little more than a reissue of the Bernard Lewis Plan.[70] How Ralph Peters seriously believes that any state which lost out in such a sacrifice of territory would not resort to armed resistance (or could remain in power if it did not resort to force, given public resistance to the change) is left unexplained. Perhaps the boundaries of states should not be sacrosanct; but unless the changes are agreed by mutual consent, the reality of international relations is that they are. It is on this basis that the system of international relations functions. It knows no other way.

This leads us to a further consideration, which is the role of trust. Andrew Kydd argues that trust is a central issue in international relations, as exemplified in the most important struggle of the second half of the twentieth century, the Cold War.[71] The basic assumption is that when states can trust each other, they can live at peace, provided that they are security seekers, uninterested in expansion for its own sake. States that are security seekers therefore pay close attention to the motivations of other states, attempting to determine which state is a fellow security seeker and which state, on the contrary, appears to be aggressive. The European states were able to cooperate with each other, the United States, and Germany after World War II because the United States was a 'trustworthy hegemon' and enabled them to overcome serious mistrust problems. Finally, the Cold War was ended through a process of costly signalling: Gorbachev made a number of dramatic gestures that increased Western trust and dispelled the suspicions that underlay the forty-year conflict.

After the terror attacks of 11 September 2001, the US administration formally abandoned containment in favour of preventive war as outlined in the 2002 National Security Strategy. The United States would now attack potential threats before they could strike it, particularly states that were suspected of developing weapons of mass destruction or of having ties to terrorist groups. The invasion of Afghanistan and especially Iraq most clearly highlight the new trends in US foreign policy. In the case of Afghanistan, the Taliban's harbouring of al-Qaeda provided a rationale for war that was credible to other nations. The case of Iraq was much more controversial. Kydd argues that the United States, with its high minimum trust threshold, favoured preventive war while many Europeans and much of the rest of the world, with much lower minimum trust thresholds, favoured a continuation of the inspections' regime and deterrence. The US and British invasion of Iraq without broader institutional backing has resulted in a serious weakening of international trust for the United States. This decline in trust is one of the most serious problems the US faces in its efforts to protect itself against terrorism. In order to counteract world suspicions about US foreign policy, Kydd argues that the US needs to implement a policy of reassurance. There is a paradox here. When Admiral

William J. Fallon, in charge of US Central Command since March 2006, did precisely this on al-Jazeera television in September 2007 – arguing that 'this constant drum beat of conflict' with Iran 'is not helpful and not useful … I expect that there will be no war and that is what we ought to be working for …' – then he was accused of being ill-suited to war and the effective use of US power, and of undercutting the Bush administration's efforts to pressure Iran with the threat of future military action.[72]

The issue of trust in international relations that Andrew Kydd has emphasized is critical for our understanding of the impact of Huntington's thesis of the clash of civilizations, and in particular whether it has become, or risks becoming, a 'self-fulfilling prophecy', as many critics contend. John Ikenberry, for example, argues that Huntington's thesis is a civilizational equivalent of a state's 'security dilemma', in which misperceptions about the other eventually increase the tension and then lead to conflict.[73] Although Huntington denies it,[74] critics accuse him of formulating a paradigm that has become both a 'successful political myth' and 'a self-fulfilling prophecy'.[75]

There is greater danger in using the term 'clash of civilizations' than Huntington is prepared to allow, particularly in the realm of perceptions. This is well illustrated by Graham E. Fuller's characterization of the 'vicious circle' affecting US foreign policy towards the Arab world:[76]

> it should not be surprising that these frustrated populations perceive the current war against terrorism as functionally a war against Islam. Muslim countries are the chief target, they contend, Muslims everywhere are singled out for censure and police attention, and US power works its will across the region with little regard for deeper Muslim concerns. A vicious circle exists: dissatisfaction leads to anti-régime action, which leads to repression, which in turn leads to terrorism, US military intervention, and finally further dissatisfaction. Samuel Huntington's theory of a 'clash of civilizations' is seemingly vindicated before the Muslim world's eyes …

For this to be reversed, and a future 'clash of civilizations' averted, there is simply no alternative but for the United States to embark upon a new era of dialogue and exchange, 'the two-way street' of public diplomacy as Oleg Svet calls it.[77] The battle with militant jihadism is a battle of ideas, not a clash of civilizations – nor will it become one, if it is recognized that the faith of Islam is not to be confused with jihadism, a political ideology seeking political objectives under the guise of religious traditionalism.

Bernard Lewis, the most senior of our 'false prophets', contended that if the dangers of regime change seemed hazardous, 'the dangers of inaction are greater that those of action'. The present author argues that the reverse is almost invariably true and that there can be no substitute for cautious analysis – taking advice from a broad spectrum of opinion and the consensus of specialists who cannot *all* be wrong. If there is an inability to distinguish between advocacy and objective policy formulation, if the intelligence reports have to be made to fit the policy rather than the other way round, then there has been a failure in a nation's foreign policy-making capability, what Halper and Clarke call a 'failure of the rational centre'.[78] While recognizing that there is need for a new jurisprudence dealing with the issues of pre-emption and preventive war,[79] Robert A. Pape's maxim that in most cases 'the risks of action outweigh the risks of deterrence' needs to be inscribed on the hearts of international statesmen in the decades to come, as the world community strives after the Iraq debacle for a return to conditions of normality.

That is the best case. The second-best case – on the assumption, as Ivo H. Daalder assures us, that pre-emption 'is here to stay' – is that there must be a genuine willingness to bring others into the deliberations. An effective alternative to multilateral paralysis and unilateral action 'is for the United States to work with its democratic partners around the world to meet and defeat the global threats of our age'. Not only must there be henceforth a real dialogue between allies, not an enforced coalition of the less than willing, but also 'when it comes to making decisions on whether or not to intervene pre-emptively' there must be reliable detailed information, probing analysis, in-depth discussion and debate, and 'a constant willingness to reassess the evidence'[80] on its own terms and not in the light of a narrow ideological viewpoint. In other words, everything that did not happen before the Iraq intervention in 2003 must happen next time if there is ever to be a next time.

# Dramatis Personae

AHMADINEJAD, Mahmoud (born 1956). Conservative Islamist elected President of Iran in 2005. Ahmadinejad took over the role of the neo-conservatives' most hated foreign ruler after the downfall of Saddam Hussein. Many neo-conservatives appeared unaware that ultimate power in Iran rested with Supreme Leader Ayatollah Ali Khamenei, whose position on some issues was more guarded than that of Ahmadinejad.

ANNAN, Kofi (born 1938). UN Secretary-General (1997–2007) and opponent of the US intervention in Iraq. Co-recipient of the Nobel Peace Prize in 2001. Supported his deputy Secretary-General Mark Malloch Brown, who openly criticized segments of the United States media in a speech on 6 June 2006.

ARMITAGE, Richard Lee (born 1945). Foreign policy adviser to President-elect Reagan 1980. Successively Deputy Assistant Secretary of Defense and Assistant Secretary of Defense under President Reagan. Ambassador to post-Communist states in Europe (1991–3). PNAC signatory to Bill Clinton urging the removal of Saddam Hussein (1998). Foreign policy adviser to George W. Bush during the presidential election campaign. Served as US Deputy Secretary of State (2001–5). Aligned closely with Colin Powell as Secretary of State, and tendered his own resignation the day after Powell's, but it became operative only in February 2005. Notoriously coerced Pakistan into an immediate decision after 9/11 to support the US in the war on terror, though denies using the words claimed by President Musharraf in his memoirs.

ATATÜRK, Kemal (1881–1938). Opponent of the imposed treaty of Sèvres (Aug. 1920), which envisaged the partition of Anatolia. Commander-in-chief during the Greco-Turkish war (1921–2), controversial founder of the modern Turkish state and its first president (1923–38). Regarded as both a strong man and a secular leader, and therefore seen as a model by some Western commentators, such as Bernard Lewis, for what is needed in a 'reformed' Middle East. Hence the adjective 'Kemalist'.

AZZAM, Abdullah Yusuf (1941–89). Of Palestinian origin, influential scholar and leader of the Afghan *jihad* against the Soviet invasion. Murdered in Peshawar by a massive bomb, possibly resulting from a conspiracy led by Ayman al-Zawahiri, one of his rivals for the leadership and direction of the nascent al-Qaeda movement.

BAKER, James Addison III (born 1930). Chief of Staff in Ronald Reagan's first administration, Secretary of the Treasury (1985–8), during the second Reagan administration and Secretary of State under President George H. W. Bush (1989–92). Awarded the Presidential Medal of Freedom 1991. Dismissed by neo-conservatives such as Daniel Pipes as too 'dictator friendly', but also condemned because of his willingness to negotiate the future of the Middle East at first without the direct participation of Israel. Co-author of the Iraq Study Group report (2006), whose recommendations were rejected by President George W. Bush. The *New York Post* depicted Baker and his co-chair, Lee Hamilton as 'surrender monkeys' on its cover page (7 December 2006).

Benedict XVI, Pope, *see* Ratzinger, Joseph Alois

Blair, Tony (born 1953). Prime Minister of the United Kingdom from 2 May 1997 to 27 June 2007. Severely criticized in the UK for his apparent subservience to George W. Bush, Blair's reputation is higher in the US than in Europe. From the start of the war on terror in 2001, Blair strongly supported US foreign policy, notably by participating in the invasions of Afghanistan in 2001 and Iraq in 2003. He was severely criticized for his claims that Iraq was developing weapons of mass destruction (which have not been discovered in Iraq). For his unwavering support for the security of the US, Blair was honoured with the Congressional Medal of Honor on 18 July 2003. On the day he stood down as prime minister, he was appointed official Envoy of the Quartet on the Middle East on behalf of the United Nations, the European Union, the United States, and Russia, but was regarded as of doubtful help to the Palestinian cause because of his long-standing support for Israel's objectives. A devout Christian, Blair announced his impending conversion to Catholicism (the faith of his wife) after his resignation as prime minister. The ceremony of conversion took place on 21 December 2007 at Archbishop's House, Westminster. Blair plans to launch his inter-faith foundation, currently run by Ruth Turner, in 2008. Along with Margaret Thatcher, he is called a neo-conservative by Irwin Stelzer (ed.) in *Neoconservativism* (2004). Beware the spoof Blair website at <http://www.tonyblairoffice.org.uk/pricing.php>

Bolton, John R. (born 1948). Senior Vice-President of the American Enterprise Institute and Under-Secretary of State for Arms Control and International Security (May 2001 to May 2005). Interim appointment as US ambassador to the United Nations (2005–6), an institution which he regularly criticizes. Bolton is, or has been, involved with a number of conservative think tanks and policy institutes, including the American Enterprise Institute (AEI), Jewish Institute for National Security Affairs (JINSA), Project for the New American Century (PNAC), Institute of East–West Dynamics, National Rifle Association, US Commission on International Religious Freedom, and the Council for National Policy. Published his memoirs under the title *Surrender is Not an Option: Defending America at the United Nations and Abroad* (2007).

Boot, Max (born 1969). American author, consultant, editorialist, lecturer, and military historian, who is a foreign policy adviser to Senator John McCain in his bid to win the 2008 US presidential election. He has been a prominent advocate for neo-conservative foreign policy, once describing his own position as support for the use of 'American might to promote American ideals' throughout the world.

Bremer, L. Paul (born 1941). Heavily criticized US proconsul in Iraq in 2003–4. Bremer's office was a division of the United States Department of Defense, and as Administrator he reported directly to the United States Secretary of Defense and the President of the United States. His most famous remark in office was 'Ladies and gentlemen ... we got him!', announcing the capture of Saddam Hussein (14 December 2003). Signed over limited sovereignty to Iraq's interim government at the end of June 2004. Awarded the Presidential Medal of Freedom December 2004. Testified before a Congressional commission about $8.8 billion missing money from Iraq and the chosen accounting method for the funds in question. Published with Malcolm McConnell, *My Year in Iraq. The Struggle to Build a Future of Hope* (2006).

Brown, Gordon (born 1951). British Prime Minister since 27 June 2007 and formerly Chancellor of the Exchequer under Tony Blair (1997–2007). Regarded as less favourable to US neo-conservative-influenced policies than his predecessor. Stated in a speech in June 2007 that he would 'learn the lessons' from the mistakes made in Iraq.

Bryen, Stephen D. JINSA's first executive director in 1978. In 1981, Bryen became Deputy Assistant Secretary of Defense (during Richard N. Perle's period as Assistant Secretary of Defense under President Reagan), remain responsible for technology security until 1988. Some observers have accused Bryen of using his insider connections in Washington to the benefit of Israel. In his book *The Armageddon Network*, Michael Saba, former director of an Arab–American organization, alleged that in 1978 he saw Bryen, then a staffer on the Senate Foreign Relations Committee, offer 'Pentagon documents on the bases' to officials of the Israeli government during a meeting in a restaurant in Washington. In addition to his political activities, which include working with a number of right-wing groups such as the AEI and the Center for Security Policy, Bryen has also worked for or headed various defense-related companies, including Finmeccanica, a British-based defence contractor. Bryen is the author of various research papers, including 'Technology Security and the Revolution in Military Affairs' and 'Cyberterrorism. The Threat and the US Response'. He is the husband of Shoshana Bryen, who has also served as head of JINSA. In a January 2002 article for National Review Online, Bryen pushed the erroneous thesis that Iraq had maintained a well-developed biological weapons programme since the first Gulf War in 1991, making it the 'leading threat' to 'global survival'.

BRZEZINSKI, Zbigniew (born 1928, Poland). National Security Adviser under President Jimmy Carter (1977–81) and friend of Samuel P. Huntington. Responsible for mobilizing the *jihad* in Afghanistan against Soviet occupation. Now considers that friendly US–Iran relations are possible and desirable.

BUCHANAN, Patrick J. ('Pat') (born 1938). Author, broadcaster, and former presidential candidate (1992, 1996, 2000). A Catholic throughout his life, attending the traditional Latin Mass. Believes that many left-wing Mexican-Americans have a revanchist view on territories lost to the United States in the Mexican–American War and has declared that their high birth-rates threaten the social cohesion of certain parts of the country. Buchanan has said that 'homosexuality is not a civil right'; and calls it unhealthy and described sex between two men as 'not only immoral, but filthy'. Further, Buchanan has said that public acceptance of homosexuality inevitably leads to societal decay and the collapse of the family. Has been accused of anti-Semitism by Norman Podhoretz and his son John Podhoretz. Critical of Yasser Arafat, but a supporter of a Palestinian state. Considers that the jihadist terror groups target the US for 'what we do, not who we are'. Outspoken critic of the Iraq war of 2003, considering that it was fought to defend Israeli interests and the interests of American oil firms.

BUSH, George H.W. (born 1924), 41st President of the US (1989–93). Director of the CIA under President Ford (1976–7) and Vice-President to Ronald Reagan (1981–8). After the dissolution of the USSR in 1991, President Bush and Soviet President Mikhail Gorbachev declared a US–Soviet strategic partnership at the summit that July, marking the end of the Cold War. President Bush declared that US–Soviet co-operation during the Persian Gulf War in 1990–1 had laid the groundwork for a partnership in resolving bilateral and world problems. Bush achieved his stated objectives of liberating Kuwait and forcing Iraqi withdrawal, then ordered a cessation of combat operations, allowing Saddam Hussein to stay in power. Bush later explained that he did not give the order to overthrow the Iraqi government because it would have 'incurred incalculable human and political costs ... We would have been forced to occupy Baghdad and, in effect, rule Iraq.'

BUSH, George Walker (born 1946). 43rd President of the US, inaugurated January 2001, son of George H.W. Bush and the first president elected without at least a plurality of the popular vote since Benjamin Harrison in 1888. Elected governor of Texas in 1994, in which position he served from 1995 to 2000. In 1998, Bush won re-election in a landslide victory with nearly 69 per cent of the vote. Within a year, he had decided to seek the Republican nomination for the presidency. In the televised Republican presidential debate held in Des Moines, Iowa on 13 December 1999, all of the participating candidates were asked 'what political philosopher or thinker do you most identify with and why?' Unlike most of the other candidates, who cited former presidents and other political figures, Bush responded, 'Christ, because he changed my heart'. Though in his autobiography ghost-written for the year 2000 presidential election, Bush states 'Reverend Graham planted a mustard seed in my soul', he had in fact been 'converted' on 3 May 1984 by Arthur Blessit, who noted in his diary: 'a good and powerful day. Led Vice-President Bush's son to Jesus today. George Bush Jr.! This is great! Glory to God.' On 25 July 2000, Bush asked Halliburton Corporation CEO Dick Cheney, then serving as head of Bush's vice-presidential search committee, to be his vice-presidential running mate. After the attacks on 11 September 2001, Bush announced a global war on terrorism and ordered an invasion of Afghanistan to overthrow the Taliban, destroy al-Qaeda, and capture Osama bin Laden. In March 2003, Bush ordered the invasion of Iraq, asserting that Iraq was in violation of UN Security Council Resolution 1441 and that the war was necessary for the protection of the US. His domestic approval has ranged from 90 per cent (the highest ever recorded by the Gallup Organization) immediately after the 9/11 attacks to a low of 24 per cent, with a disapproval rating of 65 per cent, the highest level of disfavour for any sitting president since Richard Nixon.

CARTER, Jimmy (born 1924). The first openly evangelical Christian to be elected president of the US, 39th president of the United States from 1977 to 1981, and winner of the Nobel Peace Prize in 2002. The only US President with a successful record in peacemaking in the Middle East, Carter's efforts secured the enduring peace treaty between Israel and Egypt in 1979. Prior to becoming president, Carter served two terms in the Georgia Senate, and was the 76th Governor of Georgia from 1971 to 1975. Carter won the popular vote in 1976 by 50.1 per cent to 48 per cent for Ford and received 297 electoral votes to Ford's 240. He became the first contender from the Deep South to be elected president since the 1848 election. After the Soviet invasion of Afghanistan, Carter announced what became known as the Carter Doctrine: that the US would not allow any other outside force to gain control of the Persian Gulf. The Iranian hostage crisis dominated the last year of Carter's presidency. Unsuccessful responses to the crisis were largely seen as contributing to Carter's defeat in the 1980 election. Established the Carter Center in 1982 in Atlanta to advance human rights and alleviate unnecessary human suffering. The Center promotes democracy, mediates and prevents conflicts, and monitors the electoral process in support of free and fair elections. The Center also works to improve global health through the control and eradication of diseases. Carter has become a forthright opponent of the domestic and foreign policies of President George W. Bush as well as of the role of the Religious Right in US politics. In March 2004, Carter condemned George W. Bush and Tony Blair for waging an unnecessary war 'based upon lies and misinterpretations' in order to oust Saddam Hussein. He claimed that Blair had allowed his better judgement to be swayed by Bush's desire to finish a war that George H. W. Bush had started. In August 2006, Carter criticized Blair for being 'subservient' to the Bush administration and accused Blair of giving unquestioning support to any 'radical or ill-advised' policy adopted by Bush. In June 2005, Carter urged the closing of the Guantánamo Bay prison in Cuba, which has been a focus for claims of prisoner abuse. Carter has also in recent years become a frequent critic of Israel's policies in Lebanon, the West Bank, and Gaza.

CHALABI, Ahmed (born 1944). Iraqi-born businessman and politician who moved to the UK and the US after leaving Iraq in 1956. Ph.D. from University of Chicago (1969). Enjoyed close political and business relationships with some members of the US government, including some prominent neo-conservatives within the Pentagon. Also had political contacts within the PNAC, most notably with Paul Wolfowitz. Another of Chalabi's advocates was the AEI's Iraq specialist, Danielle Pletka. Before the Iraq war, the CIA was largely sceptical of Chalabi and his party, the Iraqi National Congress, but information from his group (most famously from a defector codenamed 'Curveball') made its way into intelligence dossiers used to help convince the public in America and Britain of the need to go to war. Interim oil minister in Iraq in April–May 2005 and December–January 2006 and deputy prime minister from May 2005 until May 2006, Chalabi failed to win a seat in parliament in the December 2005 elections, and when the new Iraqi cabinet was announced in May 2006, he was not awarded a post.

CHENEY, Richard (born 1941). Vice-President in the administration of George W. Bush. Under President Gerald Ford, Cheney worked as Assistant to the President. When Donald Rumsfeld was named Secretary of Defense, Cheney became Chief of Staff to the President. Cheney and Rumsfeld successfully pushed for William Colby to be replaced by George H. W. Bush as the Director of the CIA, forging what would become a long-term relationship with the future president. Cheney was campaign manager for Ford's 1976 presidential campaign. Cheney served as Secretary of Defense from March 1989 to January 1993 under President George H. W. Bush. He directed the US's invasion of Panama and Operation Desert Storm in the Middle East. In 1991 he was awarded the Presidential Medal of Freedom for 'preserving America's defenses at a time of great change around the world'. In 1997, along with Donald Rumsfeld, William Kristol, and others, Cheney founded the Project for the New American Century, a neo-conservative US think tank whose self-stated goal was to 'promote American global leadership'. One of the PNAC positions involved urging the US to remove Saddam Hussein's regime from power in Iraq, using 'diplomatic, political and military efforts'. Member of the AEI and the board of advisers of JINSA. Halliburton Corporation CEO, 1995–2000. On 25 July 2000, George W. Bush asked Cheney, then serving as head of Bush's vice-presidential search committee, to be his vice-presidential running mate. By general consensus Cheney has been the most forceful of all vice-presidents in the modern era, and to a considerable extent has acted as the 'power behind the throne' in the Bush regime.

CHOMSKY, Noam (born 1928). Prominent American Jewish critic of US foreign policy. Considers Israel a tool of the US 'empire', with 'big oil' and the 'military-industrial complex' the main forces shaping US Middle East policy and the drivers in the Iraq war.

CLARKE, Richard A. (born 1951). Worked for the State Department during the presidency of Ronald Reagan. President Bill Clinton promoted Clarke to be the chief counter-terrorism adviser on the US National Security Council. Under President George W. Bush Clarke no longer had cabinet-level access, but continued in the same position until his retirement in Jan. 2003, serving as a member of the Senior Executive Service, specializing in intelligence, cyber security, and counter-terrorism. Stated on 26 June 2004 that the invasion of Iraq was an 'enormous mistake' that was costing untold lives, strengthening al-Qaeda, and breeding a new generation of terrorists.

CLINTON, Hillary Rodham (born 1947). Senator from New York, and candidate for the Democratic nomination in the 2008 presidential election. Since 1975 she has been married to Bill Clinton – the 42nd President of the United States – and was the First Lady of the United States from 1993 to 2001 during which time she had to endure the Monica Lewinsky scandal. Clinton has enjoyed high approval ratings for her job as senator within New York, reaching an all-time high of 72 to 74 per cent approving (including many Republicans) as against 23 to 24 per cent disapproving in December 2006, before her presidential campaign became active; by August 2007, after half a year of campaigning, it was still 64 per cent against 34 per cent. While calling for 'ending the war' in Iraq, Clinton's July 2007 position also advocates keeping US troops in Iraq for the foreseeable future, because 'we cannot lose sight of our very real strategic national interests in this region'. She favours deploying US forces to protect the Kurdish region in the north, to engage in targeted operations against al-Qaeda in Iraq, and to train and equip Iraqi forces. In supporting significant US troop levels in Iraq for the indefinite future, Clinton's position is quite close to that of the Iraq Study Group. In November 2007 she sent an open letter to President Bush, expressing concern about a possibly permanent US base-level presence in Iraq.

Clinton, William ('Bill') Jefferson (born 1946). 42nd President of the US, serving from 1993 to 2001. Before his presidency, Clinton served nearly twelve years as the 50th and 52nd Governor of Arkansas. Impeached by the US House of Representatives for perjury, he was subsequently acquitted by the United States Senate and completed his second term as president. Clinton was reluctant initially to become involved militarily in international conflicts but came to believe that the United States had a stake in the protection of human rights and the promotion of the political and economic stability of remote countries. Few American lives were lost in such military action. Clinton also spent much of his foreign policy effort in trying to end the conflicts in Northern Ireland and the Middle East, the Israeli–Palestinian conflict in particular.

Cohen, Eliot A. (born 1955). Neo-conservative who first formulated the idea that the conflict into which the US had entered post-9/11 was 'World War IV'. Robert E. Osgood Professor in American Foreign Policy at the Paul H. Nitze School of Advanced International Studies (SAIS) at Johns Hopkins University, where he came to know Paul Wolfowitz. In 1997, Cohen became a founding member of PNAC, which became known as a centre for prominent neo-conservatives. He has been a member of the Defense Policy Board Advisory Committee. Serves on the council of academic advisers of AEI. On 2 March 2007, Cohen was appointed by Secretary of State Condoleezza Rice to serve as Counsellor of the State Department.

Dershowitz, Alan (born 1938). Felix Frankfurter Professor of Law at Harvard Law School. Comments regularly on issues related to Judaism, Israel, civil liberties, the war on terror, and the First Amendment, and has engaged in highly publicized media confrontations regarding torture and the Israeli–Palestinian conflict with Noam Chomsky, Norman Finkelstein, and former President Jimmy Carter, among others.

Drumheller, Tyler. Former CIA chief of clandestine operations for Europe, who retired in 2005 having worked for the CIA for 26 years. Revealed the documentary intelligence received from Naji Sabri, Saddam's foreign minister.

Elmandjra, Mahdi (born 1933). Formerly Assistant Director-General at UNESCO (1966–9), who argued in 1991–2 that the Gulf War had 'set the stage for the first civilizational war'.

Fakhravar, Amir Abbas (born 1975). Writer, political activist, and broadcaster. Iranian dissident and opposition leader, whose popularity in Iran remains untested. Advocate of US military intervention in Iran.

Falwell, Reverend Jerry (1933–2007). American fundamentalist Christian pastor and televangelist. Founder of the Moral Majority (1979). Founder of Liberty University, Lynchburg, Virginia. Founder, Moral Majority Coalition (2004). Called the Prophet Muhammad a terrorist (2002). The Anti-Defamation League, and its leader Abraham Foxman, have expressed strong support for Falwell's staunch pro-Israel stand, sometimes referred to as 'Christian Zionism', despite repeatedly condemning what they perceive as intolerance towards Muslims in Falwell's public statements. Referring to the events of 9/11, Falwell stated that the attacks were caused by 'pagans, abortionists, feminists, gays, lesbians, the American Civil Liberties Union and the People For the American Way'. In a more moderate statement, he said that 'if we decide to change all the rules on which this Judeo-Christian nation was built, we cannot expect the Lord to put his shield of protection around us as he has in the past.' Maintained his own website (now a 'Jerry Falwell tribute site'): <http:www.falwell.com>

Feith, Douglas J. (born 1953). Author of *The Dangers of a Palestinian State*, which is published by the Zionist Organization of America and available on joining their organization: <http://www.zoabrooklyn.org/join.html>. In 2000, Feith co-founded One Jerusalem, a private American–Israeli group, with the objective of 'saving a united Jerusalem as the undivided capital of Israel'. As Under-Secretary of Defense for Policy in the Bush administration (July 2001–August 2005), Feith oversaw efforts to provide the type of 'strategic intelligence' needed to drive the neo-conservative policy agenda. An unclassified report, released in April 2007, corroborated allegations that Feith was behind efforts erroneously to connect Saddam Hussein's Iraqi regime with al-Qaeda. Maintains his own website: <http://dougfeith.com/>

FINDLEY, Paul (born 1921). Former Congressman and critic of the power of the American Jewish Lobby and founder of the Council for the National Interest, 'the anti-AIPAC', which seeks to promote US issues above pro-Israel issues. Maintained that 9/11 'would never have occurred were it not for uncritical US support of Israel'. A proponent of the Mearsheimer–Walt thesis *avant le nom*.

FINKELSTEIN, Norman G. (born 1953). American Jewish historian and critic of the Holocaust 'industry' and the writings of Alan Dershowitz. Dershowitz led the (ultimately successful) campaign to deny Finkelstein tenure at DePaul University. In its section of a joint statement issued on 5 September 2007, DePaul University called Professor Finkelstein 'a prolific scholar and an outstanding teacher'.

FOXMAN, Abraham H. (born 1940). Current National Director and chairman of the Anti-Defamation League of B'nai B'rith. Published a book against the Mearsheimer–Walt thesis in 2007.

FRIEDMAN, Murray (1926–2005). American Jewish historian who confirmed the distinctively Jewish contribution towards the neo-conservative movement in *The Neo-conservative Revolution. Jewish Intellectuals and the Shaping of Public Policy* (2005).

FUKUYAMA, Francis (born 1952). Bernard L. Schwartz Professor of International Political Economy and Director of the International Development Program at the Paul H. Nitze School of Advanced International Studies at Johns Hopkins University. Fukuyama is best known as the author of *The End of History and the Last Man* (1992), in which he argued that the progression of human history as a struggle between ideologies is largely at an end, with the world settling on liberal democracy after the end of the Cold War and the fall of the Berlin Wall in 1989. Regarded at first as a neo-conservative, he signed two PNAC letters calling for the overthrow of Saddam Hussein. By late 2003, however, he distanced himself from the Iraq intervention and called for Donald Rumsfeld's resignation as Secretary of Defense. Considered that the threat of radical Islam to the US had been overestimated; that the Bush administration failed to foresee the fierce negative reaction to its 'benevolent hegemony'; and that it had been overly optimistic in seeking to apply Western values to Iraq and the Middle East in general.

GERECHT, Reuel Marc. Former Middle East specialist at the CIA, Middle East Initiative Director of PNAC (2001–5), and now a resident fellow at the AEI. Considers that the Iranians 'have terrorism in their DNA'. Proponent of military intervention in Iraq and Iran. Argues that apologizing for 'the supposedly bad behaviour of the entire Western world toward Iran for the last 150 years' is misunderstood in Iran. 'American apologies in revolutionary clerical eyes mean only one thing – weakness. And showing weakness to power-politic-loving Iranian clerics is not astute.'

GIULIANI, Rudolph ('Rudy')(born 1944). Mayor of New York (1994–2001) at the time of 9/11, which won him national and international fame. When Saudi Prince Alwaleed bin Talal suggested that the attacks were an indication that the United States 'should re-examine its policies in the Middle East and adopt a more balanced stand toward the Palestinian cause', Giuliani asserted 'there is no moral equivalence for this [terrorist] act. There is no justification for it ... And one of the reasons I think this happened is because people were engaged in moral equivalency in not understanding the difference between liberal democracies like the United States, like Israel, and terrorist states and those who condone terrorism. So I think not only are those statements wrong, they're part of the problem.' Giuliani subsequently rejected the prince's $10 million donation to disaster relief in the aftermath of the attack. Leading Republican Party candidate for the presidential nomination in 2008. Advised by neo-cons such as Norman Podhoretz,

Daniel Pipes, and Martin Kramer; it has been suggested that his foreign policy plans make those of George W. Bush seem docile by comparison.

Graham, Billy (born 1918). Southern Baptist evangelical leader and famed evangelist who has had a personal audience with every US President since Harry Truman with the exception of the Roman Catholic J. F. Kennedy. Supporter of Richard Nixon but opponent of racial segregation and apartheid. When he refused to join Jerry Falwell's Moral Majority in 1979, he stated: 'I'm for morality, but morality goes beyond sex to human freedom and social justice. We as clergy know so very little to speak with authority on the Panama Canal or superiority of armaments. Evangelists cannot be closely identified with any particular party or person. We have to stand in the middle in order to preach to all people, right and left. I haven't been faithful to my own advice in the past. I will be in the future.' On 14 September 2001, in the aftermath of the 9/11 attacks, Graham led a prayer and remembrance service at Washington National Cathedral attended by President George W. Bush and past and present leaders. He similarly spoke at the memorial service following the Oklahoma City bombing in 1995. On 24 June 2005, Billy Graham began what he has said would be his last North American crusade, at Flushing Meadows Park in New York City. But on the weekend of 11–12 March 2006 he held a 'Festival of Hope' with his more conservative son, Franklin Graham, in New Orleans, which was recovering from Hurricane Katrina.

Hagee, The Rev. John C. (born 1940). Prominent televangelist and pastor of the 18,000-member Cornerstone Church in San Antonio, Texas and author of *Jerusalem Countdown* (which may be purchased from John Hagee Ministries' website: <http:www.jhm.org/>), a book about a nuclear-armed Iran. Founder of Christians United for Israel. Strongly anti-Muslim in his rhetoric and writings and an advocate of war with Iran.

Hoenlein, Malcolm. Executive Vice-Chairman since June 1986 and leading organizer of the Conference of Presidents of Major American Jewish Organizations (CoP), representing 52 national Jewish organizations, a prominent element within the American Jewish lobby. Considers Israel 'the corporate entity that represents the Jewish people'.

Huntington, Samuel Phillips (born 1927). Albert J. Weatherhead III Professor at Harvard University. During 1977 and 1978 he worked at the White House as co-ordinator of security planning for the National Security Council. He was a founder and co-editor for seven years of the journal *Foreign Policy*. In 1993, Huntington ignited a major debate amongst international relations theorists with the publication in *Foreign Affairs* of an extremely influential and often-cited article entitled 'The Clash of Civilizations?' The article contrasted with another political thesis regarding the core dynamics of post-Cold War geopolitics expressed by Francis Fukuyama in *The End of History*. Huntington later expanded the article into a full-length book, published in 1996, entitled *The Clash of Civilizations and the Remaking of World Order*. The article and the book articulated his views that post-Cold War conflict would occur most frequently and violently along cultural as opposed to ideological lines. He surmised that to understand conflict in our age and in the future, cultural rifts must be understood, and that cultural identity ('civilization' instead of the state) must be accepted as the potential generator of future conflict. Critics argue that the clash of civilizations thesis provides a theoretical justification to legitimize aggression by the US-led 'West' against China and the world of Islam. However, Huntington has also argued that this shift in geopolitical structures requires the West to strengthen itself internally, abandoning democratic universalism and incessant interventionism. Huntington's views have shifted significantly since 9/11 and President Bush's declaration of an open-ended 'war on terror'. Though Huntington's arguments prior to 9/11 have been used by neo-conservatives as justification for their policies, Huntington himself, a life-long conservative Democrat, has distanced himself from selective interpretation of his thesis used to bolster the legitimacy of the 'war on terror'. Nevertheless, the journal *New Internationalist* on 1 July 2004 suggested that Huntington was a 'Pontius Pilate for our age', accusing him of 'low cunning', the 'ability to champion the most reactionary ideas and play Pontius Pilate when they are put into practice'.

Hussein, Saddam (1930–2006). President of Iraq from 1979 to 9 April 2003. Repressive ruler who precipitated the Iran–Iraq war (1980–8) and the first Persian Gulf War (1991), and failed to clarify his intentions regarding WMD to the West in the run-up to the Iraq war of 2003. During the 1980s the US maintained good relations with Iraq as a bulwark against revolutionary Iran, and US presidential envoy Donald Rumsfeld met Saddam and shook hands with him on a visit in December 1983. The Reagan administration gave Saddam roughly $40 billion in aid in the 1980s to fight Iran, nearly all of it on credit. At this time, Saddam's Iraq became 'the third-largest recipient of US assistance'. The scale of the US commitment probably led Saddam to a serious miscalculation, that it would do nothing about an Iraqi invasion of Kuwait. The invasion itself was probably motivated by the need to resolve Iraq's post-war debt problem and faltering attempts to gain the resources needed for post-war reconstruction, rebuild the devastated Iraqi economy, and stabilize the domestic political situation. US suspicions of Saddam's motives remained after his defeat in the Gulf War, and there were growing human rights considerations as a result of the severe repression of the uprisings in the Kurdish north and Shi'a southern and central parts of the Iraq. No-fly zones (NFZs) were imposed on the north of Iraq shortly after the Gulf War and in the south in 1992 (expanded in 1996). As early as May 2002, both the US and British air forces stepped up their attacks on Iraqi facilities. They began to carry out offensive sorties, not only against targets that had fired on them, but upon installations that had demonstrated no hostile intent. The US claimed that these increased attacks were the result of increasing Iraqi provocations, but later, in July 2005, the British Ministry of Defence released figures showing that the number of provocations had actually dropped dramatically prior to and just after the increase in allied attacks. Their records indicate that in the first seven months of 2001, there had been 370 provocations on the part of Iraq. In the seven months from October 2001 into May 2002, only 32 such provocations were recorded. General Tommy Franks later acknowledged that the dramatic increase in offensive sorties was an attempt to destroy the Iraqi defences in much the same way as had been done at the beginning of the Gulf War. It was therefore improbable, prior to the 2003 invasion, that Saddam Hussein was in any position to threaten the Western Coalition – either with WMD or conventional forces – since the Coalition had achieved complete air supremacy. Saddam was captured by US forces on 13 December 2003 and brought to trial and convicted by the Iraqi interim government. He was executed on 30 December 2006; the execution was illegally filmed and the images distributed to al-Jazeera and the BBC.

Indyk, Martin S. (born 1951). Served for three years as AIPAC's research director after 1982 and then for eight years as founding director of the Washington Institute of Near East Policy. Special assistant to President Bill Clinton and senior director of Near East and South Asian Affairs at the US National Security Council. Served twice as US Ambassador to Israel, in 1995–7 and 2000–June 2001, and is currently a Senior Fellow and Director of the Saban Center for Middle East Policy in the Foreign Policy Studies program at the Brookings Institution.

Jackson, Senator Henry 'Scoop' (1912–83). Fiercely anti-communist Democrat senator who advocated bipartisanship in foreign and defence policy. Strong supporter of Israel around whom many neo-conservatives organized in the early 1970s in a last-ditch effort to turn the Democratic Party away from the politics of what they saw as 'appeasement' pushed by the McGovernites. When Jackson's presidential ambitions were spurned by Democrats, the neo-conservative shift to the Republican Party gained momentum. Presented with the Presidential Medal of Freedom posthumously in 1984 and the Truman–Reagan Medal of Freedom posthumously in 2007.

KAGAN, Donald (born 1932). Sterling Professor of Classics and History at Yale University. Once a liberal Democrat, Professor Kagan had changed his views by the 1970s and became one of the original signatories of the 1997 Statement of Principles of PNAC. On the eve of the 2000 presidential elections, Kagan and his son, Frederick W. Kagan, published *While America Sleeps*, a call to increase defence spending.

KAGAN, Frederick W. (born 1969). PNAC signatory and resident scholar at the AEI, and a former professor of military history at the US Military Academy at West Point. Published an article in *Foreign Affairs* on the 'crisis' in American military manpower in July 2006. Proponent of the 'limited surge' in American force levels in Iraq (2007). 'Of all the enemies that shock and awe might be effective against, al-Qaeda is absolutely not one,' Kagan writes; he goes on to explain: 'war is not about killing people and blowing things up. It is purposeful violence to achieve a political goal.' Outlined US options with regard to Pakistan's nuclear weapons in a controversial paper in 2007.

KAGAN, Kimberly. Wife of Frederick W. Kagan, director of an entity called the Institute for the Study of War, and author of *Iran's Proxy War against the United States and the Iraqi Government* (2007).

KAGAN, Robert (born 1958). Co-founder of PNAC, senior associate at the Carnegie Endowment for International Peace (where he focuses on international relations and security issues) and regular columnist in the *Washington Post*. In his book *Of Paradise and Power. America and Europe in the New World Order* (2003), he argues that 'Americans are from Mars and Europeans are from Venus: They agree on little and understand one another less and less.' Kagan claims that because Europe has benefited from 60 years of US security guarantees, it has not been forced to spend as much on defence as the United States and is softer when it comes to issues such as Iraq and other 'rogue states'.

KARZAI, Hamid (born 1957). President of Afghanistan since 7 December 2004. He became a dominant political figure after the removal of the Taliban regime. From December 2001, Hamid Karzai was Chairman of the Transitional Administration and then Interim President from 2002 until he won the 2004 presidential election. Karzai at every stage has been dependent on US military and political support. As a result, he is regarded by Osama bin Laden as an unrepresentative Quisling [= traitor or collaborator]; bin Laden uses the word 'Karzai' in this sense.

KENNAN, George F. (1904–2005). American adviser, diplomat, political scientist, and historian, best known as 'the father of containment' and a key figure in the emergence of the Cold War. He later wrote standard histories of the relations between Russia and the Western powers. Kennan served as deputy head of the US mission in Moscow from July 1944 to April 1946. At the end of that term, Kennan sent a 5,300-word telegram (the 'long telegram') from Moscow to Secretary of State James Byrnes outlining a new strategy on how to handle diplomatic relations with the Soviet Union. Unlike the 'long telegram', Kennan's well-timed article appearing in the July 1947 issue of *Foreign Affairs* under the pseudonym 'X', entitled 'The Sources of Soviet Conduct', did not begin by emphasizing 'the traditional Russian sense of insecurity'. Kennan had not intended the 'X' article as a comprehensive prescription for future policy. For the rest of his life, Kennan continued to reiterate that the article did not imply an automatic commitment to resist Soviet 'expansionism' wherever it occurred, with little distinction of primary and secondary interests. In addition, the article did not make it clear that Kennan favoured employing political and economic rather than military methods as the chief agent of containment. As late as 2007, Kennan's rhetoric was quoted by Norman Podhoretz in justification for a quite different set of arguments in the war against 'Islamo-fascism'.

KHALILZAD, Zalmay ('Zal')(born 1951). An ethnic Pashtun from the Kakar tribe, received his Ph.D. at the University of Chicago, where he studied with Albert Wohlstetter, the prominent nuclear deterrence thinker. Highest-ranking Muslim in the administration of George W. Bush. Served under President Reagan as a State Department official advising on Afghanistan and the Iran–Iraq war, and then as Deputy Under-Secretary for Policy Planning under President George H. W. Bush. Heavily involved with Paul Wolfowitz in producing the 1992 draft Defense Planning Guidance (the 'Wolfowitz Doctrine') and the final document. Between 1993 and 2000, Khalilzad was the Director of the Strategy, Doctrine, and Force Structure at the RAND Corporation. He was a PNAC signatory of the letter to President Clinton advocating the overthrow of Saddam Hussein as well as of its statement of principles. He co-authored with Wolfowitz an article in the *Weekly Standard* entitled 'Overthrow Him' (meaning Saddam), which argued for the liberation of Iraq from 'its tyranny'. Successively presidential envoy for Afghanistan (2001–3) and then US ambassador to Afghanistan (2003–5), Iraq (2005–7) and the United Nations (since April 2007).

Kirkpatrick, Jeane (1926–2006). Ardent anti-communist and long-term Democrat who turned Republican and supported the campaign of Ronald Reagan for the presidency. Once president, Reagan appointed her as the first woman US ambassador to the United Nations (1981–5). Anti-Defamation League President Abraham Foxman issued a press release upon her death which stated that she would be 'fondly remembered for her unwavering and valiant support of the State of Israel and her unequivocal opposition to anti-Semitism, especially during her tenure at the United Nations. She was always a true friend of the Jewish people.' Her highly controversial thesis that right-wing 'authoritarian' governments are more amenable to democratic reform than left-wing 'totalitarian' states, first laid out in a seminal 1979 *Commentary* magazine article, 'Dictatorships and Double Standards', split the neo-conservative movement because others, such as Joshua Muravchick and Paul Wolfowitz, were committed to the moral imperative of promoting democracies. In the short term Kirkpatrick's means-justify-the-ends logic won out with the US's support of 'friendly' dictatorships in the 'greater cause' of defeating communism. By the start of the new millennium, neo-conservatives had come to espouse ideas directly contrary to those expressed in Kirkpatrick's 1979 article. She remained sceptical of 'nation-building', but supported most of the PNAC arguments and was strongly in favour of the use of force after 9/11: 'it would be a very serious mistake for the United States not to respond with force. I do not usually ever advocate the use of force to solve problems. I just think that this is a major challenge, and that we're forced to, in order to protect our civilization. And I mean our civilization. I don't just mean American civilization, I mean modern civilization. What they are targeting is modern civilization' (*Chronicle of Higher Education*, 28 September 2001).

Kissinger, Henry (born 1923). Jewish immigrant fleeing German persecution, he was naturalized as a US citizen in June 1943. Associate Director of the Center for International Affairs at Harvard in 1957, he sought greater influence over foreign policy by acting as adviser to Nelson Rockefeller, Governor of New York, who sought the Republican nomination for president in 1960, 1964, and 1968. Richard Nixon appointed him National Security Adviser, a post he held from 1969 to 1975; he was also Secretary of State under Nixon and Gerald Ford (1973–7). Proponent of the 'realist' school of international relations, his policies were controversial, unpopular, and to a considerable extent reversed under President Reagan. He has provided guidance to George W. Bush and Dick Cheney on Iraq policy. He denies that the alternatives are 'military victory' within a short deadline or 'total withdrawal'.

Kramer, Martin (born 1954). During a 25-year career at Tel Aviv University, Martin Kramer directed the Moshe Dayan Center for Middle Eastern and African Studies. Author of *Ivory Towers on Sand. The Failure of Middle Eastern Studies in America* (2001), he supported Daniel Pipes' Campus Watch initiative and promoted bill HR 3077 to provide closer Congress control over Middle East Studies departments. He was an early advocate of attacking Saddam Hussein in the wake of 9/11, arguing in December 2001 that regardless of a possible involvement, he posed a threat to the entire Middle

East. However, by October 2002, he questioned whether the US possessed the requisite 'tools of social engineering' needed to promote an eventual democracy process in the Arab world. In 2008, he was a foreign policy adviser to Rudy Giuliani's campaign for the Republican presidential nomination. Maintains his own website: <http://www.martinkramer.org>

KRAUTHAMMER, Charles (born 1950). As with many writers associated with neo-conservatism, Krauthammer's politics originally tended toward liberalism and the Democratic Party, in particular supporting the Jimmy Carter administration. Embarked upon a journalistic career 1981; in 1985, began a weekly column for the *Washington Post* for which he won the 1987 Pulitzer Prize for commentary. In an article in *Foreign Affairs* (1990), he emphasized the 'uni-polar moment' for the United States following the demise of the Soviet Union. The 2004 Irving Kristol award winner at the AEI. Outlined the principle of strategic necessity restraining democratic idealism in his controversial 2004 Kristol Award Lecture: 'we will support democracy everywhere, but we will commit blood and treasure only in places where there is a strategic necessity – meaning, places central to the larger war against the existential enemy, the enemy that poses a global mortal threat to freedom.' Named America's most influential commentator by the *Financial Times* in 2006. Contends that the Iraqis 'chose civil war' themselves; 'we midwifed their freedom'. Winner of the 2002 Guardian of Zion Award (an annual award given since 1997 to Jews who have been supportive of the State of Israel).

KRISTOL, Irving (born 1920). Considered the father of neo-conservatism and its 'autobiographer' (1995). Before graduating, he met Gertrude Himmelfarb at a Trotskyist meeting, and they married in January 1942. He wrote in 1983 that he was 'proud' to have been a member of the Fourth International in 1940. Editor of the *Reporter* from 1959 to 1960, executive vice-president of Basic Books from 1961 to 1969, and professor of social thought at the New York University Graduate School of Business from 1969 to 1988. Co-founded the Coalition for a Democratic Majority and served as co-chair. Co-editor of *The Public Interest* (first with Daniel Bell, then with Nathan Glazer) from its founding in 1965 until 2002. John M. Olin Distinguished Fellow at the AEI since 1988, lifetime member of the Council on Foreign Relations since 1972. In July 2002, President George W. Bush awarded Kristol the Presidential Medal of Freedom.

KRISTOL, William (born 1952). Chief of Staff and Counsellor to the Secretary of Education, William Bennett (1985–8), under President Reagan; Chief of Staff to Vice-President Dan Quayle (1989–92) under President Bush Snr; and Chairman and Founder of the Project for the Republican Future (1990–3). Co-founder of the *Weekly Standard* (1995). Co-authored with Robert Kagan an influential *Foreign Affairs* article entitled 'Towards a Neo-Reaganite Foreign Policy'. Edited with Kagan *Present Dangers. Crisis and Opportunity in American Foreign Policy* (2000). In September 2007, Kristol told Fox News the neo-cons wanted military action taken against Pakistan 'over the next few weeks or months ...' Has attended Bilderberg Group meetings. In 2005, Kristol caused controversy by praising President George W. Bush's second inaugural address without disclosing his role as a consultant in the writing of the speech. Kristol praised the speech in his role as a regular political contributor during Fox's coverage of the address, as well as in a *Weekly Standard* article, without disclosing his involvement in the speech on either occasion. In August 2002, Kristol attacked the *New York Times* as part of the 'Axis of Appeasement', but he was subsequently appointed as its 'conservative columnist' (his debut column appeared on 7 January 2008). Though a confirmed Republican supporter, Kristol made it clear that he preferred the election of Barack Obama to that of Hillary Clinton as the lesser of two evils for the Democratic party candidate in the 2008 presidential elections.

LADEN, Osama bin (Usama bin Ladin, born 1957). Saudi-born militant jihadist, leader of al-Qaeda and purported mastermind behind the 9/11 attacks. Although the US supported the Afghan *jihad* against the invasion of the Soviet Union, there is no evidence that bin Laden was directly financed by the Americans, or known to them before 1996 when the Saudi government sought, and eventually obtained, his transfer from Sudan. Since by this date his Saudi citizenship had been revoked, he returned to Afghanistan. On 8 June 1998, a US grand jury indicted Osama bin Laden on charges of killing five Americans and two Indians in the 13 November 1995 truck bombing of a US-operated Saudi National Guard training centre in Riyadh. Bin Laden was charged with 'conspiracy to attack defence utilities of the United States' and prosecutors further charged that bin Laden is the head of the terrorist organization called al-Qaeda, and that he was a major financial backer of Islamic terrorists world-wide. Bin Laden denied involvement but praised the attack. On 4 November 1998, Osama bin Laden was indicted by a Federal Grand Jury for his alleged role in the 1998 United States embassy bombings in Kenya and Tanzania. Attempts at assassination and requests for the extradition of bin Laden from Taliban-controlled Afghanistan met with failure. In 1999, President Bill Clinton convinced the United Nations to impose sanctions against Afghanistan in an attempt to force the Taliban to extradite him, but again without success. Immediately after the 9/11 attacks, US government officials named bin Laden and the al-Qaeda organization as the prime suspects and offered a reward of $25 million for information leading to his capture or death. On 13 July 2007, this figure was doubled to $50 million. Bin Laden has shown himself to be a master both at a *jihadi* version of 'public diplomacy' and also at the ability frequently to change location so as to avoid capture. A letter, dated 11 December 2005, from Atiyah Abd al-Rahman to Abu Musab al-Zarqawi in Iraq indicates that bin Laden and the al-Qaeda leadership were based in the Waziristan region of Pakistan at that time.

LAHAYE, Tim (born 1926). American evangelical Christian minister, author, and speaker. Best-known for the *Left Behind* series of apocalyptic fiction, which he co-wrote with Jerry B. Jenkins and has gained 65 million in sales: <http:www.leftbehind.com> Jerry Falwell said about the first book in the series: 'in terms of its impact on Christianity, it's probably greater than that of any other book in modern times, outside the Bible.' In the 1980s, LaHaye founded the American Coalition for Traditional Values and Coalition for Religious Freedom. In 1979, he helped to establish the Institute for Creationist Research, along with Henry Morris, in Santee, California. He founded the Pre-Tribulation Research Center along with Thomas Ice in 1998. The centre is dedicated to producing material that supports a dispensationalist, pre-tribulation interpretation of the Bible: <http://www.pre-trib.org>

LAND, Richard (born 1947). President of the Ethics and Religious Liberty Commission of the Southern Baptist Convention (since 1988). Strong supporter of George W. Bush's war on terror: 'like mosquitoes, if you're going to deal with terrorists you can't just swat them or use insect repellent. You have to drain the swamp. Saddam Hussein is one of the major swamps. The US would be doing the world a favour and acting in the best interest of future citizens of the US by removing Saddam from power' (4 September 2002).

LEEDEN, Michael (born 1941). JINSA's first executive director in 1977. In the early 1980s, Ledeen appeared before the newly established Senate Subcommittee on Security and Terrorism. An outspoken proponent of taking military action against Iran, which he calls 'the mother of modern terrorism', Leeden has made a career of popularizing alarmist and often misleading charges about terrorism threats. An advocate of regime change in Iraq in 2002 (though not necessarily by the methods chosen by the Bush regime), Leeden crossed swords with former National Security Adviser Brent Scowcroft: 'if ever there were a region that richly deserved being cauldronized, it is the Middle East today. If we wage the war effectively, we will bring down the terror regimes in Iraq, Iran, and Syria, and either bring down the Saudi monarchy or force it to abandon its global assembly line to indoctrinate young terrorists. That's our mission in the war against terror.' He also claimed: 'Iran is the mother of Islamic terrorism, and it has worked hand-in-glove with Yasser Arafat and the PLO for 30 years. Therefore the only coherent strategy for the United States is one that defeats the Islamic Republic and the PLO, along with the other terror masters in Riyadh, Damascus, and Baghdad.' Leeden's most famous remark is probably that 'creative destruction is our middle name ... we must destroy [our enemies] to advance our historic mission'.

LEWIS, Bernard (born 1916). British-trained historian and naturalized American citizen (1982), Orientalist and political commentator. He is the Cleveland E. Dodge Professor Emeritus of Near Eastern Studies at Princeton University and specializes in the history of Islam and the interaction between Islam and the West. He is especially famous in academic circles for his work on the history of the Ottoman Empire. Recipient of the 2007 Irving Kristol award of the AEI. In the mid-1960s, Lewis emerged as a commentator on the issues of the modern Middle East, and his analysis of the Israeli–Palestinian conflict and the rise of militant Islam brought him publicity and aroused significant controversy. American historian Joel Beinin has called him 'perhaps the most articulate and learned Zionist advocate in the North American Middle East academic community ...' Lewis's policy advice appeared to carry particular weight because of his scholarly authority. US Vice-President Dick Cheney remarked: '... in this new century, his wisdom is sought daily by policymakers, diplomats, fellow academics, and the news media.' Professor Edward W. Said (Columbia University) defined Lewis's work as a prime example of Orientalism, in his 1978 book *Orientalism*. In an interview with *Al-Ahram Weekly*, Said suggested that Lewis's knowledge of the Middle East was so biased it could not be taken seriously, and claimed 'Bernard Lewis hasn't set foot in the Middle East, in the Arab world, for at least 40 years. He knows something about Turkey, I'm told, but he knows nothing about the Arab world.' Edward Said considered that Lewis treated Islam as a monolithic entity without the nuance of its plurality, internal dynamics, and historical complexities, and accused him of 'demagogy and downright ignorance'. Lewis has been called 'perhaps the most significant intellectual influence behind the invasion of Iraq', who urged regime change in Iraq to provide a jolt that would 'modernize the Middle East'. By interpreting the 9/11 attacks as part of a clash of civilizations that covers a thousand years or more, Lewis helped shape the war on terrorism as a war against Islamists. Seymour Hirsh asks, 'did Lewis' misconceptions lead the Bush administration to make a terrible strategic error? ... If Bernard Lewis' view of the Arab problem was in error, then America missed a chance to round up and destroy a threat – al Qaeda – that in reality existed only on the sick margins of the Islamic world.'

LIBBY, I. Lewis ('Scooter')(born 1950). Vice-President Richard Cheney's Chief of Staff from 2001 to 2007. Convicted on 6 March 2007 and sentenced for two and a half years in jail for perjury and obstruction of justice resulting from the grand jury investigation into the CIA identity leak known as the Plame Affair. Pardoned by George W. Bush. *See* PLAME, Valerie.

LIEBERMAN, Senator Joseph (born 1942). Senator from Connecticut since 1988. Orthodox Jew who was selected as Al Gore's running mate for the presidential elections of 2000. Fierce defender of the Iraq war. Called himself a 'Scoop Jackson Independent' in 2007. Consistent supporter of Israel and advocate of military strikes against Iran. Has a long history of joining forces with Republicans to support hawkish and interventionist defence policies.

MEARSHEIMER, John J. (born 1947) and WALT, Stephen M. (born 1955). Their thesis (the Mearsheimer–Walt thesis) on the power of the Jewish lobby in the US has brought down upon themselves the wrath of the various American Jewish and pro-Israel lobbies who have accused them of anti-Semitism. In 2002 Mearsheimer was one of 33 professors to sign a letter in the *New York Times* arguing against the Iraq war. Argued that invading Iraq would distract from the war against al-Qaeda, which he described as a greater threat to national security. The war was unnecessary, Mearsheimer felt, because the US could continue to contain Hussein, as it had done for over a decade since the Gulf War.

MILLER, Judith (born 1948). *New York Times* reporter who had preferential access to Ahmed Chalabi and the INC and also to Richard Perle, Paul Wolfowitz, and the Office of Special Plans. Her reporting was subsequently accused of being little more than 'plants' from the Pentagon. Jailed for 85 days in November 2005 for contempt of court for refusing to testify before a federal grand jury investigating a leak naming Valerie Plame as a covert CIA agent. Miller said of the controversy concerning Saddam's alleged WMD that her role was not 'to assess the government's information and be an independent intelligence analyst myself. My job is to tell readers of the *New York Times* what the government thought about Iraq's arsenal.' Others have criticized this position, arguing that a crucial function of a journalist is to assess information independently, question sources, and analyse the reliability of evidence before reporting it. The Miller case serves as a pre-eminent example of the failure of reporters and the American media in general to question the White House–Pentagon propaganda and manipulation of information during the 'war on terror' and the build-up to the Iraq war.

MOHAMMED, Khalid Sheikh (born 1964, known as KSM). Until his capture in Pakistan in 2003, he was an important figure in Osama bin Laden's al-Qaeda organization, where he came to head the group's propaganda operations c.1999. According to the 9/11 Commission Report he was 'the principal architect of the 9/11 attacks'. He is also thought to have had, or to have confessed to, a role in many of the most significant terrorist plots over the last twenty years, including the 1993 World Trade Center bombing, the Operation Bojinka plot ('this marked the first time KSM took part in the actual planning of a terrorist operation' according to the 9/11 Commission Report), an aborted 2002 attack on Los Angeles's US Bank Tower, the Bali nightclub bombings, the failed bombing of American Airlines Flight 63, the Millennium Plot, and the murder of Daniel Pearl. In September 2006, the US government announced it had moved Mohammed from a secret prison to the facility at Guantánamo Bay. KSM has made allegations of torture in US custody. In the Defense Department transcript, he claimed that his statement was not made under duress but both he and human rights advocates have alleged that he was tortured. CIA officials have previously told ABC News that 'Mohammed lasted the longest under water boarding, two and a half minutes, before beginning to talk'. One CIA official has cautioned that 'many of Mohammed's claims during interrogation were "white noise" designed to send the US on wild goose chases or to get him through the day's interrogation session'.

MUSHARRAF, Pervez (born 1943). President of Pakistan (scheduled until 2012). In 1998, following the resignation of General Jehangir Karamat, he was personally promoted over other senior officers by Prime Minister Nawaz Sharif. Came to power by a military *coup d'état* on 12 October 1999, ousting Nawaz Sharif. Assumed the title of Chief Executive and became Pakistan's *de facto* head of government, thereby becoming the fourth army chief of Pakistan to have assumed executive control. In 2001, Musharraf appointed himself to the office of President of Pakistan. The ousting of Nawaz Sharif was a popular measure. Following 9/11, after an ultimatum from the US, Musharraf agreed to give the US the use of three airbases for Operation Enduring Freedom. On 19 Septenber 2001, Musharraf addressed the people of Pakistan and stated that, while he opposed military tactics against the Taliban, Pakistan risked being endangered by an alliance of India and the US if it did not cooperate. On 12 January 2002, Musharraf made a landmark speech against jihadist extremism. He unequivocally condemned all acts of terrorism and also pledged to combat extremism and lawlessness within Pakistan itself. He has been subjected to at least three assassination attempts (14 and 25 December 2003; July

2007). Though criticized by the US for not doing enough, Pakistan has employed over 103,000 troops on the border with Afghanistan and suffered 680 deaths in its army during the war on terror. On 3 November 2007, only days before a bench of the Supreme Court of Pakistan was to decide on a petition challenging the constitutional validity of his re-election as president in the controversial October 2007 elections, Musharraf, as Chief of Army Staff, suspended the constitution, jailed several justices and lawyers of the Supreme Court, including Chief Justice Iftikhar Muhammad Chaudhry, ordered the arrest of political dissidents and human rights activists, and shut down all private television channels. He declared an emergency. On 24 November 2007, the Pakistan Election Commission confirmed his re-election as president and on 28 November Musharraf resigned from the army and assumed a civilian presidency.

MYLROIE, Laurie (born 1953). 'The neo-cons' favourite conspiracy theorist'. Populist writer who tried to demonstrate the connection between al-Qaeda and Saddam Hussein. Published *Bush vs. the Beltway* in 2003. Adjunct fellow at AEI.

NEUHAUS, Richard John (born 1936). Lutheran priest who converted to Roman Catholicism in September 1990. Founding editor of *First Things*, the premier Catholic neo-conservative journal. A close, yet unofficial, confidant of President George W. Bush on a range of religious and ethical matters.

NETANYAHU, Benjamin (born 1949). Controversial leader of the Likud Party and prime minister of Israel (1996–9), the first to have been born after the founding of the state in 1948. After defeat by Ehud Barak in the 1999 election, temporarily withdrew from politics. Leadership of Likud was taken over by Ariel Sharon, who appointed him successively as foreign minister (2002–3) and finance minister (2003–5). Regained leadership of Likud in 2005 when Sharon left to form the Kadima Party. Has won notoriety for his comparison of Iran to Nazi Germany in 1938 and the accusation that Iran is preparing 'another Holocaust'.

NEUMANN, Thomas. Executive director of JINSA and advocate of the US–Israel–India triumvirate against terrorism.

PERLE, Richard (born 1941). Called variously the 'prince of darkness' and 'neo-conservative high priest'. Perle objected to the arms talks between the Carter administration and the Soviet Union revolving primarily around Carter's agreement to halt all cruise missile development. He is widely credited with spearheading opposition to the treaty, which was never ratified by the Senate. Assistant Secretary of Defense under President Reagan (1981–7). Chairman of the Defense Policy Board between 2001 and 2003; served on the board from 1987 to 2004 under both Democrat and Republican administrations. Supporter of regime change in Iraq, but unwise in some of his alliances: the Iraqi defectors and the head of the INC, Ahmed Chalabi, were discredited not only by the CIA, but by the State Department at the time that Perle was supporting them. Expressed his confidence that President Bush 'would order the necessary military action' against Iran (January 2007). With David Frum, Perle states in *An End to Evil. How to Win the War on Terror* (2004) that 'there is no middle way for Americans: it is victory or holocaust'. Member of several conservative think tanks, such PNAC, JINSA, the Center for Security Policy, the Hudson Institute, the Washington Institute for Near East Policy Board of Advisers, and (as a resident fellow) the AEI. He is also a patron of the Henry Jackson Society.

PIPES, Daniel (born 1949). Self-confessed 'Islamism-ophobe' and neo-Zionist. Founder of the Middle East Forum in 1990 and its director. Ideological opponent of Edward Said. Founder of Campus Watch (2002). Winner of the 2006 Guardian of Zion Award (an annual award given since 1997 to Jews who have been supportive of the State of Israel). Pipes has joined Rudolph Giuliani's presidential campaign as an adviser. Maintains his own website: <http://danielpipes.org> and *Islamist Watch* (5 Mar. 2008).

PIPES, Richard Edgar (born 1923). Father of Daniel Pipes. Historian of the Soviet system and political activist against it. Adviser to the administration of President Reagan. In March 1981, Richard Pipes dropped the bombshell that *détente* was dead.

PLAME, Valerie (born 1963). Wife of former ambassador Joseph Wilson, who published an article in the *New York Times* criticizing the Bush administration for 'twisting' intelligence to justify war in Iraq. Plame's CIA identity was illegally leaked by the conservative political commentator Robert D. Novak on 14 July 2003 in his syndicated column in the *Washington Post*. Novak's sources were later revealed to be Richard L. Armitage, a former Deputy Secretary of State, and Karl Rove, George W. Bush's senior political adviser in the White House. Neither was charged.

PLETKA, Danielle (born 1963). Established herself as a foreign policy hawk while working as a reporter for *Insight* magazine during the George H. W. Bush administration, and later as a member of the professional staff for the Senate Foreign Relations Committee during the Clinton administration, serving as the committee's Middle East specialist. In 2002, when some 20 associates of the AEI joined the George W. Bush administration, Pletka moved from her government position to AEI, where she is vice-president for foreign and defence policy studies. Strong supporter of Ahmed Chalabi. Advocates a relatively small American troop presence in Iraq. In May 2004, she told a *Washington Post* reporter: 'I think the phrase "neo-con" is much more popular among people who think it shields their anti-Semitism. But it doesn't.'

PODHORETZ, Norman (born 1930). American neo-conservative columnist. Winner of the 2007 Guardian of Zion Award (an annual award given since 1997 to Jews who have been supportive of the State of Israel). Considers George W. Bush is 'a man who knows evil when he sees it and who has demonstrated an unfailingly courageous willingness to endure vilification and contumely in setting his face against it'. Advising Republican presidential candidate Rudy Giuliani on his views on World War IV and the struggle against 'Islamo-fascism'.

POWELL, Colin Lewis (born 1937). National Security Adviser (1987–9) under President Reagan, Chairman of the Joint Chiefs of Staff (1989–93) during the First Gulf War, and Secretary of State (2001–5). Required by the George W. Bush administration to make the case for the Iraq war before the United Nations of 5 February 2003, a speech that he later regretted and termed in September 2005 a 'blot' on his record that remained 'painful'. Awarded two Presidential Medals of Freedom and the Ronald Reagan Freedom award. Essentially outmanoeuvred by Cheney and Rumsfeld during his period in office as Secretary of State.

QUTB, Sayyid (1906–66). Leading intellectual of the Egyptian Muslim Brotherhood and prolific author of *Milestones* (1978), *In the Shade of the Qur'an* (written over a fifteen-year period, mostly while in prison; English translation by Adil Salahi in ten volumes published at Leicester by the Islamic Foundation), and other works. Executed by the Nasser regime on 29 August 1966 after a trial in which he refused to repudiate his published views. Qutb's alleged influence on Islamic Jihad in Egypt and al-Qaeda is at most indirect: his brother, Muhammad Qutb, moved to Saudi Arabia and promoted his work. Ayman al-Zawahiri was an ardent follower of Muhammad Qutb and his brother's writings. However, scholars of Sayyid Qutb dispute that he was an advocate of violence in the way espoused by Egyptian Islamic Jihad under al-Zawahiri and by al-Qaeda under bin Laden. The influence of his work extends to issues such as Westernization, modernization, political reform within the Islamic world and the theory of inevitable ideological conflict between 'Islam and the West' (= clash of civilizations), the notion of a trans-national *umma* and the nature of *jihad*.

RATZINGER, Joseph Alois (born 1927). Conservative Bavarian theologian who served as Prefect of the Congregation for the Doctrine of the Faith (1981–2005) under Pope John Paul II and was elected pope on 19 April 2005. Hostile to the entry of Turkey into the European Union, which he wishes to see remain as a Christian club. Opposes the 'dictatorship of relativism', which he sees as core challenge facing the Catholic Church. As Pope Benedict XVI, Ratzinger delivered what came to be regarded by many as a notorious lecture on 'faith and reason' at Regensburg on 12 September 2006, which was criticized by many for its apparent turn towards hostility to Islam. It was subsequently stated that the Pope's aim had been to conclude with 'a clear and radical rejection of the religious motivation for violence, from whatever side it may come. [The Pope] sincerely regrets that certain passages of his address could have sounded offensive to the sensitivities of the Muslim faithful and should have been interpreted in a manner that in no way corresponds to his intentions.

Reed, Ralph E. Jnr (born 1961). Conservative activist and executive director of the Christian Coalition 1989–97. Author of *Active Faith. How Christians are Changing the Soul of American Politics* (1996). Co-chairman with Rabbi Yechiel Eckstein of Stand for Israel. Re-emerged in 2004 as a senior member of the team campaigning for the re-election of George W. Bush and Dick Cheney.

Rice, Condoleezza (born 1954). Under President George H. W. Bush served as Soviet and East European Affairs Adviser during the collapse of the Soviet Union and the process of German reunification. Professor of Political Science at Stanford University and Provost 1993–9. Campaign adviser to George W. Bush in 2000 (leading a group known as the Vulcans, which included Richard Armitage, Richard Perle, and Paul Wolfowitz, among others). National Security Adviser to President George W. Bush (2001–5) and Secretary of State after the resignation of Colin Powell (confirmed by the Senate on 26 January 2005).

Robertson, Marion Gordon (Pat) (born 1930). Southern Baptist televangelist and founder of the Christian Coalition. An influential, but controversial, figure on the Christian Right. Agreed with Jerry Falwell when he stated that the 9/11 terrorist attacks were caused by 'pagans, abortionists, feminists, gays, lesbians, the American Civil Liberties Union and the People For the American Way'. On 21 March 2003 claimed on air that the Iraq war was 'a righteous cause out of the Bible'; subsequently has contended that 'the Lord told me it was going to be (a) a disaster and (b) messy'.

Rosen, Stephen Peter. Professor of National Security and Military Affairs at Harvard University. Associate director of the John M. Olin Institute for Strategic Studies (1990–6). Signatory of the PNAC report *Rebuilding America's Defenses* (2000).

Rosen, Steven J. The American Israel Public Affairs Committee's director of foreign policy issues for 23 years until his dismissal in March 2005 because of impending prosecution. At a lunch on 26 June 2003, Lawrence Franklin disclosed classified national defence information to Rosen and Keith Weissman.

Rove, Karl (born 1950). Deputy Chief of Staff and Senior Adviser at the White House (until August 2007); Chief Political Strategist at the White House (2001–5). The 'political brains' behind the rise of George W. Bush. His 'strategic communications' task force within the White House Iraq Group helped write and co-ordinate speeches by senior Bush administration officials prior to the Iraq war in 2003. Controversially stated in June 2005 that 'conservatives saw the savagery of 9/11 in the attacks and prepared for war; liberals saw the savagery of the 9/11 attacks and wanted to prepare indictments and offer therapy and understanding for our attackers'.

Rumsfeld, Donald (born 1932). Secretary of Defense under Gerald Ford (1975–7) and George W. Bush (2001–6). White House Chief of Staff to Gerald Ford (1974–5), a position in which he was succeeded by Dick Cheney. President Nixon, for whom he served in several roles, called him a 'ruthless little bastard'. Awarded the Presidential Medal of Freedom (1977). Served as President Reagan's special envoy to the Middle East, in which capacity he met Saddam Hussein in December 1983. Co-founder and active member of PNAC. Controversial Secretary of Defence under George W. Bush, notably with regard to his views on the necessary levels of troops for the Iraq war, his role in the prisoner abuse scandal, and also his 'information operations roadmap' (30 Oct. 2003) which provided no limits for 'information operations' at home as long as Americans were not actually 'target(s)'.

SABAN, Haim (born 1944). Egyptian-born Israeli-American billionaire, media owner, and philanthropist of political and pro-Israel causes. Funded the research organization at the Brookings Institution called the Saban Center for Middle East Policy. Quoted as stating 'I'm a one-issue guy and my issue is Israel.'

SABRI, Naji. Foreign Minister of Iraq, who confirmed secretly to the CIA prior to the Iraq war of 2003 that Iraq had no WMD. Now teaches journalism in Qatar.

SADR, Moqtada al- (born 1973). His followers are alleged to be responsible for the assassination of Imam Abdul Majid al-Khoei on 10 April 2003. Led an insurrection in 2004. Subsequently has played an intermittent political role in Iraq, while his Mahdi army has been accused of sectarian killings and penetrating various government ministries.

SAID, Edward (1935–2003). Palestinian scholar of the Middle East and critic of Orientalism; a founding figure in post-colonial theory and author of the influential *Orientalism* (1978). Hostile to Samuel P. Huntington's clash of civilizations thesis. Criticized by neo-conservatives because an unashamed champion of peace with justice for Palestinians.

SCHEUER, Michael. Former CIA employee for 22 years. Served as the Chief of the bin Laden Issue Station 1996–9, and subsequently Special Adviser to the Chief of the bin Laden unit (September 2001–November 2004). Resigned 2004. Author of two significant studies on terrorism under the title of 'Anonymous', one of which was complimented by bin Laden himself on 7 September 2007.

SCHMITT, Gary. Executive director of PNAC (1998–2005) and then moved to AEI, where in 2007 he was a resident scholar and director of its program on Advanced Strategic Studies. Co-author of *Silent Warfare. Understanding the World of Intelligence* (1991) with Abram Shulsky.

SCHULTZ, George Pratt (born 1920). Secretary of State under President Ronald Reagan (1982–9). Awarded Presidential Medal of Freedom 1989. Came to the rescue of the various pro-Israel Jewish lobbies in the United States in 2007, in the introduction to Abraham Foxman's book directed against the Mearsheimer–Walt thesis.

SCOWCROFT, General Brent (born 1925). National Security Adviser under two presidents (Gerald Ford, 1974–7, and George H.W. Bush, 1989–93), he appealed publicly to the George W. Bush administration on 15 August 2002 via the *Wall Street Journal* not to invade Iraq. Awarded the Presidential Medal of Freedom 1991. Chairman of the Foreign Intelligence Advisory Board under George W. Bush (2001–5).

SELBOURNE, David (born 1937). British historian of ideas, whose *The Losing Battle with Islam* (2005) was first turned down by a number of British publishers.

SHARON, Ariel (born 1928; incapacitated 4 January 2006). Controversial Defence Minister of Israel who failed to prevent the Sabra and Shatila massacres in Lebanon. Prime Minister of Israel (7 March 2001–incapacitation, though not declared permanently incapacitated until 14 April 2006).

SHULSKY, Abram N. Neo-conservative with long-standing ties to Paul Wolfowitz. Director of the Office of Special Plans, which reported to Douglas Feith. Straussian scholar and guru of disinformation ('truth is not the goal' of intelligence operations, only 'victory'). Co-authored with AEI's Gary J. Schmitt *Silent Warfare. Understanding the World of Intelligence* (1991).

SISTANI, Grand Ayatollah Ali al- (born 1930). Iranian citizen. Most senior Shi'ite cleric, and leader of the Shi'ite coalition, in Iraq.

SOROS, George (born 1930). Hungarian-born secular Jewish financier and philanthropist and critic of the power of the American Jewish and pro-Israeli lobbies. Allegedly 'broke the Bank of England' on Black Wednesday 1992 by speculating against the continuation of the pound sterling in the European Exchange Rate Mechanism. Chairman of both Soros Fund Management and the Open Society Institute. A supporter of Barack Obama as Democrat candidate for the 2008 presidential election.

TENET, George (born 1953). Director of the CIA from July 1997 to July 2004 under presidents Clinton and George W. Bush. Though heavily implicated in the scandal over the incorrect intelligence assessment of Iraq's WMD, awarded Presidential Medal of Freedom (14 December 2004).

WALT, *see at* MEARSHEIMER

WEIGEL, George (born 1951). Prolific Catholic author and activist. Senior Fellow of the Ethics and Public Policy Center: <http://www.eppc.org/>. Author of the controversial 'Moral Clarity in a Time of War', a public lecture that was later published in the theo-conservative journal *First Things* in January 2003. Maintains his own website: <http://www.ratzingerfanclub.com/Weigel/>

WOLFOWITZ, Paul (born 1943). Under-Secretary of Defense for Policy under George H. W. Bush (1989–93) and author of the Defense Planning Guidance of 1992 (the 'Wolfowitz Doctrine'). Deputy Secretary of Defense under George W. Bush (2001–5), widely known as 'Wolfowitz of Arabia' for his obsession with ousting Iraq's Saddam Hussein as the first step in transforming the entire Arab Middle East. Short-lived president of the World Bank (2005–7). Now visiting scholar at AEI.

WOOLSEY, R. James (born 1941). Director of the CIA under President Clinton (1993–5). In a *Washington Post* online forum on 15 April 2003, Mel Goodman called him 'a disaster as CIA director in the [19]90s [who] is now running around this country calling for a World War IV to deal with the Islamic problem'.

WURMSER, David. Co-ordinating author of *A Clean Break: a New Strategy for Securing the Realm* (1996), which advocated a new, hard line for Israel towards the Palestinians: <www.israeleconomy.org/strat1.htm> Special assistant to John Bolton at the State Department from the beginning of the George W. Bush presidency. Member of the 'Pentagon intelligence unit' appointed by Douglas Feith after 9/11. Moved in early September 2003 to the office of Vice-President Cheney and 'Scooter' Libby, where he served as Middle East policy adviser until July 2007. Advocate of regime change in Iraq and military intervention against Iran. Married to Meyrav Wurmser.

WURMSER, Meyrav. Wife of David Wurmser. Co-founder of the Middle East Media Research Institute in February 1998. Left MEMRI in 2002 to direct the Centre of Middle East Policy at the Hudson Institute.

ZARQAWI, Abu Musab al- (1966–2006). Jordanian-born al-Qaeda leader in Iraq, who led a ferocious extremist assault on the Shi'ites there. Killed 7 June 2006 while attending a meeting at a supposed safe house.

ZAWAHIRI, Ayman al- (born 1951). Second in command of al-Qaeda, having formally merged his own organization Egyptian Islamic Jihad into that body in 1998.

ZINNI, General Anthony Charles (born 1943). Retired four-star general in the United States Marine Corps and former Commander in Chief of CENTCOM. In this capacity, he envisaged the eventuality of Saddam Hussein's demise or overthrow and the resulting chaos that might follow in Iraq.

# Bibliography


Abelson, Donald E., *A Capitol Idea. Think Tanks and US Foreign Policy* (Montreal: McGill-Queen's University Press, 2006).

Abrahamian, Ervand, 'The US media, Huntington and September 11', *Third World Quarterly*, 24/3 (2003), 529–44.

Abrams, Elliott (ed.), *The Influence of Faith. Religious Groups and US Foreign Policy* (Lanham, MD: Rowan and Littlefield, 2001).

Abu Zayd, Nasr, *Reformation of Islamic Thought. A Critical Historical Analysis* (Amsterdam: Amsterdam University Press and Scientific Council for Government Policy [WRR], 2006).

Ahmed, Akbar and Forst, Brian (eds), *After Terror. Promoting Dialogue among Civilizations* (Cambridge and Malden, MA: Polity, 2005).

Ajami, Fouad, 'A Sage in Christendom. A Personal Tribute to Bernard Lewis', *Opinion Journal* (from the *Wall Street Journal* Editorial page) (1 May 2006). Web version (accessed 6 Nov. 2006) at: <http://www.opinionjournal.com/editorial/feature.html?id=110008313>

Akhavi, Shahrough, 'Islam and the West in World History', *Third World Quarterly*, 24/3 (2003), 545–62.

Alagha, Joseph, *The Shifts in Hizbullah's Ideology. Religious Ideology, Political Ideology and Political Program* (Amsterdam: ISIM/Amsterdam University Press, 2006).

Al-Azmeh, Aziz and Fokas, Effie (eds), *Islam in Europe. Diversity, Identity and Influence* (New York and Cambridge: Cambridge University Press, 2007).

Al-Djazairi, Salah Eddine Zaimeche, *The Hidden Debt to Islamic Civilisation* (Manchester: Bayt Al-Hikma Press, 2005).

——, *The Golden Age and Decline of Islamic Civilisation* (Manchester: Bayt Al-Hikma Press, 2006).

——, *The Myth of Muslim Barbarism and its Aims* (Manchester: Bayt Al-Hikma Press, 2007).

AlSayyad, Nezar and Castells, Manuel (ed.), *Muslim Europe or Euro-Islam. Politics, Culture and Citizenship in the Age of Globalization* (Plymouth: Lexington Books, 2002).

Anonymous = Scheuer, Michael.

Aysha, Emad El-Din, 'Huntington's Shift to the Declinist Camp: Conservative Declinism and the "Historical Function" of the Clash of Civilizations', *International Relations*, 17/4 (2003), 429–52.

——, 'Samuel Huntington and the Geopolitics of American Identity', *International Studies Perspectives*, 4/2 (2003), 113–32.

Bassin, Mark, 'Civilizations and their Discontents. Political Geography and Geopolitics in the Huntington Thesis', *Geopolitics*, 12/3 (2007), 351–74.

Benjamin, Daniel and Simon, Steven, *The Age of Sacred Terror* (New York: Random House, 2002).

Bensahel, Nora, 'Mission not accomplished. What Went Wrong with Iraqi reconstruction', *Journal of Strategic Studies*, 29/3 (2006), 452–73.

Berger, Peter L. (ed.), *The Desecularization of the World. Resurgent Religion and World Politics* (Grand Rapids, MI: William B. Eerdmans and Ethics and Public Policy Center, Washington DC, 1999).

Blankfort, Jeff, 'The Influence of Israel and its American Lobby over US Middle East Policy', presentation at the Islamic Human Rights Commission Conference, School of Oriental and African Studies, London, 2 July 2006 (accessed 5 Mar. 2007): <http://www.tlaxcala.es/pp.asp?reference=757&lg=en>, <http://peacepalestine.blogspot.com/2006/07/jeff-blankfort-influence-of-israel-and.html>

Blumenthal, Sidney, *How Bush Rules. Chronicles of a Radical Regime* (Princeton and Oxford: Princeton University Press, 2006).

Boase, Roger (ed.), *Islam and Global Dialogue. Religious Pluralism and the Pursuit of Peace* (Aldershot: Ashgate, 2005).

Bonney, Richard, *Jihad from Qur'an to bin Laden* (Houndmills, Basingstoke: Palgrave Macmillan, 2004).

——, *Has the War on Terror become a War on Islam?* (London: Public Policy Research Organization, 2008).

Borer, Hagit (chair), 'The Pro-Israel Lobby. The Debate between James Petras and Norman Finkelstein', Swana Collective of KPFK radio (8 Feb. 2007): <http://www.normanfinkelstein.com/article.php?pg=11&ar=978>

Bottici, Chiara and Challand, Benoît, 'Rethinking Political Myth. The Clash of Civilizations as Self-fulfilling Prophecy', *European Journal of Social Theory*, 9 (2006), 315–36.

Briody, Dan, *The Halliburton Agenda. The Politics of Oil and Money* (Hoboken, NJ: Wiley and Sons, 2004).

Bruce, Steve, 'Zealot Politics and Democracy. The Case of the New Christian Right', *Political Studies*, 48 (200), 263–82.

Byman, Daniel, 'Going to War with the Allies you have. Allies, Counter-insurgency and the War on Terrorism', Strategic Studies Institute of the US Army War College (Nov. 2005): <http://www.strategicstudiesinstitute.army.mil/pubs/display.cfm?pubID=630>

——, *The Five Front War. The Better Way to Fight Global Jihad* (Hoboken, NJ: John Wiley, 2007).

——, 'US Counter-Terrorism Options. A Taxonomy', *Survival*, 49/3 (2007), 121–50.

Carter, Jimmy, *Our Endangered Values. America's Moral Crisis* (New York: Simon and Schuster, 2005).

——, *Faith and Freedom. The Christian Challenge for the World* (New York: Simon and Schuster, 2005; London: Duckworth, 2006).

——, *Palestine. Peace not Apartheid* (New York: Simon and Schuster, 2006).

Chomsky, Noam, *Hegemony or Survival. America's Quest for Global Dominance* (Crows Nest, NSW, Aus.: Allen and Unwin, 2003).

Clarke, Richard A., *Against all Enemies. Inside America's War on Terror* (London: The Free Press, 2004).

Coates, David and Krieger, Joel, *Blair's War* (Cambridge: Polity, 2004).

Cook, Jonathan, *Israel and the Clash of Civilizations. Iraq, Iran and the Plan to Remake the Middle East* (London and Ann Arbor, MI: Pluto Press, 2008).

Crotty, William (ed.), *The Politics of Terror. The US Response to 9/11* (Boston, MA: Northeastern University Press, 2004).

Cushman, Thomas (ed.), *A Matter of Principle. Humanitarian Arguments for War in Iraq* (Berkeley and Los Angeles: University of California Press, 2005).

Daalder, Ivo H., 'Beyond Preemption. An Overview', in Daalder, Ivo H. (ed.), *Beyond Preemption. Force and Legitimacy in a Changing World* (Washington DC: Brookings Institution Press, 2007), 1–18.

Daalder, Ivo H., and Lindsay, James M., *America Unbound. The Bush Revolution in Foreign Policy* (Washington DC: Brookings Institution Press, 2003).

Dalby, Simon, 'Regions, Strategies and Empire in the Global War on Terror', *Geopolitics*, 12/4 (2007), 586–606.

Daniel, Norman, *Islam and the West. The Making of an Image* (Oxford: Oneworld Publications, 1960; repr. 2003).

Dershowitz, Alan M., *Preemption. A Knife that Cuts Both Way* (New York and London: W.W. Norton, 2006).

Domke, David, *God Willing? Political Fundamentalism in the White House, the 'War on Terror' and the Echoing Press* (London and Ann Arbor, MI: Pluto Press, 2004).

Domke, David and Coe, Kevin, *The God Strategy. How Religion Became a Political Weapon in America* (New York: Oxford University Press, 2008).

Findlay, Paul, *They Dared to Speak Out. People and Institutions Confront Israel's Lobby* (Westport, CT: Lawrence Hill, 1985).

Finkelstein, Norman G., *The Holocaust Industry. Reflections on the Exploitation of Jewish Suffering* (2nd edn.: London and New York: Verso, 2003).

——, *Beyond Chutzpah. On the Misuse of Anti-Semitism and the Abuse of History* (London: Verso, 2005).

Fox, Jonathan, 'Religion as an Overlooked Element of International Relations', *International Studies Review*, 3/3 (2001), 53–73.

——, 'Two Civilizations and Ethnic Conflict. Islam and the West', *Journal of Peace Research*, 38/4 (2001), 459–72.

——, 'Ethno-Religious Conflict in the Third World. The Role of Religion as a Cause of Conflict', *Nationalism and Ethnic Politics*, 9/1 (2003), 101–25.

——, 'Is Ethno-Religious Conflict a Contagious Disease?', *Studies in Conflict and Terrorism*, 27 (2004), 89–106.

——, *Religion, Civilization and Civil War. 1945 Through the New Millennium* (Lanham, MD: Lexington Books, 2004).

——, 'The Rise of Religion and the Fall of the Civilization Paradigm as Explanations for Intra-state Conflict', *Cambridge Review of International Affairs*, 20/3 (2007), 361–82.

——, 'The Increasing Role of Religion in State Failure: 1960 to 2004', *Terrorism and Political Violence*, 19/3 (2007), 395–414.

Fox, Jonathan and Sandler, Shmuel, *Bringing Religion into International Relations* (New York: Palgrave Macmillan, 2004).

Fox, Jonathan and Sandler, Shmuel, 'The Question of Religion and World Politics', *Terrorism and Political Violence*, 17 (2005), 293–303.

Foxman, Abraham H., *The Deadliest Lies. The Israel Lobby and the Myth of Jewish Control* (New York: Palgrave Macmillan, 2007).

Friedman, Murray, *The Neo-Conservative Revolution. Jewish Intellectuals and the Shaping of Public Policy* (Cambridge: Cambridge University Press, 2005).

Fukuyama, Francis, *The End of History and the Last Man* (New York: Avon Books; London: Profile, 1992).

——, *After the Neocons. America at the Crossroads* (London: Profile, 2006).

Gasiorowski, Mark J. and Byrne, Malcolm (eds), *Mohammad Mosaddeq and the 1953 Coup in Iran* (Syracuse, NY: Syracuse University Press, 2004).

Gauhar, Altaf, 'Arab Petrodollars. Dashed Hope for a New Economic Order', *World Policy Journal*, 4/3 (1987), 443–64.

Gerecht, Reuel Marc, 'The Last Orientalist: Bernard Lewis at 90', *The Weekly Standard* (5 June 2006; posted 30 May 2006). Web version (accessed 10 Nov. 2006) at: <http://

www.aei.org/publications/filter.all,pubID.24455/pub_detail.asp>

Gilpin, Robert, 'War is Too Important to be Left to Ideological Amateurs', *International Relations*, 19/1 (2005), 5–18.

Glass, Charles, 'Lewis of Arabia', *The Nation* (13 Sept. 2004 issue; posted 26 Aug. 2004). Web version (accessed 9 Nov. 2006) at: <http://www.thenation.com/doc/20040913/glass>

Gray, John, 'Global Utopias and Clashing Civilizations: Misunderstanding the Present', *International Affairs*, 74/1 (1998), 149–63.

——, *Al-Qaeda and What it Means to be Modern* (London: Faber, 2003).

——, *Black Mass. Apocalyptic Religion and the Death of Utopia* (London: Allen Lane, 2007).

Halper, Stefan and Clarke, Jonathan, *America Alone. The Neo-Conservatives and the Global Order* (Cambridge: Cambridge University Press, 2004).

Halper, Stefan and Clarke, Jonathan, *The Silence of the Rational Centre. Why American Foreign Policy is Failing* (New York: Basic Books, 2007).

Henderson, Errol A. and Tucker, Richard, 'Clear and Present Strangers. The Clash of Civilizations and International Conflict', *International Studies Quarterly*, 45/2 (June 2001), 317–38.

Hirsh, Michael, 'Bernard Lewis Revisited. What if Islam isn't an Obstacle to Democracy in the Middle East but the Secret to Achieving it?', *Washington Monthly* (Nov. 2004). Web version (accessed 7 Nov. 2006): <http://www.washingtonmonthly.com/features/2004/0411.hirsh.html>

Huntington, Samuel P., 'The Clash of Civilizations?', *Foreign Affairs*, 72/3 (1993), 22–49.

——, *The Clash of Civilizations and the Remaking of World Order* (New York: Simon and Schuster, 1996; London: Simon and Schuster UK, 1997: repr. The Free Press, 2002).

[Samuel P. Huntington's] *The Clash of Civilizations? The Debate* (New York–London: Council of Foreign Relations and W. W. Norton: 1996).

——, 'Robust Nationalism', *The National Interest* (20 Jan. 1999).

——, 'Religious Persecution and Religious Relevance in Today's World', in Elliott Abrams (ed.), *The Influence of Faith. Religious Groups and US Foreign Policy* (Lanham, MD: Rowan and Littlefield, 2001), 55–64.

——, 'Are We a Nation "Under God"?', *The American Enterprise*, 15/5 (July–August 2004).

——, *Who are We? America's Great Debate* (New York: Simon and Schuster, 2004).

Hussain, Iqbal S., *Islam and Western Civilization. Creating a World of Exellence* (2nd edn., Lahore: Adbistan, 2000).

Inglehart, Ronald and Norris, Pippa, 'The True Clash of Civilizations', *Foreign Policy* (Mar./Apr. 2003), 67–74.

Israeli, Raphael, *Islamikaze. Manifestations of Islamic Martyrology* (London: Frank Cass, 2003).

Jenkins, Brian Michael, *Unconquerable Nation. Knowing our Enemy. Strengthening Ourselves* (RAND Corporation, MG 454, 2006).

——, *Building an Army of Believers. Jihadist Radicalization and Recruitment* [testimony presented before the House Homeland Security Committee, Subcommittee on Intelligence, Information Sharing and Terrorist Risk Assessment] (RAND Corporation CT-278–1, Apr. 2007).

Jenkins, Philip, *God's Continent. Christianity, Islam, and Europe's Religious Crisis* (New York: Oxford University Press, 2007).

Joffé, G, 'Confrontational Mutual Perceptions and Images: Orientalism and Occidentalism in Europe and the Islamic World', *International Spectator*, 42/2 (2007), 161–78.

Kagan, Robert and Kristol, William (eds), *Present Dangers. Crisis and Opportunity in American Foreign and Defense Policy* (San Francisco: Encounter, 2000).

Kaplan, Esther, *With God on Their Side. George W. Bush and the Christian Right* (New York: New Press, 2005).

Kaufman, Robert G., *In Defense of the Bush Doctrine* (Lexington: University Press of Kentucky, 2007).

Kettell, Steven, *Dirty Politics? New Labour, British Democracy and the Invasion of Iraq* (London and New York: Zed Books, 2006).

Khan, Nasir, *Perceptions of Islam in the Christendoms. A Historical Survey* (Oslo: Solum Forlag, 2006).

Klausen, Jytte, *The Islamic Challenge. Politics and Religion in Western Europe* (New York: Oxford University Press, 2005).

LaHaye, Tim and Hindson, Ed, *Global Warning. Are We on the Brink of World War III?* (Eugene, OR: Harvest House, 2007).

LaHaye, Tim and Jenkins, Jerry B., *The Rapture. In the Twinkling of an Eye. Countdown to the Last Days* (Carol Stream, IL: Tyndale House, 2006).

Laurence, Jonathan and Vaisse, Justin, *Integrating Islam. Political and Religious Challenges in Contemporary France* (Washington DC: Brookings Institution Press, 2006).

Lawrence, Bruce (ed.), *Messages To The World. The Statements of Osama bin Laden* (London: Verso, 2005).

Lesch, David W. (ed.), *The Middle East and the United States. A Historical and Political Reassessment* (4th edn, Cambridge, MA: Westview, 2007).

Lewis, Bernard, 'The Roots of Muslim Rage', *Atlantic Monthly* (Sept. 1990). Reprinted by the Australian Centre for Independent Studies in *Policy* (summer 2001–2). Web version (accessed 6 Nov. 2006) at: <www.cis.org.au/Policy/summer01–02/polsumm01–3.pdf>

——, 'Rethinking the Middle East', *Foreign Affairs* (fall 1992). Web version by subscription only: <http://www.foreignaffairs.org/19920901faessay5893/bernard-lewis/rethinking-the-middle-east.html>

——, 'The Middle East Towards the Year 2000: Patterns of Change', B'nai B'rith World Center 'Jerusalem Address' (19 Feb. 1996). Web version (accessed 7 Nov. 2006) at: <http://ontology.buffalo.edu/smith//courses01/rrtw/Lewis96.htm>

——, *What Went Wrong? Western Impact and Middle Eastern Response* (New York: Oxford University Press, 2002).

——, *The Crisis of Islam. Holy War and Unholy Terror* (London: Weidenfeld and Nicolson, 2003).

——, 'After Saddam: Put the Iraqis in Charge. Why Iraq is Proving Much Tougher than Afghanistan', *Wall Street Journal* (29 Aug. 2003). Web version (accessed on 10 Nov. 2006) at: <http://www.opinionjournal.com/editorial/feature.html?id=110003937>

Linker, Damon, *The Theocons. Secular America under Siege* (New York: Doubleday, 2006).

Little, Douglas, *American Orientalism. the United States and the Middle East since 1945* (London: I. B. Tauris, 2003).

Malik, Aftab Ahmad (ed.), *The Empire and the Crescent. Global Implications for a New American Century* (Bristol: Amal Press, 2003).

Massing, Michael, 'Deal Breakers', *The American Prospect Magazine* (11 March 2002): <http://www.thirdworldtraveler.com/Israel/Deal_Breakers.html>

——, 'The Storm over the Israel Lobby', *New York Review of Books*, 53/10 (8 June 2006): <http://www.nybooks.com/articles/19062>

Matlock Jnr, Jack F., 'Can Civilizations Clash?', *Proceedings of the American Philosophical Society*, 143/3 (1999), 428–39.

Mearsheimer, John J. and Walt, Stephen M., 'The Israel Lobby and US Foreign Policy', Working Paper RWP06–011 (Mar. 2006): <http://ksgnotes1.harvard.edu/Research/

wpaper.nsf/rwp/RWP06-011>, <http://papers.ssrn.com/abstract=891198>; published as 'The Israel Lobby' in the *London Review of Books*, 28/6 (23 Mar. 2006; accessed 11 Jan. 2007): <http://www.lrb.co.uk/v28/n06/mear01_.html>

Mearsheimer, John J. and Walt, Stephen M., *The Israel Lobby and US Foreign Policy* (London: Allen Lane, 2007).

Miller, Mark J. and Stefanova, Boyka (eds), *The War on Terror in Comparative Perspective. US Security and Foreign Policy after 9/11* (Houndmills, Basingstoke: Palgrave Macmillan, 2007).

Musallam, Adnan A., 'Sayyid Qutb and Social Justice', *Journal of Islamic Studies*, 4/1 (1993), 52–70.

Mylroie, Laurie, *Bush vs. the Beltway. The Inside Battle over War in Iraq* (New York: Regan Books, 2003).

Nafissi, Mohammad, 'Before and Beyond the Clash of Civilizations', *ISIM Review*, 19 (2007), 46–7.

Nasr, Vali, 'When the Shiites Rise', *Foreign Affairs*, 85/4 (July–Aug. 2006).

——, *The Shia Revival. How Conflicts within Islam will Shape the Future* (New York, 2006).

Nezar, Al Sayyad and Castells, Manuel (eds), *Muslim Europe or Euro-Islam? Politics, Culture, and Citizenship in the Age of Globalization* (New York: Lexington Books, 2002).

Nirenstein, Fiamma, interview with Bernard Lewis, 'Avoid the Algerian Precedent', *Jerusalem Post*, posted on the website of the Scottish Friends of Israel (accessed 9 Nov. 2006): <http://www.scottishfriendsofisrael.org/bernard_lewis.htm>

Norton, Anne, *Leo Strauss and the Politics of American Empire* (New Haven and London: Yale University Press, 2004).

Palmer Harik, Judith, *Hezbollah. The Changing Face of Terrorism* (London: I.B. Tauris, 2002).

Pape, Robert A., *Dying to Win. Why Suicide Terrorists Do It* (London: Gibson Square Books, 2006).

Petito, Fabio and Hatzopoulos, Pavlos (eds), *Religion in International Relations. The Return from Exile* (New York: Palgrave Macmillan, 2003).

Petras, James, *The Power of Israel in the United States* (Atlanta, GA: Clarity Press, 2006).

Podhoretz, Norman, *World War IV. The Long Struggle against Islamofascism* (New York: Doubleday, 2007).

Qureshi, Emran and Sells, Michael A. (eds), *The New Crusades. Constructing the Muslim Enemy* (New York: Columbia University Press, 2003).

Ramadan, Tariq, *To Be a European Muslim. A Study of Islamic Sources in the European Context* (Leicester: the Islamic Foundation, 1999).

——, *Western Muslims and the Future of Islam* (New York: Oxford University Press, 2004).

Reed, Charles and Ryall, David (eds), *The Price of Peace. Just War in the Twenty-First Century* (Cambridge: Cambridge University Press, 2007).

Richardson, Louise, *What Terrorists Want. Understanding the Terrorist Threat* (London: John Murray, 2006).

Rosen, Gary (ed.) *The Right War? The Conservative Debate on Iraq* (New York: Cambridge University Press, 2005).

Roy, Olivier, *Globalized Islam. The Search for a New Ummah* (London: Hurst, 2004).

Ruthven, Malise, *Fundamentalism. The Search for Meaning* (Oxford: Oxford University Press, 2005).

Saad-Ghorayeb, Amal, *Hizbu'llah. Politics and Religion* (London: Pluto Press, 2002).

Sageman, Marc, *Understanding Terror Networks* (Philadelphia: University of Pennsylvania Press, 2004).

Said, Edward W., *Orientalism* (1st edn 1978; repr. Harmondsworth: Peregrine, 1985).

——, 'The Clash of Ignorance', *The Nation* (22 Oct. 2001; article posted online 4 Oct. 2001): <http://www.thenation.com/doc/20011022/said>

——, 'The Clash of Definitions', in Emran Qureshi and Michael A. Sells (eds), *The New Crusades. Constructing the Muslim Enemy* (New York: Columbia University Press, 2003), 68–87.

Saikal, Amin, *Islam and the West. Conflict or Cooperation?* (Houndmills, Basingstoke: Palgrave Macmillan, 2003).

Salvatore, Armando and Levine, Mark (eds), *Religion, Social Practice and Contested Hegemonies. Reconstructing the Public Sphere in Muslim Majority Countries* (New York: Palgrave Macmillan, 2005).

Sandole, Dennis J. D., 'The Western-Islamic "Clash of Civilizations". the Inadvertent Contribution of the Bush Presidency', *Peace and Conflict Studies*, 12/2 (2005).

Scheuer, Michael [published under 'Anonymous'], *Through Our Enemies' Eyes. Osama bin Laden, Radical Islam and the Future of America* (Washington DC: Brassey's Inc., 2002).

—— [published under 'Anonymous'], *Imperial Hubris. Why the West is Losing the War on Terror* (Washington DC: Brassey's Inc., 2004).

Selbourne, David, *The Losing Battle with Islam* (Amherst, NY: Prometheus, 2005).

Sen, Amartya, *Identity and Violence. The Illusion of Identity* (London: Allen Lane, 2006).

Shulsky, Abram N. and Schmitt, Gary J., *Silent Warfare. Understanding the World of Intelligence* (3rd edn, Washington DC: Potomac Books, 2002).

Silverstein, Paul A., *Algeria in France. Transpolitics, Race and Nation* (Bloomington and Indianapolis: Indiana University Press, 2004).

Slisli, Fouzi, 'The Western Media and the Algerian Crisis', *Race and Class*, 21 (2000), 43–57.

Smith, Christian et al., *American Evangelicalism. Embattled and Thriving* (Chicago and London: University of Chicago Press, 1998).

Solomon, Lewis D., *Paul D. Wolfowitz. Visionary Intellectual, Policymaker and Strategist* (Westport, CT: Praeger Security International, 2007).

Soros, George, *The Age of Fallibility. The Consequences of the War on Terror* (London: Weidenfeld and Nicolson, 2006).

——, 'On Israel, America and AIPAC', *New York Review of Books*, 54/6 (12 Apr. 2007 accessed 19 Apr. 2007): <http://www.nybooks.com/articles/20030>

Stelzer, Irwin (ed.), *Neo-Conservatism* (London: Atlantic Books, 2004).

Steyn, Mark, *America Alone. The End of the World as We Know It* (Washington DC: Regnery, 2006).

Strasser, Steven (ed.), *The 9/11 Investigations. Staff Reports of the 9/11 Commission. Excepts from the House–Senate Joint Inquiry Report on 9/11. Testimony from 14 Key Witnesses …* (New York: Public Affairs, 2004).

Svet, Oleg, 'Public Diplomacy: War by Other Means' (5 Nov. 2006): <http://fletcher.tufts.edu/jebsencenter/pdfs/Draft_November_5_2006_SS.pdf>

Tago, Atsushi, 'Why do States Join US-Led Military Coalitions? The Compulsion of the Coalition's Missions and Legitimacy', *International Relations of the Asia-Pacific*, 7 (2007), 179–202.

Tamimi, Azzam, *Hamas. Unwritten Chapters* (London: Hurst, 2007).

Thomas, Dominique, *Le Londonistan. La Voix du djihad* (Paris: Michalon, 2003).

Thompson, Scott and Steinberg, Jeffrey, 'Profile Bernard Lewis. British Svengali behind Clash of Civilizations', *Executive Intelligence Review* (30 Nov. 2001). Web version (accessed 6 Nov. 2006) at: <http://www.larouchepub.com/other/2001/2846b_lewis_profile.html>

Timmerman, Christiane; Hutesbaut, Dirk; Mels, Sara; Nonneman, Walter; and Van Herck, Walter (eds), *Faith-Based Radicalism. Christianity, Islam and Judaism between*

*Constructive Activism and Destructive Fanaticism* (Brussels: Peter Lang, 2007).

Visser, Reidar and Stansfield, Gareth (eds), *An Iraq of its Regions. Cornerstones of a Federal Democracy?* (London: Hurst, 2007).

Vitalis, Robert, *America's Kingdom. Mythmaking on the Saudi Oil Frontier* (Stanford: Stanford University Press, 2007).

Waldman, Peter, 'A Historian's Take on Islam steers US in Terrorism Fight', *Wall Street Journal* (3 Feb. 2004). Web version (by subscription only) at <http://www.gonline.wsj.com/article_email/0,,SB107576070484918411-IBje4Nklah3m5uvZ32GcKiEm4,00.html>

Whitaker, Brian, 'US Thinktanks Give Lessons in Foreign Policy', *The Guardian* (19 Aug. 2002).

——, 'Bush's Historian', *The Guardian* (2 May 2006). Web version (accessed 9 Nov. 2006) at: <http://commentisfree.guardian.co.uk/brian_whitaker/2006/05/the_history_man.html>

Wilkie, Andrew, *Axis of Deceit. The Story of the Intelligence Officer who Risked All to Tell the Truth about WMD and Iraq* (Melbourne: Black, 2004).

Wright, Lawrence, *The Looming Tower. Al-Qaeda's Road to 9/11* (London: Penguin, 2006).

Zeidan, David, *The Resurgence of Religion. A Comparative Study of Selected Themes in Christian and Fundamentalist Discourses* (Boston: Brill, 2003).

# Notes

*Preface*

1. Cited in Bruce Lawrence (ed.), *Messages To The World. The Statements of Osama bin Laden* (London: Verso, 2005), 124. Quoted by Michael Dunn, 'The "Clash of Civilizations" and the "War on Terror"', *49th Parallel*, 20 (2006–7): <http://www.49thparallel.bham.ac.uk/current/index.htm>

2. 'Religion, Culture and International Conflict after September 11. A Conversation with Samuel P. Huntington', EPPC Online (Washington DC, 17 June 2002): <http://www.eppc.org/programs/religionandmedia/publications/pubID.1537,programID.37/pub_detail.asp>

3. Ervand Abrahamian, 'The US Media, Huntington and September 11', *Third World Quarterly*, 24/3 (2003), 529–44.

4. Bruce Lawrence (ed.), *Messages to the World*, 121. And generally, ibid. 124–7. Bush used the expression 'this crusade, this war on terrorism is going to take a while', but subsequently apologized for it.

5. Ibid. 215.

6. Ibid. 108. Bush stated: 'we wage a war to save civilization itself. We did not seek it, but we must fight it – and we will prevail. This is a different war from any our nation has ever faced, a war on many fronts, against terrorists who operate in more than 60 different countries.'

7. Lawrence Wright, *The Looming Tower. Al-Qaeda's Road to 9/11* (London: Penguin, 2006), 208–9.

8. Toby T. Gati, quoted by Patrick E. Tyler and Elaine Sciolino, 'A Nation Challenged. Message. As UN meets, Bin Laden Tape Sets off Alarms', *New York Times* (9 Nov. 2001). Also quoted by Douglas Little, *American Orientalism. The United States and the Middle East since 1945* (London: I. B. Tauris, 2003), 315.

*Introduction: Are We Fighting World War IV Against Islamo-Fascism?*

1. Eliot A. Cohen, 'World War IV. Let's Call this Conflict What it is', *Wall Street Journal* (20 Nov. 2001).

2. <http://www.whitehouse.gov/news/releases/2006/08/20060831-1.html>

3. Josh White, 'Alleged Architect of 9/11 Confesses to Many Attacks', *Washington Post* (15 Mar. 2007).

4. Richard Bonney, *Jihad from Qur'an to bin Laden* (Houndmills, Basingstoke: Palgrave Macmillan, 2004), 282, 356–7. Azzam regarded Zawahiri as a trouble-maker, because he wanted to overthrow the Egyptian government rather than concentrate on liberating the Muslim lands, especially Palestine. Zawahiri may have been responsible for his assassination on 24 Nov. 1989: Wright, *The Looming Tower*, 130–7, 171–2. Chris Suellentrop calls Azzam 'the Lenin of international *jihad*': Suellentrop, 'Abdullah Azzam. The godfather of *jihad*', Slate.com (16 Apr. 2002).

5. Gilles Kepel, *Jihad. The Trail of Political Islam* (London: I. B. Tauris, 2002), 156.

6. Jason Burke, *Al-Qaeda. Casting a Shadow of Terror* (London: I. B. Tauris, 2003), 8, 36.

7. Marc Sageman, *Understanding Terror Networks* (Philadelphia: University of Pennsylvania Press, 2004), 20–4. Bonney, *Jihad from Qur'an to bin Laden*, 358–62.

8. Michael Scheuer, 'Osama bin Laden. Taking Stock of the "Zionist-Crusader War"', *Terrorism Focus*, 25 Apr. 2006; posted by Jamestown.org on 24 Apr. 2006.

9. 'Osama bin Laden has Given Common Identity back to the West.' 'Samuel P. Huntington is the famed Harvard professor and author of *The Clash of Civilizations and Remaking the World Order* (New York: Simon and Schuster, 1996). He spoke with NPQ editor Nathan Gardels in Oct. [2002]': <http://www.digitalnpq.org/archive/2002_winter/huntington.html>

10. <http://www.whitehouse.gov/news/releases/2005/10/20051006-3.html>

11. Joseph Sobran, 'Words in Wartime' (11 Nov. 2004): <http://www.sobran.com/columns/2004/041111.shtml>

12. Roger Scruton, 'Islamo-Fascism: Beware of a Religion without Irony', *Wall Street Journal* (20 Aug. 2006).

13. Malise Ruthven, *Fundamentalism. The Search for Meaning* (Oxford: Oxford University Press, 2005). The term 'Islamo-fascism' does not appear in the index of this work.

14. '"Islamism is Fascism". An interview with Daniel Pipes', by Eric Boehlert: Salon.Com (9 Nov. 2001).

15. John Gray, *Black Mass. Apocalyptic Religion and the Death of Utopia* (London: Allen Lane, 2007), 70. Gray contends that 'talk of "Islamo-fascism" obscures the larger debts of Islamism to western thought.' David Selbourne considers the debt to fascism in more detail: Selbourne, *The Losing Battle with Islam* (Amherst, NY: Prometheus, 2005), 482.

16. Timothy Garton-Ash, 'In Identifying those Trying to Kill Us, We should Choose our Words Carefully', *The Guardian* (22 Nov. 2007).

17. For example, by the Students' Islamic Organization of India in advertising a conference on education at Mumbai, India on its 25th anniversary: 'SIO Jihad for Redefining Education' (24 Nov. 2007).

18. Marc Sageman, 'The Normality of Global *Jihadi* Terrorism', *The International Journal of Security Affairs*, 8 (2005): <http://www.securityaffairs.org/issues/2005/08/sageman.php> Sageman is a former CIA case officer who, in the late 1980s, ran the US unilateral programmes with the Afghan *mujahadin* during the Afghan–Soviet War. He is a forensic psychiatrist and has collected over 400 biographies of al-Qaeda terrorists. His book, *Understanding Terror Networks* (Philadelphia: University of Pennsylvania Press, 2004) 'challenges the conventional wisdom on terrorism' in the sense that it analyses the terrorists in terms of networks (e.g. 'central staff', Maghreb Arabs, 'core Arabs', 'southeast Asians': ibid. 138). Ibid. 64, 69: Sageman calls the fighters 'global Salafi *mujahedin*', or '*jihad* fighters', i.e. jihadists.

19. Brian Michael Jenkins, *Unconquerable Nation. Knowing our Enemy. Strengthening Ourselves* (RAND Corporation, MG 454, 2006), 74.

20. Louise Richardson, *What Terrorists Want. Understanding the Terrorist Threat* (London: John Murray, 2006), 207.

21. Ibid. 178, 211. The PNAC document *Rebuilding America's Defenses* (2000), discussed more fully in Chapter 7, had not anticipated 9/11 but talked in terms of a 'catastrophic and catalyzing event – like a new Pearl Harbor'. *Rebuilding America's Defenses*, 51.

22. Jean Bethke Elshtain, 'Terrorism', in Charles Reed and David Ryall (eds), *The Price of Peace. Just War in the Twenty-First Century* (Cambridge: Cambridge University Press, 2007), 129, argues that 'the attacks of 9/11 present an analogous situation [to Pearl Harbor] in some important respects'. Patrick J. Buchanan writes: 'no Middle East nation has ever attacked us ... The only nation in the 20th century to attack us was Japan. And Japan lashed out, insanely, in desperation, because we had cut off her oil and convinced the British and

Dutch to cut off the vital commodities she needed to avoid imperial defeat in China. We were choking the Japanese empire to death …' Reprinted in Gary Rosen (ed.), *The Right War? The Conservative Debate on Iraq* (New York: Cambridge University Press, 2005), 202.

23. The best analysis of the selective theology in the Aug. 1996 and 23 Feb. 1998 statements is now R.W. Gwynne, 'Usama bin Ladin, the Qur'an and *Jihad*', *Religion*, 36/2 (2006), 61–90.

24. Patrick E. Tyler and Elaine Sciolino, 'A Nation Challenged. Message. As UN Meets, Bin Laden Tape Sets off Alarms', *New York Times* (9 Nov. 2001).

25. The *post-facto* justifications of George W. Bush and Mullah Omar for the Afghanistan conflict may conveniently be found in *Pak-Afghan Relations, 2005–7* (IPRI Factfile 9/2, Islamabad Policy Research Institute, 2007), 31, 44.

26. Sayyed Imam Al-Sharif, one of the most important figures in the global *jihad* movement, is explicit on this: 'Bin Laden and his followers lied to their Emir [Mullah] Muhammad Omar, betrayed him, violated [their] oath of allegiance to him, and carried out the events of 9/11 behind his back after having plotted them for more than two years in his country, Afghanistan, after Khalid Sheikh [Muhammad] suggested the idea to bin Laden. The Prophet said, "Whoever defies [a ruler] has no excuse when he meets Allah" ...' He adds elsewhere: 'Al-Qaeda bit the hand of Mullah Muhammad Omar, who had hosted them and protected them in Afghanistan, and who ordered them not to enter into a confrontation with America ...' And again: 'more than once [Mullah] Muhammad Omar ordered [bin Laden] not to clash with America, saying that he didn't have the capabilities for this, especially since Afghanistan and its people were the ones who paid the price for bin Laden's bombings in Nairobi and Dar es Salaam in 1998.' 'Major Jihadi Cleric and Author of Al-Qaeda's Shari'a Guide to Jihad: 9/11 Was a Sin; A Shari'a Court Should Be Set Up to Hold Bin Laden and Al-Zawahiri Accountable; There Are Only Two Kinds of People in Al-Qaeda – The Ignorant and Those Who Seek Worldly Gain', Memri Special Dispatch-Reform Project / Jihad and Terrorism Studies Project 1785, 14 Dec. 2007.

27. Steven Strasser (ed.), *The 9/11 Investigations. Staff Reports of the 9/11 Commission. Excepts from the House–Senate Joint Inquiry Report on 9/11. Testimony from 14 Key Witnesses* (New York: Public Affairs Reports, 2004), 377–8, 410. Ibid. 418: 'fifteen of the 19 hijackers were Saudi nationals who received visas in Saudi Arabia. Before September 11, the United States had not established heightened screening for illegal immigration or terrorism by visitors from Saudi Arabia.'

28. Richard A. Clarke recalls that in one meeting he unwisely referred to Hitler: '"they have published all of this and sometimes, as with Hitler in *Mein Kampf*, you have to believe that these people will actually do what they say they will do." Immediately Wolfowitz seized on the Hitler reference: "I resent any comparison between the Holocaust and this little terrorist in Afghanistan." … I wasn't the only one asserting an al-Qaeda threat whom Wolfowitz belittled.' Richard A. Clarke, *Against All Enemies. Inside America's War on Terror* (London: The Free Press, repr. 2004), 232–3. Lewis D. Solomon, *Paul D. Wolfowitz. Visionary Intellectual, Policymaker and Strategist* (Westport, CT: Praeger Security International, 2007), 72: 'you give bin Laden too much credit. He could not do all these things … not without a state sponsor …'

29. Alexandre de Marenches and David A. Andelman, *The Fourth World War. Diplomacy and Espionage in the Age of Terrorism* (New York: Morrow, 1992). Marenches talked of a war, waged by 'small, highly deadly units of terrorists', that has 'the very real prospect of ending civilization, at least Western civilization, as we know it'.

30. Eliot A. Cohen, 'World War IV. Let's Call this Conflict What it is', *Wall Street Journal* (20 Nov. 2001).

31. Bruce Lawrence (ed.), *Messages to the World*, 184, 255. However, in 2003, bin Laden was prepared to concede a 'convergence of interests' in fighting with the Ba'athists against the Americans.

32. 'In the end, victory over militant Islam and the terrorism it uses against us will require the transformation of an entire region of the world.' Norman Podhoretz, 'How to Win World War IV', *Commentary* (Feb. 2002).

33. Norman Podhoretz, 'World War IV: How it Started, What it Means, and Why We Have to Win', *Commentary* (Sept. 2004). Podhoretz's article is reprinted in Gary Rosen (ed.), *The Right War? The Conservative Debate on Iraq*, 102–69.

34. Joseph Rago, 'Unrepentant Neocon. Norman Podhoretz Stands IV-square for the Bush Doctrine', *Wall Street Journal* (12 Aug. 2006).

35. Norman Podhoretz, *World War IV. The Long Struggle against Islamofascism* (New York: Doubleday, 2007), 8.

36. In his State of the Union Address of 2002, George W. Bush stated: 'History has called America and our allies to action, and it is both our responsibility and our privilege to fight freedom's fight.' George Kennan, 'The Sources of Soviet Conduct', *Foreign Affairs* (1947), which may conveniently be accessed at: <http://www.historyguide.org/europe/kennan.html>

37. Podhoretz, *World War IV*, 216–17. Podhoretz, 'World War IV. How it Started, What it Means, and Why We Have to Win', in Rosen (ed.), *The Right War?*, 169.

38. James R. Woolsey, 'World War IV' (16 Nov. 2002): <http://www.globalsecurity.org/military/library/report/2002/021116-ww4.htm> For other views on World War IV: Tony Corn, 'World War IV As Fourth-Generation Warfare' (Jan. 2006): <http://www.hoover.org/publications/policyreview/4868381.html>

39. Jim Lobe, 'They're Back: Neocons Revive the Committee on the Present Danger, This Time Against Terrorism', *Foreign Policy in Focus* (22 July 2004). Tom Barry, 'The "Present Danger" War Parties', International Relations Center Special Report (16 June 2006): <http://www.irc-online.org/content/3297>

40. David Selbourne, 'This War is not about Terror, it's about Islam', *Daily Telegraph* (7 Oct. 2001). Selbourne, *The Losing Battle with Islam*, 17. Tim LaHaye and Ed Hindson, *Global Warning. Are We on the Brink of World War III?* (Eugene, OR: Harvest House, 2007). 'Bush Likens "War on Terror" to WW III', ABC News Online (6 May 2006): <http://www.abc.net.au/news/newsitems/200605/s1632213.htm>. Sheryl Gay Stolbert, 'Nuclear-Armed Iran Risks World War [III], Bush Says', *New York Times* (18 Oct. 2007).

41. Halper and Clarke emphasize the 'deliberate act of choice' on the part of neo-conservatives in embracing the concept of an endless, ongoing World War IV: Stefan Halper and Jonathan Clarke, *America Alone. The Neo-Conservatives and the Global Order* (Cambridge: Cambridge University Press, 2004), 274.

42. Downloadable at: <http://www.geocities.com/athens/forum/2496/future/kennan.html>

43. <http://www.cnn.com/SPECIALS/cold.war/episodes/01/interviews/kennan/>

44. Robert G. Kaufman, *In Defense of the Bush Doctrine* (Lexington: University Press of Kentucky, 2007), 18, 57, 117.

45. 'Terrorists – in their own words', The Claremont Institute for the Study of Statesmanship and Political Philosophy: <http://www.claremont.org/publications/pubid.47/pub_detail.asp>

46. Dan Froomkin, 'World War III', *Washington Post* (29 June 2005).

47. Dan Froomkin, 'Al-Qaeda's Best Publicist', *Washington Post* (25 July 2007).

48. Stephen Lendman, 'Terrorism Defined', Countercurrents.org (31 May 2007): <http://www.countercurrents.org/lendman310507.htm>

*Chapter One: The Context of the Clash*

1. <http://www.whitehouse.gov/news/releases/2002/06/20020601–3.html>
2. <http://www.whitehouse.gov/nsc/nssintro.html>

3. 'Full text: "Bin Laden's Letter to America"', *Observer*, 24 Nov. 2002. Variant translation in Lawrence (ed.), *Messages To The World*, 164, 169.

4. <http://www.whitehouse.gov/news/releases/2006/09/20060911-3.html>

5. Reflections on the review of Anthony Woodiwiss, *Human Rights* (London and New York: Routledge, 2005) by Dr Klejda Mulaj (Gulf Research Center): <http://www.grc.ae/>

6. Stephen Holmes, 'The Logic of a Blocked History' (23 May 2006): <http://www.opendemocracy.net/democracy-fukuyama/history_blocked_3573.jsp>

7. Bonney, *Jihad from Qur'an to bin Laden*, 8.

8. Norman Daniel, *Islam and the West. The Making of an Image* (Oxford: Oneworld Publications, 1960; repr. 2003), ch. 10.

9. Richard Holloway, 'William Montgomery Watt. A Christian Scholar in Search of Islamic Understanding', *The Guardian* (14 Nov. 2006).

10. Tomaz Mastnak, 'Europe and the Muslims. The Permanent Crusade?', in Emran Qureshi and Michael A. Sells (eds), *The New Crusades. Constructing the Muslim Enemy* (New York: Columbia University Press, 2003), 205.

11. Nasir Khan, *Perceptions of Islam in the Christendoms. A Historical Survey* (Oslo: Solum Forlag, 2006), 201. Also idem, 'Islam In Western Mirror', Countercurrents.org (19 May 2007): <http://www.countercurrents.org/khan190507.htm>

12. <http://www.zenit.org/article-16955?l=english>

13. Daniel, *Islam and the West*, 324.

14. Edward W. Said, *Orientalism* (1st edn 1978; repr. Harmondsworth: Peregrine, 1985), 204, 397.

15. Keith Windschuttle, 'Edward Said's *Orientalism* revisited', *New Criterion* (Jan. 1999).

16. Christopher de Bellaigue, 'Where Edward Said was Wrong' [review of Robert Irwin, *Dangerous Knowledge. Orientalism and Its Discontents* (London: Allen Lane, 2006)], *Times Literary Supplement* (17 May 2006).

17. Fakhreddin Azimi, 'Unseating Mosaddeq. The Configuration and Role of Domestic Forces', in Mark J. Gasiorowski and Malcolm Byrne (eds), *Mohammad Mosaddeq and the 1953 Coup in Iran* (Syracuse, NY: Syracuse University Press, 2004), 36.

18. Bernard Lewis, 'The Roots of Muslim Rage', *Atlantic Monthly* (Sept. 1990). Reprinted by the Australian Centre for Independent Studies in *Policy* (summer 2001–2). Web version at: <www.cis.org.au/Policy/summer01–02/polsumm01–3.pdf>

19. Bernard Lewis, *What Went Wrong. Western Impact and Middle Eastern Response* (New York: Oxford University Press, 2002). Juan Cole, writing in *Global Dialogue* on 27 Jan. 2003 described this as 'a very bad book from a usually very good author … a hodgepodge of muddled thinking, inaccurate assertions and one-sided punditry'.

20. John Darwin, *After Tamerlane. The Global History of Empire since 1405* (London: Allen Lane, 2007), 493.

21. Ibid. 26–7.

22. Lewis, *What Went Wrong*, 153.

23. Juan R. Cole, review of Bernard Lewis's *What Went Wrong. Western Impact and Middle Eastern Response*, *Global Dialogue* (27 Jan. 2003).

24. <http://www.globalsecurity.org/military/ops/suez.htm>

25. Eden to Eisenhower, 5 Aug. 1956, quoted at: <http://www.spartacus.schoolnet.co.uk/COLDsuez.htm>

26. Douglas Little, *American Orientalism. The United States and the Middle East since 1945* (London: I. B. Tauris, 2003), 181. For Eisenhower's view of Nasser: ibid. 27.

27. Ibid. 22–3.

28. Ibid. 49.

29. Robert Vitalis, *America's Kingdom. Mythmaking on the Saudi Oil Frontier* (Stanford: Stanford University Press, 2007).

30. 'US Saudi Arms Package Faces Fight in Congress', Agence France-Presse (20 Nov. 2007). James Petras, 'Bush's Twenty-Billion Dollar Arms Sale to Saudi Arabia Scuttled by the Israel Lobby' (29 Nov. 2007): <http://www.countercurrents.org/petras291107.htm>

31. Chalmers Johnson, 'America's Empire of Bases', Common Dreams News Center (15 Jan. 2004): <http://www.commondreams.org/views04/0115-08.htm>

32. Michael Walzer, 'Is There an American Empire?', *Dissent* (autumn 2003): <http://dissentmagazine.org/article/?article=455>

33. Martin Walker, 'America's Virtual Empire', *World Policy Journal* (summer 2002), 13–20.

34. Noam Chomsky, *Hegemony or Survival. America's Quest for Global Dominance* (Crows Nest, NSW, Aus.: Allen and Unwin, 2003): <http://www.americanempireproject.com/bookpage.asp?ISBN=0805076883>

35. Chalmers Johnson, 'Blowback', thenation.com (posted 27 Sept. 2001; published 15 Oct. 2001 issue).

36. Chalmers Johnson, *Blowback. The Costs and Consequences of American Empire* (2000 rev. edn, New York: Henry Holt, 2004); *The Sorrows of Empire. Militarism, Secrecy, and the End of the Republic* (New York: Metropolitan Books, 2004); *Nemesis. The Last Days of the American Republic* (New York: Metropolitan Books, 2006).

37. Speech of Lieutenant General Dhahi Khalfan Tamim, police chief for Dubai in the UAE at the Crans Montana Forum in Bahrain: 'Dubai Top Cop Slams US Policies', Agence France-Presse and *Kuwait Times* (21 Nov. 2007). 'Terror tactics useful for the Salafi *jihad* – explosives, casing a target, and analysis of its vulnerability – were introduced much later, around 1992': Sageman, *Understanding Terror Networks*, 56–9 ('blowback?'), particularly 59. Ibid. 57: 'no US official ever came in contact with the foreign volunteers. They simply travelled in different circles ...'

38. Max Boot, 'The Case for American Empire', *Weekly Standard*, 7/5 (15 Oct. 2001). Boot, 'American Imperialism? No Need to Run Away from Label', *USA Today* (6 May 2003).

39. Transcript of lecture by Max Boot, Council on Foreign Relations, on 'Does America Need an Empire?', 2003 Fleet Admiral Chester Nimitz Memorial Lecture at UC Berkeley (12 Mar. 2003).

40. Max Boot, 'Neither New nor Nefarious. The Liberal Empire Strikes Back', *Current History*, 102/667 (Nov. 2003): <http://www.mtholyoke.edu/acad/intrel/bush/boot.htm>

41. This term was popularized by Ian Buruma and Avishai Margalit in their book *Occidentalism. The West in the Eyes of its Enemies* (New York: Penguin Books, 2004). This work was previewed by the authors' article 'Occidentalism', *New York Review of Books*, 49/1 (17 Jan. 2002). For the term 'reverse Orientalism' see the article by Canefe and Bora cited in n. 44 below.

42. Iqbal's poetry is quoted from the English translation by Arthur J. Arberry (1948): <http://www.allamaiqbal.com/works/poetry/persian/persianpsalms/translation/index.htm>

43. Quoted by Mohammad Nafisi, 'Before and Beyond the Clash of Civilizations', *ISIM Review*, 19 (2007), 47.

44. Nergis Canefe and Taninodotl Bora, 'The Intellectual Roots of Anti-European Sentiments in Turkish Politics. The Case of Radical Turkish Nationalism', *Turkish Studies*, 4/1 (2003), 127–48 at 128, 145.

45. Jalal Al-i Ahmad, *Occidentosis. A Plague from the West*, trans. R. Campbell, ed. Hamid Algar (Berkeley, CA: Mizan Press, 1984).

46. Ibid. 29.

47. Ibid. 60.

48. Ibid. 62–3.

49. Ibid. 81, 83.

50. Ibid. 94. Wahid Akhtar, 'The Evils of Westernization. A Review Article', Shia.com: <http://www.al-shia.com/html/eng/books/miscelleneous/the-evils-of-westernization/evils.htm>

51. John C. Zimmerman, 'Sayyid Qutb's Influence on the 11 September Attacks', *Terrorism and Political Violence*, 16/2 (summer 2004), 222–52. Cf. Jenna Reinbold, 'The "Humanity" of Radical Jihad', *ISIM Review*, 18 (2006), 14–15. Paul Berman, 'The Philosopher of Islamic Terror', *New York Times* (23 Mar. 2003). Most of the correspondence approved of the article, which was said to justify the US 'war on terrorism'. A sole dissenting voice that was published (other letters were sent) was that of Hamid Algar, who wrote on 20 Apr. 2003: 'Paul Berman's article (March 23) on Sayyid Qutb failed to show any line of filiation from Qutb, executed in 1966, to al-Qaeda, established in the 1980s. Nowhere in Qutb's writings – several of which I have translated – can one find a parallel to al-Qaeda's advocacy of mass slaughter. Conversely, Osama bin Laden's statements show not a trace of Qutb's distinctive philosophy. Berman's article exemplifies the tendency to conflate into a malevolent blur all Muslims regarded as troublesome. As for the comparison of Pan-Arabists and Pan-Islamists with Fascists and Nazis, it is elsewhere in the contemporary Middle East that one might look for a closer analogy.'

52. Bonney, *Jihad from Qur'an to bin Laden*, 215–23. Qutb argued that the armed struggle was not an immediately practicable proposition; instead there should be a mental, ideological, and cultural separation in which the Islamic vanguard concentrated on consciousness-raising, nurture, growth, and strengthening group solidarity.

53. Nasr Abu Zayd, *Reformation of Islamic Thought. A Critical Historical Analysis* (Amsterdam: Amsterdam University Press and Scientific Council for Government Policy [WRR], 2006). Ahmed Bouzid, 'Man, Society and Knowledge in the Islamist Discourse of Sayyid Qutb', unpublished Ph.D. (Virginia Polytechnic Institute and State University, Blacksburg, VA, 1998).

54. Adnan A. Musallam, 'Sayyid Qutb and Social Justice', *Journal of Islamic Studies*, 4/1 (1993), 52–70 at 67.

55. Quoted by Ibrahim Abu-Rabi', *Intellectual Resurgence in the Modern Arab World* (Albany, NY: State University of New York Press, 1996), 131.

56. Ian Buruma and Avishai Margalit, *Occidentalism. A Short History of Anti-Westernism* (London: Atlantic Books, 2004), 121, 125. For these writers (ibid. 129), 'what we are witnessing now ... is a convergence between Islamic political radicals and puritanical fundamentalists. All political Islamists were puritans, but not all puritans were political Islamists.' The authors deny (ibid. 9) that Occidentalism is the same as anti-Americanism; 'rather its bigotry simply turns the Orientalist view upside down' (ibid. 10).

57. 'A Dictatorship by Stealth', *Irish Times* (2 Apr. 2005).

58. Anne Norton, *Leo Strauss and the Politics of American Empire* (New Haven and London: Yale University Press, 2004), 110.

59. Joseph Elie Alagha, *The Shifts in Hizbullah's Ideology. Religious Ideology, Political Ideology and Political Program* (Leiden: ISIM/Amsterdam University Press, 2006), 242.

60. Amal Saad-Ghorayeb, *Hizbu'llah. Politics and Religion* (London: Pluto Press, 2002), 106, 108.

61. Judith Palmer Harik, *Hezbollah. The Changing Face of Terrorism* (London: I.B. Tauris, 2002), 201–2.

62. Alagha, *The Shifts in Hizbullah's Ideology*, 181.

63. Daniel Benjamin and Steven Simon, *The Age of Sacred Terror* (New York: Random House, 2002), 127–8. Eban Kaplan, 'The al-Qaeda-Hezbollah Relationship', Council on Foreign Relations (14 Aug. 2006). Plea of Ali Mohamed in the case US vs. Ali Mohamed (20 Oct. 2000): <http://cryptome.org/usa-v-mohamed.htm>

64. 'Syrian Liberal Nidhal Na'isa on the West, Pan-Arabism, Islamism, and Al-Jazeera', Memri Special Dispatch–Syria/Reform Project, 1590 (18 May 2007): <http://memri.org/

bin/articles.cgi?Page=archives&Area=sd&ID=SP159007>

65. Thomas Cushman (ed.), *A Matter of Principle. Humanitarian Arguments for War in Iraq* (Berkeley and Los Angeles: University of California Press, 2005), 345.

66. Jenkins, *Unconquerable Nation. Knowing our Enemy. Strengthening Ourselves*, 154.

67. Ibid. 62: 'our best source of information about al-Qaeda is Osama bin Laden himself.'

68. Ibid.

69. Anonymous [= Michael Scheuer], *Imperial Hubris. Why the West is Losing the War on Terror* (Washington DC: Brassey's Inc., 2004), 241.

70. Yvonne Yazbeck Haddad, 'Islamist Perceptions of US Policy in the Middle East', in David W. Lesch (ed.), *The Middle East and the United States. A Historical and Political Reassessment* (4th edn; Cambridge, MA: Westview, 2007), 510.

71. Lawrence (ed.), *Messages To The World*, 187–8. For Sykes–Picot: David Fromkin, *A Peace to End All Peace. The Fall of the Ottoman Empire and the Creation of the Modern Middle East* (new edn, London: Phoenix, 2000), 189–95. For Nixon: Ian Rutledge, *Addicted to Oil. America's Restless Drive for Energy Security* (London: I.B. Tauris, 2005), 47. Robert Dreyfuss, 'The Thirty-Year Itch', MotherJones.com (Mar./Apr. 2003). Lizette Alvarez, 'Britain Says US Planned to Seize Oil in '73 Crisis', *New York Times* (2 Jan. 2004).

72. Scheuer quoted on the dust jacket of Lawrence (ed.), *Messages to the World*.

73. Quoted by Reuel Marc Gerecht, 'The Gospel According to Osama bin Laden': <http://www.theatlantic.com/issues/2002/01/gerecht.htm>

74. Lawrence (ed.), *Messages To The World*, 272.

75. World Crude Oil Production, 1960–2005 (millions of barrels a day): <http://www.eia.doe.gov/emeu/aer/txt/ptb1105.html>

76. Although US consumption has risen from 9.8 million barrels a day in 1960 to 20.73 million barrels a day in 2004, its proportion of the world's total consumption has fallen, since total world consumption has risen from 21.34 million to 82.59 million barrels a day. Total production in 1960 was 20.99 million barrels a day and in 2004 72.22 million. Cf. cited in n. 75 table, and also World Petroleum Consumption, 1960–2004 (million barrels a day): <http://www.eia.doe.gov/emeu/aer/txt/ptb1110.html>

77. Michael T. Klare, 'Taking Oil out of the Equation', TomPaine.com (21 Sept. 2006).

78. 'Oil on the Cusp of $100 a Barrel', *Gulf News Report* (7 Nov. 2007). 'Oil Price: the US$ 100 Barrel on its Way?', *Russia Today* (29 Oct. 2007). Simon Evans, '"The Era of Cheap Oil is Dead": $100 a Barrel is on the Way', *Independent* (11 Nov. 2007). Naseem Javed, 'Global Zerophobia has Made a Monster of $100 a Barrel Oil', GulfNews.com (14 Nov. 2007). Qatar's energy minister commented on 9 Oct. 2007 that 'if we take into account inflation from 1972 to the present day', then oil should be above $100 a barrel. ArabianBusiness.com (10 Oct. 2007).

79. Lawrence (ed.), *Messages To The World*, 239. Max Rodenbeck, 'Their Master's Voice', *New York Review of Books*, 53/4 (9 Mar. 2006).

80. Lawrence (ed.), *Messages To The World*, 112 (for banning bin Laden's words in the US), 104 (for the struggle as one of 'over 80 years').

81. Ibid. 107. Hence bin Laden could claim that the battle had been taken 'to the heart of the United States' in self-defence, 'defence of our brothers and sons in Palestine, and in order to free our holy sanctuaries'.

82. Ibid. 162–3. 'Full text. Bin Laden's "Letter to America"', *The Observer*: (24 Nov. 2002): <http://observer.guardian.co.uk/worldview/story/0,,845725,00.html>

83. Lawrence (ed.), *Messages To The World*, 169.

84. Quoted by Fouzi Slisli, 'The Western Media and the Algerian Crisis', *Race and Class*, 21 (2000), 43–57, at 50.

85. Bonney, *Jihad from Qur'an to bin Laden*, 238, 354.

86. Bernard Lewis, *The Crisis of Islam. Holy War and Unholy Terror* (London: Weidenfeld and Nicolson, 2003), 85.

87. Hugh Roberts, 'Algeria's Ruinous Impasse and the Honourable Way Out', *International Affairs*, 71/2 (1995), 247–67.

88. Daniel Byman, *The Five Front War. The Better Way to Fight Global Jihad* (Hoboken, NJ: John Wiley, 2007), 185.

89. Lawrence (ed.), *Messages To The World*, 169.

90. George Monbiot, 'The Middle East has had a Secretive Nuclear Power in its Midst for Years', *The Guardian* (20 Nov. 2007). Little, *American Orientalism*, 94–100, 102–3, 107. On 5 Oct. 1986, the *Sunday Times* reported that Israel was a nuclear power in possession 'at least 100 and [perhaps] as many as 200 nuclear weapons'. The story stated that Israel had been producing the weapons at Dimona in the Negev Desert for 20 years. The *Sunday Times* article was based on the testimony of a disaffected Israeli nuclear technician, Mordechai Vanunu, who was subsequently captured by Mossad and imprisoned for twelve years in solitary confinement. As early as 1968, the CIA concluded that Israel possessed nuclear weapons. According to records of a 1976 classified briefing given by Carl Duckett, the CIA's deputy director for science and technology from 1967 to 1976, the agency informed President Johnson of this in early 1968. Johnson's response was to order the CIA not to inform any other members of the administration, including Defense Secretary Robert McNamara and Secretary of State Dean Rusk. Israel has never ratified the non-proliferation treaty.

91. David Stout, 'Israel's Nuclear Arsenal Vexed Nixon', *New York Times* (29 Nov. 2007). Stout notes that 'the United States' reluctance to pressure Israel to disarm has made America vulnerable to accusations that it has a double standard when it comes to stopping the spread of weapons in the Middle East.' In his memoirs, Kissinger notes that 'in every crisis Nixon stood by Israel more firmly than almost any other President save Harry Truman,' while Kissinger himself 'could never forget that thirteen members of my family had died in Nazi concentration camps. I had no stomach for encouraging another holocaust by well-intentioned policies that might get out of control.' Quoted by Little, *American Orientalism*, 33.

92. Lawrence (ed.), *Messages To The World*, 265.

93. Dominic O'Connell, 'BAE Cashes in on £40bn Arab Jet Deal', *Sunday Times* (20 Aug. 2006).

94. Leslie Wayne, 'US Arms Sales Overseas Double', *International Herald Tribune* (10 Nov. 2006). David S. Cloud and Helene Cooper, 'Israeli Concerns Delay US Arms Sales to Sunni Arab States', *International Herald Tribune* (5 Apr. 2007). Dan Glaister, 'US Accused of Fuelling Arms Race with $20bn Arab Weapons Sale', *The Guardian* (30 July 2007). Associated Press, 'Administration's Plan for Large Arms Sales to Saudis Stirs Reservations in Congress', *International Herald Tribune* (18 Sept. 2007).

95. Altaf Gauhar, 'Arab Petrodollars. Dashed Hope for a New Economic Order', *World Policy Journal*, 4/3 (1987), 443–64.

96. Ibid.

97. Lawrence (ed.), *Messages To The World*, 197.

98. While bin Laden is correct in viewing Karzai as an American-backed president of Afghanistan from the outset, there is no evidence that the US instigated Musharraf's seizure of control in Pakistan on 12 Oct. 1999. Musharraf's resignation as army chief of staff on 28 Nov. 2007 'sets up the potential of competing power centres in Pakistan, with an army chief separate from the president and the recent return from exile of the country's two main opposition leaders [Benazir Bhutto and Nawaz Sharif]. That is likely to complicate Bush administration antiterrorism policy ..., something officials in Washington were hoping to avoid, and one reason they supported Mr. Musharraf for so long.' Carlotta Gall and Jane Perlez, 'For Musharraf, Reduced Power as the President', *New York Times* (29 Nov. 2007). One reason why the US was not overly concerned with the coup in 1999 was the perception that Musharraf's religious position was more 'secular' than that of Nawaz Sharif. '"Pervez is a secular-minded man", Dr. Musharraf said of his brother. "He believes in the

separation of church and state. He doesn't want a theocracy."' Celia W. Dugger, 'Pakistan Ruler seen as 'Secular-Minded Muslim', *New York Times* (26 Oct. 1999). On Nawaz Sharif's return in 2007, President Bush noted his 'good relations with Pakistan's religious parties, which raised doubts about his commitment to battling the Taliban and al-Qaeda'. Anwar Iqbal, 'US Doubts Sharif's Commitment to War on Terror', *Dawn* (29 Nov. 2007). 'Saudi Arabia blindsided the Bush administration in rapidly returning former Prime Minister Nawaz Sharif to Pakistan ... – a reflection of how regional powers are subtly jockeying for influence in Pakistan as its leadership looks shaky.' Jay Solomon, 'Saudis See Potential for Influence in Sharif', *Wall Street Journal* (29 Nov. 2007).

99. Bin Laden here refers to the treaty between Britain and Ibn Saud dated 26 Dec. 1915: Madawi Al-Rasheed, *A History of Saudi Arabia* (Cambridge: Cambridge University Press, 2002), 42.

*Chapter Two: Revisiting Huntington's 'Clash of Civilizations' Thesis Post-9/11*

1. <http://www.elmandjra.org/livre3/ENGL25.htm>

2. 'Religion, Culture and International Conflict after September 11. A Conversation with Samuel P. Huntington', EPPC Online (Washington DC, 17 June 2002).

3. <http://www.whitehouse.gov/news/releases/2004/06/20040602.html>

4. $528.7 bn out of a world total of $1,158 bn in market exchange rate (MER) terms (top 15 countries = $963.7 bn; US proportion 54.9 per cent); $528.7 bn out of a total for the top 15 countries of $1270.2 bn (or 41.6 per cent) in purchasing power parity (PPP terms). Source: 'Recent Trends in Military Expenditure', *SIPRI Yearbook 2007*. Paul Kennedy's calculations in 'The Eagle Has Landed. The New US Global Military Position', *Financial Times* (1 Feb. 2002) were deservedly criticized in a letter from Paul Robbins on 9/10 February 2002: 'in 2000, China's gross domestic product was about half of the US when measured properly (in purchasing power terms). It spent about 5% of its GDP on defence versus 3% in the US. It is simple arithmetic then that China's defence budget was about 85% of the US's. Add in India's military spending and the US does not even reach a two-power standard in terms of its defence spending.' This went unnoticed by Kaufman, *In Defence of the Bush Doctrine*, 19.

5. Kaufman, *In DefenSe of the Bush Doctrine*, 20.

6. Charles Krauthammer, 'The Unipolar Moment', *Foreign Affairs*, 70 (winter 1990–1), 23–33.

7. Intelligence Authorization Act for Fiscal Year 1994: <http://www.fas.org/irp/congress/1993_cr/h930803-ia2.htm>

8. R.N. Haass, 'Paradigm Lost', *Foreign Affairs*, 74/1 (1995), 43–58.

9. Nafissi, 'Before and Beyond the Clash of Civilizations', *ISIM Review*, 19 (2007), 46.

10. The Foundation announced it was closing its doors in May 2005. Data on John M. Olin Foundation grants at: <http://www.mediatransparency.org/recipientsoffunder.php?funderID=7> Analysis of the grants at <http://rightweb.irc-online.org/profile/653>

11. Donald E. Abelson, *A Capitol Idea. Think Tanks and US Foreign Policy* (Montreal: McGill-Queen's University Press, 2006), 33.

12. Ibid. 36.

13. Ibid. 37–9.

14. 'Fukuyama delivered his famous "end of history" lecture at Bloom's Olin Center in Chicago – and then had it published in *The National Interest*, a journal founded and maintained with Olin dollars. Fukuyama's most prominent critic has been Samuel Huntington, the national security expert who headed the John M. Olin Institute for Strategic Studies at Harvard.' John J. Miller, 'Foundation's End: the Last Days of John M. Olin's Conservative Fortune', National Review Online (6 Apr. 2005).

15. Francis Fukuyama, *The End of History and the Last Man* (London: Profile, 1992). A useful discussion piece by Fukuyama entitled 'The End of History?' was published in

*National Interest*, 16 (1989) and is consultable at various locations including <http://www.wesjones.com/eoh.htm>

16. Samuel P. Huntington, 'The Clash of Civilizations?', *Foreign Affairs*, 72/3 (1993), 22–49, at 22, reprinted in *The Clash of Civilizations? The Debate* (New York: Foreign Affairs, 1996), 1.

17. Sarah Baxter, 'He Predicted the Clash of Civilizations', *Sunday Times* (23 May 2004).

18. Elmandjra had given an interview to *Der Spiegel* dated 11 Feb. 1991. Cf. also Mahdi Elmandjra, *The First Civilizational War* (1992): <http://www.elmandjra.org/Contents.htm>

19. Reda Benkirane, 'Clash of Civilizations. The Cultural Dimension of the Current Crisis', Behind the News. Visions for Peace. Voices for Faith, 14 (14 Feb. 2002): <http://www.e-alliance.ch/culturalcrisis.jsp>

20. Roy P. Mottahedeh, 'The Clash of Civilizations. An Islamicist's Critique', in Emran Qureshi and Michael A. Sells (eds), *The New Crusades. Constructing the Muslim Enemy* (New York: Columbia University Press, 2003), 149. This paper was originally published in *Harvard Middle Eastern and Islamic Review*, 2 (1996), 1–26.

21. Ervand Abrahamian, 'The US Media, Huntington and September 11', *Third World Quarterly*, 24/3 (2003), 529–44.

22. Abrahamian, 'The US Media', 538. Fred Halliday, 'Beyond bin Laden. The Future of Afghanistan itself Should Lie at the Root of Western Political Thinking', *Observer* (23 Sept. 2001).

23. Fred Halliday, 'The "Clash of Civilizations"?: Sense and Nonsense', in Roger Boase (ed.), *Islam and Global Dialogue. Religious Pluralism and the Pursuit of Peace* (Aldershot: Ashgate, 2005), 127 (originally drafted in 1997–8).

24. Errol A. Henderson and Richard Tucker, 'Clear and Present Strangers. The Clash of Civilizations and International Conflict', *International Studies Quarterly*, 45/2 (June 2001), 317–38.

25. Peter Berkowitz, 'Re-Clash of Civilizations … and has Become a Belated Bestseller in Israel', *Boston Globe* (15 Feb. 2004). Jonathan Cook notes that within months of Samuel Huntington popularizing the term 'clash of civilizations' in 1993, Israeli politicians such as Yitzhak Rabin and Shimon Peres and military figures such as Ehud Barak (later to become a politician) 'started using the same terminology, claiming that the West and Islam were doomed to be in a permanent state of confrontation'. Israel nurtured a view of itself as 'on the frontiers of the West in an epoch-changing clash of civilizations'. Jonathan Cook, *Israel and the Clash of Civilizations. Iraq, Iran and the Plan to Remake the Middle East* (London and Ann Arbor, MI: Pluto Press, 2008), xv, 42, 106.

26. Samuel P. Huntington, 'Robust Nationalism', *The National Interest* (20 Jan. 1999).

27. 'At the start of the twenty-first century, Americans are no less committed, and are quite possibly more committed, to their Christian identity than at any time in their history': Samuel P. Huntington, 'Are We a Nation "Under God"?', *The American Enterprise*, 15/5 (July–Aug. 2004).

28. Emad El-Din Aysha, 'Huntington's Shift to the Declinist Camp. Conservative Declinism and the "Historical Function" of the Clash of Civilizations', *International Relations*, 17/4 (2003), 429–52.

29. El-Din Aysha, 'Samuel Huntington and the Geopolitics of American Identity', *International Studies Perspectives*, 4/2 (2003), 113–32, at 117. Thus, e.g., the European Union could, in certain circumstances, become a threat to American interests.

30. Part of the assertion of primacy was the lavish dispensing of flattery of the extent to which the US might have learnt from the UK: Henry Kissinger, 'Reflections on a Partnership. British and American Attitudes to Post-War Foreign Policy', *International Affairs*, 58/4 (1982), 571–87, at 585.

31. For Brzezinski: Bonney, *Jihad from Qur'an to bin Laden*, 336.

32. Edward W. Said, 'The Clash of Ignorance', *The Nation* (22 Oct. 2001; article posted online 4 Oct. 2001).

33. Edward W. Said, 'The Clash of Definitions', in Emran Qureshi and Michael A. Sells (eds), *The New Crusades. Constructing the Muslim Enemy* (New York: Columbia University Press, 2003), 72, 82, 84.

34. Huntington, *The Clash of Civilizations and the Remaking of World Order*, 24–5.

35. Mark Bassin, 'Civilizations and their Discontents. Political Geography and Geopolitics in the Huntington Thesis', *Geopolitics*, 12/3 (2007), 351–74.

36. 'Religion, Culture and International Conflict after September 11. A Conversation with Samuel P. Huntington', EPPC Online (Washington, DC, 17 June 2002).

37. Huntington, *The Clash of Civilizations and the Remaking of World Order*, 159.

38. Ibid. 26–7.

39. Amartya Sen, *Identity and Violence. The Illusion of Identity* (London: Allen Lane, 2006), 46–9, 'on seeing India as a Hindu civilization'.

40. Huntington, *The Clash of Civilizations and the Remaking of World Order*, 258 n., 263.

41. Ibid. 217. Quoted by Mohammad Nafissi, who fails to acknowledge the distinction between Huntington Mark I and Mark II: Nafissi, 'Before and Beyond the Clash of Civilizations', *ISIM Review*, 19 (2007), 46.

42. Huntington, *The Clash of Civilizations and the Remaking of World Order*, 340.

43. El-Din Aysha, 'Samuel Huntington and the Geopolitics of American Identity', 125–9. In the debate in 2002, Huntington commented: 'don't go poking into conflict elsewhere unless vital national interests are at stake (as they were, I would say, when we entered the Gulf War).'

44. In the 2002 debate he argued: 'it seems to me that the cultural/religious element is overwhelmingly preponderant. After all, Osama Bin Laden and likeminded people have denounced Western civilization. Sure, they denounced particular aspects of that civilization, claiming that we are corrupt, decadent, and so on. But I don't see much in the way of ideological content there, if you are thinking of ideology in political terms. I may be missing something, but militant Islam doesn't seem to have much in the way of a political ideology. It certainly does have a religious commitment.' Other neo-conservatives such as Daniel Pipes argue that militant Islamism is indeed an ideology: see Chapter 4. This case is also argued above, Chapter 1.

45. 'Back in the late 1950s and early 60s, all sorts of extremely well-informed, intelligent people were saying that a nuclear war between the United States and the Soviet Union was virtually inevitable. Well, that didn't happen, in part because people took the prediction seriously. They established hotlines between the Pentagon and the Kremlin, engaged in arms-control negotiations, developed informal understandings between the United States and Soviet Union of just what the rules of the game were.'

46. Huntington, *The Clash of Civilizations and the Remaking of World Order*, 253.

47. Eric O. Hanson, *Religion and Politics in the International System Today* (Cambridge: Cambridge University Press, 2006), 57–8. Hanson adds, 'the Iran–Iraq conflict of 1980–8, which occurred within Islamic Civilization, was just as brutal and resulted in many more casualties than the Yugoslavian conflict. One might escape this theoretical problem by classifying Sunni Islam and Shi'ite Islam as different religious civilizations [though this is not Huntington's classification], but Iraqi Shi'ites fought for Saddam Hussein against Shi'ite Iran.'

48. Vjekoslav Perica, *Balkan Idols. Religion and Nationalism in Yugoslav States* (New York: Oxford University Press, 2002), 166. Perica argues that the concept of *bratstvo i jedinstvo* (brotherhood and unity) served as a sort of civil religion that had legitimized socialist Yugoslavia and kept ethno-religious animus in check.

49. Norman Cigar, 'The Nationalist Serbian Intellectuals and Islam. Defining and Elimi-

nating a Muslim Community', in Emran Qureshi and Michael A. Sells (eds), *The New Crusades. Constructing the Muslim Enemy* (New York: Columbia University Press, 2003), 329.

50. 'The clash of civilizations theory itself is, at best, a fatally flawed theory that is based on two of the greatest insufficiencies of international relations theory, its failure to directly address religion and its western-centrism. Yet, the debate was successful in getting international relations scholars to at least indirectly address religion.' Jonathan Fox and Shmuel Sandler, *Bringing Religion into International Relations* (New York: Palgrave Macmillan, 2004), 135.

51. Hanson, *Religion and Politics*, 7, 59.

52. Samuel P. Huntington, 'Religious Persecution and Religious Relevance in Today's World', in Elliott Abrams (ed.), *The Influence of Faith. Religious Groups and US Foreign Policy* (Lanham, MD: Rowan and Littlefield, 2001), 55–64.

53. Ibid. 60–1.

54. 'Intel Report Says Terrorist Network among Major Perpetrators in 60 Countries' (2 June 2007): <http://www.worldnetdaily.com/news/article.asp?ARTICLE_ID=55968>

55. Cited in Allen D. Hertzke, 'The Political Sociology of the Crusade against Religious Persecution', in Abrams (ed.), *The Influence of Faith*, 89 n. 1.

56. Also quoted by Jonathan Fox, *Religion, Civilization and Civil War. 1945 Through the New Millennium* (Lanham, MD: Lexington Books, 2004), 166.

57. Ibid. 167.

58. Preface to this book. Mohammad Nafissi, 'Before and Beyond the Clash of Civilizations', *ISIM Review*, 19 (2007), 46–7.

59. 'Five Years After 9/11, The Clash of Civilizations Revisited' (18 Aug. 2006). Martha's Vineyard, Massachusetts. [Huntington was 79 at the time of the interview.] Interviewer: Mark O'Keefe, Associate Director, Editorial, Pew Forum on Religion and Public Life: <http://pewforum.org/events/index.php?EventID=125>

60. Henderson and Tucker, 'Clear and Present Strangers. The Clash of Civilizations and International Conflict', 331.

61. Ibid. 332.

62. Lawrence (ed.), *Messages To The World*, 91. Bin Laden notes that Saudi Arabia and the Gulf states pressured certain prominent scholars to issue decrees authorizing the presence of American troops, otherwise the youth would have fought them.

63. Fox, *Religion, Civilization and Civil War. 1945 Through the New Millennium*, 9. The author states that, with its 188 tables and figures, his book is probably 'the most exhaustive analysis of religion and Huntington's concept of civilization on domestic conflict'.

64. Jonathan Fox, 'Two Civilizations and Ethnic Conflict. Islam and the West', *Journal of Peace Research*, 38/4 (2001), 459–72.

65. Fox, *Religion, Civilization and Civil War*, 228.

66. Ibid. 233.

67. Ibid. 180–206, esp. 195 and figures 7.14 and 7.16 for the rise in violence within the Hindu civilization.

68. Jonathan Fox, 'The rise of religion and the fall of the civilization paradigm as explanations for intra-state conflict', *Cambridge Review of International Affairs*, 20/3 (2007), 361–382. The summary of other quantitative studies is at ibid. 366.

69. Jonathan Fox, 'The Increasing Role of Religion in State Failure: 1960 to 2004', *Terrorism and Political Violence*, 19/3 (2007), 395–414. The Joshua Project claims that 72 per cent (169 out of 235 countries) are Christian-majority, with a total population of 2.3 billion: <http://www.joshuaproject.net/great-commission-statistics.php>

70. Dieter Senghaas, *The Clash within Civilizations. Coming to Terms with Cultural Conflicts* (London and New York: Routledge, 2002), ch. 7. (An earlier version of this chapter had appeared as Senghaas, 'A Clash of Civilizations – An idée fixe?', *Journal of Peace Research*, 35/1 (1998), 127–32.)

71. Ibid. 73.

72. He adds that in view of the empirical findings, 'this conclusion is imperative; moreover, from a political perspective, and especially from the point of view of peace politics, it is strongly advisable.' Ibid. 90–1.

73. 'Distribution conflicts, in these cases, form the core of the conflicts and must be judged as primary factors. The chances for education, upward mobility, qualified positions, for status, incomes and political participation are essential, rather than the kind or intensity and even less the contents of religion.' Ibid. 75.

74. Ibid. 76.

*Chapter Three: 'Bring Them Freedom or They Destroy Us'*

1. Abrahamian, 'The US Media, Huntington and September 11', 541.

2. Bernard Lewis, 'Bring Them Freedom or They Destroy Us'. Lecture delivered by Bernard Lewis on 16 July 2006, on board the *Crystal Serenity*, during a Hillsdale College cruise in the British Isles. Posted at RealClearPolitics, 20 Sept. 2006: <http://www.realclearpolitics.com/articles/2006/09/bring_them_freedom_or_they_des.html>

3. M. Shahid Alam, *Challenging the New Orientalism. Dissenting Essays on the 'War against Islam'* (North Haledon, NJ: Islamic Publications International, 2006), ch. 1 ('Bernard Lewis: Scholarship or Sophistry?' [Feb. 2002], a critique of Lewis, *What Went Wrong?*), esp. 23.

4. Bernard Lewis was 74 when he wrote the article entitled 'The Roots of Muslim Rage' which (re)started the 'clash of civilizations' debate. His best academic work was long behind him. For the awe in which he was held by students, cf. the comment by Fouad Ajami: 'Mr. Lewis was one of the academic gods. I approached him with awe. But his grace was our bridge.' Ajami, 'A Sage in Christendom. A Personal Tribute to Bernard Lewis', *Opinion Journal* (from the *Wall Street Journal* Editorial page, 1 May 2006).

5. Bernard Lewis, 'The Roots of Muslim Rage', *Atlantic Monthly* (September 1990). Reprinted by the Australian Centre for Independent Studies in *Policy* (summer 2001–2). Web version at: <www.cis.org.au/Policy/summer01–02/polsumm01–3.pdf>

6. Charles Glass, 'Lewis of Arabia', *The Nation* (13 Sept. 2004 issue; posted 26 Aug. 2004). Web version (accessed 9 Nov. 2006) at: <http://www.thenation.com/doc/20040913/glass>

7. Quoted by Charles Glass, ibid.

8. Lewis, 'The Roots of Muslim Rage', 26.

9. Bernard Lewis, 'Other People's History', in Lewis, *Islam and the West* (New York: Oxford University Press, 1993), 130.

10. Fouad Ajami, 'A Sage in Christendom. A Personal Tribute to Bernard Lewis'.

11. Halper and Clarke also note his 'close links with neo-conservative decision-makers': Halper and Clarke, *America Alone*, 20–1, 270.

12. Brian Whitaker, 'Bush's Historian', *The Guardian* (2 May 2006). Reuel Marc Gerecht is more guarded: 'until President Bush, Vice-President Cheney, Defence Secretary Donald Rumsfeld, his former deputy Paul Wolfowitz, and White House speech writer Michael Gerson write their memoirs, we really won't know to what extent Lewis, directly or indirectly, shaped their views of the Middle East, radical Islam, al Qaeda, Saddam Hussein, and the possibilities for a post-Saddam Iraq.' Reuel Marc Gerecht, 'The Last Orientalist: Bernard Lewis at 90', *Weekly Standard* (5 June 2006).

13. Svengali is the name of a fictional hypnotist in George du Maurier's 1894 novel, *Trilby*. Svengali is, in du Maurier's words, an 'Oriental Israelite Hebrew Jew' with a cruel personality. Presumably Scott Thompson and Jeffrey Steinberg did not imply any such inference from Bernard Lewis's Jewish origins, and any such inference is categorically rejected here. The term is used to describe the extent of his influence and the wisdom of the policies advocated, no more.

14. Scott Thompson and Jeffrey Steinberg, 'Profile Bernard Lewis. British Svengali behind Clash of Civilizations', *Executive Intelligence Review* (30 Nov. 2001).

15. Peter Waldman, 'A Historian's Take on Islam Steers US in Terrorism Fight', *Wall Street Journal* (3 Feb. 2004).

16. Bernard Lewis, *What Went Wrong? Western Impact and Middle Eastern Response* (New York: Oxford University Press, 2002), 165. Quoted by Mohammad Nafissi, 'Before and Beyond the Clash of Civilizations', *ISIM Review*, 19 (2007), 46.

17. Michael Hirsh, 'Bernard Lewis Revisited. What if Islam isn't an Obstacle to Democracy in the Middle East but the Secret to Achieving it?', *Washington Monthly* (Nov. 2004).

18. So-called after Mustafā Kemal Atatürk, the founder of modern Turkey.

19. Bernard Lewis, 'Rethinking the Middle East', *Foreign Affairs* (fall, 1992).

20. 'Prof. Lewis noted that it is remarkable that in the entire region, not a single ruler or regime commands any influence or prestige outside his immediate area. Today rulers and regimes throughout the Arab world can command obedience either through repression at home or terror abroad but do not command the enormously wide support and popularity of a figure like Nasser. The old-fashioned autocratic and new style totalitarian dictatorships do not present an attractive model for the future, least of all for their own people.' Bernard Lewis, 'The Middle East Towards the Year 2000. Patterns of Change', B'nai B'rith World Center 'Jerusalem Address' (19 Feb. 1996). Web version (accessed 7 Nov. 2006) at: <http://ontology.buffalo.edu/smith//courses01/rrtw/Lewis96.htm>

21. Edward W. Said, *Orientalism* (1st edn 1978; repr. Harmondsworth: Peregrine, 1985), 316.

22. Bernard Lewis, *The Crisis of Islam. Holy War and Unholy Terror* (London: Weidenfeld and Nicolson, 2003), 70–1.

23. Ibid. 82–3. Charles Glass comments: 'fewer people died in Sabra and Shatila [than at Hama, where the Syrian government attacked an uprising of the Muslim Brotherhood], as Lewis observes, but the entire population was unarmed and undefended following the evacuation of PLO forces from Lebanon. Sharon had given his word to Philip Habib, President Reagan's envoy, that he would not invade West Beirut or attack the refugee camps. He did both. His forces delivered the Christian militias, who had a history of massacring unarmed Palestinians, to the gates of the camps and protected them while they butchered men, women and children. If the United States expressed anger at Sharon, it was because he destroyed American credibility in the Middle East.' Charles Glass, 'Lewis of Arabia', *The Nation* (13 Sept. 2004).

24. 'In pushing for the right of return, the Palestinians are essentially proposing the elimination of the Jewish state. And the UN has never proven that it differs from the Palestinians on the refugee question … With the partition [and creation of the State of Israel], 725,000 Arab refugees were relocated, and the UN immediately created a fixed institution [the United Nations Relief and Works Agency for Palestine Refugees in the Near East], which has literally prevented the Palestinians from resettling.' Fiamma Nirenstein, *Islam. La guerra e la speranza. Intervista a Bernard Lewis* (Rome: Rizzoli, 2003). Interview of Fiamma Nirenstein with Bernard Lewis, 'Avoid the Algerian Precedent', *Jerusalem Post*, posted on the website of the Scottish Friends of Israel (accessed 9 Nov. 2006): http://www.scottishfriendsofisrael.org/bernard_lewis.htm>

25. Robert Gilpin, 'War is too Important to be Left to Ideological Amateurs', *International Relations*, 19/1 (2005), 5–18, especially 4–6.

26. Posted 29 July 2005: <http://www.topdog08.com/2005/07/bernard_lewis_0.html>

27. Bernard Lewis, 'The Revolt of Islam. When did the Conflict with the West Begin, and How Could it End?', *New Yorker* (19 Nov. 2001).

28. Bernard Lewis, 'Learning the Lingo. Jihad vs. Crusade. A Historian's Guide to the New War', *Wall Street Journal* (27 Sept. 2001).

29. Peter Ford, 'Europe Cringes at Bush "Crusade" against Terrorists', *Christian Science Monitor* (19 Sept. 2001). Ford cited an editorial in *Le Monde*, which warned that 'if this "war" takes a form that affronts moderate Arab opinion, if it has the air of a clash of civilizations, there is a strong risk that it will contribute to Osama bin Laden's goal: a conflict between the Arab-Muslim world and the West.'

30. Only much later, in 2006, did he recognize that the term 'war on terrorism' was unhelpful and misleading. 'Regarding the war against terror, I am familiar with this slogan. I feel that while we are indeed engaged in a war against terror, it is inadequate and even misleading. If Churchill had informed the country in 1940, we are engaged in a war against bomber aircraft and submarines, that would have been an accurate statement but not a very helpful one. To say we are engaged in a war against terror is of the same order. Terror is a tactic. It's a method of waging war. It is not a cause, it is not an adversary, it is not anything that one can identify as an opponent, and I think we need to be more specific in fighting a war. It's useful to know who the enemy is. I think you would agree.' 'Islam and the West. A Conversation with Bernard Lewis', 27 April 2006, Hay-Adams Hotel, Washington DC. Web version at: <http://pewforum.org/events/index.php?EventID=107>

31. Christopher de Bellaigue, 'Where Edward Said was Wrong' [review of Robert Irwin, *Dangerous Knowledge. Orientalism and its Discontents* (London: Allen Lane, 2006)], *Times Literary Supplement* (17 May 2006).

32. 'It was Chalabi, after all – a foreigner, a [non-Iraqi] Arab – who persuaded the most powerful men and women in the United States to make the liberation of Iraq not merely a priority but an obsession. First in 1998, when Chalabi persuaded Congress to pass the Iraq Liberation Act (in turn leading to payments to his group, the Iraqi National Congress, exceeding $27 million over the next six years) and then, later, in persuading the Bush administration of the necessity of using force to destroy Saddam Hussein. And when it all went bad, when those nuclear weapons never turned up, the clever child shrugged and smiled. "We are heroes in error," Chalabi told Britain's *Daily Telegraph*.' Dexter Filkins, 'Where Plan A Left Ahmad Chalabi', *New York Times* (5 Nov. 2006). Chalabi commented in 2004: 'as far as we're concerned, we've been entirely successful. That tyrant Saddam is gone and the Americans are in Baghdad. What was said before is not important ...' Jack Fairweather and Anton La Guardia, 'Chalabi Stands by Faulty Intelligence that Toppled Saddam's Regime', *Daily Telegraph* (19 Feb. 2004).

33. Lewis commented the following year: 'the most notable of his open responses [to 9/11] is the increase of the bounty he pays to the families of suicide bombers from $10,000 to $25,000. This is the most public but probably not the most important of his contributions to the conflict.' Bernard Lewis, 'Time for Toppling. The Arguments against "Regime Change" are Backward', *Wall Street Journal* (28 Sept. 2002). For the bounty: 'Saddam's men summoned the families of 22 "martyrs" to receive cheques worth in total $245,000 (£160,000). The parents of 21 who died fighting the Israeli army, were given cheques for $10,000 (£7,000) – a fabulous sum in Gaza, where most of the population is unemployed and malnutrition is increasing. The family of a suicide bomber received a premium cheque of $25,000 (£18,000).' Alan Philps, 'Saddam's Palestinian Bounty', *Daily Telegraph* (13 Mar. 2003).

34. 'Saudi Arabia Arrests 208 Militants, Terror Financiers', *Arab News* (29 Nov. 2007). The militants' ideology of *takfeer* – branding other Muslims as infidels in order to legitimize violence against them – was viewed as so sinister it required an 'ideological war': 'Ideological War Needed to Fight Saudi Extremism', Agence France-Presse (30 Nov. 2007). Allegedly, 1500 detained militants had changed from 'deviant ideology' as a result of the activities of the Saudi government-appointed 'advice committee': 'Naif Asks Scholars to Fight Deviants', *Arab News* (2 Dec. 2007).

35. Even then, Lewis warned against 'premature democratization – holding elections and transferring power, in a country which has had no experience of such things for dec-

ades, can only lead to disaster, as in Algeria.' In reality, Iraq in 2004 was much closer to the model that Lewis depicted for Algeria in 1992 than Algeria itself. Bernard Lewis, 'After Saddam: Put the Iraqis in Charge. Why Iraq is Proving Much Tougher than Afghanistan', *Wall Street Journal* (29 Aug. 2003).

36. 'Few have ever described Moktada al-Sadr, the mercurial leader of Iraq's mightiest Shiite militia, as a statesman.' Sabrina Tavernise, 'Influence Rises but Base Frays for Iraqi Cleric', *New York Times* (13 Nov. 2006).

37. Amy Waldman, 'Cleric [= Sistani] wants Iraqis to write Constitution', *New York Times* (1 July 2003). 'Sistani has enormous weight', an administration official said. 'We have to hear what the Iraqis are telling us on this.' David E. Sanger and Steven R. Weisman, 'US Moves to Speed up Iraqi Vote and Shift of Power', ibid. (13 Nov. 2003). 'The American plan to turn over power in Iraq more quickly was thrown into disarray on Wednesday when the country's most powerful cleric, Grand Ayatollah Ali al-Sistani, made public his opposition to a proposal for indirect elections.' Joel Brinkley and Ian Fisher, 'US Plan to Shift Control Hits Major Snag', ibid. (27 Nov. 2003).

38. Bernard Lewis, 'The Middle East One Year after the Iraq War', Fondazione Magna Carta, Villa Piccolomini, Rome, 9 March 2004. Web version (accessed 9 Nov. 2006): <http://www.magna-carta.it/relazioni%20internazionali%20e%20democrazia/0000_Bernard_Lewis_english.asp>

39. His comments on Algeria were franker than previously: 'In Algeria, after years of bitter struggle, they decided to try democracy. They devised and promulgated a democratic constitution providing for a multiparty system. They devised an election system in two stages. In the first stage elections were held and the religious fundamentalists did very well indeed. It was perfectly clear that when the second stage was held, they would win an overwhelming majority and that would be the end of democracy in Algeria. So the army intervened and what has happened since then has been an ongoing civil war, with a series of military interventions, a series of massacres on both sides and no sign of improvement at the present time.' This time there was no hiding the fact the Lewis advocated a military *coup d'état* against a democratic victory if the victory consigned power to the Islamists.

40. 'The United Nations consensus means doing nothing. I mean it is following in the footsteps of the League of Nations that represented the international consensus at the time which did nothing about the invasions and aggressions in Africa and Asia and elsewhere and finally sank into well-deserved oblivion. The United Nations shows every sign of following the same policies and the same path and leaving matters to the United Nations would be a sure formula for total inactivity.'

41. Bernard Lewis, 'The UN is Likely to Botch the Job in Iraq', *Wall Street Journal* (12 May 2004).

42. Both Kofi Annan, Secretary-General of the United Nations, and his predecessor Boutros Boutros-Ghali, as well as several states, argued that the attack violated international law as a war of aggression since it lacked the validity of a UN Security Council resolution to authorize military force, and was not an act of defence, and so violated the UN charter, in other words that it constituted a war crime. However, none have called for the Security Council to consider sanctions against the United States or the other nations involved, both because of an effort to re-establish the relationship with the US, and because the attempt would be futile since the US has a veto in the Security Council. 'Iraq War Illegal, Says Annan', BBC News (16 Sept. 2004). Web version (accessed 9 Nov. 2006) at: <http://news.bbc.co.uk/go/pr/fr/-/2/hi/middle_east/3661134.stm>. Colum Lynch, 'US, Allies Dispute Annan on Iraq War', *Washington Post* (17 Sept. 2004).

43. Bernard Lewis, 'Freedom and Justice in the Modern Middle East', *Foreign Affairs* (May/June 2005).

44. At the time of Bonaparte's invasion in 1798, 'in Arabic usage at that time and for some time after, the word "freedom" – *hurriyya* – was in no sense a political term. It was

a legal term. One was free if one was not a slave. To be liberated, or freed, meant to be manumitted, and in the Islamic world, unlike in the Western world, "slavery" and "freedom" were not until recently used as metaphors for bad and good government.' Lewis also noted 'the absence in classical Islamic political thought and practice of the notion of citizenship, in the sense of being a free and participating member of a civic entity'.

45. Ehsan Ahrari, 'When Sistani Speaks Bush Listens', *Asia Times* (4 Jan. 2004). Web version (accessed 13 Nov. 2006) at: <http://www.atimes.com/atimes/Middle_East/FA17Ak02.html>

46. 'Islam and the West: A Conversation with Bernard Lewis', 27 April 2006, Hay-Adams Hotel, Washington DC. Web version (accessed 14 Nov. 2006) at: <http://pewforum.org/events/index.php?EventID=107>

47. No comment from Osama bin Laden seems to have infuriated American opinion as much as this ill-judged remark made in one of his first statements. Lewis commented on another occasion in 2006: 'As Osama bin Laden puts it: "In this final phase of the ongoing struggle, the world of the infidels was divided between two superpowers – the United States and the Soviet Union. Now we have defeated and destroyed the more difficult and the more dangerous of the two. Dealing with the pampered and effeminate Americans will be easy." And then followed what has become the familiar description of the Americans and the usual litany and recitation of American defeats and retreats: Vietnam, Beirut, Somalia, one after another. The general theme was: They can't take it. Hit them and they'll run. All you have to do is hit harder.' Bernard Lewis, 'Bring Them Freedom or They Destroy Us', lecture delivered by Bernard Lewis on 16 July 2006, on board the *Crystal Serenity*, during a Hillsdale College cruise in the British Isles. Posted at RealClearPolitics, 20 Sept. 2006: <http://www.realclearpolitics.com/articles/2006/09/bring_them_freedom_or_they_des.html>

48. Ibid.

49. 'Iraq-terror link [a] self-fulfilling prophecy ... What [the US] did was simply to open Iraq's international borders to international terrorists, in the sense that they dissolved the Iraqi Army, the Iraqi security forces, and now anyone can cross into Iraq from Iran, Turkey, even Syria, Saudi Arabia, and Kuwait and nobody will stop them. And this is actually a ridiculous state of affairs, that a country which was tightly controlled by a dictatorship has descended into chaos as a result of the absence of any planning for post-war Iraq.' Jeremy Bransten, 'Iraq Invasion Fuels Terrorism, Say Analysts', ISN Security Watch (15 Oct. 2003).

50. Bassam Tibi wrote this in *Welt am Sonntag*, adding that 'the problem is not whether the majority of Europeans is Islamic but rather which Islam – *sharia* Islam or Euro-Islam – is to dominate in Europe.' Christopher Caldwell, 'Islamic Europe? When Bernard Lewis Speaks ...', *The Weekly Standard* (4 Oct. 2004).

51. Is this a case of one voice for an American audience and another for one in Israel? David Machlis and Tovah Lazaroff, 'Muslims "About to Take over Europe"', International.jpost.com (29 Jan. 2007).

52. Bernard Lewis, 'Europe and Islam', 2007 Irving Kristol Lecture (AEI, 2007), 20.

53. <http://www.aei.org/publications/pubID.25814,filter.all/pub_detail.asp>

54. Gregory D. Slabodkin, 'The Secret Section in Israel's US Lobby that stifles American Debate', *Washington Report on Middle East Affairs*, 11/2 (1992), 89–91.

55. Speech of Netanyahu to the AIPAC Conference, 12 March 2007: <http://www.middleeast.org/launch/redirect.cgi?num=586&a=64>

*Chapter Four: Elijah's Mantle*

1. Jamie Glazov, 'Frontpage Interview: Richard Pipes', FrontPageMagazine.com (19 Jan. 2004).

2. Richard Pipes, *Vixi. Memoirs of a Non-Belonger* (New Haven and London: Yale University Press, 2004).

3. Murray Friedman, *The Neo-Conservative Revolution. Jewish Intellectuals and the Shaping of Public Policy* (Cambridge: Cambridge University Press, 2005), 144.

4. 'Harvard historian Richard Pipes shaped the Reagan administration's aggressive approach to the Soviet Union. His support for confrontation over containment prefigured the Bush foreign policy of today.' Sam Tanenhaus, 'The Hard-Liner [Richard Pipes]', *Boston Globe* (11 Feb. 2003).

5. In an off-the-record interview, Pipes told Reuters in March 1981 that 'Soviet leaders would have to choose between peacefully changing their Communist system in the direction followed by the West or going to war. There is no other alternative and it could go either way ... *Détente* is dead.' According to the *New York Times* on 19 March 1981, 'the interview was carried by the Reuters news agency, which did not identify the source of the comments. It was learned independently that the official interviewed was Richard V. Pipes, a Soviet specialist on the staff of Richard V. Allen, the national security adviser.' The report noted that the Secretary of State, and officials from the Department of State were particularly incensed.

6. Quotations from Sam Tanenhaus, 'The Hard-Liner [Richard Pipes]'.

7. Ibid.

8. Daniel Pipes, 'Same Difference', *National Review* (7 Nov. 1994).

'In the end, the ideological battle of the post-Cold War era instigated by fundamentalist Islam will be decided by Muslims, not by Americans. The fundamentalist challenge will succeed or fail depending on what they and their non-fundamentalist opponents do.' Pipes, 'There Are No Moderates: Dealing with Fundamentalist Islam', *National Interest* (fall 1995).

'... Only by naming militant Islam as the enemy is it possible to see the goal of defeating and marginalizing this ideology (along the lines of what was done to fascism and communism in World War II and in the Cold War).' Pipes, '[The Need to Name and] Know Thy Terrorists', *New York Post* (19 Nov. 2002).

'The Middle East has replaced the Soviet Union as the touchstone of politics and ideology. With increasing clarity, conservatives stand on one side of its issues and liberals on the other.' Pipes, 'Who Supports Israel [Conservatives or Liberals]?, *New York Post* (3 Sept. 2003).

9. Daniel Pipes, 'A Neo-Conservative's Caution', *New York Sun* (8 Mar. 2005).

10. Quoted by Getz, 'Daniel Pipes: Prophet'.

11. As is evidenced by his long campaign against Middle Eastern Studies at Columbia University. Pipes, 'Conservative Professors, an Endangered Species', *New York Sun* (12 Apr. 2005).

12. 'Daniel Pipes. Middle East Forum: founder and director. Project for the New American Century: signatory', International Relations Center, *Right Web News* (last updated 7 March 2005): <http://rightweb.irc-online.org/profile/1316> Campus Watch describes itself as 'a project of the Middle East Forum, [which] reviews and critiques Middle East studies in North America with an aim to improving them. The project mainly addresses five problems: analytical failures, the mixing of politics with scholarship, intolerance of alternative views, apologetics, and the abuse of power over students. Campus Watch fully respects the freedom of speech of those it debates while insisting on its own freedom to comment on their words and deeds. <http://www.campus-watch.org/> accessed 8 Dec. 2006. At this date, the website had on its home page a photograph of Professor Juan Cole with the comment: 'he ... claimed that free speech in academe is threatened by outsiders who criticize Middle East studies. Prof. Cole neglected to mention his unsuccessful attempts to climb the career ladder to jobs at Duke and Yale.' Why this should concern Dr Pipes and his colleagues at Campus Watch was left unclear. Also left unclarified, except through the web link itself, was the fact that in Nov. 2006 'the Middle East Studies Associa-

tion, of which Cole is the president, voted to expand the work of its academic freedom committee – which has focused on helping scholars in the Middle East – to engage in efforts on behalf of colleagues in the United States. "The subtext of these controversies is whether it is going to be allowed for Palestinians to hold positions in academe in the United States. Is it going to be allowed for people who are not Zionists to hold positions? Is there a Zionist litmus test in the United States?", said Cole in an interview Monday. He characterized the pro-Israel groups' activities as "the privatization of McCarthyism" and said that they represented the most serious threat today to academic freedom in the United States.' Scott Jaschik, 'Input or Intrusion?', *Inside Higher Ed.com News* (21 Nov. 2006).

13. Self-description of MESA in Professor Juan Cole's letter to the Secretary of State Condoleeza Rice and Under Secretary of State for Public Diplomacy and Public Affairs Karen Hughes regarding the denial of Professor Tariq Ramadan's visa application, 3 Oct. 2006: <http://www.mesa.arizona.edu/about/cafmenaletters.htm#100306>

14. Donald E. Abelson, *A Capitol Idea. Think Tanks and US Foreign Policy* (Montreal: McGill-Queen's University Press, 2006), 238.

15. Homepage of MEF <http://www.meforum.org/> accessed 8 Dec. 2006. MEF clearly sees no inconsistency in promoting American and Israeli interests simultaneously.

16. Homepage of MEQ <http://www.meforum.org/meq/> accessed 8 Dec. 2006. Of course, the MEQ makes no mention of the less politicized IJMES, which has been published since 1970 and has the prestigious Cambridge University Press imprint. This journal's remit is to publish 'original research on politics, society and culture in the Middle East from the seventh century to the present day. The journal also covers Spain, south-east Europe, and parts of the former Soviet Union for the periods in which these territories were under the influence of Middle Eastern civilization. Particular attention is paid to the history, politics, economics, anthropology, sociology, literature, and folklore of the area and to comparative religion, theology, law, and philosophy.' Note the emphasis on 'original research' which is neither claimed, nor demonstrated, by MEQ: <http://www.cambridge.org/journals/journal_catalogue.asp?mnemonic=mes> <http://www.jstor.org/journals/00207438.html>

17. Pipes particularly liked Kramer's book because it lambasted both Edward Said's study *Orientalism* and MESA. Said, Kramer contended, 'browbeat Middle Eastern studies into submission'. Kramer, 'Said's Splash' (from *Ivory Towers on Sand*), Web version (accessed 9 Dec. 2006): <http://www.geocities.com/martinkramerorg/SaidSplash.htm> Pipes, '[Middle East Scholars:] Getting it Wrong in the Middle East', *New York Post* (5 Nov. 2001).

18. Pipes and Jonathan Schanzer, 'Extremists on Campus', *New York Post* (25 June 2002).

19. Pipes, 'From the Halls of Academia. Campuses Must Reclaim Lost Ideological Ground', *Los Angeles Times* (27 Dec. 2002).

20. 'For his intellectual candour, Bernard Lewis is assaulted by Edward Said, who depicts Lewis's work as "polemical", "not scholarly", and "political propaganda".' Norvell B. De Atkine and Daniel Pipes, 'Middle Eastern Studies: What Went Wrong?', *Academic Questions* (winter 1995–6). In Pipes's and Harris's summary, Said had stated that US policy in Iraq was a 'grotesque show' perpetrated by a 'small cabal' of unelected individuals who had hijacked US policy [= the neo-conservative lobby]. He accused 'George Bush and his minions' of hiding their imperialist grab for 'oil and hegemony' under a false intent to build democracy and human rights. Said deemed Operation Iraqi Freedom 'an abuse of human tolerance and human values' waged by an 'avenging Judeo-Christian god of war'. This war, he stated, fitted into a larger pattern of America 'reducing whole peoples, countries and even continents to ruin by nothing short of holocaust'. Said's critique was sufficiently pertinent to require silencing and being declared anti-American. Pipes and Jonathan Calt Harris, 'Columbia [University] vs. America', *New York Post* (1 Apr. 2003).

21. Pipes, '[Campus Watch and] Saving Mideast Studies', *New York Post* (18 Sept. 2003).

22. Pipes, '[Middle East Studies:] Wasted Money', *New York Post* (24 June 2003). Pipes, 'Defund Middle East Studies', *New York Sun* (24 Feb. 2004).

23. Pipes, 'Five years of Campus Watch', *Jerusalem Post* (20 Sept. 2007).

24. Thus Pipes's comment on the publishing catalogue of the University of California Press in 2004: '… this finding of wisdom in only one part of the political spectrum and publishing only its views is deeply consequential: it betrays the concept of academic freedom, a concept that assumes no one outlook has a monopoly on truth, but that truth emerges from debate.' Pipes, 'California [University Press] vs. Academic Freedom', *New York Sun* (30 Mar. 2004).

25. Pipes, 'Bad News from Slippery Rock', *New York Sun* (11 Apr. 2006).

26. 'Statistics give the story in brief: my one-year mark tally stands at 1 book, 8 long articles, 80 short articles, 110 television appearances, 120 in-person lectures, 360 mentions in the media (that I know of), and 450 radio interviews. The daily visits to my web page increased from 300 per day before 9/11 to 2,000 after it. The recipients of my articles by e-mail increased from 2,000 before to 14,000.' Pipes, 'My Media Year', *National Review* (11 Sept. 2002).

27. Pipes, '[Militant Islam:] The New Global Threat', *Jerusalem Post* (11 Apr. 2001). Pipes, 'Islamists – Not Who they Say they are', *Jerusalem Post* (9 May 2001).

28. Bernard Lewis was a historian of Islamic history not a scholar of Islam *per se*. Pipes, 'What's True Islam? Not for [the] US to Say', *New York Post* (26 Nov. 2001).

29. Pipes, 'Who is the Enemy?', *Commentary* (Jan. 2002).

30. Pipes, 'War, not "Crimes". Time for a Paradigm Shift', *National Review* (1 Oct. 2001).

31. Pipes, 'Fighting Militant Islam, without Bias', *City Journal* (Nov. 2001).

32. President Discusses War on Terror at National Endowment for Democracy (6 Oct. 2005): <http://www.whitehouse.gov/news/releases/2005/10/20051006–3.html>

33. Bush repeated the speech almost exactly on Veterans' Day (11 Nov. 2005). Pipes, 'Bush Declares War on Radical Islam', *New York Sun* (11 Oct. 2005).

34. Michele Steinberg, 'The Greatest Strategic Disaster in US History', *Executive Intelligence Review* (14 Oct. 2005). <http://www.larouchepub.com/eiw/public/2005/2005_40–49/2005–41/index.html>

35. Pipes, 'Muslims Love Bin Laden', *New York Post* (22 Oct. 2001).

36. Pipes, 'Who is the Enemy?', *Commentary* (Jan. 2002).

37. Pipes and Jonathan Schanzer, 'Militant Islam's New Strongholds', *New York Post* (22 Oct. 2002).

38. Pipes, 'The Triumph of the 9/11 Commission', *New York Sun* (27 July 2004).

39. For Pipes's earlier frustration: Pipes and Mimi Stillman, 'The United States Government: Patron of Islam?', *Middle East Quarterly* (Jan. 2002). Pipes, '[President Bush and] Naming the Enemy', *New York Sun* (17 Aug. 2004).

40. Pipes, 'Identifying Moderate Muslims', *New York Sun* (23 Nov. 2004).

41. Pipes, 'Washington Finally Gets it on Radical Islam', FrontPageMagazine.com (25 Apr. 2005).

42. Pipes, 'Islamophobia?', *New York Sun* (25 Oct. 2005).

43. Pipes, 'At War with Islamic Fascists', FrontPageMagazine.com (14 Aug. 2006).

44. 'In tranquil times, organizations like the Muslim Council of Britain and the Council on American–Islamic Relations effectively go about their business, promoting their agenda to make Islam "dominant" and imposing *dhimmitude* (whereby non-Muslims accept Islamic superiority and Muslim privilege). Westerners generally respond like slowly boiled frogs are supposed to, not noticing a thing.' Pipes, 'How Terrorism Obstructs Radical Islam', *New York Sun* (23 Aug. 2005).

45. The whole wearisome tale of Pipes vs. CAIR is too long to be documented here. For some examples: Pipes and Sharon Chadha, 'CAIR: Islamists Fooling the Establishment', *Middle East Quarterly* (spring 2006). Pipes and Sharon Chadha, 'Telephoning the Enemy', *New York Sun* (18 Apr. 2006). Views quoted and apparently endorsed: 'CAIR has proven links to, and was founded by, Islamic terrorists. CAIR is not in the United States to promote the civil rights of Muslims. CAIR is here to make radical Islam the dominant religion in the United States and convert our country into an Islamic theocracy along the lines of Iran. In addition, CAIR has managed, through the adroit manipulation of the popular media, to present itself as the "moderate" face of Islam in the United States. CAIR succeeded to the point that the majority of its members are not aware that CAIR actively supports terrorists and terrorist supporting groups and nations. In addition, CAIR receives direct funding from Islamic terrorist supporting countries.' Pipes, 'CAIR Backs Down from Anti-CAIR, FrontPageMagazine.com (21 Apr. 2006).

46. '... Amnesty International has laid down the gauntlet, placing a higher priority on civil liberties than on protection from Islamist terrorism. In contrast, I worry more about mega-terrorism – say, a dirty bomb in midtown Manhattan – than an innocent person spending time in jail.' Pipes, 'To Profile or Not to Profile?', *New York Sun* (21 Sept. 2004). Pipes, 'The Enemy Within [and the Need for Profiling]', *New York Post* (24 Jan. 2003). Pipes, 'A Call for Intelligent Profiling [by Frederick Schauer]', *New York Sun* (30 Dec. 2003). Pipes, '[The Abu Ali Case and] Balancing Liberties, Security', *New York Sun* (1 Mar. 2005).

47. Leiken's view is expressed in *Bearers of Global Jihad. Immigration and National Security after 9/11* (Washington DC: Nixon Center, 2004). Pipes, 'Europe's Threat to the West', *New York Sun* (18 May 2004).

48. Pipes, 'In Muslim America: A Presence and a Challenge [= The Anti-Americanism of US Converts to Islam]', *National Review* (21 Feb. 2000).

49. Pipes, 'Sudden Jihad Syndrome [in North Carolina]', *New York Sun* (14 Mar. 2006).

50. Pipes, 'Sudden Jihad Syndrome in Seattle', *New York Sun* (8 Aug. 2006).

51. Thus praising David Cook's *Understanding Jihad* (Berkeley, CA: University of California Press, 2005) because it criticizes John Esposito's view. The fact remains in Islamic history overall that there were more years when there was no *jihad* than when one was declared, and most were purely regional phenomena. Pipes, 'Jihad through History', *New York Sun* (31 May 2005).

52. Pipes, 'Jihad and the Professors', *Commentary* (Nov. 2002). Pipes, 'What is Jihad?', *New York Post* (31 Dec. 2002). 'John Kelsay and James Turner Johnson assert (and Richard L. Rubenstein seconds them) that their scholarly work recognizes the military nature of jihad ...' Pipes, 'Letters to the Editor: Jihad and the Professors', *Commentary* (Feb. 2003).

53. In his discussion of the work of the (unrepresentative) Irshad Manji, Pipes does not mention her 'Project Ijtihad'. Pipes, '[Moderate] Voices of Islam', *New York Post* (23 Sept. 2003).

54. Pipes, 'Intimidating the West, from Rushdie to Benedict', *New York Sun* (26 Sept. 2006).

55. 'Obtaining the same rights for Christians in Islamdom that Muslims enjoy in Christendom has become the key to the Vatican's diplomacy toward Muslims': Pipes, 'The Vatican Confronts Islam', *Jerusalem Post* (5 July 2006).

56. Pipes, 'In 1796, [the] US Vowed Friendliness with Islam', *New York Sun* (7 Nov. 2006). However, the Military Intelligence Service of the US War Department considered in 1946 that 'Moslem States Represent a Potential Threat to World Peace' as noted by Pipes in an article with that title, FrontPageMagazine.com (13 Feb. 2006).

57. Pipes, 'Weak Brits, Tough French', *New York Sun* (12 July 2005).

58. Pipes, '[Nepal and France:] Two Opposite Responses to Terrorism', *New York Sun* (14 Sept. 2004).

59. Pipes, '[London Terrorism:] British "Covenant of Security" with Islamists Ends', *New York Sun* (8 July 2005). Pipes, 'Trouble in Londonistan', *New York Sun* (11 July 2006). 'While I maintain that the future of Europe – whether continuing in its historic Christian identity or becoming an adjunct of Muslim North Africa – is still an open question, the behaviour of the British public, that weakest link in the Western chain, suggests that it, at least, may be too confused to resist its Londonistan destiny.' Pipes, 'Piggybacking on Terror in Britain', *New York Sun* (29 Aug. 2006).

60. Steyn makes these assertions in *America Alone. The End of the World as We Know it* (Washington DC: Regnery, 2006). Pipes, 'Europe is Finished, Predicts Mark Steyn', *New York Sun* (14 Nov. 2006).

61. Pipes, '[Samuel Huntington and] American Purposes in Iraq', *New York Sun* (27 Apr. 2004).

62. 'The British have seemingly lost interest in their heritage while the French hold on to theirs: as the British ban fox hunting, the French ban *hijabs*. The former embrace multiculturalism, the latter retain a pride in their historic culture. This contrast in matters of identity makes Britain the Western country most vulnerable to the ravages of radical Islam whereas France, for all its political failings, has held onto a sense of self that may yet see it through.' Pipes, 'Weak Brits, Tough French.'

63. Pipes, 'Islamists, Get Out', *New York Sun* (30 Aug. 2005).

64. Pipes, 'Islamophobia?', *New York Sun* (25 Oct. 2005).

65. Pipes, 'The Politics of Muslim Anti-Semitism', *Commentary* (Aug. 1981). Pipes, 'The New Anti-Semitism' (1992). Pipes, 'The New Anti-Semitism', *Jewish Exponent* (16 Oct. 1997). Pipes, 'Deadly Denial [of Muslim Anti-Semitism]', *New York Post* (26 Oct. 2003). Pipes, 'Locus of Euro-Hate', *Jerusalem Post* (10 Dec. 2003). Pipes, 'Anti-Semitism Evolves', *New York Sun* (15 Feb. 2005).

66. Pipes, 'Letters to the Editor: Radical Islam', *Commentary* (Apr. 2002).

67. Pipes, 'Iran's Final Solution Plan', *New York Sun* (1 Nov. 2005). Pipes, 'The Mystical Menace of Mahmoud Ahmadinejad', *New York Sun* (10 Jan. 2006).

68. Pipes, 'Musharraf's Historic Speech [regarding Jews and Israel]', *New York Sun* (20 Sept. 2005).

69. Most observers do not need Daniel Pipes to warn them in order to have grave reservations about Iran's alleged 'scientific' conference on the Holocaust in December 2006. 'An international cast of established Holocaust deniers and implacable foes of Israel were given an open forum by Iran yesterday to support Mahmoud Ahmadinejad's contention that the murder of six million Jews by the Nazis was a "myth" … Iran's foreign minister, Manouchehr Mottaki, insisted the event was necessary to counter an alleged lack of free speech in the west about the Holocaust, which Iranian officials argue is used to justify Israel's oppression of the Palestinians.' Robert Tait, 'Holocaust Deniers Gather in Iran for "Scientific" Conference', *The Guardian* (12 Dec. 2006).

70. Pipes, 'The Hell of Israel is Better than the Paradise of Arafat', *Middle East Quarterly* (spring 2005).

71. '… Until that day of harmony – which I predict is about thirty years off – the outside world should focus not on showering money or other benefits on the Palestinian Arabs, but on pushing them relentlessly to accept Israel's existence.' Pipes, 'Palestinians Don't Deserve Additional Aid', *New York Sun* (21 Dec. 2004).

72. Pipes, 'Palestinians who Praise Israel', *Forward* (11 Feb. 1994).

73. 'Jews and Americans, Israel and the United States – they have merged in the minds of many around the world, so that one prejudice routinely implies the other one too …' Pipes, 'Anti-Semitism Evolves', *New York Sun* (15 Feb. 2005).

74. Pipes, 'The Lamentations in Zionist Society Can no Longer be Ignored', *Azure* (winter 5759/1999) <http://www.danielpipes.org/article/324>

75. Ilan Pappé, 'The Struggle for Survival of Traditional Zionism', in Ephraim Nimni

(ed.), *The Challenge of Post-Zionism. Alternatives to Israeli Fundamentalist Politics* (London: Zed Books, 2003), 42–62. Review article by Ned Curthoys, 'The Challenge of Post-Zionism', Borderlands e-journal, 2 (2003: Accessed 12 Dec. 2006).

76. 'The CIA first concluded that Israel had begun to produce nuclear weapons in 1968, but few details emerged until 1986 when Mordechai Vanunu, a former technician at Israel's nuclear weapons facility, gave the *Sunday Times* detailed descriptions that led defence analysts to rank the country as the sixth largest nuclear power.' Martin Hodgson, 'Olmert's Stray Comment Fuels the Nuclear Debate', *The Guardian* (12 Dec. 2006).

77. 'Israel's nuclear arsenal may provoke an arms race in the Middle East in which even moderate states could get involved, the Sa'udi intelligence chief [stated] … "The fact that Israel has nuclear weapons is the most dangerous threat against Gulf security", Intelligence chief Prince Muqrin bin Abdul-Aziz told a security conference in Bahrain, 'Sa'udi Arabia Warns of Mideast Arms Race, Blames Israel', Reuters (9 Dec. 2006). Simon Tisdall, 'How Gulf States Could Start New Nuclear Race', *The Guardian* (12 Dec. 2006). 'Estimates indicate that Israel has nearly 200 nuclear warheads. However, so far Israel has never publicly admitted the[ir] existence … In so doing, Israel has been able to receive annual financial aid of $2 billion from the United States, which constitutionally bans aid to countries with weapons of mass destruction.' 'Ehud Olmert's Nuclear Confession Causes Outrage', zaman.com (13 Dec. 2006).

78. Pipes, 'On Arab Rejectionism', *Commentary* (Dec. 1997).

79. Pipes, 'Sharon Loses his Way on Israeli "Settlements"', *New York Sun* (10 Feb. 2004).

80. Pipes, 'How Israel Can Win', *New York Sun* (4 Apr. 2006).

81. Pipes, 'The Year the Arabs Discovered Palestine', *Jerusalem Post* (13 Sept. 2000).

82. Pipes, 'Jerusalem Means More to Jews than to Muslims', *Los Angeles Times* (21 July 2000). Pipes, 'The Muslim Claim to Jerusalem', *Middle East Quarterly* (Sept. 2001). [To see the sources for this article, see the 111 endnotes in the version posted at <http://www.meforum.org/article/490>]

83. Pipes, 'Double Delusion', *Jerusalem Post* (22 Aug. 2001).

84. Pipes, 'Does Israel Need a Plan?', *Commentary* (Feb. 2003).

85. Pipes, 'Israel's Wayward Prime Ministers', *New York Sun* (29 June 2004).

86. 'Mr Sharon betrayed the voters who supported him, wounding Israeli democracy. He divided Israeli society in ways that may poison the body politic for decades hence. He aborted his own successful policies vis-à-vis the Palestinians. He delivered Palestinian, Arab, and Muslim rejectionists their greatest boost ever. And he failed his American ally by delivering a major victory to the forces of terrorism.' Pipes, 'Ariel Sharon's Folly', *New York Sun* (5 Apr. 2005).

87. Pipes, '[The Gaza Withdrawal:] A Democracy Killing Itself. Sharon Deaf to his own Words; Withdrawal "is a Recipe for War"', *USA Today* (15 Aug. 2005).

88. Pipes, 'James Baker's Terrible Iraq Report', *New York Sun* (12 Dec. 2006).

89. Pipes, 'How Israel Can Win'.

90. Pipes, '[UNRWA:] The [Palestinian] Refugee Curse', *New York Post* (19 Aug. 2003).

91. Pipes, 'Imagine a Palestinian State: A Nightmare for the Arabs and for Israel', *New York Times* (25 Apr. 1988).

92. Pipes, 'Fund the Palestinians? Bad Idea', *Jerusalem Post* (19 Dec. 2007).

93. Pipes, 'Secularism – Will it Survive?', *Free Inquiry* (Oct–Nov. 2005).

94. Response by Pipes to comments on his article 'Land for What?', *American Spectator* (Mar. 2001).

95. 'Published by the National Committee for the Heads of the Arab Local Authorities in Israel and written by members of local civil society and academia, this report aims to clearly define a collective future vision for the Arab minority in Israel.' *The Future Vision of Palestinian Arabs in Israel* (Mossawa Center in Haifa, Dec. 2006).

96. Jonathan Cook, 'The Trap of Recognising Israel', Countercurrents.org (16 Dec. 2006).

97. Pipes, 'Israel's Domestic Enemy', *New York Sun* (19 Dec. 2006).

98. Pipes and Ziad Adelnour, 'Ending Syria's Occupation of Lebanon: The US Role'. Report of the Lebanon Study Group (May 2000).

99. Pipes, '"We Don't Need Syria" in Lebanon', *Middle East Quarterly* (Sept. 2000).

100. Pipes, 'Lebanon's Liberation Approaches', *New York Sun* (22 Feb. 2005).

101. The Committee for the Liberation of Iraq (CLI) was set up in late 2002 by Bruce Jackson, a director of the Project for the New American Century (PNAC) and former Lockheed Martin vice-president. Shortly after the 2003 US invasion of Iraq, CLI closed shop, announcing on its website: 'following the successful liberation of Iraq, the committee has ceased its operations.' 'Committee for the Liberation of Iraq', IRC Right Web Profile: <http://rightweb.irc-online.org/profile/1458>

102. Pipes, 'After "Desert Storm", Barely a Footprint was Left in the Sand', *Los Angeles Times* (4 Aug. 2000).

103. Pipes, 'Memo to the Next President', *Middle East Insight* (Nov.–Dec. 2000).

104. Pipes and Jonathan Schanzer 'On to Baghdad? Yes – The Risks are Overrated', *New York Post* (3 Dec. 2001).

105. Pipes, 'A Majority of One', *New York Post* (18 Mar. 2002).

106. Under Gerald Ford from November 1975 to January 1977, and under Bush Senior throughout his term.

107. Brent Scowcroft, 'Don't Attack Saddam. It Could Undermine our Anti-Terror Efforts', *Wall Street Journal* (15 Aug. 2002).

108. Pipes and Jonathan Schanzer 'Brent Scowcroft is Wrong. We Must Attack Saddam', *FrontPage Magazine* (20 Aug. 2002).

109. Pipes, '100 Bin Ladens on the Way?', *New York Post* (8 Apr. 2003).

110. Analysis of the signatories and contributing writers by IRC Right Web (accessed 13 Dec. 2006): <http://rightweb.irc-online.org/charts/pnac-chart.php>. The letters and statements themselves are conveniently placed on PNAC's website: <http://www.newamericancentury.org/lettersstatements.htm>

111. William Kristol, Ken Adelman, Reuel Marc Gerecht, and Richard Perle were among the signatories: <http://www.newamericancentury.org/Bushletter-040302.htm>

112. Those familiar with the British legal arguments for going to war in 2003 will be surprised by Pipes's assertion that 'WMD was never the basic reason for the war. Nor was it the horrid repression in Iraq. Or the danger Saddam posed to his neighbours. Rather, the basic reason was Saddam's having signed a contract with the United States, then breaking his promise.' Pipes, 'Iraq's Weapons and the Road to War', *New York Post* (3 June 2003). Pipes found it difficult to account for Saddam's lies about WMD. The plain truth is that he could not admit to his own people that he had destroyed his WMD at the behest of the UN inspectors. Pipes, '[Saddam's] WMD Lies', *New York Post* (7 Oct. 2003).

113. The expression 'Foreign Policy as Social Work' had been used by Michael Mandelbaum in criticism of President Clinton's deployment of American troops in Bosnia and Haiti: Mandelbaum, 'Foreign Policy as Social Work', *Foreign Affairs* (Jan.–Feb. 1996). Pipes, 'War as Social Work?', *New York Post* (6 May 2003).

114. 'Why then is Afghanistan rewarded with an outpouring of aid? The reason is simple: US forces defeated Afghanistan's regime and Americans now feel responsible for fixing the country …' Pipes and Jonathan Schanzer, 'Attack US and Win Aid', *New York Post* (28 Jan. 2002).

115. Pipes, '[Samuel Huntington and] American Purposes in Iraq', *New York Sun* (27 Apr. 2004).

116. Pipes, 'Let Iraqis Run Iraq', *Jerusalem Post* (15 Oct. 2003). Pipes, 'The Case for "Iraqification"', *Jerusalem Post* (19 Nov. 2003).

117. Pipes, 'A Strongman for Iraq?', *New York Post* (28 Apr. 2003). Pipes, 'The Roots of Iraq's Rebellion', *New York Sun* (13 Apr. 2004).

118. Pipes, 'Is an Iraqi Strongman Emerging?', *New York Sun* (4 May 2004).

119. Pipes, '"Walking Back the Cat" on Chalabi', *New York Sun* (22 June 2004).

120. 'The United States cannot pass up a unique chance to remake the world's most politically fevered region. Sure, the effort might fail, but not even to try would be a missed opportunity. Secretary of State Colin L Powell last week said that American success in Iraq "could fundamentally reshape [the Middle East] in a powerful, positive way", suggesting that even the Bush team's most cautious member is rightly coming around to the ambitious point of view.' Pipes, 'After Saddam? Remaking the Mideast', *New York Post* (11 Feb. 2003).

121. Sam Tanenhaus, 'The Hard-Liner [Richard Pipes]'.

122. Pipes, 'Bush the Radical [i.e. radical conservative]', *Jerusalem Post* (12 Nov. 2003).

123. Pipes, 'Islamic Law Rules in Iraq', *New York Sun* (2 Mar. 2004).

124. 'Voting does not start the democratization process but culminates and ends it. Before Iraqis can benefit from meaningful elections, they need to leave behind the bad habits of Saddam Hussein's tyrannical rule and replace them with the benign ways of civil society. There are many steps ahead, such as creating voluntary institutions (political parties, lobby groups, etc.), entrenching the rule of law, establishing freedom of speech, protecting minority rights, securing property rights, and developing the notion of a loyal opposition. Elections can evolve with these good habits. Voting should start at the municipal level and gradually move up to the national level. Also, they should begin with legislatures and move to the executive branch.' Pipes, 'US Needs to Learn Patience [in Iraq]', *New York Sun* (30 Nov. 2004).

125. 'Give Mubarak an extra 25 years and allow the Washington administration to develop projects on a democratic transformation.' Ali H. Aslan, 'Debates Flare over "Shall We Rely on Islamists for Democracy?"', Zaman.com (26 Oct. 2005).

126. Daniel Pipes, 'A Neo-Conservative's Caution', *New York Sun* (8 Mar. 2005).

127. Pipes, 'Radical Islam as its own Antidote [argues Reuel Gerecht]', *New York Sun* (23 June 2005).

128. Reuel Marc Gerecht, *The Islamic Paradox. Shi'ite Clerics, Sunni Fundamentalists and the Coming of Arab Democracy* (Washington DC: AEI Piess, 2004), 56. Web version: <http://www.aei.org/docLib/20041115_book799text.pdf>

129. Pipes, '[The RAND Corporation] and Fixing Islam', *New York Sun* (6 Apr. 2004). Pipes acknowledges the seriousness of the Islamist challenge in Turkey. Pipes, 'Is Turkey Going Islamist?', *New York Sun* (7 June 2005).

130. Pipes, 'Turkey, still a Western Ally?', *Jerusalem Post* (5 Dec. 2007).

131. Pipes, 'Can Hezbollah and Hamas be Democratic?', *New York Sun* (22 Mar. 2005).

132. 'Arab Islamists have already achieved electoral success and takeover in Iraq, but Hamas represents the first Arab Islamist terrorist group to be legitimated through the ballot box. Comparable groups in countries such as Syria, Lebanon, Egypt, Tunisia and Morocco will watch and be encouraged, should there be any show of acceptance of Hamas by the US and other governments.' Pipes, '[The Hamas Victory and] Prospects for Peace', *Time Magazine* (6 Feb. 2006).

133. Joseph Alagha, *The Shifts in Hizbullah's Ideology. Religious Ideology, Political Ideology and Political Program* (Amsterdam: ISIM/Amsterdam University Press, 2006).

134. Pipes, '[Alastair Crooke's Conflict Forum and] Sharing Jokes with Hamas', *Jerusalem Post* (20 Apr. 2005).

135. Pipes, 'What Happened to James A. Baker III?' (5 Dec. 2006): <http://www.danielpipes.org/blog/714>

136. Pipes, '[Freedom House report on] Saudi Venom in US Mosques', *New York Sun* (1 Feb. 2005).

137. Pipes, 'The Scandal of US–Saudi Relations', *National Interest* (winter 2002/3).

138. Pipes, 'Might the Saudis Blow up their Oil Infrastructure?', FrontPageMagazine.com (11 May 2005).

139. Suzanne Goldenberg, 'If US Leaves Iraq We will Arm Sunni Militias, Saudis Say', *The Guardian* (14 Dec. 2006). 'White House Denies Saudi Iraq Plan Report', Agence France-Presse (14 Dec. 2006).

140. Pipes, 'Support the Lesser Evil [in Saudi Arabia]', *The Australian* (31 May 2004).

141. Pipes, 'Defending and Advancing Freedom', *Commentary* (Nov. 2005).

142. Pipes, '[Lee Harris on Why the US is] Discarding War's Rules', *New York Post* (22 July 2003).

143. Pipes, 'In the Mideast, Bush Dared to be Different', *Philadelphia Inquirer* (24 Oct. 2004).

144. 'What an amazing bloody catastrophe. The Bush administration's policy towards the Middle East over the five years since 9/11 is culminating in a multiple train crash. Never in the field of human conflict was so little achieved by so great a country at such vast expense. In every vital area of the wider Middle East, American policy over the last five years has taken a bad situation and made it worse.' Timothy Garton Ash, 'Bush has Created a Comprehensive Catastrophe across the Middle East', *The Guardian* (14 Dec. 2006).

145. 'The core of Pipes' argument is that a fratricidal conflict between Sunni and Shi'ite Iraqis, whatever the death toll and however tragic for the Iraqi people, would have definite benefits for American strategic, economic and military interests in the Middle East.' James Cogan, 'Daniel Pipes and the Unfolding Civil War in Iraq', World Socialist Web Site (11 Apr. 2006). Pipes, 'Civil War in Iraq?', *New York Sun* (28 Feb. 2006). In a subsequent television interview, Pipes clarified: 'I do not want them to be shooting each other. I wish that the communities found a way to work together. I'm just saying should there be a civil war, it is not necessarily all that bad for our interests. By no means am I endorsing it, by no means do I want one. I'm looking at it in a cool way and saying there are advantages to it. Let me emphasise that does not mean I want it to happen.'

146. 'Civil War Likely in Iraq: Pipes', Australian Broadcasting Corporation (2 Mar. 2006): <http://www.abc.net.au/lateline/content/2006/s1582736.htm>

147. Whom was Pipes trying to fool by his propaganda for naked militarism? He wrote: 'like gangland capos, Mullah Omar and Saddam Hussein disappeared (will Arafat be next?). The outcome of these operations is not in doubt. The rights of victims are as important as the safety of police. Not using excessive force is a paramount concern … the two democracies at the cutting edge of this type of fighting, the United States and Israel, have creative and humane militaries that are proving themselves worthy of this challenge.' Pipes, 'War's New Face', *New York Post* (16 Apr. 2003).

148. Pipes, 'What if the United States had Not Invaded Iraq?' *Philadelphia Inquirer* (11 Sept. 2005).

149. 'Only after absorbing catastrophic human and property losses will Left-leaning Westerners likely overcome this triple affliction and confront the true scope of the threat. The civilized world will likely then prevail, but belatedly and at a higher cost than need have been.' Pipes, 'How the West Could Lose', *New York Sun* (26 Dec. 2006).

*Chapter Five: The Real American Special Relationship*

1. Bernard Reich, 'The United States and Israel. The Nature of a Special Relationship', in David W. Lesch (ed.), *The Middle East and the United States. A Historical and Political Reassessment* (4th edn: Cambridge, MA: Westview, 2007), 205.

2. Lawrence (ed.), *Messages To The World*, 168.

3. Sen. Ernest Hollings, 'Bush's Failed Mideast Policy is Creating More Terrorism', *Charleston Post and Courier* (10 May 2004) reprinted at: <http://www.antiwar.com/orig/hollings.php?articleid=2536>

4. Avi Shlaim, 'It is not only God that will be Blair's judge over Iraq. His cravenly pro-US policy on the Middle East misunderstood Bush's real agenda and resulted in catastrophic failure', *The Guardian* (14 May 2007): <http://www.guardian.co.uk/commentisfree/story/0,,2078846,00.html>

5. Hagit Borer (chair), 'The Pro-Israel Lobby. The Debate between James Petras and Norman Finkelstein', Swana Collective of KPFK radio (8 Feb. 2007): <http://www.normanfinkelstein.com/article.php?pg=11&ar=978>

For a relatively straightforward account claiming that it was Israel's war: Mark Weber, 'Iraq: A War for Israel' (4 May 2007, accessed 21 May 2007): <http://www.arsenalofhypocrisy.com/blog/?p=80>

6. The webpage <http://aipac.org/documents/unitedefforts.html> cited by Mearsheimer and Walt as having been consulted in Jan. 2006 has been moved: John J. Mearsheimer and Stephen M. Walt, 'The Israel Lobby and US Foreign Policy', Working Paper RWP06–011 (Mar. 2006), n 11: <http://ksgnotes1.harvard.edu/Research/wpaper.nsf/rwp/RWP06–011> <http://papers.ssrn.com/abstract=891198>; published as 'The Israel Lobby' in the *London Review of Books*, 28/6 (23 Mar. 2006; accessed 11 Jan. 2007): <http://www.lrb.co.uk/v28/n06/mear01_.html>

7. Abraham H. Foxman, *The Deadliest Lies. The Israel Lobby and the Myth of Jewish Control* (New York: Palgrave Macmillan, 2007).

8. Abraham H. Foxman, *The Deadliest Lies,* 14. Patricia Cohen, 'Free Speech or Conspiracy Theory? Backlash over Book on Policy for Israel', *New York Times* (16 Aug. 2007).

9. Mearsheimer and Walt, 'The Israel Lobby'. Mearsheimer and Walt, *The Israel Lobby and US Foreign Policy* (London: Allen Lane, 2007), 112, where they comment: 'one might more accurately dub this the "pro-Israel community" or even the "help Israel movement" because the range of activities that different groups undertake goes beyond simple lobbying.'

10. G. Neuburger, 'The Difference between Judaism and Zionism' (nd): <http://www.jewsnotzionists.org/differencejudzion.html>

11. Based on the Annual Surveys of Jewish Opinion on the website of the AJC: <http:www.ajc.org/>

12. Jeff Blankfort, 'The Influence of Israel and its American Lobby over US Middle East Policy', presentation at the Islamic Human Rights Commission Conference, School of Oriental and African Studies, London (2 July 2006).

13. Michael Massing, 'Deal Breakers', *American Prospect Magazine* (11 Mar. 2002).

14. George Soros, 'On Israel, America and AIPAC', *New York Review of Books*, 54/6 (12 Apr. 2007).

15. Norman G. Finkelstein, 'It's Not Either/Or the Israel Lobby', *Counter Punch* (1 May 2006): <http://www.counterpunch.org/finkelstein05012006.html>

16. Noam Chomsky, 'The Israel Lobby?', ZNet Foreign Policy (28 Mar. 2006): <http://www.chomsky.info/articles/20060328.htm>

17. James Petras, *The Power of Israel in the United States* (Atlanta, Ga: Clarity Press, 2006), 169. Petras, 'Why Condemning Israel and the Zionist Lobby is so Important' (22 Dec. 2006): <http://petras.lahaine.org/articulo.php?p=1688&more=1&c=1>

18. Editorial entitled 'Dear John', *Forward* (8 Dec. 2006): <http://www.forward.com/articles/dear-john/>

19. According to the indictment of Lawrence Franklin, 'as the Director of Foreign Policy Issues, Rosen lobbied on behalf of AIPAC, primarily with officials within the Executive Branch of the US government. During the time period of this indictment, Rosen did not have a US government security clearance and was not authorized to receive or possess US government classified information.' Indictment dated Aug. 2005: <http://www.globalsecurity.org/intell/library/reports/2005/franklin_indictment_04aug2005.htm>

20. Mearsheimer and Walt, *The Israel Lobby and US Foreign Policy*, 156, citing 'Taming Leviathan', *The Economist* (15 Mar. 2007).

21. Paul Findlay, *They Dared to Speak Out. People and Institutions Confront Israel's Lobby* (Westport, CT: Lawrence Hill, 1985), 25.

22. Ibid. 85–90, 93–7, 109–13.

23. <http://cnionline.org/about/>

24. Petras, *The Power of Israel in the United States*, 36 (without citing sources).

25. Murray Friedman, 'The Changing Jewish Political Profile', *American Jewish History*, 91 (Sept.–Dec. 2003), 423–38.

26. 'This year, pro-Israel forces are targeting Senator Lincoln Chafee of Rhode Island': Michael Massing, 'The Storm over the Israel Lobby', *New York Review of Books*, 53/10 (8 June 2006).

Raphael J. Sonenshein, 'How will GOP Fare with Jewish Voters in '08?': <http://www.jewishjournal.com/home/preview.php?id=17652>

27. Ron Kampeas, 'Pro-Israel Funds Target Candidates no Matter what Party' (6 Oct. 2006): <http://www.jewishsf.com/content/2–0-/module/displaystory/story_id/30519/format/html/displaystory.html>

28. The website of CoP is at: <http://www.conferenceofpresidents.org/> The quotation is from: <http://israeloncampuscoalition.org/aboutus/members/cpmajo.htm>

29. Michael Massing, 'Deal Breakers', *American Prospect Magazine* (11 Mar. 2002).

30. <http://news.bbc.co.uk/1/hi/programmes/newsnight/3010371.stm>

31. Accessed 29 May 2007: <http://www.haaretz.com/hasen/pages/QA.jhtml?qaNo=108>

32. Malcolm Hoenlein, 'Investigation of AIPAC Crosses Line', JewishJournal.com (14 Jan. 2005).

33. Petras, *The Power of Israel in the United States*, 73–5.

34. Accessed 29 May 2007: <http://www.haaretz.com/hasen/pages/QA.jhtml?qaNo=108>

35. *Jerusalem Post* (23 Jan. 2007 and 17 May 2007), both comments directed against Mearsheimer and Walt's publication on 'The Israel Lobby'.

36. <http://www.washingtoninstitute.org/templateC11.php?CID=70>

37. Blankfort, 'The Influence of Israel and its American Lobby over US Middle East Policy'.

38. Saban Centere website: <http://www.brookings.edu/fp/saban/sabancenter_hp.htm>

39. Andrew Ross Sorkin, 'Schlepping to Moguldom', *New York Times* (5 Sept. 2004).

40. <http://www.campaignmoney.com/contributors.asp?pg=1>

41. <http://www.jinsa.org/about/agenda/agenda.html> <http://www.jinsa.org/home/home.html>

Analysis at: <http://rightweb.irc-online.org/profile/1508>

42. Mark H. Milstein, 'Strategic Ties or Tentacles?', *Institute for National Security Affairs* (Oct. 1991): <http://www.wrmea.com/backissues/1091/9110027.htm>

43. 'This Goes Beyond bin Laden', JINSA press release (13 Sept. 2001).

44. JINSA report, 'It is the Same War' (6 Mar. 2003).

45. Thomas Neumann, 'Israel, India, and the United States. A New Partnership against Terrorism', JINSA article (5 Nov. 2003): <http://www.jinsa.org/articles/articles.html/function/view/categoryid/1949/documentid/2258/history/3,2360,1947,1949,2258>

46. Halper and Clarke, *America Alone*, 106. Matthew Dorf, 'Is Irving Moskowitz a Hero or just a Rogue', Jewish Telegraphic Agency (26 Sept. 1997): <http://www.jewishsf.com/content/2–0-/module/displaystory/story_id/7083/edition_id/133/format/html/displaystory.html>

47. Halper and Clarke, *America Alone*, 108. Brian Whitaker, 'Selective MEMRI. Is the "Independent" Media Institute quite what it seems?', *The Guardian* (12 Aug. 2002). *The Guardian* published a letter from Col. Yigal Carmon on 21 Aug. 2002.

48. 'Saudi Academic: Muslim Organizations, Leaders Must Condemn Terrorism – Our Enemies Are Translating Statements of Each and Every [Islamic] Scholar, Imam, and Charity Spokesman', Memri Special Dispatch-Reform Project 1789, 20 Dec. 2007.

49. Juan Cole, 'Repressive MEMRI' (24 Nov. 2004): <http://www.antiwar.com/cole/?articleid=4047>

50. 'Some current or former MEMRI staffers or contributors are Israelis, including Yotam Feldner, MEMRI's director of media analysis. Like Carmon, Feldner worked in military intelligence while serving with the Israeli Defence Forces. Another MEMRI staff member, Aluma Solnik, also worked in military intelligence before joining MEMRI. Other MEMRI staffers come to the organization from various Zionist and Israeli organizations, including the World Zionist Organization.' The archived webpage deleted after 9/11 in which MEMRI stated that 'in its research, the institute puts emphasis on the continuing relevance of Zionism to the Jewish people and to the state of Israel' is particularly significant: <http://rightweb.irc-online.org/profile/1511>

51. David Wurmser, *Tyranny's Ally. America's Failure to Defeat Saddam Hussein* (Washington DC: AEI Press, 1999).

52. Profile of David Wursmer at <http://rightweb.irc-online.org/profile/1392>

53. 'It is important that Jews reach out to him, especially if we want him to deal with the various issues that concern us' (15 Dec. 2000): <http://www.jewishsf.com/content/2-0-/module/displaystory/story_id/15156/edition_id/294/format/html/displayst>

54. Mearsheimer and Walt, 'The Israel Lobby'. Mearsheimer and Walt, *The Israel Lobby and US Foreign Policy*, 251.

55. Profile of Douglas Feith at <http://rightweb.irc-online.org/profile/1146>

56. Julian Borger, 'The Spies who Pushed for War', *The Guardian* (17 July 2003). Jim Lobe, 'Pentagon Office Home to Neo-Con Network', Inter-Press Service (7 Aug. 2003). <http://www.commondreams.org/headlines03/0807-02.htm>

57. R. Jeffrey Smith, 'Hussein's Pre-war Ties to al-Qaeda Discounted', *Washington Post* (6 Apr. 2007).

58. Grant F. Smith, 'Let the AIPAC Spy Trial Begin. Why Prosecuting Weissman and Rosen Matters' (21 Apr. 2006): <http://www.irmep.org/rosweiss.htm>

59. 'Dangerous Prosecution', *Washington Post* (23 Mar. 2006). 'Espionage Lite. Talking about Secrets Becomes a Crime', *Washington Post* (15 Aug. 2006).

60. Dorothy Rabinowitz, 'First they Came for the Jews. A Prosecution under the Espionage Act Threatens the First Amendment', *Wall Street Journal* (2 Apr. 2007). Justin Raimondo, 'First they Came for the Spies. Why is the *Wall Street Journal* in Favour of Espionage?' (4 Apr. 2007): <http://www.antiwar.com/justin/?articleid=10764>

61. Oren Yiftachel, 'Democracy or Ethnocracy. Territory and Settler Politics in Israel/Palestine', *Middle East Report*, 207: <http://www.merip.org/mer/mer207/yift.htm> Extended as '"Ethnocracy". The Politics of Judaizing Israel/Palestine', *Constellations*, 6/3 (1999), 364–90. Oren Yiftachel, *Ethnocracy. Land and Identity Politics in Israel/Palestine* (Philadelphia: University of Pennsylvania Press, 2006). The Palestinian state is perceived as ethnic too, in the sense of being non-Jewish, though Arab nationalism in Palestine has traditionally been multi-confessional: Virginia Tilley, 'From "Jewish State and Arab State" to "Israel and Palestine"? International Norms, Ethnocracy and the Two-State Solution', *Arab World Geographer*, 8/3 (2005), 140–6, at 145.

62. Quoted in the profile of Natan Sharansky at <http://rightweb.irc-online.org/profile/1352>

63. Ian Black, 'Netanyahu Confirms Secret Attack on Syria', *The Guardian* (21 Sept. 2007). Uzi Mahnaimi, Sarah Baxter, Michael Sheridan, 'Israelis "Blew apart Syrian Nuclear Cache". Secret Raid on Korean Shipment', *The Times* (16 Sept. 2007). Uzi Mahnaimi and Sarah Baxter, 'Israelis Seized Nuclear Material in Syrian Raid', *Sunday Times* (23 Sept. 2007).

64. James Petras, 'Why Condemning Israel and the Zionist Lobby is so Important' (22 Dec. 2006): <http://petras.lahaine.org/articulo.php?p=1688&more=1&c=1>

65. For the exaggeration and evidential weakness of Dershowitz's work, the fullest documentation is Norman G. Finkelstein, *Beyond Chutzpah. On the Misuse of Anti-Semitism and the Abuse of History* (London: Verso, 2005).

66. Mearsheimer and Walt 'The Israel Lobby', *London Review of Books*, 28/9 (11 May 2006).

67. Mearsheimer and Walt, *The Israel Lobby and US Foreign Policy*, 346.

68. Ibid. 163. Little, *American Orientalism*, 110. James D. Bessert, 'Lieberman didn't Draw Many Extra Jewish Votes', *Jewish News Weekly of North California* (10 Feb. 2000).

69. 'Jewish Vote a Key Factor in Narrow Bush Victory', Israelinsider.com (3 Nov. 2004), which put the figure at 25 per cent. 'The American Jewish Vote', National Jewish Democratic Council (26 Mar. 2006): <http://www.njdc.org/> provides a conclusive analysis of the 2004 result. This estimates that, among subgroups in the Jewish population, men under 30 (Bush 35%) and Jews who attended synagogue weekly were the most likely to vote Republican. Jewish women under 30 gave 88% of their votes to Kerry and those over 60 gave 90% of their votes to Kerry.

70. Mearsheimer and Walt, *The Israel Lobby and US Foreign Policy*, 341.

71. See above, 68, n. 55. Cook, *Israel and the Clash of Civilizations*, 90–2. Mearsheimer and Walt note that Pastor John Hagee repeated these words at the AIPAC conference in March 2007 and drew 'multiple standing ovations': Mearsheimer and Walt, *The Israel Lobby and US Foreign Policy*, 301.

72. <www.aipac.org/Publications/SpeechesByPolicymakers/Hagee-PC-2007.pdf>

73. Cook, *Israel and the Clash of Civilizations*, 53. Press conference by the President, 17 October 2007: <http://www.whitehouse.gov/news/releases/2007/10/20071017.html>

74. Cook, *Israel and the Clash of Civilizations*, 76–7. According to the translation by Professor Juan R. Cole in May 2006 (before Olmert's speech was delivered), Ahmadinejad had stated on 26 October 2005: 'the Imam [Khomeini] said that this regime occupying Jerusalem (*een rezhim-e ishghalgar-e qods*) must [vanish from] from the page of time (*bayad az safheh-ye ruzgar mahv shavad*).' <http://www.juancole.com/2006/05/hitchens-hacker-and-hitchens.html> MEMRI had translated the same passage as: 'Imam [Khomeini] said: 'this regime that is occupying Qods [Jerusalem] must be eliminated from the pages of history.' The term 'eliminated' sounded more threatening than 'vanish', which was ambiguous. Even so, even MEMRI's translation does not include the word 'Holocaust': <http://www.memri.org/bin/articles.cgi?Page=archives&Area=sd&ID=SP101305>

75. <http://www.rense.com/general77/noor.htm> Is Ahmadinejad a second Hitler, as Netanyahu claims? Mearsheimer and Walt argue merely that his 'irresponsible statements and bellicose attitudes have made a difficult situation worse' (*The Israel Lobby and US Foreign Policy*, 304).

*Chapter Six: 'Rapture', the Theo-cons ,and the Christian Right in US Politics*

1. Peter Stothard, 'The Town of the Rising Son', Times Online (17 July 2004): <http://www.timesonline.co.uk/tol/comment/article703896.ece>

2. Ibid.

3. Frontline interview with Richard Land, 18 Nov. 2003 and 4 Feb. 2004: <http://www.pbs.org/wgbh/pages/frontline/shows/jesus/interviews/land.html>

4. Stothard, 'The Town of the Rising Son'.

5. Tim LaHaye and Jerry B. Jenkins, *In the Twinkling of an Eye. The Rapture. Countdown to the Earth's Last Days* (Carol Stream, IL: Tyndale House, 2006), 275, 333, 343.

6. The official website is at <http://leftbehind.com/>

7. *Concerning the Coming of our Lord Jesus Christ and our being Gathered to Him* ... (2

*Thess. 2:1). A Lutheran Response to the 'Left Behind' Series* (A Report of the Commission on Theology and Church Relations of the Lutheran Church – Missouri Synod, Apr. 2004).

8. Nicholas D. Kristof, 'Jesus and *Jihad*', *New York Times* (17 July 2004).

9. Tim LaHaye and Ed Hindson, *Global Warning. Are We on the Brink of World War III?* (Eugene, OR: Harvest House, 2007), 89, 97, 99, 118, 127, 133, 138, 139, 205. Ezra HaLevi, 'Israel Warns World War III May be Biblical War of Gog and Magog', IsraelNN.com (18 Oct. 2007): <http://www.israelnationalnews.com/News/News.aspx/123961>

10. In Edward Irving's London church, in 1830, a young girl named Margaret McDonald uttered an ecstatic prophecy in which she claimed there would be a special *secret* coming of the Lord to 'rapture' those awaiting His return. LaHaye thus rejects this prophecy and the theology associated with it.

11. LaHaye and Hindson, *Global Warning*, 167–8.

12. Ian S. Markham, 'Engaging with the Theology that Really Sells', *Conversations in Religion and Theology*, 1/2 (2003), 115–23, at 120.

13. John Nelson Darby, 'The Rapture of the Saints and the Character of the Jewish Remnant': <http://www.stempublishing.com/authors/darby/PROPHET/11007E.html>

14. 'Why Christians Must Keep Israel Strong. Southern Baptist Leader Richard Land Explains the Theological Reasons behind Evangelical Christian Support of Israel.' Interview by Deborah Caldwell: <http://www.beliefnet.com/story/106/story_10697_1.html>

15. Bill Berkowitz, 'Christian Right Steps up Pro-Israel Lobby', IPS News (26 July 2006). <http://ipsnews.net/news.asp?idnews=34110>

16. Rebecca Spence, 'As Evangelical Firebrand Hooks up with Federations, Liberals Speak out', *Forward. The Jewish Daily* (4 May 2007).

17. Berkowitz, 'Christian Right Steps up Pro-Israel Lobby'.

18. <http://www.cufi.org/> (accessed 31 May 2007).

19. Vali Nasr and Ray Takeyh, 'The Costs of Containing Iran. Washington's Misguided New Middle East Policy', *Foreign Affairs*, (Jan./Feb. 2008).

20. 'W. A. Criswell, perhaps aside from Billy Graham the most famous Southern Baptist, was travelling to Israel and met with David Ben Gurion in the early 1950s and was leading trips over there and was preaching from his Dallas pulpit in the early 1950s that the Jews going back into the land was a fulfilment of biblical prophecy.' 'Why Christians Must Keep Israel Strong'.

21. Charles Y. Glock and Rodney Stark, *Christian Beliefs and Anti-Semitism* (New York: Harper and Row, 1966), 120, 146.

22. William Martin, 'Is Billy Graham an Anti-Semite?' <http://www.beliefnet.com/story/102/story_10213_1.html>

23. Ibid.

24. Richard Land, 'Keep the Faith': <http://www.beliefnet.com/story/102/story_10211_1.html>

25. Norman G. Finkelstein, *The Holocaust Industry. Reflections on the Exploitation of Jewish Suffering* (2nd edn: London and New York: Verso, 2003), 31–2.

26. 'Why Christians Must Keep Israel Strong'.

27. Robert Ruby, 'A Six-Day War. Its Aftermath in American Public Opinion', Pew Forum on Religion and Public Life (30 May 2007): <http://pewresearch.org/pubs/491/six-day-war>

28. Clyde Wilcox, 'Radical Dreams and Political Realities. Religion and Social Movements in the United States', in Christiane Timmerman, Dirk Hutesbaut, Sara Mels, Walter Nonneman, and Walter Van Herck (eds), *Faith-based Radicalism. Christianity, Islam and Judaism between Constructive Activism and Destructive Fanaticism* (Brussels: Peter Lang, 2007), 241.

29. <http://www.liberty.edu/index.cfm?PID=6921>

30. <http://www.moralmajority.us/>

31. John Hagee, 'Dr Jerry Falwell. A Pioneer of Christian Zionism': <http://www.cufi.org/hagee-falwell.aspx>

32. 'ADL Condemns Falwell's Anti-Muslim Remarks; Urges Him to Apologize' (4 Oct. 2002): <http://www.adl.org/PresRele/DiRaB_41/4168_41.htm> Cf. Bonney, *Jihad from Qur'an to bin Laden*, 45.

33. Friedman, *The Neo-Conservative Revolution*, 225.

34. <http://www.adl.org/special_reports/buchanan_own_words/buchanan_intro.asp>

35. Patrick J. Buchanan, 'Whose War? A Neo-Conservative Clique Seeks to Ensnare our Country in a Series of Wars that are not in America's Interest', *The American Conservative* (24 Mar. 2003).

36. 'Robertson Suggests God Smote Sharon. Evangelist Links Israeli Leader's Stroke to "Dividing God's Land"' (6 Jan. 2006): <http://www.cnn.com/2006/US/01/05/robertson.sharon/>

'What they are Saying: Evangelicals Speak Out on Pat Robertson' (9 Jan. 2006): <http://www.adl.org/main_Interfaith/Evangelicals.htm>

37. Murray Friedman, *The Neo-Conservative Revolution. Jewish Intellectuals and the Shaping of Public Policy* (New York: Cambridge University Press, 2005), 218.

38. <http://www.cc.org/about.cfm>

39. Richard John Neuhaus, 'Ralph Reed's Real Agenda', *First Things* (Oct. 1996).

40. Jim Lobe, 'Conservative Christians in US Biggest Backers of War on Iraq' (Oct. 2002): <http://www.twnside.org.sg/title/2414.htm>

41. Friedman, *The Neo-Conservative Revolution*, 221.

42. <http://www.theocracywatch.org/taking_over.htm>

43. Christian Smith et al., *American Evangelicalism. Embattled and Thriving* (Chicago and London: University of Chicago Press, 1998), 150–1.

44. Steve Bruce, 'Zealot Politics and Democracy. The Case of the New Christian Right', *Political Studies*, 48 (2000), 263–82.

45. Friedman, *The Neo-Conservative Revolution*, 221.

46. Frontline interview with Richard Land, 18 Nov. 2003 and 4 Feb. 2004: <http://www.pbs.org/wgbh/pages/frontline/shows/jesus/interviews/land.html>

47. Robert Parham, executive director of the Baptist Center for Ethics in Nashville, Tenn., quoted by Bill Berkowitz, 'Land Roving', Media Transparency.org (7 Apr. 2007).

48. Robert Parham quoted by Louis Jacobson 'Evangelical Christian lobbyist Richard Land '69' (14 Dec. 2005): <http://www.princeton.edu/~paw/web_exclusives/plus/plus_121405land.html>

49. 'Carter and Clinton Call for "New Baptist Covenant"', *Baptist Press* (10 Jan. 2007): <http://www.bpnews.net/bpnews.asp?id=24745>

'Baptist Leaders Convene at the Carter Centre. Announce Plans for 2008 Convocation in Atlanta': <http://www.newbaptistcovenant.org/release010907.icm>

50. Quoted by David Domke, *God Willing? Political Fundamentalism in the White House, the 'War on Terror' and the Echoing Press* (London and Ann Arbor, MI: Pluto Press, 2004), 16.

51. Bush in February 2003, quoted ibid. 63.

52. Blumenthal, *How Bush Rules. Chronicles of a Radical Regime*, 110–11.

53. *Washington Times*, 23 Oct. 2006, quoted at <http://rightweb.irc-online.org/profile/1343>

54. Domke, *God Willing? Political Fundamentalism in the White House*, 3–4.

55. <http://www.newbaptistcovenant.org/about.icm>

56. Jimmy Carter, 'Americans Need to Know the Facts about the Abominable Oppression of the Palestinians', *The Guardian* (12 Dec. 2006).

57. Proclamation of the Third International Christian Zionist Congress (1996): <http://christianactionforisrael.org/congress.html>

58. According to Arnold G. Fruchtenbaum the invasion of Israel in Ezekiel chs. 38 and 39 is a pre-tribulational event, though not necessarily pre-rapture: <http://www.tribulation.com/prt_gog.htm>

59. Statement by the Patriarch and Local Heads of Churches in Jerusalem entitled 'The Jerusalem Declaration on Christian Zionism' (22 Aug. 2006): <http://www.voltairenet.org/article144310.html> The signatories were: His Beatitude Patriarch Michel Sabbah, Latin Patriarchate, Jerusalem; Archbishop Swerios Malki Mourad, Syrian Orthodox Patriarchate, Jerusalem; Bishop Riah Abu El-Assal, Episcopal Church of Jerusalem and the Middle East; and Bishop Munib Younan, Evangelical Lutheran Church in Jordan and the Holy Land.

60. Jeremiah Hineman, 'A Few Simple Reasons why God is not a Democrat' (May 2004): <http://www.driventoone.com/May2004.html>

61. <http://www.raptureready.com/republican.html> accessed 4 June 2007.

62. Mark Stricherz, 'Primary Colours. How a Little-Known Task Force Helped Create Red State/Blue State America' (23 Nov. 2003): <http://www.boston.com/news/globe/ideas/articles/2003/11/23/primary_colors/>

Mark Stricherz, 'The Anti-Christianity Party' (Apr. 2007): <http://www.crisismagazine.com/april2007/book1.htm>

This is a review of David Carlin, *Can a Catholic be a Democrat? How the Party I Loved Became the Enemy of my Religion* (Manchester, NH: Sophia Institute Press, 2006). Carlin argues 'that on issues of human life, sex, faith, morality, suffering – and the public policies that stem from them – the modern, secularist Democratic Party has become the enemy of Catholicism; indeed, of all traditional religions.'

63. Ross Douthat, 'Theocracy, Theocracy, Theocracy', *First Things* (Aug./Sept. 2006).

64. Jeffey M. Stonecash, Mark D. Brewer, R. Eric Petersen, Mary P. McGuire, Lori Beth Way, 'Class and Party. Secular Realignment and the Survival of the Democrats outside the South', *Political Research Quarterly*, 53/4 (Dec. 2000), 731–52.

65. William Rusher, 'Are the Theocons Taking Over?' (26 Oct. 2006): <http://www.townhall.com/columnists/WilliamRusher/2006/10/26/are_the_theocons_taking_over>

66. <http://www.theocracywatch.org/>

67. <http://www.SeekGod.ca/ect3.htm>

68. David Martin, 'Beware, Beware', *Times Literary Supplement* (15 Dec. 2006), 10.

69. <http://www.adherents.com/largecom/com_romcath.html>
<http://www.adherents.com/rel_USA.html#Pew_branches>

70. Blumenthal, *How Bush Rules. Chronicles of a Radical Regime*, 111. Blumenthal's contention was that Bush won 55% of the Catholic vote in 2004. This has been amended to 52% here, based on '63% of Catholics voted in the 2004 Presidential Election' (Centre for Applied Research in the Apostolate, Georgetown University, 22 Nov. 2004): <www. cara.georgetown.edu/Press112204.pdf> Robert Worcester, 'America's Crucial "Swing"', *Tablet* (13 Nov. 2004). There was a 3.5% swing among Catholic voters as against 2000, when 47% of Catholics voted for Bush (only 2% less than for Gore, at 49%).

71. From 1996 to 2005, the IRPL received close to $9 million in grants from right-wing organizations such as the Lynde and Harry Bradley Foundation, the Sarah Scaife Foundation, the John M. Olin Foundation, Castle Rock Foundation, and Carthage Foundation, mostly to assist the publication *First Things*: <http://mediatransparency.org/recipientgrants.php?recipientID=175>

72. Friedman, *The Neo-Conservative Revolution*, 133.

73. <http://www.eppc.org/about/pageID.1/default.asp>

74. Richard John Neuhaus, 'Iraq and the Moral Judgement', *First Things* (Oct. 2005): <http://www.firstthings.com/>

75. Richard John Neuhaus, 'The Sounds of Religion in a Time of War', *First Things* (May 2003).

76. Right Web profile of Richard John Neuhaus: rightweb.irc-online.org.

77. Richard John Neuhaus, 'Religious Freedom in a Time of War', *First Things* (Jan. 2002).

78. Richard John Neuhaus, 'The Two Hundred-Year War', *First Things* (Apr. 2006).

79. George Weigel, 'World Order. What Catholics Forgot', *First Things* (May 2004).

80. Brian Orend, 'Is there a Supreme Emergency Exemption?', in Mark Evans (ed.), *Just War Theory. A Reappraisal* (Edinburgh: Edinburgh University Press, 2005), 151.

81. Damon Linker, *The Theocons. Secular America under Siege* (New York: Doubleday, 2006), 123–4.

82. Ibid. 124.

83. The Editors [= Richard John Neuhaus], 'In a Time of War', *First Things* (Dec. 2001).

84. Norman Russell, 'Regensburg Revisited', *Tablet* (8 Sept. 2007), 9.

85. Tom Henegen, 'Vatican Disappoints Muslim Scholars', *Tablet* (27 Oct. 2007). John Hooper, 'Pope Agrees to Talks with Muslim Leaders', *The Guardian* (1 Dec. 2007). The Pope had been 'particularly impressed by the attention given in the letter [from the 138 Muslim scholars] to the two-fold commandment to love God and one's neighbour'.

86. Linker, *The Theocons*, 64.

87. <http://www.ird-renew.org/site/apps/nl/content2.asp?c=fvKVLfMVIsG&b=391221&ct=4410995>

88. Andrew J. Weaver, 'Neo-Con Catholics Target Mainline Protestants. Institute on Religion and Democracy Leads to [a] Serious Breach of Ecumenical Good Will', Media Transparency.org (11 Aug. 2006).

89. 'Vatican links "Christianophobia" to war on terror', *Tablet* (11 Dec. 2004), 31.

90. Based on reports in *the Tablet* dated 30 Aug. 2003, 7 Aug. 2004, 23 Oct. 2004, 23 July 2005, 18 Nov. 2006, 25 Nov. 2006, 26 May 2007, 2 June 2007, and 30 June 2007. Nina Shea, 'Iraq's Endangered Minorities', *Washington Post* (27 Aug. 2007). Michael Luo, 'Iraq's Christians Flee as Extremist Threat Worsens', *New York Times* (17 Oct. 2006). Peter Ford, 'Iraqi Christians wary of Islamists', *Christian Science Monitor* (21 Apr. 2003). 'Pope Greatly Concerned about the Fate of Christians in Iraq', *International Herald Tribune* (21 June 2007).

91. Keith Roderick, 'Iraq's Christian Exodus. Targeted by All Sides, Christians Must Choose to Leave, or Stay and Face Death', National Review Online (30 July 2007).

92. Damon Linker, 'Mitt Romney's theo-conservatism', *The Guardian* (7 Dec. 2007). Robert Weitzel, 'Mitt Romney: Tabernacle Choirboy or Blackwater Mercenary?', Countercurrents.org (19 Dec. 2007).

93. 'The War over the Wonks', Washingtonpost.com (2 Oct. 2007).

94. Kevin Zeese, 'Will Republicans nominate an Evangelical Minister to be Commander In Chief?', Countercurrents.org (22 Dec. 2007). Also Stan Moody, 'President Huckabee: "No Room In The Inn". Gov. Mike Huckabee shows all the signs of being a Christian Zionist', ibid. (20 Dec. 2007).

95. Michael Finnegan, 'Christian Right is Split over GOP Field', *Los Angeles Times* (1 Oct. 2007). Daniel Pipes, 'Giuliani's Fresh Start', published under the title 'Rudy Giuliani is no George W. Bush', *Jerusalem Post* (17 Oct. 2007). Amy Schatz, 'Republicans Court a Sceptical Bloc', *Wall Street Journal* (20 Oct. 2007). Jason Horowitz, 'I, Podhoretz: Mr World War IV Tutors Giuliani. Neo-Con Patriarch Sells Rudy Islamo-fascism and Thirty Years' War', *New York Observer* (23 Oct. 2007). Michael Cooper and Marc Santora, 'Mideast Hawks Help to Develop Giuliani Policy', *New York Times* (25 Oct. 2007). Mary Shaw, 'Is God Running For President?', Countercurrents.org (31 Oct. 2007). Michael Tomasky, 'This is One Dangerous Man. It's George Bush with Brains', *The Guardian* (5 Nov. 2007). Rick Klein and Jennifer Parker, 'Christian Right Split Over GOP. Christian Conservatives in Disarray Over 2008 Republican Candidates', ABC News (7 Nov. 2007). Libby Quaid, 'Analysis. Right Splinters on GOP Field', Associated Press (7 Nov. 2007). 'Pat Robertson

endorses Giuliani. Conservative Religious Leader's Nod Seen as Helpful on Social Issue Concerns', MSNBC.com (7 Nov. 2007). Michael D. Shear and Alec MacGillis, 'Consensus Lacking in GOP Endorsements. Evangelical Vote still Appears Divided', *Washington Post* (8 Nov. 2007). Mary Jacoby and Susan Davis, 'Robertson's Support of Giuliani Underscores Evangelical Divide', *Wall Street Journal* (8 Nov. 2007). Suzanne Goldenberg, 'Rightwing Televangelist Boosts Giuliani's Presidential Hopes', *The Guardian* (8 Nov. 2007). Ewen MacAskill, 'Giuliani Leaves Trail of Doubt amid Republican Applause', *The Guardian* (9 Nov. 2007).

96. Karen Armstrong interviewed by Andrea Bistrich, 'Divisions in our World are not the Result of Religion', Countercurrents.org (14 Nov. 2007).

97. Jimmy Carter interviewed by Bill McGarvey and Mike Hayes, nd, BustedHalo.com.

98. Jimmy Carter, *Our Endangered Values. America's Moral Crisis* (New York: Simon and Schuster, 2005), 45. Carter, *Faith and Freedom. The Christian Challenge for the World* (New York: Simon and Schuster, 2005; London: Duckworth, 2006), 32. *Faith and Freedom* is basically the same book as *Our Endangered Values*, but directed towards an international rather than a domestic audience.

99. Ayelish McGarvey, 'Carter's Crusade. Jimmy Carter Explains how the Christian Right isn't Christian at All', Prospect.Org (5 Apr. 2004). Bob Allen, 'Carter Blasts Fundamentalism, Southern Baptist Leaders, in New Book', EthicsDaily.com (4 Nov. 2005). 'I think it was in 1979 when future fundamentalists took control of the Southern Baptist Convention,' and it became increasingly fundamentalist: Jeff Fleischer, 'The Former President Traces America's "Moral Crisis" to the Rise of Fundamentalism', MotherJones.com (2 June 2006).

100. David Domke and Kevin Coe, *The God Strategy. How Religion Became a Political Weapon in America* (New York: Oxford University Press, 2008), 19, 26, 107, 115. The authors' website contains appendices of the main terms analysed as well as the full list of speeches: <http://www.thegodstrategy.com/book.htm>

101. Bill Berkowitz, 'Slouching toward Theocracy. President Bush's Faith-Based Initiative is Doing Better than You Think', Dissidentvoice.org (9 Feb. 2004).

102. The title of the initiative: <http://www.whitehouse.gov/news/reports/faithbased.html>. The official site for the Office of Faith-Based and Community Initiatives: <http://www.whitehouse.gov/government/fbci/>

103. Hanna Rosin, 'Beyond Belief', *Atlantic Monthly* (Jan./Feb. 2005). Bob Allen, 'Southern Baptist Leader Cites Affinity for Pope', EthicsDaily.com (12 Jan. 2005). Brian Kaylor, 'Richard Land Doesn't Get Baptist "Covenant"', ibid. (15 Jan. 2007).

104. Ewen MacAskill, 'Manual Exposes Divide-and-Rule Tactics in Camp Delta', *The Guardian* (15 Nov. 2007). *The Guardian* website offered its readers the chance to download the .pdf file of the manual.

105. Carter's published comments on the 'rapture' theology were more restrained: Carter, *Our Endangered Values*, 144–5. Carter, *Faith and Freedom*, 114.

106. James Traub, 'Does Abe Foxman Have an Anti-Anti-Semite Problem?', *New York Times* (14 Jan. 2007).

107. Jimmy Carter, *Palestine. Peace not Apartheid* (New York: Simon and Schuster, 2006), 194.

108. Anders Strindberg, 'Forgotten Christians. Not all Displaced Palestinians are Muslims', *American Conservative* (24 May 2004).

109. Riah Abu El-Assal, *Caught in Between. The Extraordinary Story of an Arab Palestinian Christian Israeli* (London: SPCK, 1999), 154. Belatedly, the Rt Rev. Rowan Williams, Archbishop of Canterbury, has condemned Christian neo-Zionist theology, but in a little-known Muslim magazine not in an interview for the Christian media: Abul Taher, 'US is "Worst" Imperialist: Archbishop', *Sunday Times* (25 Nov. 2007). Ruth Gledhill, 'Archbishop

of Canterbury … Gets Political Blessing for his Attack on America's Foreign Policy', *The Times* (26 Nov. 2007). Williams told his interviewer that he found Christian Zionism 'not at all easy to accept', adding that it was connected with the 'chosen national myth of America, meaning that what happens in America is very much at the heart of God's purpose for humanity'. Stephen Bates, 'Archbishop Thrown into Row over US Middle East Policy', *The Guardian* (26 Nov. 2007).

110. Ron Suskind, 'Faith, Certainty and the Presidency of George W. Bush', *New York Times Magazine* (17 Oct. 2004).

111. Frank Luntz Republican Playbook – Searchable Text Version: New Ameican Lexicon – Part X, 'Appendix: The 14 Words Never to Use': <http://www.politicalcortex.com/special/Luntz_NAL_Appendix_14_Words>

112. Matt Bai, 'The Framing Wars', *New York Times Magazine* (17 July 2005).

113. Jim Wallis, 'The Message Thing', *New York Times* (4 Aug. 2005).

114. Jim Wallis, 'Dangerous Religion. George W. Bush's Theology of Empire', *Sojourners Magazine* (Sept.–Oct. 2003).

115. 'Rumsfeld on Terrorists: Drain the Swamp they Live in', American Forces Press Service (18 Sept. 2001): <http://www.defenselink.mil/news/newsarticle.aspx?id=44863>

116. Wallis, 'Dangerous Religion'.

117. 'Senator Feinstein Urges Defense Department Action on General Boykin's Remarks', 21 Oct. 2003: <http://feinstein.senate.gov/03Releases/r-boykin.htm>

118. 'Rumsfeld Defends General who Commented on War and Satan', Cnn.com (17 Oct. 2003). After a ten-month investigation the Department of Defense concluded that he had broken three rules in giving the speeches but did not consider his actual remarks because 'freedom of expression considerations under the First Amendment to the US Constitution apply in this case'.

119. 'General Faulted for Satan Speeches. Boykin's Remarks on Terrorism and Religion Violated Pentagon Rules', CBSnews.com (19 Aug. 2004).

120. Esther Kaplan, *With God on Their Side. George W. Bush and the Christian Right* (New York: New Press, 2005), 21.

121. Ibid. 281.

*Chapter Seven: Regime Change? Assertive Nationalism Captures the White House Post-9/11*

1. Interview with William Kristol (14 Jan. 2003): <http://www.pbs.org/wgbh/pages/frontline/shows/iraq/interviews/kristol.html>

2. Irving Kristol, 'The Neoconservative Persuasion. What it was, and What it is', *Weekly Standard*, 8/47 (25 Aug. 2003).

3. Michael Lind, 'A Tragedy of Errors', *The Nation* (23 Feb. 2004).

4. Gregory Bruce Smith, 'Leo Strauss and the Straussians. An Anti-Democratic Cult?', *Political Science and Politics*, 30/2 (1997), 180–9, at 187.

5. The jury remains out: Edward Rothstein, 'Democracy's Best Friend or Anti-Democratic Elitist?', *New York Times* (10 July 2006). Robert Alter, 'Neo-Con or Not?', *New York Times* (25 June 2006). James Atlas, 'The Nation. Leo-Cons. A Classicist's Legacy. New Empire Builders', *New York Times* (4 May 2003). For Fukuyama: *After the Neocons*, 21. For Wolfowitz: 'It's a product of fevered minds who seem incapable of understanding that September 11th changed a lot of things and changed the way we need to approach the world. Since they refused to confront that, they looked for some kind of conspiracy theory to explain it. I mean I took two terrific courses from Leo Strauss as a graduate student. One was on Montesquieu's spirit of the laws, which did help me understand our Constitution better. And one was on Plato's laws. The idea that this has anything to do with US foreign policy is just laughable … Wohlstetter is a much more relevant figure and it's interesting too, by the way, that the same fellow who, or one of the same fellows who discovered the

Straussian Conspiracy kind of throws Wohlstetter in as a Straussian when Wohlstetter was actually philosophically a student of Quine. If there was anything anathema to Leo Strauss it was analytical philosophy ... Wohlstetter was somebody who really just almost painfully resisted being labelled even as to political party. He was so insistent on ascertaining the facts. He had a very fact-based approach to policy ...' Deputy Secretary Wolfowitz's interview with Sam Tannenhaus, *Vanity Fair*, 9 May 2003: <http://www.defenselink.mil/transcripts/transcript.aspx?transcriptid=2594>

6. Anne Norton, *Leo Strauss and the Politics of American Empire* (New Haven and London: Yale University Press, 2004), 10, 16, 18.

7. Seymour M. Hersh, 'Selective Intelligence. Donald Rumsfeld has his own Special Sources. Are they Reliable?' *New Yorker* (12 May 2003).

8. Abram N. Shulsky and Gary J. Schmitt, *Silent Warfare. Understanding the World of Intelligence* (3rd edn Washington DC: Potomac Books, 2002), 176.

9. 'Danny Postel Interviews Shadia Drury – a Leading Scholarly Critic of Strauss – and Asks her about the Connection between Plato's Dialogues, Secrets and Lies, and the United States-led War in Iraq', OpenDemocracy (18 Oct. 2003). Jim Lobe, 'Leo Strauss' Philosophy of Deception', AlterNet (19 May 2003). Jim Lobe, 'Neocons Dance a Strauss Waltz', Asia Times.com (9 May 2003).

10. John G. Mason, 'Leo Strauss and the Noble Lie. The Neo-Cons at War' (Mar. 2004): <http://www.logosjournal.com/mason.htm>

11. 'Danny Postel Interviews Shadia Drury ...'

12. Irving Kristol, 'The Neo-Conservative Persuasion'. Cf. also Norton, *Leo Strauss and the American Empire*, 176–9.

13. Knowledge of the President's remarks, and the closure of PNAC and its integration into AEI, would have altered some of the conclusions in Abelson's useful study, which went to press too early to include them: Donald E. Abelson, *A Capitol Idea. Think Tanks and US Foreign Policy* (Montreal: McGill-Queen's University Press, 2006). Ibid. 239–41, Abelson notes that 23 individuals at AEI have held government positions. Remarks by the President on the Global War on Terror, 15 Feb. 2007: <http://www.aei.org/publications/pubID.25630,filter.all/pub_detail.asp>

14. <http://www.mediatransparency.org/recipientgrants.php?recipientID=19>

15. Abelson, *A Capitol Idea*, 238.

16. Ibid. 157.

17. Ibid. 172–8.

18. Ibid. 217–18, 221, 223.

19. Ibid. 221, 223–4. Ivo H. Daalder and James M. Lindsay, *America Unbound. The Bush Revolution in Foreign Policy* (Washington DC: Brookings Institution Press, 2003), 16.

20. Ibid. 15.

21. Stephen Eric Bronner, 'Is Neo-Conservatism Dead?', *The Guardian* (31 Aug. 2007).

22. Robert G. Kaufman, *In Defense of the Bush Doctrine* (Lexington: University Press of Kentucky, 2007), 112.

23. <http://lieberman.senate.gov/newsroom/release.cfm?id=276719>

24. Lewis D. Solomon, *Paul D. Wolfowitz. Visionary Intellectual, Policymaker and Strategist* (Westport, CT: Praeger Security International, 2007), 15.

25. Friedman, *The Neo-Conservative Revolution*, 158–60. Ibid. 79, where Friedman traces the beginning of Irving Kristol's move away from his earlier liberal beliefs.

26. Michael Novak, 'Neo-Cons. Some Memories', National Review Online (20 May 2003).

27. Friedman, *The Neo-Conservative Revolution*, 137. Friedman states the late 1960s, Michael Lind, 'A Tragedy of Errors', *Nation* (23 Feb. 2004), the early 1970s.

28. <http://www.ips.org/blog/jimlobe/?p=60>

29. Daniel Pipes, 'A Neo-Conservative's Caution', *New York Sun* (8 Mar. 2005).

30. Bizarrely, given its aggressive tenor, the article from *Foreign Affairs* was reprinted on the website of the Carnegie Endowment for International Peace. This was explicable only because Robert Kagan was at the institution concerned: <http://www.carnegieendowment.org/publications/index.cfm?fa=view&id=276>

31. Walter A. McDougall, 'Why Some Neo-Cons are Wrong about US Foreign Policy' (Dec. 1997): <http://www.fpri.org/pubs/nightthoughts.199712.mcdougall.neoconswrong.html>

32. But cf. Norton, *Leo Strauss and the Politics of the American Empire*, 191–2.

33. Robert Kagan and William Kristol (eds), *Present Dangers. Crisis and Opportunity in American Foreign and Defense Policy* (San Francisco: Encounter, 2000), 307, 316. Solomon quotes from the essay briefly, and states that 'Wolfowitz, perhaps with a slight exaggeration, asserted that the 1992 document formed a consensus view of America's post-Cold War strategy'. Solomon, *Paul D. Wolfowitz*, 53.

34. Kagan and Kristol (eds), *Present Dangers*, 200.

35. Ibid. 309.

36. Ibid. 318. Cf. ibid. 112, 132–3, 134, 136–7. Gerecht noted that Saudi Arabia and Pakistan had more to answer for than Iran, at least in so far as bin Laden was concerned. 'Neither the Sa'udi terrorist Osama bin Laden nor other Sa'udi Wahhabi fundamentalists are ecumenical: they hate Shi'ites' (ibid. 132).

37. Ibid. 333–4.

38. <http://www.newamericancentury.org/statementofprinciples.htm>

39. <http://rightweb.irc-online.org/profile/1315>

40. The report could still be accessed from the PNAC website on 14 June 2007: <http://www.newamericancentury.org/defensenationalsecurity.htm>

41. Letter to Clinton, 26 Jan. 1998:
<http://www.newamericancentury.org/iraqclintonletter.htm>
Letter to Lott and Gingrich, 29 May 1998:
<http://www.newamericancentury.org/iraqletter1998.htm>

42. Peter Bergen, 'Armchair Provocateur. Laurie Mylroie, the Neo-Cons' Favourite Conspiracy Theorist', *Washington Monthly* (Dec. 2003). Richard A. Clarke found it extraordinary that Paul Wolfowitz supported her discredited theories: Clarke, *Against All Enemies*, 95, 232.

43. Laurie Mylroie, 'The Iraqi Connection', *Wall Street Journal* (13 Sept. 2001).

44. Laurie Mylroie, *Bush vs. the Beltway. The Inside Battle over War in Iraq* (New York: Regan Books, 2003). AEI had published her previous book: Laurie Mylroie, *Study of Revenge. Saddam Hussein's Unfinished War against America* (Washington DC: American Enterprise Institute, 2000).

45. PNAC letter to President Bush on the war on terrorism, 20 Sept. 2001: <http://www.newamericancentury.org/Bushletter.htm>

46. Reuel Marc Gerecht, 'Crushing al-Qaeda is Only a Start', *Wall Street Journal* (19 Dec. 2001).

47. PNAC letter to President Bush on Israel, Arafat, and the war on terrorism, 3 Apr. 2002: <http://www.newamericancentury.org/Bushletter-040302.htm>

48. First PNAC statement on Post-War Iraq, 19 Mar. 2003: <http://www.newamericancentury.org/iraq-20030319.htm>

Second PNAC statement on Post-War Iraq, 28 Mar. 2003: <http://www.newamericancentury.org/iraq-20030328.htm>

49. <http://www.nato.int/issues/iraq-assistance/index.html>

50. Paul Reynolds, 'End of the Neo-Con Dream', BBC News (21 Dec. 2006): <http://news.bbc.co.uk/go/pr/fr/-/1/hi/world/middle_east/6189793.stm>

51. PNAC letter to President Bush on the defence budget, 23 Jan. 2003: <http://www.newamericancentury.org/defense-20030123.htm>

52. PNAC letter to Congress on increasing US ground forces, 28 Jan. 2005: <http://www.newamericancentury.org/defense-20050128.htm>

53. Danielle Pletka, 'More isn't Better', *New York Times* (23 Sept. 2003).

54. Frederick W. Kagan, 'The US Military's Manpower Crisis', *Foreign Affairs* (July/Aug. 2006).

55. Frederick W. Kagan, 'Donald Rumsfeld's Self-Inflicted Wounds', *Los Angeles Times* (12 Nov. 2006).

56. Michael Rubin, 'Our Intelligence Community Could Use More Competition', *Weekly Standard* (5 Feb. 2007).

57. <http://www.mediatransparency.org/recipientgrants.php?recipientID=258>

58. Jim Lobe, '"New American Century" Project Ends with a Whimper' (13 June 2006): <http://www.antiwar.com/lobe/?articleid=9132>

59. Richard Perle, 'Four Broad Lessons from Iraq' (7 Apr. 2005; testimony of 6 Apr. 2005): <http://www.aei.org/publications/pubID.22273,filter.all/pub_detail.asp>

60. Oliver Burkeman and Julian Borger, 'War Critics Astonished as US Hawk Admits Invasion was Illegal', *The Guardian* (20 Nov. 2003).

61. Andrew F. Krepinevich, Jr., 'How to Win in Iraq', *Foreign Affairs* (Sept./Oct. 2005).

62. Frederick W. Kagan, 'Choosing Victory. A Plan for Success in Iraq' (5 Jan. 2007): <http://www.aei.org/publications/filter.all,pubID.25396/pub_detail.asp>. Frederick W. Kagan, 'Send More Troops to Baghdad and We'll Have a Fighting Chance', *Sunday Times* (24 Dec. 2006).

Frederick W. Kagan and Jack Keane, 'The Right Type of "Surge"; Any Troop Increase Must be Large and Lasting', *Washington Post* (27 Dec. 2006).

63. Fukuyama, 'After Neo-Conservatism'.

64. Of course, this was not how the National Intelligence Estimate of Jan. 2007 expressed it, but it was how this statement was interpreted. 'Several major American newspapers have interpreted this consensus judgment of all US intelligence agencies as a declaration of defeat': Anwar Iqbal, 'US no Longer in Position to Win Iraq War: Report', *Dawn* (13 Feb. 2006): <http://www.dawn.com/2007/02/13/top15.htm> In the *New York Times*, Nicholas D. Kristof argued that 'maybe a phased withdrawal will nudge Iraqis back from the brink and make a cataclysm less likely': Nicholas D. Kristof, 'Iraqis Show us the Door', *New York Times* (13 Feb. 2007). The NIE of Jan. 2007 was accessed from <http://www.dni.gov/> on 13 Feb. 2007. Eighteen months earlier, Andrew J. Bacevich argued that 'the Bush administration's insistence on staying the course also implicitly assumes that a US withdrawal would leave a dangerous political vacuum in the region. But this assumption too is suspect. More likely, the American departure would foster a political dynamic in which Iraq's neighbours would exert themselves to keep Iraq from spinning out of control – not out of any concern for the well-being of the Iraqi people but out of sheer self-interest.' Andrew J. Bacevich, 'Call it a Day. We've Done All We Can Do in Iraq', *Washington Post* (21 Aug. 2005, page B01).

65. William Kristol, 'The GOP's Moment of Truth. You Get no Credit for Timidity', *Weekly Standard*, 12/22 (19 Feb. 2007).

66. Frederick W. Kagan, 'What We've Accomplished', *Daily Standard* (19 Sept. 2007).

67. Steven R. Weisman, 'Europe Resists US Push to Curb Iran Ties', *New York Times* (30 Jan. 2007). Ian Traynor and Jonathan Steele, 'Europeans Fear US Attack on Iran as Nuclear Row Intensifies', *The Guardian* (31 Jan. 2007), 17.

'US Signals Gulf Allies that Attack on Iran is Possible this Year', Geostrategy.com (by subscription, accessed 19 Jan. 2007): <http://www.geostrategy-direct.com/geostrategy%2Ddirect/secure/2007/01_24/1.asp>

68. 'Perle Confident Bush "Would Order the Necessary Military Action" against Iran', Geostrategy.com (by subscription, accessed 26 Jan. 2007): <http://www.geostrategy-direct.com/geostrategy-direct/secure/2007/01_31/1.asp?>

69. Richard Perle, 'Why did Bush Blink on Iran? (Ask Condi)', AEI Online (21 July 2006): <http://www.aei.org/publications/filter.all,pubID.24691/pub_detail.asp>

70. 'Iranian Dissidents Say Population Ready for Regime Change: Mullahs would "Flee Immediately"', Geostrategy.com (by subscription, accessed 26 Jan. 2007): <http://www.geostrategy-direct.com/geostrategy-direct/secure/2007/01_31/me.asp>

71. David Machlis and Tovah Lazaroff, 'Muslims "About to Take Over Europe" [Lewis]', *Jerusalem Post* (29 Jan. 2007).

72. Francis Fukuyama, 'The Neo-Cons have Learned Nothing from Five Years of Catastrophe', *The Guardian* (31 Jan. 2007), 27.

73. Con Coughlin, 'Ready for War', *Daily Telegraph* (24 Feb. 2007).

74. Ali Ansari, 'Only the US Hawks can Save the Iranian President Now', *The Guardian* (30 Jan. 2007).

75. Helene Cooper and Mark Mazzetti, 'Sceptics Doubt US Evidence on Iran Action in Iraq', *New York Times* (13 Feb. 2007). Julian Borger, 'US Intelligence on Iran does not Stand up, Say Vienna Sources', *The Guardian* (23 Feb. 2007).

76. <http://www.aei.org/publications/pubID.26760/pub_detail.asp>

77. <http://www.weeklystandard.com/Content/Public/Articles/000/000/014/030aryoy.asp>

78. 'Shia extremists, backed by Iran, are training Iraqis to carry out attacks on our forces and the Iraqi people. Members of the Qods Force of Iran's Islamic Revolutionary Guard Corps are supplying extremist groups with funding and weapons, including sophisticated IEDs ... Some say Iran's leaders are not aware of what members of their own regime are doing. Others say Iran's leaders are actively seeking to provoke the West. Either way, they cannot escape responsibility for aiding attacks against coalition forces and the murder of innocent Iraqis. The Iranian regime must halt these actions. And until it does, I will take actions necessary to protect our troops. I have authorized our military commanders in Iraq to confront Tehran's murderous activities.'

79. 'Bush Must Face Trial over Iraq: Iran Leader', Agence France-Presse (15 Sept. 2007).

80. 'US praises Iran curbs on militias in Iraq', Agence France-Presse (24 Dec. 2007).

81. Joshua Frank, 'Hillary's Neocon. The Imperial Vision of Richard Holbrooke', Counterpunch.org (25 July 2007).

82. Jeff Berg, 'Holbrooke's Revelation', Countercurrents.org (29 Nov. 2007). Holbrooke's speech was made at the Toronto Design Exchange on 27 Nov. 2007.

83. 'Fear of US "Grand Bargain" with Iran Sends Saudis to Moscow', Geostrategy-Direct (5 Dec. 2007), by subscription only: <http://www.geostrategy-direct.com/geostrategy-direct/headlines.html>.

84. Zbigniew Brzezinski, 'Hegemonic Quicksand', *National Interest* (winter 2003/4), 15.

85. Frank Rich, 'Noun + Verb + 9/11 + Iran = Democrats' Defeat', *New York Times* (4 Nov. 2007).

86. David Albright and Jacqueline Shire, 'Why a military attack on Iran is not an option', *Arms Control Today* (Nov. 2007).

87. Bruce Riedel, 'Iran: the lesson of September 6', Saban Center for Middle East Policy, Brookings Institution (16 Nov. 2007).

88. Daniel Pipes, 'That NIE Makes War against Iran *More* likely' [JP title: 'Their own worst nightmare'], *Jerusalem Post* (13 Dec. 2007). The reverse position was taken by the Spiegel Online analysts: Erich Follath, Cordula Meyer, and Christoph Schult, 'Intelligence Agencies put brakes on Bush's Iran Plans', SpiegelOnline (10 Dec. 2007).

89. It was termed by those with short memories 'the most politically-motivated assessment by the community since at least the Vietnam War': 'How an intelligence deficit on Iran led to the hijaking of the National Intelligence Estimate', Geostrategy-Direct.com (week of 19 Dec. 2007, by subscription only). The Chairman of the National Intelligence

Council, Thomas Fingar, was allegedly 'highly suspicious of foreign intelligence, particularly that supplied by Israel', while 'CIA director Michael Hayden [was] regarded as inexperienced on, and even hostile to, human intelligence'. Allegedly the Saudis believe that the CIA has fallen to an Iranian disinformation campaign.

90. <http://rawstory.com/news/2007/Neocon_Bill_Kristol_urges_Bush_to_0712.html>

91. William Kristol, 'Why Bush will be a Winner', *Washington Post* (15 July 2007).

92. Pervez Musharraf, *In the Line of Fire. A Memoir* (London and New York: Simon and Schuster, 2006), 201. 'We'll bomb you to Stone Age, US told Pakistan. Musharraf reveals post-9/11 threat in book serialised by *The Times*', *The Times* (22 Sept. 2006).

93. Masood Haider, 'Maleeha Recalls Meetings with Armitage after 9/11', *Dawn* (5 Aug. 2007): <http://www.dawn.com/2007/08/05/top16.htm>

94. Editorial: 'The General's Best Chance', *Washington Post* (29 Aug. 2007).

95. Anthony C. Zinni, 'Musharraf Matters. Stand by our Man in Pakistan', *Washington Post* (9 Sept. 2007).

96. Declan Walsh, 'Bin Laden Tape Urges Uprising against "Infidel" Musharraf as Poll Date is Set', *The Guardian* (21 Sept. 2007). Zahid Hussain and Jeremy Page, 'Bin Laden Calls for *jihad* against Musharraf', *The Times* (21 Sept. 2007). Noor ul Haq (ed.), *Lal Masjid Crisis* (Islamabad: IPRI Factfile, Sept. 2007), 97.

97. Adrian Levy and Cathy Scott-Clark, 'Bush Handed Blueprint to Seize Pakistan's Nuclear Arsenal', *The Guardian* (1 Dec. 2007). Frederick W. Kagan and Michael O'Hanlon, 'Pakistan's Collapse, Our Problem', *New York Times* (18 Nov. 2007) and AEI website. In an interview for *Dawn*, Kagan denied that there was a 'blueprint' or that anything had been handed over to the Bush administration: Anwar Iqbal, '"Joint Force" for Nuke Safety', *Dawn* (2 Dec. 2007). The Pakistan Foreign Office spokesman stated that 'our strategic assets are as safe as those of any other nuclear state. As for the irresponsible conjectures about external contingency plans, suffice it to say that Pakistan possesses adequate retaliatory capacity to defend its strategic assets and sovereignty.' 'US President Advised to Seize N-Assets, says Paper', *Dawn* (2 Dec. 2007).

98. Frederick W. Kagan, 'Spend Whatever it Takes on the War on Terror', *Los Angeles Times* (14 Oct. 2007) and AEI website.

99. 'EU election monitors visit Abbottabad', *Dawn* (18 Jan. 2008). 'Opposition BJP condemns US Policy in Afghanistan [and] Pakistan', India-Defence.com (22 Jan. 2008). Shadaba Islam, 'Musharraf decries West's "obsession" with democracy', *Dawn* (22 Jan. 2008). Mujtaba Ali Ahmad, 'EU to monitor Pakistan poll', Rediff.com (22 Jan. 2008). Khaleeq Kiani, 'President faces tough time defending judges' removal', *Dawn* (25 Jan. 2008). Eric Schmitt and David E. Sanger, 'Pakistan rebuffs secret US plea for CIA buildup', *New York Times* (27 Jan. 2008). Masood Haider, 'Musharraf rejects proposals for US military action', *Dawn* (28 Jan. 2008). 'Security at nuclear facilities boosted', *Dawn* (27 Jan. 2008). Pervez Hoodbhoy, 'Pakistan's Nuclear Threat', *International Herald Tribune* (28 Jan. 2008).

*Chapter Eight: 'Making the World Safer and Better'?*

1. Neta C. Crawford, 'The Justice of Pre-emption and Preventive War Doctrines', in Mark Evans (ed.), *Just War Theory*, 37.

2. Anne-Marie Slaughter, 'A Chance to Reshape the UN', *Washington Post* (13 Apr. 2003), 7.

3. William Crotty, 'On the Home Front. Institutional Mobilization to Fight the Threat of International Terrorism', in Crotty (ed.), *The Politics of Terror. The US Response to 9/11* (Boston, MA: Northeastern University Press, 2004), 194.

4. Richard J. Powell, 'The Presidency Responds. The Implication of 9/11 for the Bush Administration's Policy Agenda', ibid. 261.

5. Crotty, 'On the Home Front', 195.

6. Ibid. 193.
7. Conveniently reprinted by Kaufman, *In Defense of the Bush Doctrine*, 157–83.
8. Crawford, 'The Justice of Pre-emption and Preventive War Doctrines', 25–7, 47.
9. Mark Evans, 'Moral Theory and the Idea of a Just War', ibid. 12–13.
10. Patrick Hayden, 'Security beyond the State. Cosmopolitanism, Peace and the Role of Just War Theory', ibid. 169.
11. Andrew Rigby, 'Forgiveness and Reconciliation in Jus Post Bellum', ibid. 180–1.
12. Mary Kaldor, 'From Just War to Just Peace', in Charles Reed and David Ryall (eds), *The Price of Peace. Just War in the Twenty-First Century* (Cambridge: Cambridge University Press, 2007), 272.
13. Terrence K. Kelly, 'The Just Conduct of War against Radical Islamic Terror and Insurgencies', ibid. 201–15.
14. 'Former Saudi Dissident Slams bin Laden', Agence France-Presse (17 Sept. 2007). The former dissident was Shaikh Salman Al Odah.
15. 'Major Jihadi Cleric and Author of Al-Qaeda's Shari'a Guide to Jihad: 9/11 Was a Sin; A Shari'a Court Should Be Set Up to Hold Bin Laden and Al-Zawahiri Accountable; There Are Only Two Kinds of People in Al-Qaeda – The Ignorant and Those Who Seek Worldly Gain', Memri Special Dispatch-Reform Project / Jihad and Terrorism Studies Project 1785, 14 Dec. 2007.
16. Terrence K. Kelly, 'The Just Conduct of War against Radical Islamic Terror and Insurgencies', 215.
17. George Weigel, 'Moral Clarity in Time of War', *First Things* (1 Jan. 2003). An earlier version of this was delivered as the William E. Simon Lecture (24 Oct. 2002).
18. Aquinas, *Summa Theologiae*, II, II, Q. 40, Art. 1.
19. George Weigel, 'The Development of Just War Thinking in the Post-Cold War World. An American Perspective', in Reed and Ryall (eds), *The Price of Peace*, 34. Much of this is repeated in Weigel, 'Iraq: Then and Now', *First Things* (Apr. 2006).
20. John Langan, 'Justice after War and the International Common Good', in Reed and Ryall (eds), *The Price of Peace*, 228.
21. Ibid. 232–3.
22. Darrin W. Belousek, 'Deconstructing the Reigning Paradigm' (30 Oct. 2005): <http://www.ekklesiaproject.org/content/view/29/46/>
23. Andrew Wilkie, *Axis of Deceit. The Story of the Intelligence Officer who Risked All to Tell the Truth about WMD and Iraq* (Melbourne: Black, 2004), 70. Clarke, *Against All Enemies*, 31.
24. William B. Quandt, 'New US Policies for a New Middle East?', in Lesch (ed.), *The Middle East and the United States*, 497.
25. Ed Pilkington, 'Articles of Faith' [interview with Mearsheimer and Walt], *The Guardian* (15 Sept. 2007).
26. Graham Paterson, 'Alan Greenspan Claims Iraq War was Really for Oil', *Sunday Times* (16 Sept. 2007). Richard Adams, 'Invasion of Iraq was Driven by Oil, says Greenspan', *The Guardian* (17 Sept. 2007). JoAnne Allen, 'Greenspan Clarifies Iraq War and Oil Link', Reuters (17 Sept. 2007).
27. Clarke, *Against All Enemies*, 30–1, 270.
28. Richard Norton-Taylor, 'The Calamity of Disregard', *The Guardian* (4 Aug. 2007).
29. Colin Brown and Andy McSmith, 'Diplomat's Suppressed Document Lays Bare the Lies behind Iraq War', *Independent* (15 Dec. 2006).

Butler inquiry, 2004: supplementary evidence submitted by Mr Carne Ross, Director, Independent Diplomat, released 15 Dec. 2006: <http://news.independent.co.uk/uk/politics/article2076142.ece>

30. Richard Norton-Taylor and Vikram Dodd, 'Kelly: No. 10 Exaggerated the Case for War', *The Guardian* (14 Aug. 2003).

31. <http://www.number-10.gov.uk/output/Page281.asp> Cf. the BBC's own timeline on the claim: <http://news.bbc.co.uk/1/hi/uk_politics/3466005.stm>

32. David Leigh and Richard Norton-Taylor, 'Iraqi who Gave MI6 45-Minute Claim Says it was Untrue', *The Guardian* (27 Jan. 2004). Richard Norton-Taylor and Patrick Wintour, 'Hoon Dismisses 45-Minute Claim as Insignificant', *The Guardian* (6 Feb. 2004). Patrick Wintour and Sam Jones, 'Straw Drops 45-Minute Claim', *The Guardian* (13 Oct. 2004).

33. Stephen Moss, 'Diplomat at Large', *The Guardian* (20 June 2005).

34. Sidney Blumenthal, *How Bush Rules. Chronicles of a Radical Regime* (Princeton and Oxford: Princeton University Press, 2006), 402. Aram Roston and Lisa Myers, 'Iraqi Diplomat Gave US Prewar WMD Details', Msnbc.msn.com (20 Mar. 2006).

35. Sidney Blumenthal, 'Bush Knew Saddam had no Weapons of Mass Destruction' (6 Sept. 2007): <http://www.salon.com/opinion/blumenthal/2007/09/06/bush_wmd/>

36. David Coates and Joel Krieger, *Blair's War* (Cambridge: Polity Press, 2004), 129.

37. Steven Kettell, *Dirty Politics? New Labour, British Democracy and the Invasion of Iraq* (London: Zed Books, 2006), 156–7.

38. David Coates and Joel Krieger, *Blair's War*, 128.

39. Kettell, *Dirty Politics?*, 158–9.

40. Rafid Ahmed Alwan arrived in a German refugee centre in 1999 where he lied to win asylum: 'Iraq War Source's Name Revealed', BBC News 24 (2 Nov. 2007). Alex Koppelman, '"The Man who Sold the War". *Curveball* Author Bob Drogin Talks about the Iraqi Defector Responsible for Much of the CIA's Bogus Pre-war Intelligence about Iraqi WMD', Salon.Com (16 Oct. 2007). For the significance of Curveball: Luke Harding, 'Germans Accuse US over Iraq Weapons Claim', *The Guardian* (2 Apr. 2004). Edward Helmore, 'US Relied on "Drunken Liar" to Justify War', *Observer* (3 Apr. 2005). Also the ABC News images: <http://abcnews.go.com/WNT/popup?id=2948620>

41. Colin L. Powell, 'US Forces: Challenges Ahead', *Foreign Affairs* (winter, 1992).

42. Mark Danner, 'A Doctrine Left Behind', *New York Times* (21 Nov. 2004).

43. Halper and Clarke, *America Alone*, 153.

44. 'Powell regrets UN speech on Iraq WMDs' (ABC News Online, 9 Sept. 2005): <http://www.abc.net.au/news/newsitems/200509/s1456650.htm>

45. Fred Kaplan, 'The Tragedy of Colin Powell. How the Bush Presidency Destroyed him', Slate.com (19 Feb. 2004): <http://www.slate.com/id/2095756/>

46. Steven Strasser (ed.), *The 9/11 Investigations. Staff Reports of the 9/11 Commission. Excepts from the House–Senate Joint Inquiry Report on 9/11. Testimony from 14 Key Witnesses* … (New York: Public Affairs, 2004), 473.

47. '"Why we Know Iraq is Lying". A Column by Dr Condoleezza Rice', *New York Times* (23 Jan. 2003).

48. 'Rice Defends Decision to Go to War in Iraq' (CNN, 22 Oct. 2004): <http://web.archive.org/web/20041117054631/http://www.cnn.com/2004/ALLPOLITICS/10/22/rice.speech.ap/>

49. Halper and Clarke, *America Alone*, 218, 321–2.

50. Not least because Chalabi blurted out to the *Washington Post* that the INC intended to reward its American friends: 'American companies will have a big shot at Iraqi oil', he proclaimed. Robert Dreyfuss, 'Tinker, Banker, NeoCon, Spy. Ahmed Chalabi's Long and Winding Road from (and to?) Baghdad', *American Prospect* (18 Nov. 2002).

51. Seymour M. Hersh, 'Selective Intelligence. Donald Rumsfeld has his own Special Sources. Are they Reliable?' *New Yorker* (12 May 2003).

52. Michael Massing, 'Now they Tell us', *New York Review of Books* (29 Jan. 2004).

53. Neil A. Lewis, 'Libby Given 30 Months for Lying in CIA Leak Case', *New York Times* (6 June 2006); Ewen MacAskill, '"Scooter" Libby Gets 2 1/2 years in Jail for Perjury', *The Guardian* (6 June 2006). Amy Goldstein, 'Bush Commutes Libby's Prison Sentence', *Washington Post* (3 July 2007).

54. Plame told Congress on 16 Mar. 2007 that the leak of her identity as a CIA covert operative had 'jeopardized and even destroyed entire networks of foreign agents': 'Plame Wilson: Leak Severely Hurt US Intelligence', CNN.com (17 Mar. 2007). 'Valerie Plame Wilson: No Ordinary Spy. In her First Interview, Former CIA Officer Speaks to Katie Couric', CBS News (21 Oct. 2007).

55. George Packer, 'Rove's Legacy', *New Yorker* (13 Aug. 2007).

56. Quoted by Blumenthal, *How Bush Rules*, 233.

57. <www.usinfo.state.gov/topical/pol/arms/03031945.htm>

58. Ibid.

59. <www.pm.gov.uk/output/Page3280.asp>

60. 'I accept that in military action such as this there will be innocent civilians that have lost their lives. But I would say to people in Iraq, the numbers that have lost their lives are only a small number compared with the hundreds of thousands that have lost their lives under Saddam': <www.pm.gov.uk/output/page3421.asp>

61. Inayat Bunglawala, 'We Won't Forget the Terrible Things Done in our Name', *The Times* 25 Mar. 2003.

62. Jan Narveson, '"Regime Change". the Case of Iraq', in Cushman (ed.), *A Matter of Principle*, 63–4.

63. Cushman (ed.), *A Matter of Principle*, 338–9.

64. The CIA estimated the population of Iraq in 2007 as 27.5 million, so Blair's figure is probably too low.

65. 'Number of Iraqi Displaced Tops 4.2 million; Shanty Towns Mushroom', Reuters (5 June 2007). Suzanne Goldenberg, 'Refugees in their Own Land: 2m Iraqis Forced to Flee their Homes ... Ethnic Map Redrawn, Says Red Crescent Report', *The Guardian* (20 Sept. 2007).

66. <http://www.iraqbodycount.org/>

67. Gilbert Burnham, Shannon Doocy, Elizabeth Dzeng, Riyadh Lafta, Les Roberts (principal authors), 'The Human Cost of War in Iraq. A Mortality Study, 2002–2006': <web.mit.edu/cis/human-cost-war-101106.pdf>. However, the British had little to be proud of in Iraq either. Jonathan Steele, 'Britain "as inept as US" in failing to foresee post-war Iraq insurgency. Revelation undermines British blaming Rumsfeld. Experts stressed danger of tribalism to Blair in 2002', *The Guardian* (21 Jan. 2008).

68. 'For the single most important category – the total number of deaths by violence during the war – the confidence interval ranges from 426,369 to 793,663. That means that we are 95% certain that the correct number is between those two, and 601,027 is the statistically most probable number.' The methodology of the Iraq Study was defended in a letter dated 14 Oct. 2006 from the Burnet Institute and International Rescue Committee (IRC), which had used the same methods to estimate mortality in the Democratic Republic of Congo. The findings of the IRC study received widespread media attention and were accepted without reservation by the US and British governments because the issue was uncontroversial from their point of view: <http://www.scoop.co.nz/stories/HL0610/S00204.htm>

69. <http://www.opinion.co.uk/Newsroom_details.aspx?NewsId=78>

70. The rates were 3.2 deaths/1000/year (March 2003–April 2004); 6.6 deaths/1000/year (May 2004–May 2005); 12.0 deaths/1000/year (June 2005–June 2006).

71. <http://www.oxfam.org.uk/what_we_do/issues/conflict_disasters/bp105_iraq.htm>

72. John Gray, 'The Death of this Crackpot Creed is Nothing to Mourn', *The Guardian* (31 July 2007).

*Chapter Nine: 'We Don't Do Nation-Building'*

1. Speech to the Veterans of Foreign Wars 103rd National Convention, 26 Aug. 2002. Cf. John Donnelly and Anthony Shadid, 'Iraq War Hawks Have Plans to Reshape Entire Mideast', *Boston Globe* (10 Sept. 2002).

2. <http://www.defenselink.mil/transcripts/transcript.aspx?transcriptid=3144> On 14 Feb. 2003, Rumsfeld delivered an address entitled 'Beyond Nation-Building': <http://www.defenselink.mil/utility/printitem.aspx?print=http://www.defenselink.mil/speeches/speech.aspx?speechid=337>

3. Deputy Secretary of Defense Paul Wolfowitz, interview with the *Jerusalem Post*, 22 Sept. 2003: <http://www.defenselink.mil/transcripts/transcript.aspx?transcriptid=3173>

4. 'New State Department Releases on the *Future of Iraq Project*' (1 Sept. 2006): <http://www.gwu.edu/~nsarchiv/NSAEBB/NSAEBB198/index.htm>

5. Halper and Clarke, *America Alone*, 223.

6. Galbraith, *The End of Iraq*, 118.

7. Con Coughlin and Neil Tweedie, 'Gen Sir Mike Jackson Attacks US over Iraq', *Daily Telegraph* (1 Sept. 2007).

8. Nora Bensahel, 'Mission Not Accomplished. What Went Wrong with Iraqi Reconstruction', *Journal of Strategic Studies*, 29/3 (2006), 452–73, at 459.

9. Thomas E. Ricks, *Fiasco. The American Military Adventure in Iraq* (New York and London: Penguin Press, 2006), 135.

10. Galbraith, *The End of Iraq*, 113.

11. Quoted by Ricks, *Fiasco*, 136.

12. Halper and Clarke, *America Alone*, 93, 222.

13. 'Iraq: What Could Have Been, What Should Have Been ...' *Soldiers for the Truth* (28 Feb. 2007): <http://www.sftt.org/cgi-bin/csNews/csNews.cgi?database=Unlisted%20 2007.db&command=viewone&id=12>

14. Ricks, *Fiasco*, 97. Shinseki added: 'it takes a significant ground force presence to maintain a safe and secure environment so as to ensure that people are fed, that water is distributed, all the normal responsibilities that go along with administering a situation like this.'

15. Halper and Clarke, *America Alone*, 222.

16. Calculated on a ratio of 20 soldiers per 1000 inhabitants (as in Bosnia and Kosovo in 1995 and 1999–2000 respectively), on the assumption of a population of Iraq of nearly 25 million: James T. Quinlivan, 'Burden of Victory. The Painful Arithmetic of Stability Operations', *Rand Review* (summer 2003): <http://www.rand.org/publications/randreview/issues/summer2003/burden.html>

17. Ricks, *Fiasco*, 160. David Nummy interviewed by Larry Plotkin (United States Institute of Peace. Association for Diplomatic Studies and Training. Iraq Experience Project, 14 Oct. 2004): <www.usip.org/library/oh/sops/iraq/rec/nummy.pdf>

18. Galbraith, *The End of Iraq*, 119.

19. Ricks, *Fiasco*, 162–3.

20. David E. Sanger and Eric Schmitt, 'US has a Plan to Occupy Iraq, Officials Admit', *New York Times* (10 Oct. 2002).

21. In March 2006, Secretary of Defense Donald Rumsfeld started something of a stir by stating on the third anniversary of the beginning of the Iraq war that 'turning our backs on post-war Iraq ... would be the modern equivalent of handing post-war Germany back to the Nazis. Both Henry Kissinger and Zbigniew Brzezinski pointed out that the situations were not analogous in that in 1945 the Germans were totally crushed: <http://www.cnn.com/2006/POLITICS/03/19/rumsfeld.nazis/>

22. Bensahel, 'Mission Not Accomplished', 458.

23. L. Paul Bremer III with Malcolm McConnell, *My Year in Iraq. The Struggle to Build a Future of Hope* (New York: Simon and Schuster, 2006). Reviewed by Michiko Kakutani, 'A View from the Center of the Iraq Maelstrom', *New York Times* (12 Jan. 2006).

24. Ellen Knickmeyer, 'US Has End in Sight on Iraq Rebuilding. Documents Show Much of the Funding Diverted to Security, Justice System and Hussein Inquiry', *Washington Post* (2 Jan. 2006).

25. Text of US Security Adviser's Iraq Memo (8 Nov. 2006): <http://www.nytimes.com/2006/11/29/world/middleeast/29mtext.html?ex=1187841600&en=9df38374d4b15335&ei=5070>

26. Guido Steinberg, 'Iraq on the Path to a Shi'ite Dictatorship', Spiegel Online (21 Aug. 2007).

27. Bensahel, 'Mission Not Accomplished', 459–60.

28. Rajiv Chandrasekaran, 'How Cleric Trumped US Plan for Iraq …', *Washington Post* (26 Nov. 2003).

29. Ray A. Moore and Donald L. Robinson, *Partners for Democracy. Crafting the New Japanese State under MacArthur* (New York and Oxford: Oxford University Press, 2002), 336–7.

30. Ibid. 335–6.

31. Ibid. 337.

32. Gareth Stansfield, 'Divide and Heal', *Prospect*, 122 (May 2006).

33. For the significance of Kirkuk: 'Iraq and the Kurds. The Brewing Battle over Kirkuk', ISN Middle East Report, 56 (18 July 2006): <http://www.crisisgroup.org/home/index.cfm?id=4267> Dominic Moran, 'Kirkuk Arabs Fear Government Expulsion', ISN Security Watch (9 Feb. 2007): <http://www.isn.ethz.ch/>

34. Galbraith heard the story from two of the participants in a meeting between Bush and three named Iraqi Americans. 'So two months before he ordered US troops into the country, the president of the United States did not appear to know about the division among Iraqis that has defined the country's history and politics. He would not have understood why non-Arab Iran might gain a foothold in post-Saddam Iraq. He could not have anticipated US troops being caught in the middle of a civil war between two religious sects that he did not know existed.' Peter W. Galbraith, *The End of Iraq. How American Incompetence Created a War without End* (New York: Simon and Schuster, 2006), 83.

35. Christian Avard, 'Ambassador Claims Shortly Before Invasion Bush Didn't know there were Two Sects of Islam', Rawstory.com (4 Aug. 2006).

36. Ehsan Ahrari, 'When Sistani Speaks, Bush Listens', Asia Times Online (17 Jan. 2004).

37. Though he denies the likelihood of a 'Shi'ite crescent', Kamran Taremi argues that important consequences follow from the Shi'ite-dominated government in Iraq. Taremi, 'Is a Shi'ite Crescent Soon to Slice through the Middle East?', *Daily Star* (7 Feb. 2005)

38. <http://www.lemonde.fr/cgi-bin/ACHATS/acheter.cgi?offre=ARCHIVES&type_item=ART_ARCH_30J&objet_id=909697> Translated at: <http://nuralcubicle.blogspot.com/2005/07/shiite-crescent.html>

39. Ghassan Charbel, 'Former Iranian President Khatami to *Al-Hayat*: "The Shi'ite Crescent Doesn't Exist …"', *Al-Hayat* (19 June 2006).

40. Robin Wright and Peter Baker, 'Iraq, Jordan See Threat to Election from Iran. Leaders Warn against Forming Religious State', *Washington Post* (8 Dec. 2004).

41. Lionel Beehner, 'Shiite Muslims in the Middle East', *Council on Foreign Relations* (16 June 2006): <http://www.cfr.org/publication/10903/shiite_muslims_in_the_middle_east.html> Also Anthony O'Mahony, 'The rise of the Shia', *Tablet* (26 July 2006).

42. Edward Wong and Dexter Filkins, 'The Reach of War. Sectarian Strife. In an About-face, Sunnis Want US to Remain in Iraq', *New York Times* (17 July 2006).

43. Jim Rutenberg, 'Baghdad Chaos Pushes Bush to Shift US Troops', *New York Times* (26 July 2006). Michael R. Gordon, 'Battle for Baghdad Boils down to Grabbing a Slice at a Time', ibid. Ewen MacAskill and Richard Norton-Taylor, 'Iraqi PM Admits Failure to Contain Growing Violence', *The Guardian* (25 July 2006).

44. <http://www.foreignpolicy.com/story/cms.php?story_id=3924&page=1&fpsrc=ealert070820_02><http://www.foreignpolicy.com/story/cms.php?story_id=3924&page=3>

45. 'America has won an important battle in the war on terror. We turned an imminent victory for al-Qaeda in Iraq into a humiliating defeat for them and thereby created an opportunity for further progress not only in Iraq, but also in the global struggle. In the past five months, terrorist operations in and around Baghdad have dropped by 59%. Car bomb deaths are down by 81%. Casualties from enemy attacks dropped 77%. And violence during the just-completed season of Ramadan – traditionally a peak of terrorist attacks – was the lowest in three years. Winning a battle is not the same as winning a war. Our commanders and soldiers are continuing the fight to ensure that al-Qaeda does not recover even as they turn their attention to the next battle: against Shi'a militias sponsored by Iran.' Frederick W. Kagan, 'Winning One Battle, Fighting the Next', *Weekly Standard* (5 Nov. 2007).

46. Ahmed Janabi, 'Dismembering the Body Politic in Iraq', English Aljazeera.net (27 June 2006).

47. Gareth Stansfield, 'Divide and Heal', *Prospect*, 122 (May 2006). The same author adds: 'there are, however, powerful forces refusing to contemplate partition or "hard federalism". The radical Shi'a movement led by Muqtada al-Sadr, emerging as one of the most powerful groups in Iraq, rejects federalism as a divide-and-rule tactic and defends Iraqi identity in traditional nationalist terms. Opposition among the Arab Sunnis who have traditionally dominated the state is even stronger. Whether radical Islamists, ex-Ba'athists or secularists, Arab Sunnis see federalism as undermining everything they have stood for in nearly a century of Iraqi history.'

48. Samuel Berger, 'Foreign Policy for a Democratic President', *Foreign Affairs* (May–June 2004).

49. 'Mideast Conference Should not Aim to Help US in Iraq: GCC', Agence France-Presse (19 Sept. 2007).

50. Ellen Knickmeyer, 'US Has End in Sight on Iraq Rebuilding. Documents Show Much of the Funding Diverted to Security, Justice System and Hussein Inquiry', *Washington Post* (2 Jan. 2006).

51. 'Rebuilding Iraq "Will Cost $100 Billion"', *Gulf Times* (21 Aug. 2007).

52. James T. Quinlivan, 'Burden of Victory. The Painful Arithmetic of Stability Operations', *Rand Review* (summer 2003).

53. James Dobbins, 'Nation-Building. The Inescapable Responsibility of the World's Only Superpower', ibid.

54. Naomi Klein, 'Why Failure is the New Face of Success', *The Guardian* (12 Sept. 2007).

55. Peter W. Singer, 'Outsourcing War', *Foreign Affairs* (1 Mar. 2005).

56. T. Christian Miller, 'Private Contractors Outnumber US Troops in Iraq', *Los Angeles Times* (4 July 2007).

57. Sabrina Tavernise, 'US Contractor Banned by Iraq over Shootings', *New York Times* (18 Sept. 2007). Ewen MacAskill, 'Iraq Orders Expulsion of US Security Firm', *The Guardian* (18 Sept. 2007).

58. John M. Broder and James Risen, 'Armed Guards in Iraq Occupy a Legal Limbo', *New York Times* (20 Sept. 2007). Ewen MacAskill, 'Joint Inquiry Could Resolve Blackwater Standoff', *The Guardian* (20 Sept. 2007).

59. Michael Rubin, 'Less is More in Iraq', *Washington Post* (9 Aug. 2005).

60. *A More Secure World. Our Shared Responsibility*. Report of the UN High-level Panel on Threats, Challenges and Change (Dec. 2004: A/59/565), 57–8. <www.un.org/secureworld/>

61. Richard Bonney, 'Impossible to Reconcile? Christian Just War Theory and the Second Iraq War', *Encounters. Journal of Inter-cultural Perspectives*, 9 (Mar. 2003), 69–91, at 81.

62. 'Andrew White, the Anglican vicar of Baghdad, a diplomat, a hostage negotiator

and an adviser to the US government, remains a firm supporter of the war – "Saddam had to be got rid of, and there was no way the Iraqi people could do it themselves" – but he accepts that what followed was a disaster. The result has been terrible and we have to take some responsibility for everything that has happened. We made three big mistakes. One, we didn't close the borders, so all the insurgents and bad guys got in. Two, we got rid of all the Iraqi security forces – the police, the army, the intelligence. And three, the CPA [Coalition Provisional Authority] ended too soon because of American domestic issues like the presidential election.' Stephen Moss, 'I Don't Just Work with Nice People', *The Guardian* (17 July 2006).

63. '"I am viscerally opposed to a prolonged occupation of a Muslim country at the heart of the Muslim world by Western nations who proclaim the right to re-educate that country," said the former secretary of state, Henry A. Kissinger, who as a young man served as a district administrator in the military government of occupied Germany.' Quoted by David E. Sanger and Eric Schmitt in their *New York Times* report on 11 Oct. 2002.

64. Juan Cole: 'Clarke: Invasion of Iraq an Enormous Mistake' (27 June 2004): <http://www.juancole.com/2004/06/clarke-invasion-of-iraq-enormous.html>

65. Michael Walzer, *Arguing about War* (New Haven and London: Yale Univesity Press, 2004), 163–4.

66. David E. Kellogg, '*Jus Post Bellum*. The Importance of War Crimes Trials', *Parameters* (autumn 2002), 87–99.

67. Kenneth R. Himes, 'The Case of Iraq and the Just War Tradition', *Washington Theological Union* (12 Feb. 2007): <http://www.wtu.edu/news/TheologiansCorner/12–3-02-Himes-JustWar-Iraq.htm>

68. Brian Orend, '*Jus Post Bellum*', *Journal of Social Philosophy*, 31 (2000), 117–37.

69. Timothy L. Challans, 'Birth of a Nation. Planning for Regime Change Operations' (2005): <http://www.usafa.af.mil/jscope/JSCOPE05/Challans05.html>

70. Louis V. Iasiello, '*Jus Post Bellum*. The Moral Responsibilities of Victors in War', *Naval War College Review*, 57 (summer/autumn 2004).

71. Henry Kissinger, 'How to Exit Iraq. At First, Iraqi Soldiers Should Augment US Forces, Not Replace Them', *Washington Post* (18 Dec. 2005).

72. The five in Muslim states or provinces were: Somalia, Bosnia, Kosovo, Afghanistan, and Iraq.

73. Dobbins, 'Nation-Building. The Inescapable Responsibility of the World's Only Superpower'. James Dobbins served as US special envoy for Somalia, Haiti, Bosnia, Kosovo, and Afghanistan. He directs the International Security and Defense Policy Center at RAND. Dobbins et al., *America's Role in Nation-Building. From Germany to Iraq* (Santa Monica, CA: RAND, 2003), ch. 10 on Iraq (2003). <http://www.rand.org/pubs/monograph_reports/MR1753/>

74. James Rothenberg, 'The Iraqi Miracle – From Invasion To "Partnership"', Countercurrents.org (29 Nov. 2007). 'US, Iraq Set Stage for Long US Presence', Agence France-Presse (27 Nov. 2007).

*Chapter Ten: Towards 'Eurabia' or the Co-Habitation of Civilizations?*

1. Bassam Tibi, 'Muslim Migrants in Europe. Between Euro-Islam and Ghettoization', in Nezar AlSayyad and Manuel Castells (eds), *Muslim Europe or Euro-Islam. Politics, Culture and Citizenship in the Age of Globalization* (Plymouth: Lexington Books, 2002), 37–8.

2. Orla Lynch, 'Fundamentalism, Psychology and the European Threat', in Christiane Timmerman, Dirk Hutesbaut, Sara Mels, Walter Nonneman, and Walter Van Herck (eds), *Faith-Based Radicalism. Christianity, Islam and Judaism between Constructive Activism and Destructive Fanaticism* (Brussels: Peter Lang, 2007), 207–8.

3. Bassam Tibi, *The Challenge of Fundamentalism. Political Islam and the New World Disorder* (Berkeley and Los Angeles: University of California Press, 1998; repr. 2002), 4–5.

4. Timothy M. Savage, 'Europe and Islam. Crescent Waxing, Cultures Clashing', *Washington Quarterly*, 27/3 (2004), 25–50, at 46–7.

5. G. Joffé, 'Confrontational Mutual Perceptions and Images: Orientalism and Occidentalism in Europe and the Islamic World', *International Spectator*, 42/2 (2007), 161–178.

6. Mark Mazzetti, 'Accountability. CIA Lays out Errors it Made before 11 Sept.', Spiegel Online (22 Aug. 2007).

7. <http://select.nytimes.com/gst/abstract.html?res=F00912F63B540C7B8EDDAA0894DC404482>

8. Mark Steyn, *America Alone. The End of the World as We Know it* (Washington DC: Regnery, 2006), 146–7, 207–8.

9. Christopher Caldwell, 'Islamic Europe? When Bernard Lewis Speaks ...', *Weekly Standard* (4 Oct. 2004).

10. Steyn, *America Alone*, 107.

11. All of which serves to show that you cannot trust alarmist sources of information: *Mapping the Global Future. Report of the National Intelligence Council's 2020 Project based on Consultation with Non-governmental Experts around the world* (Washington DC: National Intelligence Council, 2004), 57, 61, 83. <http://www.dni.gov/nic/NIC_globaltrend2020.html>

12. Bat Ye'or, *Eurabia. The Euro–Arab Axis* (Cranbury, NJ: Fairleigh Dickinson University Press/Associated University Presses, 2005). *Eurabia* was originally the title of a newsletter published by the Comité européen de coordination des associations d'amitié avec le monde Arabe.

13. <http://www.dhimmitude.org/>; <http://www.dhimmi.org/>

14. Michael A. Sells, 'Christ Killer, Kremlin, Contagion', in Emran Qureshi and Michael A. Sells (eds), *The New Crusades. Constructing the Muslim Enemy* (New York: Columbia University Press, 2003), 366.

15. Steyn, *America Alone*, 15.

16. Ibid. 38, 40, 55.

17. 'The US Census population pyramids suggest countries with high birth rates – i.e. Muslim – are made up of 23% male 0–19 year olds, and 15% male 20–39 year olds.' Paul Weston, 'Is European Civil War Inevitable By 2025?': <http://atangledweb.squarespace.com/httpatangledwebsquarespace/is-european-civil-war-inevitable-by-2025-part-1.html>

18. George Weigel, 'Europe's Problem – and Ours', *First Things* (Feb. 2004).

19. Daniel Pipes, 'Europe's Stark Options', *National Interest* (Mar.–Apr. 2007).

20. Philip Jenkins, *God's Continent. Christianity, Islam, and Europe's Religious Crisis* (New York: Oxford University Press, 2007), 16.

21. Ibid. 21.

22. Ibid. 19: Jenkins talks of a figure of 20 per cent 'late in the present century'. The point is made more explicitly in Philip Jenkins, 'Islam and Muslims in Europe Today. Some Key Issues': <www.divinity.cam.ac.uk/cip/documents/IslamandMuslimInEuropeToday.pdf>

23. Konrad Pedziwiatr, 'Europe's Muslims. Their Impact on EU Foreign Policy and Transatlantic Relations' (15 Jan. 2007):<http://www.europeancourier.org/26.htm>

Unlike the alarmists, this author has published on the subject already: Konrad Pedziwiatr, *From Islam of Immigrants to Islam of Citizens. Muslims in the Countries of Western Europe* (Cracow: Nomos, 2005) [in Polish: *Od islam imigrantow do islamu obywateli: muzulmanie w krajach Europy Zachodniej*].

24. Bruce Bawer, *While Europe Slept. How Radical Islam is Destroying the West from Within* (New York: Doubleday, 2007), quoted by Jenkins, *God's Continent*, 17. Eliot Weinberger and John Freeman's criticisms of Bawer are cited by Patricia Cohen, 'In Books, a Clash of Europe and Islam', *New York Times* (8 Feb. 2007).

25. Richard Bonney and William Le Goff, 'Leicester's Cultural Diversity in the Context

of the British Debate on Multiculturalism', *International Journal of Diversity in Organizations, Communities and Nations*, 6 (2006).

26. Richard Bonney, 'British and French Muslims. Between Assimilation and Segregation?', in Richard Bonney and D. J. B. Trim (eds), *The Development of Pluralism in Modern Britain and France* (Oxford/Bern: P. Lang, 2007), 344.

27. Robert A. Pape, *Dying to Win. Why Suicide Terrorists Do it* (London: Gibson Square, 2006), vi, 125.

28. Steyn, *America Alone*, 74.

29. Ibid. 85.

30. Daniel Pipes, 'Islamophobia?', *New York Sun* (25 Oct. 2005).

31. Full text: writers' statement on cartoons (1 Mar. 2006): <http://news.bbc.co.uk/1/hi/world/europe/4764730.stm>

32. Robin Richardson (ed.), *Islamophobia. Issues, Challenges and Action. A Report by the Commission on British Muslims and Islamophobia* (Stoke on Trent: Trentham Books and Uniting Britain Trust, London, 2004).

33. Quoted by Lee Sustar, 'European Islamophobia', Countercurrents.org (1 Nov. 2006): <http://www.countercurrents.org/eu-sustar011106.htm>

Glyn Ford, *Fascist Europe. The Rise of Racism and Xenophobia* (London: Pluto Press, 1992). This work has been criticized as one of those which conflates the radical Right with neo-fascism: Roger Karapin, 'Radical Right and Neo-Fascist Political Parties in Western Europe', *Comparative Politics*, 30/2 (1998), 213–34, at 216, 232 n. 11.

34. Peter D. Salins, 'Assimilation, American Style', *Reason* (Feb. 1997). His book with the same title was published in the same year (New York: Basic Books, 1997).

35. <http://www.cre.gov.uk/diversity/wordsandmeanings/essay9.html>

36. Bassam Tibi, 'Europeanization, not Islamization. Bassam Tibi Argues for Euro-Islam as a Bridge between Civilizations' (22 Mar. 2007): <http://www.signandsight.com/features/1258.html>

37. Bassam Tibi, 'Muslim Migrants in Europe. Between Euro Islam and Ghettoization', 38.

38. 'British Muslims and the *Ummah*' (1 Sept. 2005): <http://news.bbc.co.uk/1/hi/programmes/panorama/4171328.stm>

39. Olivier Roy, *Globalized Islam. The Search for a New Ummah* (London: Hurst, 2004).

40. Tariq Ramadan, *To Be a European Muslim. A Study of Islamic Sources in the European Context* (Leicester: the Islamic Foundation, 1999). Ramadan, *Western Muslims and the Future of Islam* (New York: Oxford University Press, 2004).

41. Bassam Tibi, 'Euro-Islam. The Quest of Islamic Migrants and of Turkey to Become European in a Secular Europe', *Turkish Policy Quarterly* (Spring 2004).

42. Bahtiar Effendy, *Islam and the State in Indonesia* (Singapore: Institute of Southeast Asian Studies, 2003), 78–7.

43. Dominique Thomas, *Le Londonistan. La Voix du djihad* (Paris: Michalon, 2003). <http://www.melaniephillips.com/>

44. Paul A. Silverstein, *Algeria in France. Transpolitics, Race and Nation* (Bloomington and Indianapolis: Indiana University Press, 2004).

45. Jonathan Laurence, 'Islam in France', US–France Analysis (Dec. 2001): <http://www.brookings.edu/fp/cusf/analysis/islam.htm>

46. Jonathan Laurence and Justin Vaisse, *Integrating Islam. Political and Religious Challenges in Contemporary France* (Washington DC: Brookings Institution Press, 2006), 4.

47. Jocelyne Cesari, 'Muslims identities in Europe: the snare of exceptionalism', in Aziz Al-Azmeh and Effie Fokas (ed), *Islam in Europe. Diversity, Identity and Influence* (Cambridge: Cambridge University Press, 2007), 49–67 at 56: '... there now exists a French Islam, an English Islam, a Belgian Islam, etc.' Jorgen Nielsen questions whether 'Euro-Islam' is a

conscious choice or a government-imposed agenda: Nielsen, 'The question of Euro-Islam: restriction or opportunity?', ibid. 34–48.

48. Neil MacMaster, 'Islamophobia in France and the "Algerian Problem"', in Emran Qureshi and Michael A. Sells (eds), *The New Crusades. Constructing the Muslim Enemy* (New York: Columbia University Press, 2003), 309.

49. Quoted by Laurence and Vaisse, *Integrating Islam*, 110.

50. Quoted by Jonathan Laurence, 'From the Elysée Salon to the Table of the Republic. State–Islam Relations and the Integration of Muslims in France', *French Politics, Culture and Society*, 23/1 (2005), 36–63, at 58.

51. Nikki R. Keddie, Review of Shireen T. Hunter, *The Future of Islam and the West. Clash of Civilizations or Peaceful Coexistence* (Westport, CT: Praeger, 1998). Also review of Bassam Tibi, *The Challenge of Fundamentalism. Political Islam and the New World Disorder* (Berkeley: University of California Press, 1998), in *International Journal of Middle East Studies*, 32/1 (2000), 180–3, at 183.

52. Olivier Roy, *Globalized Islam. The Search for a New Ummah* (London: Hurst, 2004), 139. Roy notes that 'almost everywhere fertility rates are falling to European levels (Iran, Tunisia, Algeria, and of course within the immigrant community) ...'

53. Ronald Inglehart and Pippa Norris, 'The True Clash of Civilizations', *Foreign Policy* (Mar./Apr. 2003), 67–74.

54. Priscilla Offenhauer, 'Women in Islamic Societies. A Selected Review of Social Scientific Literature' (Library of Congress, Nov. 2005): <www.loc.gov/rr/frd/pdf-files/Women_Islamic_Societies.pdf>

55. Farzaneh Roudi-Fahimi and Mary Mederios Kent, 'Challenges and Opportunities – the Population of the Middle East and North Africa, *Population Bulletin*, 62/2 (June 2007), 8, accessed at <www.prb.org>

56. <http://www.spiegel.de/international/spiegel/0,1518,druck-440340,00.html>

57. Queen Noor of Jordan, 'Security through Dialogue', in Akbar Ahmed and Brian Forst (eds), *After Terror. Promoting Dialogue among Civilizations* (Cambridge and Malden, MA: Polity, 2005), 129. The UN General Assembly decided on 7 Sept. 2001 that the International Day of Peace thereafter should be observed on 11 September. Kofi Annan issued his message for 11 Sept. 2001 the day before.

58. Akbar Ahmed and Brian Forst (eds), *After Terror*, 3. Bernard Lewis, 'Clash or Dialogue among Cultures?', ibid. 157–8.

59. Kofi Annan, 'Dialogue among Civilizations', ibid. 94–97.

60. <http://www.unesco.org/dialogue2001/en/annan.htm>

61. <http://www.un.org/Pubs/chronicle/2001/issue1/0103p71.htm>

62. Brett D. Schaefer represented it as a self-interested plot engineered by Kofi Annan. Schaefer, 'The US Should Oppose the Proposed UN Alliance of Civilizations' (22 Feb. 2007): <http://www.heritage.org/Research/InternationalOrganizations/bg2009.cfm>

63. 'Alliance of Civilizations. Final Report of the High-Level Group' (13 Nov. 2006): <http://www.unaoc.org/aoc.php?page=7&PHPSESSID=d94da33a34cfe2ee4c45a2d8c6a82ab7>

64. The authors of the report note that 'for global terrorist groups, a "clash of civilizations" is a welcome and potent slogan to attract and motivate a loosely knit network of operatives and supporters. We must make it clear that, in our view, no political end, whether arising from historical injustice or contemporary provocation, and whether committed by resistance organizations, global militant groups, or by states, can justify the targeting of civilians and non-combatants. Such actions must be condemned unequivocally.'

65. The authors of the report do not talk of religious pluralism so much as reaffirm freedom of religion (para 5.15). This phrasing does not quite cover the situation where, as in Iraq, political conflict is marked by a sectarian religious character: reaffirming religious and political pluralism addresses such issues.

66. <http://www.unaoc.org/aoc.php?page=10&id=90>

67. In total 28,389 citizens in Argentina, Australia, Brazil, Canada, Chile, China, Egypt, France, Germany, Great Britain, Greece, Hungary, India, Indonesia, Italy, Kenya, Lebanon, Mexico, Nigeria, the Philippines, Poland, Portugal, Russia, South Korea, Turkey, the United Arab Emirates, and the United States were interviewed between 3 Nov. 2006 and 16 Jan. 2007. Polling was conducted for the BBC World Service by the international polling firm GlobeScan and its research partners in each country. In 10 of the 27 countries, the sample was limited to major urban areas. The margin of error per country ranges from +/-2.5 to 4%. (Significantly the pollsters did not canvas opinions in Saudi Arabia, Pakistan, Iraq, or Iran, nations considered by some to be at the heart of tensions between the West and Islam.) Details of the poll were made available on 19 Feb. 2007: <http://www.worldpublicopinion.org/pipa/articles/home_page/317.php?nid=&id=&pnt=317&lb=hmpg1>.

When this book was at press, the findings of the Gallup West–Muslim Dialogue poll for 2007, which was based on nine questions asked of those surveyed in 21 Muslim and non-Muslim majority countries, became available. In this case, the pollsters canvassed opinions in three of the most volatile Muslim-majority countries (Saudi Arabia, Pakistan, and Iran) as well as Bangladesh, Indonesia, Malaysia, Palestine, and Turkey. In answer to the question 'do you think violent conflict between the Muslim and Western worlds can be avoided or not?', majorities in all countries (with the exception of Pakistan, where the majority 'did not know') believe that violent conflict can be avoided. *Islam and the West: Annual Report on the State of Dialogue*. January 2008 (World Economic Forum, Geneva, 2008), 140.

68. <http://www.globescan.com/news_archives/bbciswest/>.

69. Rashmee Roshan Lall, 'India Undecided about Clash of Civilizations', *Times of India* (19 Feb. 2007).

70. Hasan Suroor, 'Islam–West conflict', *The Hindu* (20 Feb. 2007).

71. Damien McElroy, 'Politics Causes Divide between Islam and West', *Daily Telegraph* (20 Feb. 2007).

72. Amartya Sen, *Identity and Violence. The Illusion of Identity* (London: Allen Lane, 2006), 17, 20, 21.

73. Ibid. 175.

74. Ibid. 16.

75. <http://europa.eu/scadplus/leg/en/lvb/l29017.htm>

76. Sen, *Identity and Violence*, 156–60.

77. Bassam Tibi, 'Muslim Migrants in Europe. Between Euro-Islam and Ghettoization', 47–8.

*Conclusion: Demise of the False Prophets?*

1. Huntington, *The Clash of Civilizations and the Remaking of World Order*, 312.

2. Quoted by Stefan Halper and Jonathan Clarke, *America Alone. The Neo-Conservatives and the Global Order* (Cambridge: Cambridge University Press, 2004), 133.

3. Patrick J. Buchanan, '"Stay the Course!" is Not Enough', repr. in Gary Rosen (ed.), *The Right War? The Conservative Debate on Iraq* (New York: Cambridge University Press, 2005), 202.

4. <http://www.brainyquote.com/quotes/quotes/s/samuelphu218282.html>

5. Clare Dyer, 'There is No War on Terror', *The Guardian* (24 Jan. 2007).

6. Louise Richardson, *What Terrorists Want. Understanding the Terrorist Threat* (London: John Murray, 2006), 252.

7. Jane Mayer, 'Outsourcing Torture. The Secret History of America's "Extraordinary Rendition" Program', *The New Yorker* (14 Feb. 2005). Andrew Cohen, 'Extraordinary Rendition. Outsourced Torture Victims a Legal Hot Potato', CBSNews.com (18 Feb. 2005). American Civil Liberties Union Fact Sheet: Extraordinary Rendition (6 Dec. 2005): <http://www.aclu.org/safefree/extraordinaryrendition/22203res20051206.html>

8. Osama bin Laden's Video Message to the American People (Memri Special Dispatch 1709, 10 Sept. 2007): <http://memri.org/bin/articles.cgi?Page=archives&Area=sd&ID=SP170907>

Here, the author has referred to the complete transcript of the video issued by the SITE Intelligence Group on 9 Sept. 2007: <http://www.siteinstitute.org/> (by subscription only).

9. Except in relation to the American Jewish lobby, we have not featured the criticisms of Noam Chomsky significantly in this study. This is because his views are long-standing, dating from the Vietnam War, whereas the emphasis of this discussion is on specific reactions to Huntington post-1993. However, for a useful summary of Chomsky's criticisms of the George W. Bush world view: Noam Chomsky, *Hegemony or Survival. America's Quest for Global Dominance* (Crows Nest, NSW, Aus.: Allen and Unwin, 2003), ch. 2, 'Imperial Grand Strategy'.

10. 'Bin Laden Takes Liberties with Contents of Guardian Video', *The Guardian* (11 Sept. 2007). The issue was whether a US soldier in Iraq was wiping away tears in his eyes (bin Laden) or was wiping away sweat from his forehead (the account of Sean Smith, *The Guardian*'s cameraman).

11. Tim Shipman, 'Bin Laden Sidelined as al-Qaeda Threat Revives', *Daily Telegraph* (16 Sept. 2006). This report suggested that Ayman al-Zawahiri had taken over the propaganda operations of al-Qaeda and that bin Laden had not chaired an al-Qaeda ruling *shura* meeting for two years.

12. 'We are very fortunate to know enough about the Kennedy assassination to be able to confirm the fact that he was murdered because he opposed the Vietnam war to the point where he had forecasted withdrawal by 1965. At the same time, it is important to note that the detailed truth is buried in a mountain of secrecy.' <http://surftofind.com/specialgroup>

13. John Kenneth White, 'Terrorism and the Remaking of American Politics', in William Crotty (ed.), *The Politics of Terror. The US Response to 9/11* (Boston: Northeastern University Press, 2004), 47–8.

14. Sidney Blumenthal, *How Bush Rules. Chronicles of a Radical Regime* (Princeton and Oxford: Princeton University Press, 2006), 215. Text of the Speech at Online NewsHour (28 June 2005): <http://www.pbs.org/newshour/bb/middle_east/jan-june05/bush_6–28.html>

15. Jean Bethke Elshtain, 'Terrorism', in Charles Reed and David Ryall (eds), *The Price of Peace. Just War in the Twenty-First Century* (Cambridge: Cambridge University Press, 2007), 129.

16. Richardson, *What Terrorists Want*, 10–11.

17. Quoted by Byman, 'US Counter-Terrorism Options. A Taxonomy', *Survival* 49/3 (2007), 121–50, at 145.

18. Richardson, *What Terrorists Want*, 216.

19. Ibid. 246–81.

20. Ibid. 210.

21. Robert Dreyfuss, 'Just the Beginning. Is Iraq the Opening Salvo in a War to Remake the World?', *American Prospect* (1 Apr. 2003).

22. He was head of the CIA's bin Laden desk from 1996 to 1999 and was named as the author, e.g. by Erich Marquardt, 'Why the US Supports the State of Israel' (7 Oct. 2004): <www.isn.ethz.ch/infoservice/sw/details.cfm?ID=9879>

23. Michael Scheuer, *Imperial Hubris. Why the West is Losing the War on Terror* (Washington DC: Brassey's Inc., 2004), xviii–xix. (The same author used the term 'imperial hubris' in 2002: Scheuer, *Through our Enemies' Eyes. Osama bin Laden, Radical Islam and the Future of America* (Washington DC: Brassey's Inc., 2002), 24.)

24. Halper and Clarke, *America Alone*, 7.

25. Ayman al-Zawahiri goaded the Americans: 'I ask [Bush], why send 20,000 [troops] only – why not send 50 or 100,000? Aren't you aware that the dogs of Iraq are pining for your troops' dead bodies? So send your entire army to be annihilated at the hands of the *mujahideen* to free the world from your evil ... because Iraq, land of the caliphate and *jihad*, is able to bury ten armies like yours, with Allah's help and power.' 'Al-Qaeda Deputy Mocks US Iraq Plan', Al-Jazeera (22 Jan. 2007): <http://english.aljazeera.net/NR/exeres/441CEFCD-E19E-4EAF-80C2-B8AFEBD06102.htm>

26. Richardson, *What Terrorists Want*, 227.

27. 'It's Time to Talk to Qaeda: Doha Debates', *Peninsula* (6 Sept. 2007): <http://www.gulfinthemedia.com/index.php?id=340337&news_type=Top&lang=en> For the list of Doha Debates: <http://www.thedohadebates.com/output/page12.asp>

28. Ibid. 104, quoting Bruce Hoffman.

29. 'A stepped up military offensive that targets mosques, religious leaders and Islamic customs is leading many Iraqis to believe that the US-led invasion really was a "holy war". Photographs are being circulated of black crosses painted on mosque walls and on copies of the Qur'an, and of soldiers dumping their waste inside mosques. New stories appear frequently of raids on mosques and brutal treatment of Islamic clerics, leading many Iraqis to ask if the invasion and occupation was a war against Islam.' Dahr Jamail and Ali al-Fadhily, 'The War Becomes More Unholy', Inter Press Service (20 Jan. 2007): <http://countercurrents.org/iraq-jamail200107.htm>

30. 'The conflicts in Iraq, Somalia, Afghanistan, Kashmir, Chechnya, and the Pakistani tribal regions are all examples of "rancorous Crusader war". These struggles prove that "war is continuing against the messenger of God, may the peace and blessings of God be upon him, and his religion and nation" ... Of all these fights, bin Laden claims that the war in Iraq is going "from good to better" and is the most important struggle because Iraq is the historical "seat of the caliphate". "Their [the Crusaders'] failure there will be failure for all their wars and attacks, God willing," bin Laden says, "and the beginning of the recession of the Zionist-Crusader wave against us."' Michael Scheuer, 'Osama bin Laden. Taking Stock of the "Zionist-Crusader War"', *Terrorism Focus*, 25 Apr. 2006 (posted by Jamestown.org on 24 Apr. 2006): <http://www.jamestown.org/news_details.php?news_id=177>

31. Bruce Lawrence (ed.), *Messages To The World*, 255.

32. Ibid. 272.

33. Donald Byman, *The Five Front War. The Better Way to Fight Global Jihad* (Hoboken, NJ: John Wiley, 2007), 101. Marc Sageman, *Understanding Terror Networks* (Philadelphia: University of Pennsylvania Press, 2004), 180–1.

34. Donald Byman, 'Going to War with the Allies you have. Allies, Counter-Insurgency and the War on Terrorism', Strategic Studies Institute of the US Army War College (Nov. 2005): <http://www.strategicstudiesinstitute.army.mil/pubs/display.cfm?pubID=630>

35. Donald Byman, 'US Counter-Terrorism Options. A Taxonomy', 145.

36. Byman, *The Five Front War*, 190. Cf. ibid. 180.

37. Paul Rogers, 'The Costs of America's Long War', openDemocracy.net (9 Mar. 2007 accessed at ISN Security Watch at date): <http://www.isn.ethz.ch/news/sw/details.cfm?id=17343>

38. The assertion of Tod Lindberg, editor of the Hoover Institution's *Policy Review*. Lindberg, 'In Full Pursuit of Democracy', *Washington Times* (21 Mar. 2006). Also quoted by Kenneth Anderson, 'Doomed International' [review of Fukuyama, *After the Neocons*], *Times Literary Supplement* (22 Sept. 2006), 4.

39. Francis Fukuyama, *After the Neocons. America at the Crossroads* (London: Profile, 2006), 48–9.

40. '(1) Our struggle is moral, against an evil enemy who revels in the destruction of innocents. Knowing this can help us assess our adversaries correctly and make appropriate strategic choices. Saying it convincingly will strengthen our side and weaken theirs. (2)

The conflict is global, and outcomes in one theatre will affect those in others. (3) While we should always prefer non-violent methods, the use of force will continue to be part of the struggle. (4) The spread of democracy offers an important, peaceful way to weaken our foe and reduce the need for force.' Joshua Muravchik, 'The Past, Present, and Future of Neo-Conservatism', *Commentary* (Oct. 2007).

41. Fukuyama, *After the Neocons*, 102. William Kristol and Robert Kagan, 'Introduction. National Interest and Global Responsibility', in Kagan and Kristol (eds), *Present Dangers. Crisis and Opportunity in American Foreign and Defense Policy* (San Francisco: Encounter, 2000), 22.

42. Fukuyama, *After the Neocons*, 104–5.

43. Fukuyama, 'After Neo-Conservatism'.

44. Godfrey Hodgson argues, plausibly, that 'the US' predicament is that one side of its dualist face has come to predominate. But bullying will not forever eclipse idealism.' But he adds: 'America is no longer a profoundly civilian society occasionally goaded into war, which is the way Americans used to see their country. It is a profoundly militarized society, one faction of whose leaders openly proclaim that they intend to maintain military supremacy over all comers for the 21st century.' Godfrey Hodgson, 'America against Itself', ISN Security Watch (21 Feb. 2007): <http://www.isn.ethz.ch/news/sw/details.cfm?id=17275>

45. Fukuyama, 'After Neo-Conservatism'.

46. Richardson, *What Terrorists Want*, 11.

47. Ibid. 230–1, 233. Lewis D. Solomon, *Paul D. Wolfowitz. Visionary Intellectual, Policymaker and Strategist* (Westport, CT: Praeger Security International, 2007), 80. Cf. Clarke, *Against All Enemies. Inside America's War on Terror*, 264: 'in the new administration's discussion of terrorism, Paul Wolfowitz had urged a focus on Iraqi-sponsored terrorism against the US, even though there was no such thing.'

48. Richardson, *What Terrorists Want*, 233. Vali Nasr, *The Shia Revival. How Conflicts within Islam will Shape the Future* (New York: Norton, 2006), 243: 'a Shia–Sunni civil war would destroy America's project in Iraq far more quickly and thoroughly than al-Qaeda's terrorism could by itself.'

49. Fukuyama, 'After Neo-Conservatism'.

50. Clifford Longley, 'The Neo-Con Illusion', *Tablet* (6 Sept. 2003), 2.

51. Fukuyama, *After the Neocons*, 9, notes the 'neo-conservative principle that neo-conservatives seem to have forgotten in the lead-up to the Iraq war: namely, that ambitious social engineering is very difficult and ought always to be approached with care and humility'.

52. Ibid. 63. Fukuyama, 'After Neo-Conservatism': 'This over-optimism about post-war transitions to democracy helps explain the Bush administration's incomprehensible failure to plan adequately for the insurgency that subsequently emerged in Iraq. The war's supporters seemed to think that democracy was a kind of default condition to which societies reverted once the heavy lifting of coercive regime change occurred, rather than a long-term process of institution-building and reform. While they now assert that they knew all along that the democratic transformation of Iraq would be long and hard, they were clearly taken by surprise. According to George Packer's recent book on Iraq, *The Assassins' Gate*, the Pentagon planned a drawdown of American forces to some 25,000 troops by the end of the summer following the invasion.'

53. Patrick Wintour, 'Brown Emphasises Reconstruction as Main Aim of Foreign Policy', *The Guardian* (13 Nov. 2007). Prime Minister's speech at the Lord Mayor's Banquet (12 Nov. 2007): <http://www.pm.gov.uk/output/Page13736.asp>

54. *War at Any Price? The Total Economic Costs of the War beyond the Federal Budget. A Report by the Joint Economic Committee* (Nov. 2007). Accessed at: <http://www.cfr.org/publication/14794/>. Even higher costs are calculated by Joseph Stiglitz and Linda Bilmes,

*The Three Trillion Dollar War* (London: Allen Lane, 2008).

55. Charles Krauthammer, 'Who's to Blame for The Killing?', *Washington Post* (2 Feb. 2007), repr. in *The Guardian* (12 Feb. 2007), 28, under the more contentious title 'They Chose Civil War'. For Zakaria's views: Fareed Zakaria, 'We Might "Win", But Still Lose', *Newsweek* (15 Jan. 2007): <http://www.fareedzakaria.com/articles/newsweek/011507.html>; Zakaria, 'The Road to Reformation', *Newsweek* (5 Feb. 2007): <http://www.fareedzakaria.com/articles/newsweek/020507.html>

56. Vali Nasr, *The Shia Revival*, 245.

57. Vali Nasr, 'When the Shiites Rise', *Foreign Affairs*, 85/4 (July–Aug. 2006).

58. The statements were issued at Amman (July 2005), Mecca (Oct. 2006), and Doha (Feb. 2007).

59. Vali Nasr, *The Shia Revival*, 253–4.

60. Orla Lynch, 'Fundamentalism, Psychology and the European Threat', in Christiane Timmerman, Dirk Hutesbaut, Sara Mels, Walter Nonneman, and Walter Van Herck (eds), *Faith-based Radicalism. Christianity, Islam and Judaism between Constructive Activism and Destructive Fanaticism* (Brussels: Peter Lang, 2007), 207.

61. Willfried Spohn, 'Nationalism and Religion in a Globalizing World. A Multiple Modernities Perspective', ibid. 29–30. Cf. Shmuel N. Eisenstadt (ed.), *Multiple Modernities* (New Brunswick: Transaction, 2002).

62. Robert Dreyfuss and Thierry LeMarc, *Hostage to Khomeini* (New York: New Benjamin Franklin House Publishing, 1980), 157–8. Jonathan Duffy, 'Bilderberg. The Ultimate Conspiracy Theory', BBC News Online Magazine (3 June 2004). Kaveh Farrokh, 'Pan-Turanianism Takes Aim at Azerbaijan. A Geopolitical Agenda', *Rozaneh Magazine* (Nov.–Dec. 2005). Dreyfuss and LeMarc fail to make the link between the Bernard Lewis plan presented to the Bilderberg meeting in 1979 and the emergence of the Sharon doctrine to 'Ottomanize' the Middle East, starting with Lebanon, by 1982. The dissident Israeli scholar Israel Shahak translated Oded Yinon's article into English, and the importance of this aggressive doctrine is emphasized by Jonathan Cook. However, Cook fails to link the continuity of the thinking in current American strategic discussions such as that of Ralph Peters (see below, n. 68), although he mentions a conference held at the American Enterprise Institute in October 2005, which hosted Iran's Kurdish, Azeri, and Baluchi opposition groups in exile. Cook, *Israel and the Clash of Civilizations*, 84, 106–15. Oded Yinon, 'The Zionist Plan for the Middle East' (Feb. 1982), trans. and ed. Israel Shahak: <http://www.geocities.com/alabasters_archive/zionist_plan.html#pn> (accessed 28 Jan. 2008). For a fuller discussion of the link between the ideas and why they might be seen by the Islamic world as an attack on 'Islam', Richard Bonney, *Has the War on Terror become a War on Islam?* (London: Public Policy Research Organization, 2008).

63. Thomas P. M. Barnett, *The Pentagon's New Map. War and Peace in the Twenty-First Century* (New York: G.P. Putnam, 2004).

64. Thomas P. M. Barnett, 'The Pentagon's New Map', *Esquire* (Mar. 2003), 174–9; web version (consulted 9 Jan. 2007): <http://www.thomaspmbarnett.com/published/pentagonsnewmap.htm>

65. Mackubin T. Owens, 'Review of *The Pentagon's New Map*' (May 2004): <http://www.ashbrook.org/publicat/oped/owens/04/newmap.html>

66. Simon Dalby, 'Political Space. Autonomy, Liberalism, and Empire', *Alternatives. Global, Local, Political*, 30/4 (2005).

67. Simon Dalby, 'Regions, Strategies and Empire in the Global War on Terror', *Geopolitics*, 12/4 (2007), 586–606, at 595, 596, 602.

68. In January 2007, the article included a relatively detailed map of the proposed changes: Ralph Peters, 'Blood borders: how a better Middle East would look', *Armed Forces Journal* (June 2006; accessed 5 Jan. 2007): <http://www.armedforcesjournal.com/2006/06/1833899>. However, by January 2008, though the article remained at the

URL, the maps had been moved. They could be accessed, together with a copy of the article, at: <http://www.militaryphotos.net/forums/showthread.php?t=91628>

69. 'What Afghanistan would lose to Persia in the west, it would gain in the east, as Pakistan's Northwest Frontier tribes would be reunited with their Afghan brethren (the point of this exercise is not to draw maps as we would like them but as local populations would prefer them). Pakistan, another unnatural state, would also lose its Baluch territory to Free Baluchistan. The remaining "natural" Pakistan would lie entirely east of the Indus, except for a westward spur near Karachi.'

70. Kaveh Farrokh, 'Professor Bernard Lewis', Justice for all (14 July 2007): <http://iranzamin2529.blogspot.com/2007/07/professor-bernard-lewis.html>

71. Andrew H. Kydd, *Trust and Mistrust in International Relations* (Princeton and Oxford: Princeton University Press, 2005).

72. 'US Centcom Commander Raises Eyebrows in al-Jazeera Interview', based on a briefing by 'a senior Bush administration official': Geostrategy-Direct (21 Nov. 2007), by subscription only <http://www.geostrategy-direct.com/geostrategy-direct/> It is alleged that Fallon has vowed privately that there would be no attack on Iran while he was commander at CENTCOM: 'Many in the US Military Think Bush and Cheney Are Out of Control', Spiegel Online (15 Oct. 2007): <http://www.spiegel.de/international/world/0,1518,511492,00.html>

73. G. John Ikenberry, 'The West, Precious Not Unique. Civilizations Make for a Poor Paradigm just like the Rest', *Foreign Affairs*, 76/2 (Mar.–Apr. 1997), 162–3. Cited by Engin I. Erdem, 'The "Clash of Civilizations" Revisited after September 11', *Alternatives. Turkish Journal of International Relations*, 1/2 (2002): <http://www.alternativesjournal.net/volume1/number2/erdem.htm>

74. 'That's nonsense; no prophecy or forecast is inherently self-fulfilling. It depends on how people react to it. I said in my book, look, there's a real possibility of local conflict between groups of different civilizations, and there's a possibility that these local conflicts can escalate into much broader sorts of conflicts ...'

75. Chiara Bottici and Benoît Challand, 'Rethinking Political Myth. The Clash of Civilizations as Self-Fulfilling Prophecy', *European Journal of Social Theory*, 9 (2006), 315–36.

76. Graham E. Fuller, 'The Future of Political Islam', *Foreign Affairs* (Mar.–Apr. 2002), 54.

77. Oleg Svet, 'Public Diplomacy. War by Other Means' (5 Nov. 2006): <http://fletcher.tufts.edu/jebsencenter/pdfs/Draft_November_5_2006_SS.pdf>

78. Stefan Halper and Jonathan Clarke, *The Silence of the Rational Center. Why American Foreign Policy is Failing* (New York: Basic Books, 2007), 128–9.

79. Alan M. Dershowitz, *Preemption. A Knife that Cuts Both Ways* (New York and London: W.W. Norton, 2006). The fact that the main historical examples cited by Dershowitz, apart from the attack on Iraq in 2003, arise from the relations between Israel and its neighbours does not inspire confidence that the maxim of caution should be displaced by that of intervention. First, Israel is a small state surrounded by hostile neighbours: extrapolating from the circumstances of a small state, with no 'strategic depth', to that of a great power such as the United States makes little sense. Secondly, as everyone knows (although some care to ignore it), the fact that Israel has established its military supremacy in the region through a successful exercise of preventive war in 1967 has not led, and will not lead, to the establishment of peace in the region until there is a just settlement of the Palestine issue.

80. Ivo H. Daalder, 'Beyond Preemption. An Overview', in Daalder (ed.), *Beyond Preemption. Force and Legitimacy in a Changing World* (Washington DC: Brookings Institution Press, 2007), 1–18.

# Index

*Individuals marked * have an entry in the 'Dramatis Personae' section.*